Argumentation

Understanding and Shaping Arguments

Argumentation

Understanding and Shaping Arguments

sixth edition

James A. Herrick

Hope College

Strata Publishing, Inc.
State College, Pennsylvania

Argumentation: Understanding and Shaping Arguments

9 8 7 6 5 4 3 2 1

Pearson Education, Inc., previously published this book. The updated (second), third, fourth, fifth, and sixth editions are published by Strata Publishing, Inc.

Strata Publishing, Inc.
P.O. 1303
State College, PA 16804
USA

1-814-234-8545

http://www.stratapub.com

Grateful acknowledgment is made for permission to use the following:
Excerpts: Ryan Jaslow, "Pediatricians Warned Children of Military Personnel Face Mental Health Risks." CBS News online, May 27, 2013. Reprinted by permission.
Excerpts: Jean Twenge, "How Long Can You Wait to Have a Baby?" *The Atlantic,* July/August 2013. Used by permission.
Excerpts: Fred Alvarez, "Ban Could Make Breathing Easier." *Los Angeles Times,* July 26, 2004. Copyright © 2004. Los Angeles Times. Used with Permission.
Sample policy case essay in Appendix A: Leah Asen, "Twenty-First Century Slavery," adapted student editorial originally written for Communication 160 at Hope College, Fall 2016. Reprinted by permission of the author.
Red Eagle and Logan Glaciers, 1914. E. C. Stebinger, courtesy of GNP Archives.
Red Eagle and Logan Glaciers, 2009. Lisa McKeon, USGS.
"Where imagination sprouts." Image courtesy Ad Council and United States Forest Service.
"Unemployment Rates and Earnings by Educational Attainment, 2017" chart. U.S. Bureau of Labor Statistics, Current Population Survey.
Direct Correlation chart. Data from Temperature change from 1901–2000 baseline: NOAA National Centers for Environmental information, Climate at a Glance: Global Time Series, published March 2018, retrieved on April 4, 2018 from http://www.ncdc.noaa.gov/cag/ and Atmospheric CO_2: NOAA Earth System Research Laboratory and Scripps Institute of Oceanography, file created March 5, 2018.
"Taking a Stand in Baton Rouge." Jonathan Bachman/Reuters.
"You Don't Need to Be Famous to Be Unforgettable. Make More. Teach." Image courtesy of TEACH.org.
"A Syrian refugee child . . . ." Giorgos Moutafis/Reuters.
Cover photo and photo page ii: Stephane Bidouze/Shutterstock.com.
Photo page 1: goodluz/Shutterstock.com.
Photo page 61: iStock.com/Rklfoto.
Photo page 87: Rido/Shutterstock.com.
Photo page 139: livertoon/Shutterstock.com.
Photo page 173: iStock.com/Steve Debenport.
Photo page 195: iStock.com/Tassii.
Photo page 283: iStock.com/IPGGutenbergUKLtd.

ISBN 13: 978-1-891136-42-9

Brief Contents

Contents

Preface

My goal in the sixth edition of *Argumentation: Understanding and Shaping Arguments*, as in previous editions, is to provide an accessible, up-to-date, ethically grounded, and audience-centered guide to arguments as they occur in public and private settings: in personal conversation and professional meetings, in civic and political discourse, in the mass media and on the internet, through digital and social media. This text's practical treatment of marketplace argumentation remains grounded in classical and contemporary rhetorical theory, and promotes the standards of constructive public discourse that inform the rhetorical tradition as well as contemporary approaches to critical thinking. Conversations with colleagues suggest that faculty seek a clear, engaging, yet intellectually rigorous book that helps students participate confidently in public discourse, while at the same time nurturing the ethical values essential to a flourishing democracy. Students indicate that they appreciate a serious, useful guide to evaluating the vast array of persuasive writing and speaking they encounter. I have sought to integrate these concerns in developing the sixth edition of *Argumentation: Understanding and Shaping Arguments* for the twenty-first century classroom and our increasingly digital culture.

Writing in response to my own teaching needs, feedback to earlier editions, and the best contemporary practices of public discourse, I have tried to maintain the basic approach and foundational pedagogical features that colleagues tell me they have found helpful in their own classrooms. I have also updated examples throughout the book and developed new sections to reflect current issues and media, such as social media and podcasts, as well as recent theoretical insights. I hope you will find this new edition to be a thorough, intellectually challenging aid to teaching courses such as argumentation, rhetoric, critical thinking, public speaking, and expositional writing.

I believe that the most effective teaching of argumentation keeps the proven practices of everyday argumentation in view, focusing particularly on the most reliable ways that we actually reason in public and private settings. The guidelines students encounter here for evaluating arguments are thus flexible suggestions rather than rigid prescriptions. Students are encouraged to see them as standards of critical assessment that should always be employed with a corresponding concern for audience, ethics, and context. As this approach acknowledges how we actually reason with one another, it also encourages students to become rational judges of arguments rather than fallacy detectives. Although fallacies are discussed, these reasoning mistakes do not occupy a central place in the discussion of arguments. Similarly, the principles and language of debate are addressed in an appendix, but I have not written with a guiding concern for the technicalities of formal debate. At the heart of *Argumentation: Understanding and Shaping Arguments* is a focused concern for how people reason with one another every day, as well as how our reading and writing practices can be improved through a solid introduction to the principles of sound, ethically grounded argument.

The ethics of argument plays a key role in the book. Students are reminded that arguments emerge in contexts that include audiences and advocates, both of whom possess personal values and moral responsibilities. Students are encouraged to consider the ethical obligations they incur whenever they enter the public arena as advocates. These obligations include respect for the audience, fidelity to the truth, and regard for the settings in which arguments develop. This ethical orientation is introduced in an early chapter and maintained throughout the text.

As any classroom instructor knows, relevant and timely examples are crucial to student engagement and thus to successful teaching. In keeping with my focus on marketplace argument, this new edition reflects a determined effort to provide examples that are contemporary, pertinent to student concerns, and derived from the actual practice of public discourse. Examples are drawn from business, sports, medicine, technology, politics, interpersonal relationships, international affairs, religion, environmental issues, and personal decision-making; from oral conversation, printed sources, the mass media, the internet, social media, and other digital discourse.

In addition to addressing the traditional concerns of argument studies—linguistic clarity, validity, evidence, ethics, fallacies—*Argumentation* explores narrative and visual elements that are important to much contemporary discourse. Moreover, the internet and social media are situated here as arenas for radically expanded public discourse. This new edition also recognizes the need for contemporary students to develop digital literacy. Toward this end, it sets characteristic digital forms of argument—for example, texts and tweets—in the context of the broader concerns of public discourse. Such communication innovations shape how we interact about ideas and policies, and are here integrated into the discussion of public advocacy.

FEATURES OF THE BOOK

This new edition of *Argumentation: Understanding and Shaping Arguments* retains the central features that characterized earlier editions, and that instructors have told me worked well in their classrooms. These include:

- An emphasis on the importance of sound, principled, open public discourse in rational, democratic decision-making.
- An accessible, foundational theory of argument rooted in classical and contemporary rhetorical tradition.
- Clear explanations of how various types of arguments—from formal syllogisms to simple comparisons—develop in diverse public and private settings.
- A practical and adaptable approach to developing and evaluating arguments, based on the criteria of evidence (support), validity (sound structure), and linguistic consistency (clear and consistent definitions of key terms).
- A focus on argument ethics, with an early chapter on ethics and attention throughout the book to the ethical responsibilities of advocates.
- Emphasis throughout on preparing students to be skilled practitioners of written and spoken public discourse, as well as fully equipped critics of the arguments they encounter.
- Discussions of narrative and visual argument that explore how stories and images are incorporated into persuasive cases, and that provide guidance for evaluating such approaches to argument.
- A presentation of the internet and social media as sources of evidence and as important locations for public discourse.
- A detailed discussion of the Toulmin Model and its value to advocates and critics, with examples showing how this model can be used to discover unstated reasons and evaluate public arguments.

FEATURES OF THE NEW EDITION

This sixth edition adds several new features that enhance its content and clarity. These revisions are in response to my own experiences with the book and to suggestions from colleagues.

- Many updated examples and exercises, reflecting current issues, recent events, and new media forms.

- Expanded discussion of internet resources and discourse, including social media, as well as a new section on podcasts, as resources for advocates and as locations for public discourse.

- An expanded discussion of visual evidence and visual argument, with illustrations of contemporary uses.

- A new discussion of conspiracy theories that treats these persistent and misleading narratives as problems of evidence and its critical evaluation.

PEDAGOGICAL FEATURES

Several pedagogical features are designed to engage student interest, enhance understanding, and emphasize salient points:

- A practical vocabulary of more than 200 terms that provides students with categories and concepts crucial to composing and evaluating arguments. Key terms are listed at the beginning of each chapter and in the glossary at the end of the book.

- Numerous application exercises at the end of each chapter that allow students to practice new skills.

- Epigrams to engage student interest at the beginning of each chapter.

- Pull quotes and boxed figures to underscore key points and help engage students visually.

- Photographs introducing each part division, adding visual interest and underscoring the pervasiveness of argument in everyday life.

- Recommended websites listed at the end of each chapter, providing resources for extending the discussion of crucial topics covered in the text.

- An Instructor's Manual with sample syllabus, additional exercises, suggested written assignments, and other teaching resources, available to instructors who adopt the book.

ORGANIZATION

This sixth edition of *Argumentation: Understanding and Shaping Arguments* consists of eighteen chapters, organized in six parts that reflect the book's central concerns, plus two appendices that may be employed at any point in the semester.

Part I, "Goals, Skills, and Functions of Argumentation," consists of three chapters that introduce the basic language and theory of argument, as well as analytic tools that help students grasp the inferential structure of arguments.

Chapter 1, "An Introduction to Argumentation," explores ways in which argumentation functions in the deliberation and decision-making of individuals and groups. This chapter also considers the crucial role of values and agreements in argumentation, as well as how the internet and social media function as forums for public discourse.

Chapter 2, "The Elements of Arguments," sets out a foundational theory of argument, including various types of claims and how each type of claim may be reasonably supported. The chapter also discusses interpretations of evidence, and how such interpretations may vary according to the diverse values that individuals bring to the argumentative situation.

Chapter 3, "Tools for Analyzing Arguments," presents students with practical analytic tools for grasping the structure and content of any argument. The discussion of the Toulmin Model, an important tool of argument analysis, reveals its potential for assessing truncated arguments such as those found in digital media.

Part II, "The Conditions of Constructive Argumentation," consists of two chapters that examine the qualities of sound arguments and the characteristics of ethical advocates.

Chapter 4, "Ethical Advocacy," prompts students to consider advocates' ethical obligations and provides an ethical foundation for subsequent topics taken up in the text. The chapter's centerpiece is the discussion of a virtues approach to ethics, focusing on the moral commitments that ethical advocates exhibit in argumentative situations.

Chapter 5, "Reasonable Arguments, Reasonable People," sets out three considerations relevant to assessing any argument: evidence, structure, and clear language. The chapter also examines characteristics of reasonable people, such as an attitude of openness to the views of others.

Part III, "Support: The Content of Arguments," addresses the crucial topic of evidence in argument. The chapter addresses the issues of online research, while also offering detailed information about using traditional sources such as books and periodicals.

Chapter 6, "Evaluating Evidence," provides a guide to assessing the quality of evidence, including tests such as accessibility and recency. The discussion of visual evidence, expanded in this edition, reflects current research on its use in argumentative cases. A new section considers conspiracy theories as a problem of evidence misuse.

Chapter 7, "Locating and Evaluating Sources of Evidence," explores methods of evaluating a range of sources, from books and magazines to interviews and websites, and includes a new section on podcasts. The chapter also includes a section on assessing a source's political perspective.

Chapter 8, "Using Statistics as Evidence," considers the issues and mechanics of generalizing from a sample. The chapter also helps students to determine when statistical evidence is used well—or employed carelessly to mislead an audience.

Chapter 9, "Using Testimony as Evidence," sets out basic types and tests of testimony to assist students in evaluating and employing testimonial evidence.

Part IV, "Validity: The Structure of Arguments," considers the important and often overlooked issue of argument structure.

Chapter 10, "Validity in Conditional and Enumeration Arguments," examines the structure of arguments that develop around necessary and sufficient conditions, as well as arguments that follow an enumeration or partition pattern.

Chapter 11, "Validity in Categorical Arguments," takes up the structure of arguments that manage categories or definitions, and introduces a set of validity tests to help students navigate a sometimes complex process of testing validity.

Part V, "Linguistic Consistency: Language in Argument," is made up of two chapters that explore issues ranging from definition and ambiguity to common problems of expression such as redundancy and mixed metaphor.

Chapter 12, "Definition in Argument," takes up the central role played by strategic definitions in argumentative settings. Sources of definitions as well as their various uses in argumentation are considered.

Chapter 13, "Ambiguity, Equivocation, and Other Language Considerations," helps students recognize and avoid common language mistakes that cloud the clarity of thinking, writing, and speaking.

Part VI, "Types and Tests of Arguments," covers the types of arguments encountered in public and private settings, and presents practical and accessible methods of evaluating these arguments.

Chapter 14, "Analogies, Examples, Metonymy, and Narratives," explores ways of reasoning from one or a limited set of cases, reasoning by comparison of cases, reasoning from part to whole, and the role of narrative in argument.

Chapter 15, "Reasoning about Causes," presents an accessible guide to the difficult issue of establishing the cause of individual occurrences or classes of events, and to assessing arguments from sign.

Chapter 16, "Moral and Practical Arguments," covers four arguments that are often discovered in advertising and political discourse, and that engage our moral commitments or pragmatic inclinations.

Chapter 17, "Essential Nature Arguments," addresses arguments built around claims regarding the essential nature of institutions, individuals, and documents. The discussion of reasoning from images and other visual representations, often used to sum up essential nature, has been expanded and updated in this edition.

Chapter 18, "Fallacies and Appeals," surveys erroneous approaches to reasoning. It also discusses the difficult issue of appeals to the emotions and to authority.

The Appendices, "Developing and Adapting Your Case," discusses and provides guidelines for developing a case and presenting it to an audience.

Appendix A, "Policy Case Construction," discusses the elements of an effective case supporting a proposal and covers the basic vocabulary of policy debate. Basic debate terms and concepts are explored through a case study, which is new to this edition.

Appendix B, "Adapting Arguments to an Audience," provides students with a highly practical guide to audience adaptation, including the audience's demographics, moral commitments, and relationship to the topic and the advocate. A case study for analysis, with commentary, illustrates the principles discussed in this appendix.

Argumentation: Understanding and Shaping Arguments is designed to encourage students to assume the role of capable, responsible, and informed advocates who participate effectively and ethically in the public arena. The text's tested approach is intended to help students become better, more self-assured producers and consumers of public and private discourse. It is my hope that, as a result of our helping a new generation of students to understand and practice argumentation, the crucial reasoning processes that keep democracy vibrant will be enhanced. I offer this new edition in the belief that we all stand to gain when the citizens of our democracy are well equipped to read, think, write, listen, and speak with skill and confidence.

ACKNOWLEDGMENTS

Many individuals have had a hand in forming this new edition of *Argumentation: Understanding and Shaping Arguments* and the editions that preceded it. As the present book would not have been possible without their assistance, I would like to take this opportunity to acknowledge their help and to thank them.

Teaching at least one section of argumentation every semester provides me with continuous opportunity to test material and solicit the reactions of students to the text. I would like to thank the many students in my Analytic Skills course here at Hope College whose suggestions and comments have improved both topic presentation and the quality of exercises in each chapter.

A number of colleagues at colleges and universities across the country have also provided helpful feedback that contributed in important ways to enhancing every aspect of the sixth edition of *Argumentation.* My thanks to Jennifer Biedendorf, California State University, Stanislaus; Martin Camper, Loyola University Maryland; George Dionisopolous, San Diego State University; Michaela Frischherz, Towson University; Jill James, Tarrant County College; Sarah Kornfield, Hope College; Christopher Leland, Colorado Christian University; Sarah T. Partlow Lefevre, Idaho State University; Heather May, Emerson College; Margaret M. Michels, Pennsylvania State University; Samuel Mayer Nelson, Cornell University; David Romanelli, Loyola University Chicago; and Joel S. Ward, Geneva College.

I would also like to acknowledge the contributions of reviewers of previous editions. These include Stephen Andon, Nova Southeastern University; R. V. Barello, Lewis University; Diane M. Blair, California State University, Fresno; Robert Boller, University of Hawai'i Manoa; Diana I. Bowen, University of Houston–Clear Lake; Beth Brunk-Chavez, University of Texas at El Paso; Michael L. Butterworth, Ohio University; Martha S. Cheng, Rollins College; George N. Dionisopoulos, San Diego State University; Larry Eby, Goldey-Beacom College; James M. Farrell, University of New Hampshire; Michael Fleming, Mount San Jacinto College; Douglas Fraleigh, California State University, Fresno; Adam Gaffey, Texas A&M University; Morgan Ginther, University of Memphis; Robert Greenstreet, East Central University; Lisa M. Gring-Pemble, George Mason University; Cory Hillman, Central Michigan University; Treva Hodges, Indiana University Southeast; Erica Hollander, Metropolitan State College of Denver; Deborah L. Hoover, Tiffin University; Randall Iden, Northwestern University; Brandon Inabinet, Furman University; Carl Isaacson, Bethany College; Bryan P. Jacobs, Dixie State University; Lenore Langsdorf, Southern Illinois University; Ilon Lauer, Western Illinois University; Karen King Lee, University of Nebraska–Lincoln; Thomas M. Lessl, University of Georgia; Charles Lester, Palm Beach Atlantic University; Ryan Louis, Ottawa University; Beth Innocenti Manolescu, University of Kansas; Cynthia Martin, James Madison University; Nancy Nichol Meyer, Metropolitan State College of Denver; Margaret M. Michels, Pennsylvania State University; David Moss, Crafton Hills and Mt. San Jacinto Colleges; Carroll Ferguson Nardone, Sam Houston State University; Samuel Mayer Nelson, Cornell University; Clark Olson, Arizona State University; Frank O'Mara, State University of New York, College at Oneonta; Jennifer Reem, Nova Southeastern University; Kevin Stein, Southern Utah University; Fred Sternhagen, Concordia College; Abbie Syrek, University of Nebraska at Omaha; Phillip Voight, Gustavus Adolphus College; Dennis L. Wignall, Dixie State College; Joel Worden, Goldey-Beacom College; David Worthington, DePauw University; and David Zarefsky, Northwestern University.

Thanks are also due to the Hope College Communication Departmental office manager Linda Koetje for her careful attention to various aspects of manuscript preparation and correspondence with the publisher. I also want to thank Kathleen Domenig of Strata Publishing for the extraordinary care and high level of professionalism she brought to every detail of production, and for a number of important recommendations regarding the text's structure, tone, and appearance. Finally, my deepest gratitude to my wife for her good nature and patience.

I

Goals, Skills, and Functions of Argumentation

1 An Introduction to Argumentation

> Only through our connectedness to others can we really know
> and enhance the self. And only through working on the self
> can we begin to enhance our connectedness to others.
> *Harriet Lerner (1944–)*
> *United States psychologist*

> Give everyone the power to share anything with anyone.
> *Mark Zuckerberg (1984–)*
> *Founder of Facebook*

KEY TERMS

advocacy   audience   public discourse

argument   pluralistic culture   rule of reason

argumentation   power   values

    procedures

The online world provides access to many forums for encountering new ideas, gathering information, and interacting with others. On any given day you might receive and send text messages, follow individuals on Twitter, explore online news sources, or look up a fact on Wikipedia. You may visit websites to read music reviews, follow a favorite sports team, or listen to a favorite political podcast. Social media such as Facebook and Twitter generate controversy, provide a platform for political discussion, and dramatically increase our connection with a wide range of people.

Traditional print sources also continue to play an important role as sources of ideas, information, and opinion: we read books and magazines, browse newspapers with our morning coffee, and receive mail from a variety of political groups, charitable organizations, or other causes.

Many of these experiences in the contemporary world of ideas are marked by urgent persuasive appeals from corporations or political organizations. The range of ideas available to us today is extraordinary, the volume of information beyond anyone's capacity to estimate accurately. More than ever, the dissemination of ideas, opinions, and information is constantly present in our personal and public lives. This abundance of news, ideas, and data presents us with important moral and ethical questions: Which sources are worthy of my attention? Do I have an obligation to act in response to what I've heard? Which groups or individuals are likely to be affected by my responses?

All this idea-driven communication often involves us directly in the activity discussed in this book—**argumentation,** *the cooperative activity of developing and advancing arguments and of responding to the arguments of others.*

We often associate argumentation with a rather narrow range of activities such as politics, commerce, or religion, but most other activities of human interaction also exhibit our characteristically human inclination to present our ideas to others and to support those ideas with reasons. Think, for instance, of the many opinions you hear expressed during a typical week about education, art, sports, or employment.

We might say that any subject that people care deeply about is a subject about which they also make arguments. Let's define an **argument** as *a claim advanced with a reason or reasons in its support.* Whereas our reasoning may be conducted privately,

> Any subject that people care deeply about is a subject about which they also make arguments.

argumentation is usually a public activity, that is, something we do in the presence of other people. *Those people for whom we develop our arguments* constitute our **audience.** Notice, then, that an audience may consist of one person or a thousand people. Whether it is small or large, that audience—far from being passive recipients—often has a significant impact on how we go about making our arguments. For example, we typically adapt our arguments to the people in an audience based on what we know of their interests and attitudes, and even in response to their reactions.

This activity of reasoning with others—whether our goal is persuading or simply expressing our views—characterizes our conversations about sports or music as clearly as it does those about politics or commerce. When you suggest that one baseball team is better than another or that a certain singer did not deserve an award from the music industry, you are engaged in making arguments just as surely as when you make a statement in support of a new approach to national defense or speak up in favor of affirmative action. All these situations, and many others, involve you in the process of making arguments. As soon as someone responds to your arguments with another argument, the process of argumentation has begun.

Indeed, it is difficult to imagine any interest or activity that does not at some point involve setting out our views and supporting those views with our reasons. Business, medicine, sports, relationships, education, art, and even science are all subjects that involve people in making and hearing arguments.

The enterprise of making arguments can take many forms. We may think immediately of conversation, public speaking, nonfiction writing, podcasts, or radio and television talk shows as situations in which people present and justify their thinking. Other methods of expression, however, are just as clearly ways of setting out our opinions and the reasons we hold them. Many songs involve efforts to advance and defend a point of view. An example from the Vietnam War era would be folk singer Pete Seeger's anti-war songs.[1] More recently, singers such as Bono and bands such as Green Day have continued this tradition of making arguments through music. The same can be said of other art forms, particularly movies and novels. First published in 1852, abolitionist Harriet Beecher Stowe's novel *Uncle Tom's Cabin* was immediately recognized as a powerful argument against slavery. When President Abraham Lincoln was introduced to Stowe he reportedly said, "So, you're the little woman who wrote the book that made this great war."[2] Lincoln, skilled as he was in argumentation, recognized that Stowe's argument in her novel was as powerful as any ever advanced on the floor of the Senate. In recent years, popular books such as Margot Lee Shetterly's *Hidden Figures* (now a major movie) have advanced arguments against racism and sexism. We will take a close look at narrative argument in Chapter 14. Argumentation also takes place in visual media such as photographs and movies, as we shall also discuss later.

No endeavor is more characteristic of human social interaction or more satisfying to the human spirit than expressing our views and hearing others' views in response. This activity of argumentation—presenting our ideas and opinions, supporting them with our reasons, and hearing others' arguments in response—stimulates our thinking, energizes our conversations, and makes democracy possible. Argumentation is not simply a satisfying and energizing process; it is also essential to maintaining a healthy egalitarian and diverse society.

ARGUMENTATION IN A DEMOCRATIC SOCIETY

There is a close connection between the flourishing of democracy and a nation's willingness to test its foundational principles in the arena of public debate. The success of such testing of ideas depends on how well citizens are prepared to participate in **public discourse,** *open discussion of those issues that potentially affect everyone.*

Argumentation, perhaps more clearly than any other enterprise, is essential to the conduct of personal and public life in free societies. Our right to express our views and to support these views with reasons is guaranteed in the First Amendment to the United States Constitution, and for a good reason: democracy depends on the free expression and continuous interaction of differing points of view. The First Amendment's guarantee that "Congress shall make no law . . . abridging the freedom of speech . . . ." protects vigorous interaction in the public sphere. Through collaboration in argumentation, we discover solutions to problems, test the merits of ideas, moderate extreme views, convince others to work cooperatively toward a common goal, and ensure that no single way of thinking achieves a dominance that can lead to stagnation or tyranny.

Free societies encourage **advocacy,** *the activity of promoting or opposing an idea in public settings.* Each one of us is at some time an advocate. For example, if we believe an idea is a good one—that art programs should be funded in the local schools, that a particular candidate should be elected, that recycling should be mandatory in our community—we may develop arguments to advocate that idea. If, on the other hand, we think certain ideas are unjust or dangerous—that women's sports programs receive less funding than men's, that a ban on dumping toxins into a river might be lifted—we feel obliged to express the reasons that led us to these conclusions.

Advocacy and argument are inseparable activities, for advocacy depends on the presentation of arguments. *Successful* advocacy depends on the *skillful* presentation of arguments. Social movements such as the civil rights movement and the women's movement, as one component of their efforts, have advocated change via public arguments. By argument, supporters of these and other causes have also vigorously opposed ideas and practices that limit freedoms. Such groups have changed the ways we think, speak, and act, and they have done it in large measure by presenting arguments, by setting out their views and supporting those views with reasons and evidence. Less reputable organizations pursue their agendas in the same way—by making arguments. The arguments may not be good ones, but they are arguments nonetheless. Differentiating between good and bad ideas is often a matter of differentiating between good and bad arguments in the public arena.

Advocacy, Power, and Free Societies

Argumentation characterizes nearly every aspect of your life as a member of a free society. In a conversation with a friend about your favorite movie, you provide your reasons. While commending the mayor's handling of a recent crisis, you might build a case from the best arguments you can make. In writing a letter to the editor of the local paper about a problem at a municipal park, you present reasons and conclusions. While making a classroom speech about nuclear power plants or addressing a large audience from your community about a new business opportunity, you will find yourself engaged in making and responding to arguments. This is how democracy functions—citizens present their arguments in public settings to the best of their ability, and other citizens are given the opportunity to respond.

What do these observations about the role of argument and advocacy in a free society suggest? Just this: in a democracy, argumentation is the preferred means of winning a hearing and convincing others of our perspectives. However, we also cannot ignore the role that **power** plays in democratic decision-making processes. Let's define power as *the capacity to wield influence, to shape important decisions that affect the lives of others.* Most people realize that wealth brings political influence or power, regardless of how strong or weak the wealthy individual's arguments are. Similarly, fame may lend credibility to celebrities' opinions despite the fact that they may not be in possession of the facts. Thus, power must enter the equation when we consider how decisions are made, even in free societies.

Nevertheless, knowledge of argumentation processes serves as a counter-balance to sources of power, such as wealth and fame. The more the members of an audience know about what goes into a good argument, the more resistant they become to efforts to employ power to persuade. The greater skill at argument that advocates possess, the better prepared they will be to answer unsubstantiated claims, regardless of their sources. Although power cannot be discounted as a factor in our public discourse, power need not have the last word. Indeed, the capacity to argue effectively is itself a kind of power in a democracy—the power to improve public discourse and in this way move toward a more just and rational society.

As this discussion of the relationships among argumentation, power, and public discourse suggests, serious problems arise when citizens lack training and skill in argumentation. The likelihood of bad ideas prevailing in public discourse increases, as does the probability that good ideas will be ignored. The individual citizen also becomes more susceptible to manipulation and deception. If skill in argument is itself a source of power—as it very clearly is—then the absence of this skill renders you more vulnerable to people who do possess it.

Argumentation in a Pluralistic Culture

The examples of the Civil Rights movement, the women's movement, and arguments in local settings underscore a central reality of our private and public lives today: We live in a **pluralistic culture,** *a society composed of groups who see the world from different perspectives, value different activities, hold disparate religious beliefs, and aspire to different goals.* No other fact of modern social life demands our attention more than social pluralism does. Let's consider why this is.

Our success in arriving at working agreements, despite our differences and potential disagreements, will determine the future course of our society. For this reason, the central focus in this book will be on how to improve the whole process of public discourse, that is, of argumentation as it takes place in a variety of public settings, before various kinds of audiences, and on issues of general concern. Drawing examples from a range of activities and about a host of issues, we will explore how to improve public discourse through constructing better arguments, advocating our ideas in an ethical fashion, and testing the soundness of arguments we read and hear.

> Our success in arriving at working agreements will determine the future course of our society.

What means are available to us for discussing and resolving vital issues, while still preserving diversity and a plurality of views? The best means is free public discussion, the exchange of reasoned views, the interaction of ideas that thoughtful people have considered carefully and presented well. Through skillful public argumentation we can pursue a synthesis of our thinking that incorporates the best of our ideas and accommodates differences in a reasonable manner. These reflections suggest that our success as a democratic and pluralistic society depends on our success, individually and collectively, as producers and critics of the good public discourse that results when sound arguments are presented to competent audiences.

The Internet and Public Discourse

The internet has vastly increased access to public discourse. The sheer number of people participating in websites, blogs, chat rooms, social media, and other online forums vastly exceeds anything previously imagined as a means of involving citizens in discussions of important topics. These highly accessible forums for expressing opinions and advancing arguments also mean that more people are writing arguments on topics of interest to them than ever before. Simply the ability to respond to a news story in a major online newspaper such as the *Los Angeles Times* brings thousands of people into a debate, people who in past decades might never have participated in such discussions. The internet has drawn millions of citizens into a broad discussion of issues that are important to everyone.

Because of this enormous increase in the size and scope of the public square, this rebirth of the citizen as active participant in public discussions, it is more important than ever to propagate standards of ethical advocacy and to discuss standards for a reasonable argument. The need for civility in online discussions—an ethical concern—is also evident to nearly everyone who has ever entered such an exchange. Similarly, the line between assertion and argument is sometimes blurred online, particularly as heated discussions of everything from politics to sports characterize the digital world. The leading themes of this text take on additional urgency in the face of the internet's development into our new public sphere.

GOALS OF STUDYING ARGUMENT

Argumentation traditionally is built of units of written and spoken language called arguments. In the next chapter we will take a close look at how reasons and conclusions come together to make an argument. Understanding their basic structure makes us more skillful in developing and responding to arguments. Skill in argument not only prepares us to be more effective advocates, but also makes us more able to participate in the democratic process.

This text sets the practice of argumentation in its social context. The general goal of the text is to improve your abilities in the essential public activity of reasoning with others, that is, of argumentation. Three specific objectives that contribute to accomplishing this goal are:

1. To help you to understand and evaluate the arguments you hear or read.
2. To equip you to compose and present your own arguments more effectively.
3. To enhance your appreciation of the ethical use of arguments.

It is hoped that when you enter the public arena as an advocate or as a member of an audience, everything we discuss will assist you in making public discourse more reasonable and ethical.

As you read the text, you will be introduced to concepts such as what makes an argument reasonable, the attitudes of reasonable people, the ethics of argument, the many types of arguments we encounter every day, and methods for evaluating each type. We will also consider topics such as evidence and where to find it, construction of a convincing argumentative case, and clear and effective use of language. We will analyze examples of arguments as they develop in the worlds of politics, business, religion, science, sports, international affairs, history, the arts, and other domains. Before we address these important topics, however, let's look more closely at the basic reasons that motivate us to create arguments in both public and private settings.

WHAT ARGUMENTS DO: PERSUADE, JUSTIFY, DISCOVER

We have been considering arguments as essential to both everyday life and the vibrancy of democracy. Some scholars have gone so far as to suggest that making arguments may be the most characteristically human activity.[3] This contention raises the question: Why do we make arguments? That is, what functions does this type of communicating perform for us? Three goals seem to underlie our efforts to develop and present arguments.

1. We present arguments when we want to persuade. Perhaps the first reason that comes to mind for making arguments is the goal of persuading someone else to agree with us. Most people recognize that sound arguments and ethical persuasion are preferable to lies, violence, and coercion. For example, if I want you to agree with me that animals have rights that must be respected, I will seek to present you with *reasons* such as: "Animals are living things, and all living things have rights that should be respected."

Our political processes depend on this activity of persuading through arguments. In a democracy, we change people's views and achieve working agreements on the issues by making arguments. In the most productive settings our arguments should invite a response, a counter-argument, thus leading to an exchange of views. That is to say, persuasion by means of argument ought to be a two-way street.

2. We develop arguments to justify our positions on issues. Our goals in making arguments are not always persuasive goals. Arguments are often advanced simply to clarify or to support our views on issues, to let others know what we are thinking and why. You may want to explain to a friend why you support spending on education, why you think concerts should not be allowed in a local park, or why you voted against a particular candidate for judge. Your goal may not be to change anyone's mind, but simply to explain, inform, or invite a response. As you present

FIGURE 1.1 Reasons to Advance Arguments

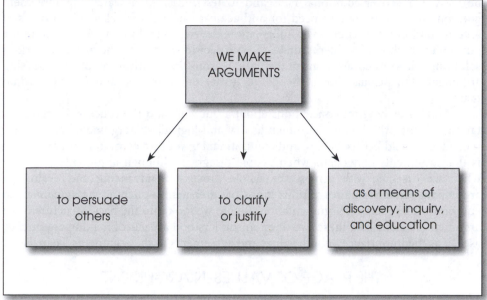

your arguments, you clarify your position on the topic for a listener—perhaps even for yourself—and your point of view is shown to be one a reasonable person can hold.

The topic of argument as justification has recently received a lot of attention. Researchers Hugo Mercier and Dan Sperber have concluded that our real goal when making arguments is to demonstrate to other people that we actually have good rational support for our views. In other words, making arguments is not principally a matter of trying to persuade someone else, but of creating a sound justification of our views for an audience that may be listening to opposing arguments, as well. The idea is "that the primary function for which [reasoning] evolved is the production and evaluation of arguments in communication."[4]

> Making arguments is not principally a matter of trying to persuade someone else, but of creating a sound justification of our views for an audience.

3. We use arguments as a means of inquiry. Although we often think that argumentation depends on having a store of clear facts readily at hand, through advancing, hearing, and responding to arguments we also discover facts, develop solutions to problems, inquire into a topic, and become educated about a subject. For example, a committee of community residents, engineers, and airline executives may seek the best way to deal with the problem of noise from jet engines at the municipal airport. Members of the committee inquire into the relevant facts about airport noise. Arguments are advanced about the severity of the problem, possible solutions, and the costs and feasibility of various plans. Through this process of public argumentation, facts come to light, ideas that were previously taken to be facts may be shown false, and the relative merits of proposed solutions are evaluated. However, our private reasoning is also a means of discovery. If I am considering a new job, I will go through a private reasoning process with the goal of making a good decision. In other words, argument as a means of inquiry can have a private as well as a public side.

Argumentation depends on the prior existence of some facts, but it can also be used to discover additional facts and to test ideas. As a search for agreement goes on, arguments are advanced for and against various proposals. The process of argumentation helps us uncover information, develop our thinking on issues, refine our understanding of problems, make reliable decisions, and test the merits of various solutions. These, then, are some of the basic reasons that motivate all of us to develop arguments—to persuade an audience, to justify our thinking, and to inquire into issues.

Many of us have misconceptions about arguments and the process of argumentation. We may think of an argument as dry and logical; yet, arguments engage our most deeply held beliefs, values, and commitments. Another common misconception is that arguments only occur when people disagree. Although arguments do occur when we disagree with others, the whole process of advancing and evaluating arguments actually requires various kinds of agreements—such as the agreement to enter into the process of argumentation. Before we look into the basic structure of an argument, let's consider these two often misunderstood aspects of making arguments, as well as the importance of both values and agreements in the arguments we make.

THE PLACE OF VALUES IN ARGUMENT

Military robots are now a reality: The technology has advanced to the point that robots are capable of making autonomous decisions under battlefield conditions. Some weaponized robots—including drones—are capable of deciding to fire on enemy troops without the intervention of a human agent. This capability has divided experts familiar with the technology. Some see autonomous robots as a way to save the lives of troops in the field, because a robot could act instantly in response to a threat. Other experts raise ethical concerns about machines in combat situations making life-and-death decisions without human input. The same evidence—that robots are now capable of autonomous actions—leads different individuals to remarkably different conclusions.

Our beliefs, values, and assumptions play a major role in how we interpret the world we encounter each day. Much argumentation is undertaken because we are presented with choices—whether to pursue a certain career, what car to purchase, which candidate to vote for, how to understand someone else's action, what to believe. Choices, and the arguments that accompany them, engage our **values,** which we define here as *deeply held moral commitments acquired from family, cultural background, religious training, and personal experience.* Values inform our thinking when we are faced with a choice. Values for privacy, justice, free speech, sexual responsibility, self-determination, majority rule, and many other things animate and inform virtually all public and private controversies and decision-making. Rendering our decisions more complex is the fact that we all adhere to conflicting values. For example, our values that stem from religious convictions may clash with the values we are exposed to in our work environment.

Values drive us to make arguments that advocate one idea as preferable to another, one policy as more desirable than another. As we have seen, the same piece of evidence may lead different people to quite different conclusions, depending on the values those people bring to bear on interpreting that evidence. Moreover, a piece of evidence may leave us in two minds about how best to interpret it: To which value ought I adhere in this case?

Suppose that in a speech you advance evidence that organs from animals such as pigs and baboons, modified with human DNA, can produce organs suitable for transplant into human beings. Such procedures, called "xenotransplants," have already been performed experimentally. From this evidence, one member of your audience concludes that there has been a breakthrough in transplant technology that will one day alleviate the shortage of human donors. Another member of your audience concludes that science has opened the way for dangerous experimentation in animal and human DNA mixing. Each individual has used a different value or set of related values in deriving a conclusion from the same evidence. On the basis of a value for helping to overcome disease by technology, you decide to advocate for the procedure, even if you have a personal reservation rooted in a distinction between animals and humans.

Values themselves are contested in the public arena and subject to change. For example, Facebook and other social networking services have sparked debate about whether privacy is still an important value.

The fact that we adhere to conflicting values can show up in reasoning through a choice. Here is an example:

> Lisa works as a sales representative for a supplier that distributes precision airplane parts internationally. Lisa's company has recently begun ordering turbine blades from a new supplier that offers lower prices for the same parts, but that also runs fewer tests on them. Lisa understands the incentive for her company's cost-cutting measures, but she is also troubled that customers are not being informed about the new manufacturer and its less rigorous quality control standards. Lisa is not aware of any quality deficiency in the new parts. However, she questions whether she should challenge her company's policy and risk her job, or simply remain silent and let her supervisors decide what to tell customers.

Lisa's reasoning through this choice will bring many of her values into play. These values will suggest different ways of interpreting her options and making her decision. Which personal values might be relevant to this situation? The process of reasoning—of argumentation—can help us decide. Thus, argumentation can be a means of self-discovery.

Values are crucial to reasoning and making choices. They often provide the link between a fact and a conclusion drawn from that fact. Values also give us a frame for interpreting evidence and assessing options that are presented to us. Being aware of the place of values in argument can help us understand our own reasoning as well as others' reasoning, and thus can make us more skilled in making and assessing arguments. Understanding the place of values in argument also can help us appreciate the nature of argumentation in a diverse cultural context.

Values can be crucial to argumentation in at least one other important way. Many of the disagreements that mark life in a pluralistic society result from differences in values. Resolving controversies peacefully often requires us to search for common, unifying values. People who are interested in helping diverse groups work through differences and find satisfying compromises must be attentive both to differences in values and to the possibility that groups who disagree on many issues may have some values in common.

> Social and political conflicts can illustrate the need to discover unifying values to resolve controversies.

Social and political conflicts can illustrate the need to discover unifying values to resolve controversies. For instance, the United States is embroiled in a fundamental political disagreement often referred to as the red state–blue state divide. People working for agreement between the two points of view seek to articulate unifying values such as the desire for justice, respect for the dignity of all people, and the social and economic benefits of national unity. These common values can become the foundation of public arguments in support of harmony.

Consider another example: Ethicist Charles C. Camosy emphasized the common values that help create a space for dialogue on the highly divisive subject of abortion. Camosy arranged a meeting of opinion leaders representing different perspectives on the issue. He wrote, "We talked honestly about our differences, but also explored areas where some of us might be able to come together." The commonly held values of respect for conscience, for not causing pain, and for providing needed medical resources opened the way for productive conversation. Camosy suggests that the success of such discussions depends on other qualities as well, such as humility, recognizing that we have something to learn from opponents, avoiding binary thinking that recognizes no common ground, eschewing "dismissive words and phrases," and emphasizing commonly held values. Commenting on this last quality, Camosy wrote that participants in the conversation were "actually after very similar things."[5]

Not only do we adhere to values; not only do these values influence our decisions and reasoning; we also arrange values into hierarchies—some at the top and some further down the scale of importance. For example, I may hold a value for both privacy and security in the online world, but consider privacy to be a more important value than security. In this case I may be unwilling to give up elements of privacy— for example, to allow more surveillance of personal data—even though such a sacrifice would increase security. In my investing, I might hold both safety and potential profit as important monetary values, but prioritize safety over potential profit. Though buying stocks could increase my potential for profit, it also introduces risk by increasing my potential for loss. Thus, I might purchase relatively safe money market funds, even though the risk in buying stocks comes with potential for greater profit.

Unifying values can be employed in argument to help resolve conflict and nurture agreement. Our discussion of the role of values in argument has brought us to the topic of the relationship between agreement and argumentation. We have seen how agreement can be one goal of argumentation. What other roles does agreement play in argumentation, which often begins with disagreement?

AGREEMENT AND COOPERATION IN ARGUMENTATION

Argumentation is an ongoing, interactive process of advancing and responding to arguments. It can occur any time a claim or statement is in dispute. If I advance the claim that life exists on other planets or that Democrats have a better plan to revive the economy than Republicans do, and someone hearing my argument disagrees, the process of argumentation might begin. I may be asked to provide reasons for my claims. My reasons can then be challenged with opposing reasons. I will then have an opportunity to answer the challenge, and so on. Because disagreement marks nearly every aspect of our lives, argumentation is one of the most common, and perhaps the most characteristically human, of all human endeavors.

> Argumentation is a cooperative process, rooted in the agreement that it is the preferred means of resolving disagreements.

Though disagreement attends argumentation, the process of argumentation also requires some basic agreements. Argumentation is fundamentally a cooperative process, rooted in the agreement to advance and hear arguments as the preferred means of resolving

FIGURE 1.2 Argument Involves Agreement

These agreements include:
- The agreement to resolve disagreement through argumentation
- Agreements about procedures
- Agreements about goals
- Agreements about evidence

disagreements. The most basic agreement involved in reasoning with another person is the **rule of reason,** *the agreement to engage in the cooperative process of argumentation rather than to resolve disagreement by other means.* This commitment involves the intentional choice of argumentation over coercion, intimidation, passivity, or violence. The rule of reason forms the foundation of all productive argumentation.

Following the rule of reason may require us to overcome a long-held cultural understanding of argument as a competition with winners and losers. Why do we tend to see argumentation as something other than a means of seeking agreements? Linguists George Lakoff and Mark Johnson point out that the language we use to talk about argument reflects the influence of an analogy between argument and warfare. We talk about winning or losing an argument, about defeating an opponent in a debate. This way of talking can blind us to the fact that argumentation also requires quite a lot of cooperation. Lakoff and Johnson point out that "in the midst of a heated argument, when we are intent on attacking our opponent's position and defending our own, we may lose sight of the cooperative aspects of arguing." They go on to explain that "someone who is arguing with you can be viewed as giving you his time, a valuable commodity, in an effort at mutual understanding. But when we are preoccupied with the battle aspects, we often lose sight of the cooperative aspects."[6]

What other agreements provide a foundation for constructive argumentation? Argumentation often involves agreement about **procedures,** *the rules or guidelines according to which argumentation will take place.* We see agreement about procedures in courts of law, in which each argument, each piece of evidence, must be presented according to recognized rules. The judge is supposed to ensure that the rules are followed. Procedures may also be agreed upon in other settings. Some student and civic organizations follow rules about how debate or discussion will take place within the organization. For instance, a student group sponsoring a discussion about sexuality might require that participants avoid labels, clichés, personal attacks, or emotional appeals, in order to make discussions more productive and less contentious.

Argumentation also may involve agreements about the *goals* of the exchange of arguments. For instance, in some disputes legislators may agree that the goal of their deliberations is to craft laws that benefit the largest number of people. In court, advocates agree that their goal is a just resolution of the case at hand. Even a disagreement between friends about what to do for an evening's entertainment may involve an unstated agreement that the goal is to have the most fun within the limits set by the available money and time.

Argumentation often also exhibits some agreements about *evidence,* although there may be disagreements about its quality or interpretation. For instance, both parties to a court case might agree that the defendant wrote a particular letter, though they might disagree about the intent, interpretation, or significance of the letter. Legislators might agree about evidence that their state is facing a serious waste disposal problem, but disagree about how the problem should be solved. Two friends may agree that one of them made a particular comment about the other, but disagree about what the comment meant.

Any productive process of argumentation occurs within a framework of agreements. Even participants in argumentation over controversial topics such as nuclear power or gun control can agree on some points that can make meaningful argumentation possible.

A COMMITMENT TO ETHICAL ADVOCACY

Achieving argumentative goals involves ethical and rational obligations associated with advancing and responding to arguments in public settings. Because argumentation provides the very foundation of democratic processes, we all incur a responsibility to prepare ourselves to be rational participants in public life. Studying the basic principles of argumentation is an important part of that preparation. Because argumentation often is undertaken in an effort to persuade others—to change another person's way of thinking, indeed, to make that person's thinking more like our own—we should aim not to deceive or in other ways take advantage of our audience members. We have a moral responsibility to advance arguments that are sound and to provide our audiences with accurate, up-to-date evidence and information.

Argumentation also involves a commitment to share our reasons with others as we seek to resolve disagreements. We incur the responsibility to present our views clearly and in such a way that others have a chance to respond with their own views. This commitment to the process of argumentation carries with it an obligation to view others as capable of reasonable argument and rational decision making. These and other ethical and rational responsibilities of advocates will be explored in detail in Chapters 4 and 5.

The next step toward accomplishing the three goals mentioned at the outset of this chapter is to develop a basic vocabulary for discussing arguments and to consider the structure of arguments. These topics are taken up in Chapter 2.

CHAPTER REVIEW

This chapter introduces the social activity known as argumentation, which we defined as the cooperative activity of developing and advancing arguments and of responding to the arguments of others. Arguments are typically advanced before an audience. We adapt our arguments to what we know of the audience's beliefs, values, and assumptions.

Arguments and argumentation characterize nearly every area of our lives, including our increasingly online existence. Argumentation is crucial to a vibrant democratic and pluralistic society, because democracy itself depends on the free expression and continuous interaction of differing points of view. For this reason, free societies protect and encourage the public advocacy of diverse viewpoints. The desire to be successful advocates for our own ideas and the goal of improving public discourse provide important reasons for studying argumentation. This text is intended to help you understand and evaluate arguments you encounter, learn how to compose and present your own arguments more effectively, and enhance your appreciation of the ethical use of arguments.

The chapter has considered our three major goals in developing and advancing arguments—to persuade others, to justify positions we hold, and to discover new information on important issues. We also explored the important place that both values and agreements have in the argumentative process. A value shared by all responsible advocates is the agreement to resolve disagreement through argumentation, the rule of reason.

EXERCISES

A. Provide definitions for the following terms.

advocacy

argument

argumentation

audience

pluralistic culture

power

procedures

public discourse

rule of reason

values

B. Identify four of your own values that might influence how you interpret information you hear or read. How did you acquire these values? Identify and describe a situation in which one or more of these values informed an argument you advanced.

C. Suggest one conclusion that you might draw from each the following facts. Identify the value that led you from the fact to your conclusion.

1. The National Cancer Institute estimates that 480,000 people die in the United States every year from tobacco-related illnesses.

2. More than 2,000 new religions emerged in the United States during the twentieth century.

3. There are 250,000 deaths each year in the United States due to medical error on the part of doctors, nurses, pharmacists, and hospital staff. Thus, medical error is the nation's third leading cause of death.

4. More than 60 percent of all deaths from gunshots each year in the US are suicides.

5. Cases of adult onset or type 2 diabetes rose from 2 percent of the population in 1973, or 4.2 million Americans, to 7 percent, or 21 million Americans, in 2010.

6. China has the fastest-growing economy in the world.

7. The abortion rate has dropped to its lowest point—15 per 1,000 women— since the 1973 *Roe v. Wade* decision.

8. The United States incarcerates more than 2.3 million people—1 in every 150 of its adult citizens, the highest percentage of any country in the world.

9. The world's oceans have risen by seven inches in the last century.

10. A total of $102 billion was spent on ads sent to mobile phones and tablets worldwide in 2017. That's a fourfold increase over 2013.

ENDNOTES

[1]Seeger's song, "Waist Deep in the Big Muddy," for example, was a criticism of President Lyndon Johnson's policies in Vietnam.

[2]The quotation is attributed to Lincoln in Carl Sandburg's book, *Abraham Lincoln: The War Years* (New York: Harcourt & Brace, 1939). It is often misquoted as, "So, you're the little lady who started this big war."

[3]See, for example, Michael Billig, *Arguing and Thinking,* 2nd ed. (Cambridge, U.K.: Cambridge University Press, 1996).

[4]Hugo Mercier and Dan Sperber, "Why do Humans Reason? Arguments for an Argumentative Theory," *Behavioral and Brain Sciences* 34 (2011): 57–111, 58.

[5]Charles C. Camosy, "5 Tips for Creating Civil Discourse in an Era of Polarization," *Seattle Times,* July 19, 2012, http://seattletimes.com/html/opinion/2018728414_guest20charlescamosy.html.

[6]George Lakoff and Mark Johnson, *Metaphors We Live By* (Chicago: University of Chicago Press, 1980, 2003), 10.

RECOMMENDED WEBSITES

Institute for Civic Discourse and Democracy

www.k-state.edu/icdd

Many universities and other organizations have established working groups that are attempting to improve the quality of public discourse on controversial issues. This website introduces one such effort at Kansas State University.

The OpEd Project Byline Report

www.theopedproject.org

The OpEd Project approaches the question of public discourse by examining the writers who shape public opinion.

2 The Elements of Arguments

How can I tell what I think till I see what I say?
E. M. Forster (1879–1970)
British novelist

We haven't got the money, so we've got to think!
Ernest Rutherford (1871–1937)
British physicist

KEY TERMS

case	cues	propositions of fact
claim	evidence	propositions of policy
conclusion	fact	propositions of value
connectives	indicators	reason
criteria of evaluation	inference	reservation
	logical sense	structure of inferences
	predictive	

The word "argument" has at least two common meanings, so we need to clarify what we mean by that term. When we speak of people "having an argument," we mean they are disagreeing, perhaps angrily, about some matter. We also speak of someone "making an argument," "advancing an argument," or even "crafting an argument," suggesting that he or she is presenting reasons in support of a conclusion or claim. In the midst of the first kind of argument, the second kind of argument is often advanced. Understanding, composing, and evaluating this second kind of argument are among the main concerns of this text.

Let's look more closely at what goes into such arguments. In the process we will develop a basic theory of argument that we will come back to throughout the book.

ARGUMENTS: CONCLUSIONS AND THEIR REASONS

A first step toward understanding and evaluating arguments is knowing what an argument is and recognizing the elements from which arguments are composed. We defined an argument in Chapter 1 as a claim advanced with a reason or reasons in its support. This definition suggests that an argument is a composite of different kinds of statements—claims and reasons. When someone advances an argument,

FIGURE 2.1 Definitions: Claim, Argument, Reason, and Conclusion

Claim: A statement the advocate believes or is in the process of evaluating.

Argument: A claim advanced along with a reason or reasons in its support.

Reason: A statement advanced for the purpose of establishing a claim.

Conclusion: A claim that has been reached by a process of reasoning.

typically that person is, at the minimum, presenting a **claim**—which we define here as *a statement the advocate believes or is in the process of evaluating*—and also providing a reason or reasons for believing or considering that claim. A **reason** is *a statement advanced for the purpose of establishing a claim*. A **conclusion** is *a claim that has been reached by a process of reasoning. The rational movement from a particular reason or reasons to a particular conclusion* is called an **inference**. When we make an argument, we are translating an internal and private activity of reasoning into a public statement tailored to a particular audience.

The term "argument" may also refer to a series of reason-conclusion units that all tend to support the same assertion. Thus, a single sentence in a newspaper editorial might advance an argument if it includes a claim and a supporting reason. The entire editorial may also be referred to as "advancing an argument." A **case** is *a series of arguments, all advanced to support the same general contention or set of conclusions.* Thus, an advocate for nuclear power plants advances a case that includes arguments about safety issues, costs, environmental issues, and gaining community acceptance for a particular plant.

Let's consider another example. If a man tells a joke with a sexual theme to a group that includes a woman, is that a form of sexual harassment? The following is an argument for answering this question affirmatively:

> Making sexual jokes in conversations with women is a form of sexual harassment. This is because such jokes are almost always demeaning to women. Any activity that demeans women is a case of harassment.

Which statements are the reasons in this argument? Which statement is the conclusion? You probably identified the first statement as the point of the argument, its conclusion. You also may have identified the other statements as reasons.

Here's another brief example of an argument:

> Competency tests should be required of all public school teachers, because these tests would establish a standard of performance for all teachers and also identify the least capable teachers.

The first part of the sentence states a conclusion. The second part of the sentence—introduced by the word "because"—advances reasons for the conclusion.

Assertion vs. Argument

Our definition of an argument suggests that not all assertions or contentions qualify as arguments. When we make an argument in public, we ask an audience to believe that a statement is true on the basis of other statements. We owe our audience—whether it is one person or many—the presentation of our own reasons for believing the statement.

Thus, a series of assertions, even if they all seem to express the same view, does not by itself count as an argument. In order to call a series of statements an argument, we have to see the reason-conclusion relationship emerge. Suppose you see the following letter to the editor of your local paper:

> Dear Editor:
> Global warming is the greatest threat to our security and safety as a nation. It is also the greatest threat to the other nations of the world. The United States has done relatively little to address this important issue.

Though the author of this letter is clearly concerned about global warming, and though there is certainly an argumentative feel to the letter, there are no clear reason-conclusion relationships among the statements here, only a series of assertions. This letter does not count as an argument because it does not satisfy the basic criterion of providing a claim along with a reason or reasons in its support.

Identifying Reasons and Conclusions

How do we know which statement in an argument is the conclusion and which statements are the reasons? First, *your sense of how arguments develop,* which we call **logical sense,** suggests to you what the argument's conclusion is. You have been making and evaluating arguments most of your life, so you have a fairly well-developed sense of what other people are advancing as claims and what they are presenting as support for these claims. Logical sense probably suggested to you that the first example argument on page 18 advanced a claim about the nature of sexual jokes and that the conclusion of the argument was this statement: Making sexual jokes in conversations with women is a form of sexual harassment.

Logical sense may not always be sufficient for accurately distinguishing reasons from conclusions, however. Fortunately, arguments often include **indicators,** *words and phrases such as "because" and "therefore" that provide important clues to identifying reasons and conclusions in an argument.* Indicators, when present, mark important points in a **structure of inferences,** *the relationships among the reasons and the conclusions in an argument.* An indicator signals that a reason or a conclusion is being, or has been, advanced. When used in an argument, words and phrases such as "since," "because," "the following evidence shows," and "my reason being" signal that a reason will follow. Other indicators for reasons include "for," "consider that," and "is shown by." Indicators for conclusions include "therefore," "thus," "hence," "so," "which shows that," "which leads me to conclude that," and many others.

Like logical sense, indicators are not always sufficient to reveal the structure of an argument. Some reasons or conclusions in an argument may be signaled by indicators; others may not. Moreover, indicators tell us only where a speaker or writer intended an inference, not whether the inference is a good one. Indicators only suggest the presence of reasons and conclusions, not their quality.

Other words may also help us to detect an argument's structure. **Cues** in arguments are *words or phrases that signal something, other than a reason or a conclusion, about the content of an argument.* For instance, the cue "and" may signal the parallel status of two reasons or two conclusions, as in the example:

> Because it requires the killing of animals *and* because I believe it is bad for your health, I don't eat meat.

Here the cue "and" tells us that the first two statements perform similar functions in the argument. By itself, however, "and" does not tell us that these statements are reasons. The indicator "because" does that.

FIGURE 2.2 Indicators and Cues

Indicators

Provide important clues to identifying an argument's reasons and conclusions. For example:

> *Because, since,* and phrases such as *the following evidence shows* signal that a reason will follow.

> *Therefore, thus, so,* and *hence* indicate that a conclusion will follow.

Cues

Signal something about an argument's content other than reasons or conclusions. For example:

> *And* frequently indicates a parallel relationship between two statements.

> *Although* and *nevertheless* often signal that the author is aware of a counter-argument.

> *In addition* and *moreover* can signal the introduction of a new line of argument.

> *First, second,* and *finally* are quantitative cues, designating a series of reasons for a conclusion.

A cue such as "although" or "nevertheless" may signal that the person advancing the argument is aware of a counter-argument. The following is an example of "although" signaling the acknowledged presence of a counter-argument:

> Although cosmetic companies allege that such tests are necessary to protect consumers, I believe that testing cosmetics on the skin of living animals is immoral because it violates the animal's right to live its life free of artificially inflicted pain.

The first statement in the argument—which we will call a **reservation**—is included in the argument, not because it is a reason or a conclusion but, rather, because it is *a statement that acknowledges the existence of an argument, evidence, or an attitude opposing the conclusion being advanced.* Other important cues include "moreover" and "in addition," which signal the introduction of a new line of argument, a second conclusion, or perhaps an additional item of information. Similarly, quantitative cues such as "first," "second," and "finally" may point to a series of reasons that all tend to support a single conclusion. In some cases, quantitative cues may designate several conclusions derived from a single set of evidence.

TWO TYPES OF REASONS: EVIDENCE AND CONNECTIVES

We have said that arguments are composed of reasons and conclusions. This isn't the whole story, though. There are at least two kinds of reasons and several different types of conclusions. This section considers two types of reasons that work together in arguments. The next section considers three types of propositions that may serve as the conclusion of an argument.

The first type of reason, **evidence,** is *a reason rooted in observation,* either your own or someone else's. The observation may be as systematic as a carefully conducted study of cancer cells in a Petri dish, or as casual as the observation that the weather is getting colder. Evidence may be derived from expert testimony, eyewitness reports, statistical reports, surveys, examples, or comparisons. Statements serving as evidence can usually be shown to be true or false in some definite or demonstrable way. In some arguments, however, the evidence can be identified only because it is the most specific statement or statements in the argument. In the following example, the first sentence is presented as evidence supporting the second sentence, which begins with a reservation and then presents the argument's conclusion:

> National Highway Traffic Administration statistics indicate that more than ten thousand people in the United States were killed in automobile accidents caused by drunk drivers in 2016. This figure represents the first time since 2012 that drunk-driving deaths have exceeded ten thousand. Clearly we still need strong laws to protect us from drunk drivers.

Not all reasons can be classified as evidence. **Connectives** are *reasons that consist of beliefs, values, assumptions, or generalizations that link evidence to a conclusion.* Unlike evidence, connectives cannot always be demonstrated to be true or false—they are often assumed, presupposed, or taken for granted. For instance, the belief that human beings have certain basic rights is not so much an observation as it is a belief about people. Similarly, a value for fairness or honesty cannot be proved the way the distance between the earth and moon can. If you believe that people should not kill animals for food, that war is never justified, that working hard is the only way to be successful, or that the government should not legislate moral behavior, these beliefs are, for you, potential connectives in arguments. Widely accepted generalizations, such as that people need food and water to survive, that mammals are warm-blooded, or that vaccinations tend to prevent the spread of childhood diseases, may also serve as connectives in arguments. Such generalizations are sometimes capable of rigorous proof, much as evidence is. Connectives, then, are reasons that reflect personal commitments, such as beliefs and values, or generalizations that are widely accepted. Their function is to connect evidence to conclusions.

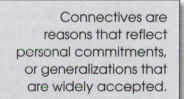

Connectives are reasons that reflect personal commitments, or generalizations that are widely accepted.

Even a very simple argument typically incorporates both evidence and a connective. The mental process of making an inference usually involves combining some bit of evidence with a connective—a belief, value, assumption, or generalization—and deriving a conclusion from this combination of reasons. Evidence and connectives are each necessary to complete an inference, even in cases where one of these two reasons is assumed rather than directly stated.

Let's look again at the argument about drunk driving. It involved an unstated reason, specifically, an unstated connective. The argument presents evidence and a conclusion, but no stated connective. We can try to supply the missing connective to show how the complete argument might look, but bear in mind that we are guessing about the connective in the mind of the argument's author:

> **Evidence:** Bureau of Transportation statistics indicate that for the first time since 2012 more than ten thousand people in the United States were killed in automobile accidents caused by drunk drivers.
>
> **Connective:** [When a clear threat to public safety is present and growing, strong laws are still needed for protection from that threat.]
>
> **Conclusion:** Clearly we need strong laws to protect us from drunk drivers.

The brackets indicate that the missing connective was added to an argument that did not originally state it. Notice how this connective represents a personal belief or value—that laws are needed to protect the public from significant dangers. Others might not hold this view; they might object that we should protect ourselves from dangers and not rely so much on the government. The connective was not presented in the original argument, perhaps because the writer thought the idea expressed in the connective was obvious and did not have to be articulated.

Although the beliefs, values, assumptions, and generalizations that connect evidence to a conclusion are often left unstated in an argument, they are always present and at work in the reasoning process. Moreover, changing the connective results in different conclusions from the same evidence. The following set of brief arguments illustrates this point. The four cases start with the same piece of evidence, but arrive at four different conclusions by following different connectives:

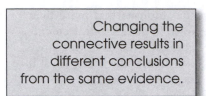

Changing the connective results in different conclusions from the same evidence.

> **Evidence:** More than two thousand new religions emerged in the United States in the twentieth century.
>
> **Connective:** [People seek alternatives when they are dissatisfied with the status quo.]
>
> **Conclusion:** There must have been widespread dissatisfaction with traditional religions in the twentieth century.

> **Evidence:** More than two thousand new religions emerged in the United States in the twentieth century.
>
> **Connective:** [People only explore alternatives to established beliefs when they are in a free and open environment for inquiry.]
>
> **Conclusion:** The United States in the twentieth century must have provided people with a free and open environment to explore new ideas.

> **Evidence:** More than two thousand new religions emerged in the United States in the twentieth century.
>
> **Connective:** [A diverse population will produce diverse belief systems.]
>
> **Conclusion:** The United States in the twentieth century was becoming a highly diverse culture.

> **Evidence:** More than two thousand new religions emerged in the United States in the twentieth century.
>
> **Connective:** [New communication technologies expose people to a wider range of ideas.]
>
> **Conclusion:** Emerging technologies allowed propagation of a wide range of alternative religious beliefs in the twentieth century.

As these examples show, connectives play a crucial role in the reasoning process and have a dramatic impact on which conclusions we draw from the available evidence.

PROPOSITIONS OF FACT, VALUE, AND POLICY

Argumentation is the means by which we advance our conclusions and back them up with our reasons. The conclusions of arguments can be categorized under the three headings of: (1) propositions of fact, (2) propositions of value, and (3) propositions of policy. As the kinds of arguments needed to support each type of proposition vary in some respects, these categories help us determine what to expect or require in support of a particular type of conclusion. How, then, can we identify each type of proposition?

Propositions of Fact

Some conclusions are **propositions of fact,** *statements that report, describe, predict, or make causal claims.* Examples include statements such as:

> Support for a cap on pharmaceutical costs will increase over the next five years.

> Shanghai is the most populous city in the world.

> Housing starts were up in August.

> Melting polar ice caps are a direct result of global warming.

To call a statement a proposition of fact is not the same as to say the statement is true. For instance, controversy has always surrounded the assassination of John F. Kennedy in November 1963. Claims and counter-claims have been advanced endlessly, particularly surrounding the question of whether Lee Harvey Oswald acted alone in murdering the president. Nevertheless, the claim "Lee Harvey Oswald acted alone in killing President John F. Kennedy" still counts as a proposition of fact, as do other statements that purport to describe historical events. You may be thinking that "Oswald acted alone in killing President John F. Kennedy" is not a fact, that it is only a theory, an opinion, or a hypothesis, but the word **fact** as we are using it here applies to *a claim that can potentially be verified as either true or false.* This claim about Oswald is either true or false despite the fact that experts on the assassination disagree about its accuracy; Oswald either did or did not act alone in killing the president.

Causal claims are categorized as propositions of fact. For example, "The extinction of the dinosaurs was caused by an asteroid striking the earth off the coast of the present-day Yucatan peninsula" is a proposition of fact. The claim that "The extinction of the dinosaurs was caused by emerging mammal species eating their eggs" is also a proposition of fact, though it may not be widely accepted as an accurate theory. Because causal relationships between events are potentially verifiable as either true or false, all causal claims are propositions of fact.

> All causal claims are propositions of fact.

Propositions of fact may be **predictive,** *making claims about the future.* The statement "San Francisco will be destroyed by an earthquake sometime in the next century" is a predictive factual claim. This event either will or will not occur, so this predictive claim is a proposition of fact.

What kind of extended argument or "case" provides support for a proposition of fact? Briefly, the case supporting a proposition of fact should satisfy the following three criteria:

1. Advance sufficient evidence to support the factual claim.

2. Clarify and interpret the evidence for the audience.

3. Ensure that the evidence's relevance to the claim is made clear.

Let's apply these criteria briefly to one of our examples. The theory that the dinosaurs were wiped out by an asteroid striking the earth was first proposed in the 1970s by the team of Nobel Prize–winning physicist Luis Alvarez, his son Walter, and other scientists from the University of California. The principal fact this team brought forward was the existence of an extensive subterranean layer of clay in various parts of the world. This clay showed very high levels of the rare chemical iridium. Added to this observation was a second one—iridium is found in large amounts in meteors and asteroids. The scientists interpreted the iridium as evidence of a massive asteroid strike. Because of the amounts and vast extent of the iridium, the asteroid was estimated to have been four to eight miles in diameter. Judging from the depth of the clay in the earth's crust, scientists believed the asteroid strike must have occurred about sixty-five million years ago, the time when dinosaurs are known to have started disappearing. At this point, the evidence for a particular factual claim had been both advanced and interpreted.

The next step was to relate the evidence to the claim that this asteroid strike could have led to the demise of the dinosaurs. A strike of such magnitude would have sent enormous amounts of dust and other debris into the atmosphere, leading to global cooling. Temperatures dropped precipitously: the earth would suddenly have been too cool to allow the survival of cold-blooded reptiles such as dinosaurs, though warm-blooded mammals would have been relatively unaffected. The Alvarezes and their colleagues thus successfully connected their evidence to their factual claim. Their theory about the disappearance of the dinosaurs is still the most widely accepted.

Propositions of Value

Propositions of value are *statements that advance judgments about morality, beauty, merit, or wisdom.* These propositions can be identified by the presence of an evaluative term. For example, the following is a proposition of value:

> The US decision not to intervene during the Syrian revolution was unconscionable.

The reasons supporting this conclusion might include:

> because intervention could have saved the lives of hundreds of thousands of people, and because our failure to intervene sent the signal to the world that the West does not care about the fate of the Syrian people.

Other propositions of value include:

> The Pittsburgh Steelers team of the 1970s was the best football team ever.
>
> *Allegiant* was a terrible movie.
>
> Capital punishment is immoral.

Value claims also may compare the relative merit of two objects. Recently, for example, the Social Security system has received a great deal of attention because it had been suggested that the funding in the system was inadequate to cover Social Security payments to the large number of baby boomers who would soon be retiring. Several experts assert, however, that the Medicare crisis is much more serious than the Social Security crisis. These experts are advancing a value claim that makes a comparative evaluation of the seriousness of two similar situations. Other examples of comparative evaluations include:

> Robert Downey Jr.'s *Sherlock Holmes* films are better than his *Iron Man* films.
>
> Social programs that provide early childhood education are more important than military projects.

Paying for products with cash is a better idea than accumulating credit card debt.

Just as a case supporting a proposition of fact should meet specific standards, a fully developed case in support of a proposition of value should satisfy three criteria:

1. Clarify the **criteria of evaluation**—*the standards on which a value judgment is based.*

2. Provide evidence supporting the evaluation.

3. Set out evidence to show that the criteria of evaluation have been satisfied.

Let's look first at the issue of clarifying criteria of evaluation. If I assert, "*La La Land* was a great movie," my argument in support of this claim should advance criteria defining the term "great" when applied to a movie. These criteria might include the following:

A great movie will exhibit (1) good acting, (2) excellent writing, (3) high quality cinematography, and (4) a strong plot.

These are my four criteria of "movie greatness." As long as I have not neglected an obviously important criterion, I have satisfied the first requirement of an argument supporting a proposition of value. Others may disagree with my criteria or advance a different set of criteria for greatness in a movie, but I have made my criteria clear. Of course, each of these criteria also contains an evaluation that may need to be clarified as well. For instance, how will "good acting" or "excellent writing" be defined?

The second requirement of an argument supporting a value claim is that it would advance evidence to support the evaluation. We will talk in greater detail about evidence later in the text; for now, though, we can point out that my case should provide evidence of the movie's greatness. For example, I might point out that the movie received dozens of awards from groups such as the American Film Institute, the National Society of Film Critics, and the National Board of Review.

The third criterion requires applying the criteria directly to the object being evaluated. For example, one criterion was excellent writing. I could point out that Damien Chazelle's screenplay won a Golden Globe award, as evidence that the movie satisfies this criterion. I might also provide evidence from a recognized expert about the high quality of Linus Sandgren's cinematography and point out that his work was nominated for an American Society of Cinematographers award.

Now I have explained my criteria for evaluation, provided evidence in support of the evaluation, and used the evidence to connect the criteria to the object being evaluated.

Let's look at another example where criteria of evaluation come into play in supporting value judgments, this time for a comparative evaluation. Each year, *U.S. News and World Report,* a highly regarded magazine, publishes its rankings of the top universities in the United States. These rankings are available on the magazine's web site (www.usnews.com). Recently the magazine ranked Princeton University as the nation's top university, followed by Harvard and then the University of Chicago.

But suppose that a member of the audience, hearing this claim about Princeton in a speech, happens to be from the West Coast. Her suspicion is aroused about the evidence because Cal Tech, Stanford, and the University of California at Berkeley were not listed among the nation's top three universities. She asks herself, "What factors were considered in arriving at these rankings?" That is, she wants to know the criteria of evaluation *U.S. News* employed in arriving at its rankings.

Fortunately for the speaker involved, *U.S. News* publishes not only its rankings but also its criteria of evaluation. The magazine's website provides an easy link to a complete discussion of its selection criteria, with the title "Best Colleges Ranking Criteria and Weights." Criteria are clearly discussed on the web page and include academic reputation, retention, faculty resources, student selectivity, and financial resources. Even if the audience member still disagrees with the evaluation of graduate programs, the criteria of evaluation have been made clear and evidence has been provided that links the criteria to the schools in question.[1]

Propositions of Policy

Propositions of policy are *statements that urge that an action be taken or discontinued.* Thus, "The US space program should be abandoned," is a proposition of policy. Reasons presented in support of this policy claim might include "because the money spent on the program is needed to solve social problems." Other examples of propositions of policy are:

> You should recycle.
>
> We ought not to discriminate in hiring on the basis of sexual orientation.
>
> Arizona must develop a new water policy.
>
> The US Senate should ratify the Paris Accords.

As with propositions of fact and value, an argument supporting a proposition of policy should accomplish specific goals:

1. Provide evidence that a problem exists as a result of the present way of doing things.
2. Show that the problem is serious and in need of immediate attention.
3. Outline a proposal for changes that will solve the problem without causing additional problems.

You may have noticed that the first goal would involve proving a proposition of fact and that the second goal would involve arguing for a proposition of value. Typically, propositions of fact and value are advanced and supported as part of the effort to establish a proposition of policy. For example, imagine that you are arguing that the United States should take a more aggressive response to the AIDS crisis in Africa. You may need to show that AIDS currently affects millions of people in Africa, which is a proposition of fact. From this fact you might conclude that AIDS is the most serious health crisis facing Africa, a proposition of value. Both points would have to be established before you could expect your audience to accept the proposition of policy, "The United States should respond more aggressively to the AIDS crisis in Africa."

Because arguing for propositions of policy is so characteristic of public debate settings, this topic is treated in detail in Appendix A.

CHAPTER REVIEW

We all make, hear, and evaluate arguments. To develop and assess arguments effectively, we need to understand their nature and structure, especially the relationships among reasons and conclusions that reflect inferences. Logical sense, indicators, and cues play roles in helping us to ascertain the structure of an argument.

We have been introduced to two different types of reasons: evidence and connectives. Evidence is a reason rooted in an observation. A connective is a reason that reflects a belief, value, assumption, or generalization, and links evidence to a conclusion.

We have also noted that conclusions are categorized under three headings: propositions of fact, value, and policy. Each type of proposition requires a specific kind of case in its support.

EXERCISES

A.   Provide a brief definition for each of the following terms, then check your definitions against those in the text:

reason

conclusion

case

inference

logical sense

indicators

cues

reservation

B.   In the following arguments, <u>underline</u> indicators and cues. Draw wavy lines under the conclusions. For example:

Legalizing drugs would radically reduce crime <u>because</u> it <u>would</u> eliminate the high cost of these substances.

1. Failing to address climate change puts future generations at risk. Thus, failure to address climate change is immoral.

2. You must have a dream to act, and you must act to live. Thus, you must have a dream to live.

3. The only way to deal with habitual criminals is incarceration. This is because there are only two possibilities: incarceration or rehabilitation. Though incarceration is expensive and difficult, rehabilitation simply does not work.

4. "Wherever there are laws, there will be lawyers, and where there are lawyers, there will be arguments, for it is by argument that they earn their livings. Thus, where there are laws there will be arguments."[2]

5. Fines and suspensions are often handed out when athletes turn violent during a game, but widely publicized brawls involving players as well as fans provide clear evidence that tougher measures are needed. Athletes who assault other athletes or fans during a game must be prosecuted under existing criminal statutes.

C.   Identify each of the following claims as a proposition of fact (F), value (V), or policy (P).

1. James Watson and Francis Crick discovered the complex double-helix structure of the DNA molecule in 1959.

2. Pictures beamed back from the Hubble Telescope reveal the universe to be a place of exquisite beauty.

3. The United States should immediately pass stiffer laws regulating the development of human-level artificial intelligence.

4. The Hennessey Venom GT is the fastest production car on the market.

5. It is only fair to legalize same-sex marriages.

6. At the current rate of consumption, Earth's reserves of crude oil will be depleted by 2080.

7. Moving forward with natural gas extraction using fracking is more important than developing solar energy technologies.

8. There has been a 30 percent increase in arrests of women for drunk-driving infractions since 1997.

9. We must pass stiffer handgun legislation immediately.

10. Russian intervention in US elections poses a grave threat to US security.

D. Underline any indicators or cues in each of the following examples. Draw a wavy line under the conclusion. Then, label the conclusion as a proposition of fact, value, or policy:

1. A recent poll by the Pew Research Center revealed that 48 percent of US voters view the Republican Party as friendly to religion, while only 28 percent view the Democratic Party the same way. Thus, Democrats should start now to develop a strategy for winning over the deeply religious voter.

2. The number of prisoners serving life sentences has now risen to a record 160,000, compared with 34,000 in 1984. This dramatic increase proves that new, stiffer sentencing guidelines are working to keep criminals off the street.

3. Nuclear arms have prevented war in the past, so they will do the same in the future.

4. State lotteries are morally unacceptable as they tend to cheat the poorest members of society out of their much-needed monetary resources.

5. A recent examination of databases from more than 125 US colleges and universities receiving government funds for programs designed to reduce the number of rapes on campus revealed that fewer than one in three men responsible for a sexual assault were expelled.

6. Decisions in Japanese corporations are made by groups rather than individuals. Thus, decisions in Japanese corporations are made more fairly than in US corporations.

7. Gambling is an activity that cannot be stopped. Therefore, gambling should be legalized.

8. The United States's failure to intervene in Myanmar is unconscionable, as this failure revealed an utter disregard for human rights.

9. US citizens have gained twenty-eight years in life expectancy in the past century. This finding proves that the current system of medical care is working to preserve and improve health.

10. Instituting a military draft should take place immediately because this is the only equitable way to staff our armed forces.

E. Explain how the value judgment "better" is defined differently in the following examples:

1. Online reading programs function better than traditional teachers because they can cater to individual student needs in the elementary school classroom. No teacher can tailor a customized reading program for twenty-eight students, but that is exactly what the new programs do. Online programs are vastly more efficient educators than teachers are.

2. Education is an inherently relational activity. Online reading instruction programs are not better at teaching children, they are just more efficient at delivering a certain kind of content to kids. The teacher is vastly better at detecting individual student learning styles and emotional needs—concerns that are at the very heart of teaching.

ENDNOTES

[1]Robert Morse and Eric Brooks, "Best Colleges Ranking Criteria and Weights," September 12, 2016, http://www.usnews.com/education/best-colleges/articles/ranking-criteria-and-weights.

[2]Michael Billig, *Arguing and Thinking: A Rhetorical Approach to Social Psychology,* 2nd ed. (Cambridge, U.K.: Cambridge University Press, 1996), 28.

RECOMMENDED WEBSITES

National Institute for Civil Discourse

nicd.arizona.edu

The mission of the University of Arizona's National Institute for Civil Discourse is "fostering an open exchange of ideas and expression of values that will lead to better problem-solving and more effective government." (nicd.arizona.edu/purpose) The website explores a variety of topics introduced in this chapter.

Pew Research Center for the People & the Press

people-press.org

The Pew Research Center for the People & the Press, an organization that works to improve the quality of public debate and to track trends in public opinion, provides this helpful website.

3 Tools for Analyzing Arguments

Why should you mind being wrong
if someone can show you that you are?
A. J. Ayer (1910–1989)
British philosopher

I dislike arguments of any kind.
They are always vulgar, and often convincing.
Oscar Wilde (1854–1900)
Irish playwright

KEY TERMS

backing

claim

complementary
  reasons

data

deductive argument

diagramming

inductive argument

inductive leap

intermediate
  conclusion

linguistic link

modal qualifiers

necessary conclusion

premise

probable conclusion

rebuttals

scanning

standardizing

statement

straw man argument

warrant

Over morning coffee a friend argues that the apparent design of nature means there must be a God. At lunch another friend states that all the pain and suffering in the world makes him think there must *not* be a God. At the office, a coworker argues for a new health insurance plan because of the broader coverage it would provide; another argues against it based on cost. On a weekend visit, a family member makes a case for investing in real estate; another argues, just as persuasively, that you should invest your extra money in solar energy. On the ride home, a radio commentator argues that the Dallas Cowboys are destined to win the Super Bowl.

We encounter arguments continuously, day in and day out. Most of us are constantly evaluating arguments. We advance our own, as well, to support our views on everything from music to medicine, from sports to social issues, from religion to relationships. As Chapter 1 points out, presenting, hearing, and evaluating arguments are activities central to our public and private lives, and for good reasons. The cooperative process of argumentation helps us forge agreements between groups embracing disparate values, facilitates the discovery of new facts, resolves misunderstanding, and moves us toward solutions to social and personal problems.

Entering the process of argumentation involves effort. For example, virtually all arguments—our own as well as others'—invite different interpretations. To understand an argument accurately, we must ascertain the connections between reasons and conclusions, set arguments in their appropriate contexts, and sometimes search for missing background information. Our effort is reduced and the accuracy of our understanding is increased, however, if we can approach arguments systematically.

Most of the time we approach arguments rather unsystematically. We hear or read an argument and quickly form a judgment based on our sense or intuition as to whether it is reasonable or unreasonable. This is not a problem when little is at stake. When a decision is important, though, an informed understanding of arguments can help us identify what we are being asked to accept, and on what basis. Setting out our own arguments clearly and persuasively is also important. We want others to understand our points of view on important issues. Sometimes we want to convince others that our perspective on a topic is worthy of their acceptance.

> An informed understanding of arguments can help us identify what we are being asked to accept, and on what basis.

You may feel unsure of your ability to present your point of view adequately, whether to friends or to a large group. Here we encounter yet another reason for studying argumentation—having a basic grasp on the structure of arguments and on the principles of sound reasoning can help you feel more confident in presenting your own arguments.

To be an effective producer and critic of arguments, it helps to possess a systematic understanding of arguments as well as some terminology and principles for discussing, interpreting, and evaluating them. Chapter 2 introduced you to the basic components of arguments—reasons, conclusions, and the indicators and cues that, when present, mark an argument's structure of inferences. This chapter provides additional tools for understanding the structure and content of arguments you encounter. You can also use these tools in developing your own arguments.

As you begin to analyze arguments, you will notice that they don't all work the same way. People have different preferred ways of reasoning, employing different kinds of arguments, and advancing various types of evidence. Some people prefer to reason from moral principles, others from practical consequences. Some people like generalizations, while others appreciate a good, specific example. Some people are drawn to comparisons or analogies; others are always suspicious of them.

In this chapter, we'll consider when and in what contexts we are most likely to encounter other people's arguments and to develop arguments of our own. We will examine the two major divisions of arguments—deductive and inductive arguments—and three tools for analyzing arguments. The chapter also examines the Toulmin model, a popular model for displaying the various parts of an argument. We will conclude the chapter by exploring the important issue of supplying parts of an argument that have been left unstated.

WHEN ARGUMENTS ARE AND ARE NOT LIKELY

Knowing the contexts or settings in which arguments typically occur—and where they are less likely—can assist you in distinguishing arguments from other kinds of discourse, such as reports, explanations, and unsubstantiated assertions. Let's consider some of the settings in which we all find ourselves from time to time, and in which arguments are likely to occur.

When We Expect Arguments

First, and most generally, we expect to hear or read arguments when an assertion seems to require reasoned support. Sometimes we have a sense that a statement must have reasons to support it, that most reasonable people in most contexts would not accept it uncritically. Statements such as "abortion is wrong," "Ronald Reagan was the best president of the twentieth century," "the earth's climate is gradually warming," or "there should be no speed limit laws" require reasoned support in the form of evidence for many people to consider accepting them as true or accurate. You also might imagine settings in which any of these statements would be accepted without evidence. For instance, a pro-life organization might not require a speaker to provide proof for the statement that abortion is wrong. Nevertheless, any time it makes sense to ask, in response to an assertion, "Why do you think that?" the statement probably requires reasons to undergird it.

Once that support is presented, we have an argument—a claim advanced with a reason or reasons to support it. This is not to say that once we hear reasons, we have heard a *good* argument. The quality of arguments varies dramatically from one instance to another, and the criteria satisfied by good arguments will be discussed in subsequent chapters.

Second, arguments are expected in the context of controversy or disagreement. If someone says, "The high cost of medical insurance is destroying our medical establishment," we would expect that reasons will be advanced to substantiate this conclusion. Similarly, arguments arise from controversy surrounding topics such as global warming, gay marriage, teaching evolution in public schools, energy policy, United States foreign policy, and many others. Controversies always involve advocates advancing and defending claims, efforts to persuade uncommitted individuals, and a search for solutions to problems—three common functions of arguments.

Third, many statements of personal opinion are accompanied by arguments. Expressing an opinion, especially a contested opinion, signals to others that you are prepared to provide supporting reasons. A statement such as "I think excessively violent video games should be banned from sale to people under the age of eighteen" might be followed by a reason such as "because such games have the potential for suggesting violent or otherwise dangerous behavior to young people." Any time you ask others—that is, an audience—to accept a claim you have made, they are entitled to ask you for your reasons before making up their minds on the issue. When you offer those reasons you are making an argument.

Fourth, inferences and predictions based on observations are also arguments. For example, if I were to say, "Someone is home because the lights are on in the house," I would be making a simple argument that involved an observation used as evidence and an explanation that serves as my conclusion. Such explanations of observations are a kind of argument. Similarly, a prediction such as, "Current economic trends, including renewed activity in the housing market and new jobs, lead me to believe that the US economy will recover in the next year," is also an argument that uses an observation as its evidence.

When We Don't Expect Arguments

We are not always interested in justifying a claim, persuading others to adopt our views, or looking for solutions to problems. Certain situations do not call forth arguments, even though the language used in these settings sometimes resembles that employed in arguments. When do we *not* expect to read or hear an argument?

First, when the cause of an event is well known, we usually expect reports or descriptions, not arguments. For example, if someone tells me that "Tides occur because of the gravitational pull of the moon on large bodies of water," I would be wrong to think I was hearing an argument. The cause of tides is so well established that an argument usually need not be set out to support the idea, even though the word "because" was used in presenting the explanation. Of course, an audience that had never heard an explanation of their cause—or that thought there was another cause—might need to hear reasons before accepting the idea that the moon causes tides. In that case, an argument would be advanced to make the case for the moon as the cause of tides, and perhaps to disprove other supposed causes.

Second, when an audience already accepts an idea as true, arguments are not needed to support the idea. Some concepts are accepted by virtually everyone, even when they are debated for academic purposes. In most contexts and for most audiences the claim "other people exist" does not require reasons to support it. On hearing such a claim, most people respond, "Of course they do. Who ever doubted that other people exist? I work with some people and live with some other people." Some philosophers *have* debated whether other people exist, or whether their existence can be proved. In this debate arguments are offered to support claims, inferences, and counter-arguments.

Some claims are accepted as true by a more limited circle. At a meeting of the National Rifle Association, the claim "the Constitution guarantees every citizen

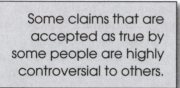

Some claims that are accepted as true by some people are highly controversial to others.

the right to own a gun" might be accepted as a statement of uncontested fact, an idea that does not require defense and that should not elicit counter-arguments. This same statement, however, would be highly controversial before a group favoring handgun registration. With this second audience, the statement would require reasoned defense and elicit strenuous counter-arguments.

Third, we might not expect arguments when neither side in a controversy wishes to challenge a claim. Imagine a criminal trial in which both the prosecution and the defense agree that the defendant killed another person. The question is not whether the act occurred, but what kind of act it was: murder, manslaughter, self-defense, or accidental homicide. Thus, the claim that "the defendant killed Mr. Watson on the evening of December 12" may not require argumentative support and may not even elicit a counter-argument. Other claims in the same case, however, will certainly be advanced to gain the jury's agreement, require reasoned support, and elicit counter-arguments. "The defendant was acting in self-defense when he killed Mr. Watson" is such a claim.

Similarly, suppose a candidate in a mayoral contest asserts that a debate between the two candidates would help the city's residents decide how to vote. If the other candidate agrees not to challenge this claim, then no arguments about whether to have a debate would be expected. The debate itself, however, would undoubtedly raise issues that would elicit arguments from each candidate.

DEDUCTIVE AND INDUCTIVE ARGUMENTS

People who study arguments have long acknowledged a difference between two basic types: deductive and inductive arguments. These two basic approaches to reasoning are common to public discourse.

Deductive arguments are *arguments that lead to necessary conclusions when their reasons are true.* Traditionally, *the reasons in a deductive argument* are called **premises.** The typical structure of a deductive argument involves moving from a general principle (sometimes called a "major premise") and a more specific observation (sometimes called a "minor premise") to a conclusion that applies the general principle to a particular case.

The conclusion of a deductive argument is said to be a **necessary conclusion,** *a particular conclusion to which the reasons or premises in a deductive argument—when accepted as true—unavoidably lead.*

Let's begin with this principle as the first reason in a deductive argument:

Men and women should receive equal pay for equal work.

Now, we can add this piece of evidence as a second reason in an argument:

Stephen and Dolores do equal work as editors for the paper.

As you can probably anticipate, the conclusion drawn from these reasons is:

Thus, Stephen and Dolores should receive equal pay.

This is a typical deductive argument, as it moves from a general principle to a specific application of that principle in a particular case. Notice that in a deduction, the conclusion does not introduce any information that is not already present in the reasons.

Inductive arguments, by contrast, are *arguments whose reasons lead to probable conclusions.* A **probable conclusion** is *a conclusion that can be shown to be more or less likely, but not necessary.* An inductive argument typically moves from specific observations to a general conclusion.

For example, a newspaper reporter writes:

In a salary audit of thirty major US businesses conducted by an independent accounting firm, male executives were paid, on average, 20 percent more than their female counterparts in comparable positions.

She then draws this probable conclusion from her evidence:

It appears that many US companies are still paying men more than women for similar work.

Notice that the conclusion of this inductive argument, which is based on the author's interpretation of the evidence, says considerably more than the evidence alone says. From the thirty businesses observed, a conclusion is drawn about US companies in general. Inductive arguments are often said to involve an **inductive leap,** *a reasoning process in which the conclusion of an inductive argument moves beyond its stated evidence.* Deductive arguments involve no such leap beyond their evidence—their conclusion is contained or "entailed" in their reasons.

This inferential movement beyond evidence is typical of inductions, and illustrates the distinction between induction and deduction. Deductions arrive at necessary conclusions, whereas inductions arrive at more or less probable conclusions. Look again at the example of a deduction:

Men and women should receive equal pay for equal work.

Stephen and Dolores do equal work as editors for the paper.

Thus, Stephen and Dolores should receive equal pay.

If we accept the two reasons in this argument as true or accurate, we cannot avoid the conclusion. This is a defining quality of deductions—when their reasons are accepted as true, their conclusions are "necessary" or unavoidable.

FIGURE 3.1 Deductive and Inductive Arguments

Deductive Arguments

- Draw *necessary* conclusions when their reasons are true.
- Typically involve moving from general principles to specific cases. For example:

  All members of the military are bound by the Uniform Code of Military Justice. Mr. Green was a member of the army last year, so he was bound by the Uniform Code at that time.

Inductive Arguments

- Draw *probable* conclusions when their reasons are true.
- Typically involve moving from specific observations to general conclusions. For example:

  The past three Republican state senates have sought to restrict the size of state programs. We just voted in another Republican state senate, and the leaders are promising to cut state programs. Clearly one goal of our state's Republican legislators is to see the size of government shrink.

Inductions, however, arrive at probable conclusions. They establish their conclusions to one degree or another of likelihood. This does not mean that inductions are inherently weaker arguments than deductions are, only that induction is appropriate in some instances, deduction in others. When I am in the initial stages of gathering evidence on a topic, I am almost compelled to operate inductively. Look again at our example of an induction:

> In an independent salary audit of thirty major businesses in the United States, male executives were paid, on average, 17 percent more than their female counterparts were. Thus, many US companies probably pay male executives more than they pay female executives for similar work.

The conclusion here expresses that the practice of disparate pay for men and women "probably" remains a problem in "many US companies." An induction is intended to show what is likely or probable—or, conversely, what is unlikely or improbable—not what is necessarily the case.

THREE TOOLS FOR ANALYZING ARGUMENTS

The three analytic tools introduced in this section can help you understand clearly how an argument—your own or someone else's—is constructed and what, exactly, it is affirming. Our discussion of inductive and deductive arguments suggests that, in addition to presenting their content, arguments also exhibit an underlying structure. Both content and structure are important in developing and evaluating arguments, a point we will return to later in the text.

Tool 1: Scanning

Sometimes it is helpful to have a method for marking and tracking the reasons, conclusions, and other elements in an argument, particularly when the statements making up an argument are similarly worded, their meanings uncertain, or their relationships to the argument's claim unclear. Once mastered, such a method can become a habitual way of thinking about arguments.

One method, **scanning,** simply involves *identifying and marking the statements in an argument, as well as underlining indicators and cues.* A **statement,** as we define it here, is *any phrase or sentence that supplies a portion of the argument's content or meaning.* Statements may be reasons, conclusions, or other considerations, such as reservations. Some appear as full sentences or clearly stated claims, others as brief phrases or even questions. In some instances a "statement" may remain unstated because it is strongly implied by other statements.

When scanning arguments, we underline indicators and cues. Individual statements are marked, using numbers, letters, or other symbols. We will be using letters. Here's an example of a scanned argument in which the indicators and cues are underlined and the statements are marked with letters:

> A: We are beginning to realize that the architecture of the brains of whales and other cetaceans is similar to that of humans. <u>This means that</u> B: such higher mammals may be self-aware. <u>Thus</u> C: it's time we recognize the basic rights of such nonhuman persons, <u>because</u> D: self-awareness is a fundamental aspect of personhood.

We can see now that this argument consists of four statements.

Here is another example:

> <u>Because</u> A: the Fed has just lowered interest rates <u>and because</u> B: banks are now anxious to revive the new home loan market, <u>we can expect that</u> C: mortgage loans will increase soon. <u>Therefore,</u> D: home sales can also be expected to increase in the last quarter of this year.

This argument has four statements. Statements A and B are reasons. Statements C and D apparently are conclusions.

Scanning can help us gain a preliminary grasp of the structure and content of an argument, but it does not reveal the precise relationships among all the elements in the argument. To find those relationships, we need additional analytic tools.

Tool 2: Standardizing

When you are writing or evaluating an argument, it can be helpful to set out the argument's statements systematically—all of its reasons, conclusions, and reservations. The method for doing this, our second analytic tool, is called **standardizing** the argument, which involves *making each statement or implied statement in the argument a complete sentence, changing indefinite references such as pronouns to the definite nouns they represent, and placing reasons above the conclusions they support.*[1] Standardizing helps us grasp an argument's logical structure, and is thus an aid to understanding, evaluating, and responding to it. When an argument is standardized, the letters assigned to statements when the argument was scanned are retained. For example:

Step 1:

> A: We are beginning to realize that the architecture of the brains of whales and other cetaceans is similar to that of humans.
>
> <u>This means that</u>
>
> B: Such higher mammals may be self-aware.
>
> <u>Thus</u>
>
> C: It's time we recognize the basic rights of such nonhuman persons.
>
> <u>Because</u>
>
> D: Self-awareness is a fundamental aspect of personhood.

The indicators and cues have been separated out to make the argument's structure easier to see. Here is how the example concerning interest rates looks after the first step in standardizing:

Because

A: The Fed has just lowered interest rates.

and because

B: Lenders are anxious to revive the home loan market.

we can expect that

C: Mortgage loans will increase soon.

Therefore,

D: Home sales can also be expected to increase in the last quarter of this year.

The second step in standardizing is to place reasons above the conclusion they support. In a finished standardization, a conclusion follows the reasons advanced in its support. *This step may require you to rearrange the reasons and conclusions in an order different from the order in the original argument.* For example:

Step 2:

A: We are beginning to realize that the architecture of the brains of whales and other cetaceans is similar to that of humans.

This means that

B: Such higher mammals may be self-aware.

Because

D: Self-awareness is a fundamental aspect of personhood.

Thus

C: It's time we recognize the basic rights of such nonhuman persons.

The order of statements in our example concerning interest rates and home sales does not have to be changed in the second step, as its reasons already precede its conclusions. When all the argument's reasons precede its conclusion, standardizing is a simple process. If an argument is written clearly, we may not have to standardize it in order to understand its inferential structure. In cases where the relationships among reasons and conclusions are not clear, however, standardizing can help clarify them.

When standardizing a longer argument, you can follow the same scanning and standardizing procedure with each set of reasons and conclusions. Here is an example of a longer argument that has been scanned:

A: Recently the exploration of space has received little attention from politicians. However, B: the US space exploration program must be pursued aggressively. C: Scrapping the space program would mean the loss of thousands of jobs in the aerospace industry. Moreover, D: the research benefits of the space program should also be considered, because E: who knows what technological advances would come of a project such as landing a research team on Mars? In addition, F: our capitalist economic system requires cultivating a spirit of adventure in order to survive and move forward, and G: such a spirit is inherent to space exploration. Finally, H: a developed space program will have numerous benefits for future generations.

What is the argument's conclusion? Logical sense and careful attention to indicators and cues suggests that the second statement, B, is the argument's final conclusion:

B: The US space exploration program must be pursued aggressively.

(Notice that statement A acknowledges opposition to this argument. We'll come back to statement A momentarily.) The first reason in support of this argument's conclusion apparently is statement C, which constitutes the argument's first "line of reasoning" or "line of argument" about the space program. We can standardize this line as follows:

[Because]

C: Scrapping the space program would mean the loss of thousands of jobs in the aerospace industry.

[thus]

B: The US space exploration program must be pursued aggressively.

Notice that statements B and C themselves constitute a brief argument because they include a reason in support of a conclusion.

The cue "moreover" suggests the beginning of a second line of argument. The indicator "because" signals that statement E is a reason for statement D. We can change statement E from a question into the statement it implies:

Moreover, because

E: Technological advances [might result from] a project such as landing a research team on Mars.

[thus]

D: The research benefits of the space program should also be considered.

The argument now takes a turn toward a discussion of capitalism. Because this discussion is not directly related to the second line of argument, dealing with technological advances, we probably have a third line of argument developing. The cue "and" suggests a parallel structure between statements F and G. In standardizing, the indefinite phrase "such a spirit" should be changed to the definite phrase "a spirit of adventure" to which it refers. Standardized, this third line of argument looks like this:

In addition

F: Our capitalist economic system requires cultivating a spirit of adventure in order to survive and move forward.

and

G: [A spirit of adventure] is inherent to space exploration.

The fourth and last line of argument is introduced by the cue "finally." This argument involves the single claim advanced in support of conclusion B:

Finally,

H: A developed space program will have numerous benefits for future generations.

We now can put together the full standardization of this argument. This process involves arranging each of the lines of argument in order above the argument's final conclusion, which is placed last in the standardization. The reservation is placed at the top of the standardization:

A: Recently the exploration of space has received little attention from politicians.

However

[Because]

C: Scrapping the space program would mean the loss of thousands of jobs in the aerospace industry.

Moreover

because

E: Technological advances [might result from] a project such as landing a research team on Mars.

[thus]

D: The research benefits of the space program should also be considered.

In addition

F: Our capitalist economic system requires cultivating a spirit of adventure in order to survive and move forward.

and

G: [A spirit of adventure] is inherent to space exploration.

Finally,

H: A developed space program will have numerous benefits for future generations.

[thus]

B: The US space exploration program must be pursued aggressively.

Now we can easily see that this conclusion about the space program is supported by four lines of argument or reasoning—the first having to do with jobs, the second with technological advances, the third with the nature of capitalism, and the fourth with benefits to future generations.

Tool 3: Diagramming

Occasionally we read an argument that is hard to track—it is not clear which statements serve as evidence and which as conclusions. The technique known as diagramming can help us to create a visual image of the argument's flow from its reasons to its conclusion. **Diagramming** an argument consists of *mapping the argument, using only the letters assigned during scanning, and drawing lines from reasons to the conclusion they support.* This process produces a sketch of an argument's inferences and other qualities such as reservations. It thus allows us to see the argument's structure: how some statements are supported by other statements, which reasons are not provided with additional support, how many lines of argument are developed, and which statements do not contribute to supporting the conclusion.

Basic Patterns

Diagramming is a relatively straightforward process. Despite the elaborate diagrams that sometimes result, it only involves a few possible combinations. These possibilities, called patterns, are represented below, with explanations.

Pattern 1: The simplest pattern is employed when one statement (in this case A) is presented as a reason for another statement (in this case B). This pattern is represented with the reason above its conclusion, as is always the case in diagramming:

A
↓
B

The following argument exhibits this basic structure:

> <u>Because</u> A: many parents express doubts about the side effects of vaccinations,
> B: the government should begin educating parents about their safety.

This brief diagram would represent a unit of argument reading "A *thus* B," or the equivalent. Of course, we could keep adding inferences to this string. So, for example, "A is true, therefore B, and thus C." This set of statements would be diagrammed this way:

A
↓
B
↓
C

For example:

> <u>Because</u> A: many parents express doubts about the side effects of vaccinations,
> B: the safety of vaccinations should be carefully presented to the public. <u>So</u>,
> C: the government should begin educating parents about their safety.

If we read an argument worded as "A *because* B," the pattern would be reversed to keep the reason above the conclusion:

B
↓
A

Pattern 2: When two or more statements (in this case A and B) are independent reasons for another statement (in this case C), a diagram of the three would look like this:

This diagram would represent a unit of argument reading: "A is the case and B also has been observed, *thus* it is likely that C is also true." This diagram represents separate pieces of evidence leading to a *probable* conclusion, that is, an inductive unit of argument.

If the original argument had read, "A is the case *because* B has been observed and *because* C is also true," the diagram would appear as follows:

Other reasons could be added to this pattern, all contributing independently to the same conclusion. This is the pattern of an *inductive* argument.

Pattern 3: When two statements (in this case A and B) work together to support a third statement (in this case C), the diagram appears as follows:

This diagram represents an argument that reads: "Because A is the case *and because* B is also the case, *it is therefore certain* that C must be true." For instance:

> A: Small businesses create jobs, <u>and</u> B: jobs are crucial in the economy. <u>So,</u>
> C: small businesses are crucial to the economy.

This unit of argument reflects the movement from closely related reasons to a necessary, rather than probable, conclusion. This is a description of a *deductive* argument.

Had the original argument read, "A must be true because B is the case and C is also the case," the diagram would appear as follows:

Thus, this diagram would describe the following order of reasons and conclusions:

> A: Small businesses are crucial to the economy <u>because</u> B: small businesses create jobs, <u>and</u> C: jobs are crucial to the economy.

Pattern 4: It is possible for a single reason to result in two or more conclusions. If we were to read an argument that asserted, "A is true, *so* B is the case, *and* C must also be true," the diagram would appear this way:

This diagram would describe, for example, the following argument:

A: Online dating services generated $1.9 billion in profit last year. <u>Therefore,</u>
B: People clearly accept this new way of meeting potential partners, <u>and</u>
C: such online services have become an important part of the economy.

Pattern 5: This pattern is used to represent a reservation, a statement that does not support or perhaps actually works against the argument's conclusion. A reservation is often employed to acknowledge an obvious counter-argument. Here we use a dashed line to show lack of support. For example, we read: "Even though A is the case, B is still true." These two statements would be diagrammed as:

A
┊
┊
B

<u>Even though</u> A: we are fascinated by space, B: space exploration must be temporarily terminated.

We can now combine this set of patterns to diagram several additional brief example arguments.

As noted, when one statement is offered as a reason for another statement in an argument, the diagram is simple. This argument:

A: Competency tests would improve the quality of education in our schools,
<u>therefore</u> B: they should be required of all public school teachers.

results in the diagram we saw in pattern 1:

A
|
↓
B

As discussed in Chapter 2, many arguments contain reservations, which are statements that acknowledge counter-arguments, significant opposition, or contrary evidence. Reservations often are introduced by cues such as "although" or "even though" or are followed by cues such as "but," "nevertheless," or "however." We can add a reservation to the brief argument above:

A: Competency tests would improve the quality of education in our schools.
<u>Therefore</u> B: they should be required of all public school teachers, <u>even though</u>
C: unions have strongly opposed the concept.

In this diagram, as in pattern 5, we use a broken line to represent the reservation's relationship to the conclusion:

In diagramming a reservation, a broken line is drawn back to the argument's final conclusion, as has been done here.

Let's take another look at the argument concerning space exploration and build a diagram of it. Here is that argument again:

> A: Recently the exploration of space has received little attention from politicians. <u>However</u>, B: the US space exploration program must be pursued aggressively. C: Scrapping the space program would mean the loss of thousands of jobs in the aerospace industry. <u>Moreover</u>, D: the research benefits of the space program should also be considered, <u>because</u> E: who knows what technological advances would come of a project such as landing a research team on Mars? <u>In addition</u>, F: our capitalist system requires cultivating a spirit of adventure in order to survive and move forward, <u>and</u> G: such a spirit is inherent to space exploration. <u>Finally</u>, H: a developed space program will have numerous benefits for future generations.

The cue "however" suggests that statement A represents a reservation in this argument. We'll return to it shortly. Let's begin with the clear reason-conclusion relationship between statements D and E. The relationship is standardized with the reason, E, above its conclusion, D:

> <u>because</u>
>
> E: Technological advances [might result from] a project such as landing a research team on Mars.
>
> [<u>thus</u>]
>
> D: The research benefits of the space program should also be considered.

and thus is diagrammed this way:

E
↓
D

When we add the conclusion, B, we get this diagram (pattern 1):

E
↓
D
↓
B

Statements C and H support B directly (following pattern 2), so we can easily add them to the diagram:

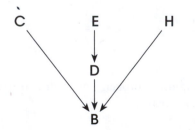

Complementary Reasons

Some arguments contain **complementary reasons,** sometimes also called dependent reasons. These are *pairs of reasons that must work together to lend support to their conclusion.* Complementary reasons are characteristic of deductive reasoning. Statements F and G from our example are:

> F: Capitalism requires cultivating a spirit of adventure in order to survive and move forward.
>
> <u>and</u>
>
> G: [A spirit of adventure] is inherent to space exploration.

Neither reason by itself produces the argument's conclusion, but together they do. In a diagram, complementary reasons can be represented this way, following pattern 3:

F w/ G

This combination is read, "reason F with reason G." Again, complementary reasons work together to lend support to their conclusion, in this case, statement B. Complementary reasons may appear as deductive units in longer arguments, as they do here. Notice also that statement F presents a general principle of which G presents a particular application, another common mark of deductive reasoning.

Complementary reason pairs can be hard to spot. Three clues tell us that reasons are complementary. First, one reason, without the other, will not produce the conclusion in question. Second, the statements deal with the same idea, as revealed by a **linguistic link,** *a repeated phrase or term that links statements to one another.* In this case, the linguistic link is "spirit of adventure." Third, complementary reasons often, though not always, are joined by the word "and."

When we combine all the elements in the diagram, including the reservation, A—which is connected to the conclusion with a dashed line—the finished product looks like this:

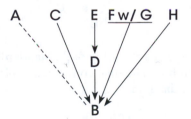

Notice that statement D serves as both a conclusion and a reason. It is an **intermediate conclusion,** *a conclusion that is then used as a reason for some additional conclusion.*

The argument above begins with reservation A, then employs independent reasons (C, E, and H), a pair of complementary reasons (F and G), and an intermediate conclusion (D).

Another example of an argument with several reasons of different types, as well as a reservation, is:

> <u>Even though</u> A: teachers' unions object to their use, B: competency tests should be required for all public school teachers. This is <u>because</u> C: studies show that these tests improve the quality of education, <u>and</u> D: the School Board is on record as claiming that whatever improves the quality of

education should be pursued aggressively. <u>In addition</u>, E: teachers should back the idea <u>because</u> F: competency tests allow the better teachers some objective evidence for proving their quality.

This argument can be standardized as follows:

<u>Even though</u>

A: Teachers' unions object to their use.

<u>because</u>

C: Studies show that these tests improve the quality of education.

<u>and</u>

D: The School Board is on record as claiming that whatever improves the quality of education should be pursued aggressively.

<u>In addition,</u>

<u>because</u>

F: Competency tests allow the better teachers some objective evidence for proving their quality.

[<u>Thus</u>]

E: Teachers should back the idea [of competency tests].

[<u>Therefore</u>]

B: Competency tests should be required for all public school teachers.

The argument would be diagrammed as follows:

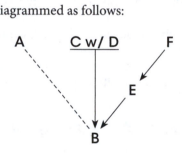

As before, the reservation appears at the top of the standardization, and is represented in the diagram by a broken line. The final conclusion is placed at the bottom of both the standardization and the diagram.

Using Diagramming to Clarify Structure

As noted, diagramming allows us to grasp the underlying structure of inferences in an argument, even when that structure is not immediately apparent. Consider the following example of an argument that makes a clear point, but in a somewhat indirect manner:

> The Senate should pay careful attention to the military spending bill unveiled last week by a bipartisan group of leaders in Congress. The bill extends funding for current military campaigns. It also reduces military expenditures over the next five years. Thus, the bill will satisfy lawmakers on both sides of the aisle. The bill's allocation for treating veterans who are experiencing emotional and mental issues as a result of combat duty is less than is needed, but the new bill still deserves Senate endorsement.

Clearly the argument favors the new bill, but the reasons and claims are not set out in an orderly way. Thus making sense of the argument is a challenge.

To bring a little clarity to the argument, let's begin by scanning it:

A: The Senate should vote to pass the military spending bill unveiled last week by a bipartisan group of leaders in Congress. B: The bill extends funding for current military campaigns. C: It also reduces overall military expenditures over the next five years. <u>Thus</u>, D: the bill will satisfy lawmakers on both sides of the aisle. E: The bill's allocation for treating veterans who are experiencing emotional and mental issues as a result of combat duty is less than needed, <u>but</u> F: the new bill still merits Senate endorsement.

What is this argument's conclusion? Is it statement A or statement E, or perhaps even statement D? Here our categories of types of claims—fact, value, and policy—are of some assistance. Because policy claims often are supported by factual and evaluative claims, we might begin with statement A—a policy statement—as the argument's likely final conclusion. Statements B and C look like evidence supporting this claim. However, we also notice that statement D is preceded by the indicator "thus," which suggests that B and C lead first to statement D. The reasons and conclusions are out of order, but a diagram helps us to see this structure:

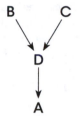

This diagram still omits statements E and F. Where do they belong? Statement E is pretty clearly a reservation, a statement of a counter-argument or of some hesitation on the writer's part. But what about statement F? It also sounds like a conclusion, but perhaps not the argument's final conclusion.

The fact that this argument's reasons and conclusions are out of order makes it difficult to sort out, but diagramming can help. Evaluative statements such as F typically precede policy claims such as A, so we will insert F as an intermediate conclusion. We can then add E as a reservation for the final conclusion. The inferences in the argument, then, yield the following diagram:

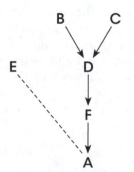

Why develop skill with this diagramming technique? It provides a useful means of determining the point and the reasoning process in a brief argument, but the principal benefit may be found elsewhere—in the development of reading and writing habits when evaluating expositional discourse. First, diagramming reinforces the understanding that arguments consist principally of reasons and conclusions, and that reasons are intended to support conclusions. This practical insight can assist us in assessing someone else's argument or in clarifying our own writing and speaking. Second, the process of diagramming cultivates the mental habit of asking about an author's main point (or our own), as well as which other statements are intended as support for that point. Finally, diagramming can help us *visualize* the structure of an argument, which in turn may reveal the various lines of arguments and missing reasons, as well as embedded rhetorical strategies such as mentioning counter-arguments. This visualization process assists us in understanding and responding to an argument. Whether or not you take the time to create a diagram of a particular argument—your own or someone else's—diagramming develops habits important to critical reading and listening.

THE TOULMIN MODEL
AND THE HIDDEN ELEMENTS OF ARGUMENTS

Our discussion of diagramming and standardizing arguments raises issues that take us beyond the structure of the argument. For instance, there are hidden elements in some arguments, components that are implied rather than stated. In public discourse, arguments often are incomplete as presented, lacking a crucial component such as a reason—evidence or connective—or even a directly stated conclusion. We often supply what is missing without even knowing we are doing it. One frequently hidden element is some deeply held value on which an entire argument may rest.

For example, we read: "Because of new studies revealing the highly complex brain structures of many animals, we need to pay more attention to animal rights." We may guess at the connection between reason and conclusion in this argument, but something seems to be missing. What is it, and how would we discover this missing element?

One widely used approach to discovering the hidden components of everyday arguments—and grasping the structure of arguments generally—was developed by British philosopher Stephen Toulmin.[2] He noted that any sound argument consisted of at least three parts, which he labeled data, warrant, and claim. The **claim** was *the assertion being advanced;* the **data** was *the evidence presented in its support;* and the **warrant** was *the broader assumption linking the claim and the data.* In our example, the data or evidence is the observation that many animals have highly complex brain structures. The claim that follows from this observation is that we need to pay much closer attention to animal rights.

What broader assumption upholds the movement from complex brain structures to rights? We might guess that the person advancing the argument believes that complex brains suggest a level of self-awareness and self-determination that deserves protection through rights. This belief may be the warrant to which Toulmin would draw our attention. We can set out this much of the argument using the model Toulmin suggested:

data	*claim*
Many animals possess complex brain structures.	So, we need to pay more attention to animal rights.

warrant

Complex brains suggest a level of self-awareness and
self-determination that deserve protection through rights.

This model reveals the basic structure and content of the argument.

The warrant seems to rest on the belief that enunciated rights are needed to protect an individual, a "self," from harm or exploitation. Such a value is enshrined in the US Constitution. The need for protection by enunciated rights is also under-lined by examples of exploitation when rights were not expressly applied to an individual or group. A closer look at Toulmin's Model helps us understand how he analyzed the surface as well as the deeper content of the arguments we make every day.

Toulmin was particularly interested in an argument's use to justify an everyday claim. He sought to demonstrate that there is considerable rational strength in ordinary arguments, but that such arguments often conceal elements that would help us appreciate this quality. For example, when a claim is advanced with a single piece of evidence, it may appear more fully justified when various components that are just out of view but strongly suggested by the claim and its context are examined.

These three basic elements—data, warrant, and claim—are common to many of the arguments we encounter every day. In addition, arguments imply **backing,** *foundational assumptions or presuppositions that support a warrant.* Toulmin noted as well that many arguments include or imply **rebuttals,** *possible answers or exceptions to the inference being drawn.*

If we add these elements we get the following more elaborate and revealing analysis:

data	*claim*
Many animals possess complex brain structures.	We need to pay more attention to animal rights.

warrant	*rebuttal*
<u>Since</u>	<u>Unless</u>
Complex brains suggest a level of self awareness and self-determination that deserves protection through rights.	Humans alone can be said to possess rights.

backing

<u>On account of</u>

Scientific findings regarding brain complexity, self-awareness and self-determination.

As you can see, this model allows the argument critic to account for the various elements of most everyday arguments. It provides a convenient vocabulary for discussing arguments and can also help us detect when an argument is concealing a crucial element. For instance, consider this brief argument:

The average US worker spends 445 hours driving to and from work each year. This number is steadily increasing. Therefore, radio will remain an important medium of communication for the foreseeable future.

Here we have an argument consisting only of data and claim:

data

The average US worker spends 445 hours driving to and from work each year. This number is steadily increasing.

claim

Therefore, radio will remain an important medium of communication for the foreseeable future.

What is missing? It's the warrant that connects these two statements. That warrant is apparently the following idea:

warrant

When people drive, they typically listen to the radio.

Let's pursue that idea of missing pieces further.

How would this model be employed in understanding everyday arguments? The following example sets out, on the Toulmin Model, an argument that we might encounter in conversation:

> I recently visited Mount Rushmore and was not impressed. The monument is certainly sexist. No effort on the part of the National Park Service to hide this fact changes the basic message of this massive sculpture. Mount Rushmore depicts four men and no women as the nation's greatest leaders. It thus leaves the impression that women have taken no important national leadership roles. That is a plainly sexist message.

It is pretty clear what this individual is advancing as evidence in support of his claim: the faces of four presidents that make up the Mount Rushmore monument, and the absence of any women's faces. (Notice that the evidence or data in this argument is an object rather than a verbal statement. We will explore such arguments in greater detail in subsequent chapters.) According to Toulmin's approach, we would designate the physical features of the monument as the "data" in this argument.

The argument's conclusion or, in Toulmin's terms "claim," is equally clear: the monument is sexist. We can set out these two components using Toulmin's Model:

data	*claim*
Mount Rushmore depicts four men and no women as the nation's greatest leaders.	Mount Rushmore is sexist.

The data represent an observation. The conclusion represents an inference from that observation; in Toulmin's terms, a "claim." In this case, as in many cases, we have to make an educated guess as to the warrant intended by the individual advancing the argument. Looking at what is asserted in the data and claim provides an important clue. We can ask ourselves, "What must someone believe in order to move from this observation about Mount Rushmore to this claim?" We can also draw on our knowledge of widely held beliefs and values.

Thus, one possibility for a warrant in this argument would be:

warrant

Any national monument that acknowledges the contributions of men while failing to acknowledge the contributions of women is sexist.

Critics might disagree about the precise wording of the warrant in the argument, but this phrasing certainly constitutes a likely possibility, based on what we know about the data, claim, and certain widely held values. As you can see, if you accept this warrant or generalization, then the data would indeed lead to the claim.

The Toulmin Model allows us to see in greater detail the warrants, or assumptions, at work below the surface of everyday arguments. Toulmin suggested that warrants themselves are based on even deeper assumptions, such as widely acknowledged cultural values or legal principles, that Toulmin termed "backing." Here is a possible formulation for the warrant in the argument we are considering.

backing

A social consensus that sexism is an immoral practice that leads us to emphasize, in public and private settings, the rights and contributions of one gender to the exclusion of those of the other.

Toulmin also drew attention to **modal qualifiers,** *terms that indicate the intended strength of a conclusion.* The modal qualifier for this argument—"certainly"—reveals that the individual making the argument sees little or no possibility for the conclusion being wrong. Here is the argument set out in its entirety on the Toulmin Model:

data	*claim*
	qualifier
Mount Rushmore depicts four men and no women as the nation's greatest leaders.	Mount Rushmore is <u>certainly</u> sexist.

warrant

Any national monument that acknowledges the contributions of men while failing to acknowledge the contributions of women is sexist.

backing

A social consensus that sexism is an immoral practice that leads us to emphasize, in public and private settings, the rights and contributions of one gender to the exclusion of those of the other.

At this point we have a reasonable presentation of the original argument, complete with a couple of crucial elements that were embedded or suggested in its original form. We should note again that advocates typically leave out such important details, either because they believe they are clearly enough understood or because they wish to involve their audience in completing the argument.

The final element in Toulmin's model, a rebuttal, is often introduced with the term "unless." For example, if the person making this argument agreed that we should acknowledge certain historical circumstances and overlook the practices of a past generation, rather than judging them by contemporary standards, then this argument might reasonably encounter a rebuttal. We could insert the following as a potential rebuttal to this argument:

rebuttal

Unless the practices of an earlier generation should not, in this case, be judged by contemporary moral standards.

The rebuttal is included in the Toulmin model to indicate that warrants almost always carry within them an embedded reservation, a limit on how generally they are to be applied. This element in the model also suggests that every argument implies a potential counter-argument, another important hidden element in the argument itself.

data ─────────────────────────┬────────── *claim*

qualifier

Mount Rushmore depicts
four men and no women as
the nation's greatest leaders.

Mount Rushmore is <u>certainly</u> sexist.

rebuttal

Unless the practices of an earlier
generation should not, in this case, be
judged by contemporary moral standards.

warrant

Any national monument that acknowledges the contributions of men while
failing to acknowledge the contributions of women is sexist.

backing

A social consensus that sexism is an immoral practice that leads us to
emphasize, in public and private settings, the rights and contributions of one
gender to the exclusion of those of the other.

Let's consider another example of an argument set out on the Toulmin Model.
Suppose you want to advance an argument regarding global warming. You do considerable research and come to the conclusion that the situation requires immediate action
by the federal government concerning emission standards on all automobiles. Your
claim might be something like the following:

> *claim:* The federal government must require that all automobiles sold in the
> United States achieve a gas mileage goal of fifty miles per gallon by 2025.

As it stands, this is a claim without any evidence, an assertion without an
argument. The next step in the process of developing an argument to justify this
claim, using the Toulmin Model as a guide, would be to provide data in the claim's
support. Thus, you supply evidence such as the following:

> *data:* Requiring all automobiles in the United States to achieve at least a fifty
> miles per gallon level of fuel efficiency would cut our total national energy
> consumption by 15 percent and reduce production of greenhouse gases by
> 25 percent.

What would count as a warrant for this argument? It is likely that some broadly
held value regarding the need for reducing energy consumption and greenhouse gases
would link this data to the claim:

> *warrant:* Reducing our energy consumption and greenhouse gas emissions
> are both crucial components in developing a sustainable and environmentally
> responsible approach to the use of fossil fuels.

Such a warrant would receive backing from broad moral or legal commitments,
such as an obligation to preserve the environment for future generations. Backing
might take this form:

> *backing:* Our moral obligation to preserve the environment.

We can at this point see an argument taking shape. The argument offers support
for the claim, as well as the cohesiveness and persuasive appeal that comes from

being connected to broad audience values and long-standing moral commitments. Nevertheless, there is always the possibility of a rebuttal or of limits on an audience's willingness to accept even a well-supported claim. The presence of a rebuttal in the Toulmin Model allows for these possibilities. For instance, an objection to our argument might run something like this:

> *rebuttal:* Unless the costs of forcing compliance with such a directive would place an insurmountable barrier in the way of the recovering automobile industry.

Now we can see the full argument. It includes a claim needing justification, reasons in its support in the form of both data and warrant, the backing that provides a foundation for the warrant, and the rebuttal that acknowledges possible objections to the claim. Our argument takes the following form:

data ———————————————————————— *claim*

Requiring all automobiles in the United States to achieve at least a fifty miles per gallon level of fuel efficiency would cut our total national energy consumption by 15 percent and reduce production of greenhouse gases by 25 percent.	The federal government must require that all automobiles sold in the United States achieve a gas mileage goal of fifty miles per gallon by 2025.

rebuttal

Unless the costs of forcing compliance with such a directive would place an insurmountable barrier in the way of the recovering automobile industry.

warrant

Reducing our energy consumption and greenhouse gas emissions are both crucial components in developing a sustainable and environmentally responsible approach to the use of fossil fuels.

backing

Our moral obligation to preserve the environment.

As we have noted, arguments involve evidence, a connective, and a conclusion. These terms correspond to Toulmin's terms data, warrant, and claim. As noted, in many arguments one or more of these elements is unstated but strongly implied. Frequently the unstated element is the connective or warrant—a belief, value, or assumption that links the evidence to the conclusion.

Supplying such missing and hidden reasons can help us to grasp the structure and content of an argument, and may be the only way to really know what someone is arguing. Only when we know what advocates are assuming as they argue can we know whether we agree with them or reject their reasoning. Consider our earlier example of an argument with a missing component:

> Because of new studies revealing the highly complex brain structures of many animals, we need to pay much greater attention to animal rights.

Apparently the individual making this argument assumes that basic rights and higher-order brain structures are related. It would seem plausible that the missing reason connecting these two ideas is some formulation of the following:

> Higher-order brain structures suggest the possibility of self-awareness, a quality often linked to rights such as protection from unnecessary suffering.

This is a guess, but perhaps a reasonable guess, regarding the missing reason in the original argument.

Supplying an element that is missing from another person's argument can be a risky process: it should be approached with care. Unless we can ask the author for verification, perhaps we can never be certain that the missing element we supply is what the author intended. Two guidelines are helpful, though:

1. Add only statements that seem to be part of the argument as its author intended it. Don't add reasons or other statements that clearly violate an author's motives in writing or speaking, or that reflect your own rather than the author's assumptions. For example, suppose a friend argues that the United States should implement a military draft that applies equally to all males between the ages of eighteen and twenty-three. The evidence offered is that under the current volunteer military system, minority groups and members of the lower economic classes are overly represented in the military. What is the missing assumption in this argument, the connective that links evidence to conclusion?

The missing connective (or warrant) in this argument might be that it is not fair to place the burden of military service more heavily on minorities and the poor than on the majority population and the well off. It is also possible, though, that your friend believes all citizens should share equally in the defense of their country so as to learn the value of patriotism. If you believe the first idea, you might be more likely to fill it in as the missing reason, but only through listening to more of the argument or asking directly for clarification could you actually know what your friend has in mind. We must exercise care in supplying what is missing in someone else's argument.

2. Give the argument a strong reading. One important rule of argument analysis is that we should avoid creating a **straw man argument,** *a weak interpretation of someone else's argument in order to make it easier to refute.*

Suppose you read an editorial in which the author argues that the complexity of biological life on earth suggests that an intelligent designer stands behind the physical world that we observe. You are impatient with such an idea and immediately dismiss the argument as reflecting a "creationist" idea that the entire universe was created in six days. The author has not actually given you reason to believe that this is his view, however. He may only believe that complexity in a system suggests intelligence of some kind behind the system. The argument you attributed to him may be easier to refute, but it is not actually *his* argument.

DIGITAL PUBLIC DISCOURSE

It is estimated that 205 billion emails are sent each day (though recipients consider only 14 percent to contain important information). US residents now send 200 billion text messages each month. What about tweets? Estimates run to more than 500 million each day, which works out to about 15 billion tweets each month.[3] Such numbers make it clear that we like to communicate employing digital media. They also suggest that much advocacy of important ideas is now taking place in these formats.

The great advantages of the new media of personal communication include immediacy and a better sense of the opinions of the broader public as contrasted to the opinions of experts. Digital forms of communication also promote participation in public discourse and encourage the give and take of debate on important issues. But while emails, texts, and tweets are fast and nearly effortless forms of communication, most are brief in comparison to, say, a speech or an editorial. Because of their brevity and the speed with which they are formed as messages, digital messages might also undercut the quality of that discourse.

Perhaps the principal challenge to advocates employing such popular digital forms of communication is presenting evidence, especially fully developed evidence such as substantiated statistics or testimony from a qualified expert. Despite the restraints of these media, an argument must still exhibit good evidence, clear definitions, and a sound structure.

Is there a solution to this dilemma of brevity vs. soundness of argument? In the digital age, sound public discourse is still built on shared values and good support. There must still be a clear line from evidence to conclusion, but important elements in an argument may be obscured by the brief form and highly personal tone of a digital message.

> In the digital age, sound public discourse is still built on shared values and good support.

Twitter, for example, has emerged as an important forum for public discourse. The service's potential for easy and immediate response to developing events has attracted millions of subscribers. Like other online and mobile formats, Twitter tends to erase the speaker-audience relationship that characterizes more traditional argument formats, such as public speeches or debates. However, the enforced constraint of 280 characters requires extraordinary economy of expression, which means that effective tweets require careful word choice, a direct writing style, and abbreviation. Such requirements can be advantageous, as they render writing more engaging and vibrant. At the same time, enforced brevity means that the audience for tweets must supply more of the message through a kind of informed reading, even educated guessing.

Here we may turn to Toulmin's model for help. As we have seen, Toulmin encourages us to expand public arguments so their hidden components are open to view. This model reminds us that even the truncated message of a text or tweet requires convincing evidence and convictions that speaker and audience share.

Examining a few tweets prompted by a recent Canadian legal decision will help us to develop approaches to understanding and evaluating arguments that are advanced in this and similar formats. In this case, the Toulmin approach can suggest how missing or implied elements might be supplied to complete a fragmentary argument.

Canada's Supreme Court struck down legal barriers to prostitution, a decision that prompted thousands of divergent Twitter messages. The numerous opinions expressed reflected a desire to participate in a public discussion of the issue, as well as some of the challenges associated with abbreviated online and mobile formats such as texts.

One apparently straightforward tweet on the Court's decision reads:

> I would like to thank the Supreme Court of Canada for declaring sex workers to be persons.

This may be—as the author suggests—simply a note of thanks; but it sounds as if the writer has also embedded an argument in this brief sentence. If we assume that what we are reading is a conclusion about the decision, the Toulmin approach would prompt us to ask about implied elements for the argument, such as data and warrant.

It is clear that the writer suggests a connection between the Court's decision and the issue of personhood, but what warrant (belief, value or assumption) would connect the concepts? We will formulate the apparent assumption as follows:

> When one's occupation is recognized as legal by government institutions, one's personhood is affirmed.

Admittedly, this is a guess, but it is probably close to what the writer intended.

The data or evidence for the implied argument is likely as simple as the Court's decision itself: Prostitution will now be legal in Canada. Thus, the complete argument, with implied warrant and data supplied, might develop as follows:

> *Data:* Canada's Supreme Court struck down laws against prostitution, thus declaring that prostitution is legal in Canada.
>
> *Warrant:* When one's occupation is recognized as legal by government institutions, one's personhood is affirmed.
>
> *Claim:* Thus, the Canadian Supreme Court has declared sex workers to be persons.

It appears that this tweet, presented as a note of thanks, in fact expresses the conclusion of an implied argument. Clearly the message conveys more than an affirmation of the Court's decision—the data and warrant of a complete argument are both implied. The argument's brevity requires extra effort on the part of the reader to apprehend, as contrasted to what is required in a longer argument such as a speech. Understanding and responding to the full message of the tweet, however, necessitate supplying these missing elements.

A second example poses a different challenge: providing the missing historical data to which the writer alludes. The tweet reads:

> In thinking about the Supreme Court decision, never forget the background: Pickton killing fields & countless dead & missing sex workers.

The reference to Pickton killing fields is dramatic and cryptic, but the message makes little sense without certain background knowledge. An internet search reveals that Robert Pickton is a serial killer, convicted in 2007, who preyed on prostitutes in Vancouver, British Columbia. What, then, does the tweet mean?

Once the missing background information has been supplied, we can see that the author suggests that making prostitution legal in Canada will protect prostitutes, who will no longer have to work in obscure areas and fear arrest if they report a threat to police. The reasoning thus moves from an infamous criminal case and related incidents (the stated data), to an implied warrant—criminalizing prostitution places prostitutes at risk—and finally to the implied claim that the Supreme Court decision will save many lives. As in the first example, much more is suggested than stated in the tweet, so our reconstruction of the argument remains an educated guess. Ordinarily we would supply missing information in such abbreviated arguments without even being aware of what we are doing. The approach outlined here helps clarify what we are supplying, and thus allows for more accurate understanding and a more effective response.

Advocacy conducted in digital formats involves more people in public discourse than do traditional forms such as the speech or the published editorial. Digital advocacy also encourages the back-and-forth quality that makes public debate productive of compromise and new insights. Digital formats make developing sound evidence difficult, however, and can obscure the line dividing mere assertion from actual argument. Toulmin reminds us that although we are presenting truncated arguments in these newer formats, we still construct sound persuasive discourse out of the raw material of evidence and shared belief.

CHAPTER REVIEW

The chapter considers when we do and do not expect arguments. For example, when an assertion seems to need support, we expect that an argument will follow. When the cause of an event is well known, however, we do not expect an argument to be advanced to support the causal claim.

We have also examined the difference between deductive and inductive arguments, or arguments whose reasons—when accepted as true—lead to necessary or probable conclusions. Inductive arguments typically move from specific observations to general conclusions, while deductive arguments usually move from general observations to specific conclusions. Some reasons are complementary; that is, they must work together to provide support for their conclusion. Others are independent, which means that by themselves they lend support to their conclusion.

Three tools that can clarify the structure of arguments we are reading or composing are: (a) scanning, (b) standardizing, and (c) diagramming. These tools can help you to understand and evaluate the arguments you hear and read, as well as to strengthen your own arguments.

When reasons are missing from an argument we can often supply them in order to understand the structure and content of the argument.

Stephen Toulmin's model provides a means of exploring an argument's deeper structure and content. Its chief components—data, claim, warrant, and backing—provide insights into the way everyday arguments operate. The model also underlines the importance of the hidden elements in arguments that we hear and read. The Toulmin Model also provides guidance for understanding and improving advocacy presented in digital formats.

EXERCISES

A.   Scan the following arguments. Draw a wavy line under the conclusion of each example.

1. The Federal Reserve Board controls all monetary policy, and thus functions as a fourth branch of government.

2. Because it constitutes an illegal search, and thus is unconstitutional, genetic testing should not be required of anyone applying for life insurance policies.

3. Because drones will soon be used for everything from product delivery to crowd surveillance, the FAA must move quickly to enact legislation governing drone use.

B.   Scan, standardize, and diagram the following arguments. Which argument is deductive? Which is inductive? Your diagrams should also show either independent or complementary reasons.

1. The sport of boxing should be banned from the Olympic Games because it places athletes at risk and promotes violence among young people.

2. Because it promotes violence, and because violent sports are not appropriate for international games, the sport of boxing should be banned from the Olympics.

C. Scan, standardize, and diagram the following arguments.

1. We currently spend less than one-tenth as much protecting ourselves from cyberattacks as we do preventing conventional terrorist attacks. Yet, our military readiness currently depends entirely on the internet. Banking institutions also rely almost entirely on digital communication with consumers and with one another. It is also true that major transportation systems could be crippled if the internet went down. So, it is safe to say that the United States is under far greater threat from cyberattacks than from conventional terrorist attacks that employ explosives. It's time to increase our investment in preventing an attack where we are most vulnerable—in critical systems dependent on the internet.

2. Even though opposition to cloning human embryos is heard from some quarters, it is certain that a majority of people will soon support the practice. First, the public will back any research that promises cures for serious, genetically conveyed diseases. Embryo cloning will hasten the eradication of such diseases. In addition, moral objections to human cloning will evaporate because the public will come to understand that cloning embryos does not mean creating human beings in a test tube. Finally, the economic potential of human embryo cloning will provide yet another incentive for broad public acceptance of the technology.

3. Movies portraying acts of violence are consistently among the most financially successful. The violence in many of the most popular new movies, however, develops around the impulse to seek revenge. These same movies connect taking revenge with masculinity. Thus, a cultural definition of masculinity is emerging that incorporates a virtual obligation to do violence to anyone who opposes or offends you. It is also well established that physical violence causes vastly more social problems than it solves, so it is time to develop a new definition of masculinity that recognizes that taking revenge violently is not a sign of true manhood.

4. The amount of information in the human genome exceeds that contained in all the internet sites in the world. It is also the case that such a vast amount of information could not have been accumulated as the result of purely random processes, so it is clear that there must have been a designing intelligence behind the creation of life on earth. Therefore, the genome offers some evidence for the existence of God.

D. Set out the following arguments using Toulmin's model, identifying the data, claim, warrant, and backing for each. If an element is hidden, suggest how it might be stated.

1. A national health care plan is vital, because many people in the United States currently cannot afford adequate health care. When citizens cannot afford a vital service, the government must assist them.

2. It is wrong to deny the right to marry to gay people. Such a prohibition violates a fundamental right to the pursuit of happiness.

3. The canyon area ought to be developed, because then more people would have access to it.

ENDNOTES

[1] This treatment of standardizing was suggested by Trudy Govier, *A Practical Study of Argument* (Belmont, Calif.: Wadsworth, 1985), 21–25.

[2] Stephen Toulmin, *The Uses of Argument* (Cambridge, U.K.: Cambridge University Press, 1958).

[3] "Our Mission," http//about.twitter.com/company (Accessed May 10, 2014).

RECOMMENDED WEBSITES

ProCon.org: Pros and Cons of Controversial Issues

www.procon.org

ProCon.org is an independent, nonpartisan site devoted to exploring both sides of issues that are of public interest.

ChangingMinds.org

changingminds.org/disciplines/argument/making_argument/toulmin.htm

This website contains a great deal of useful information on argument, persuasion, and related topics. The site's discussion of the Toulmin Model is particularly helpful.

II

The Conditions of Constructive Argumentation

4 Ethical Advocacy

Moral cowardice that keeps us from speaking our minds
is as dangerous to this country as irresponsible talk.
The right way is not always the popular and easy way.
Margaret Chase Smith (1897–1995)
United States senator

The opinions that are held with passion
are always those for which no good ground exists.
Bertrand Russell (1872–1970)
British mathematician

KEY TERMS

argumentative contexts

argument virtues

cooperation

courage in argument

dialogic perspectives

honesty

human nature perspectives

pluralism

political perspectives

regard for contexts

respect for persons

situational perspectives

virtues

Some political observers, having witnessed an apparent disregard for truth on the part of some political campaigns and candidates, suggest that we have entered a new era of "post-truth" politics in the United States. We hear talk of "fake news" and "alternative facts" as part of our political discourse. It may be harder now for a politician to tell the truth and be elected, but it is also easier for voters to check the accuracy of political claims. Countless blogs and websites dedicated to checking the truthfulness of politicians' claims have brought a new standard of awareness to the public sphere, but what counts as a "fact" can be difficult to ascertain at times, and facts require interpretation. Even the meaning of the term "fact" is contested. Moreover, "false balance"—the journalistic tendency to treat all opposed claims as equally legitimate—adds yet another dimension of difficulty to achieving an ethical practice of public discourse.

Most public controversies pose serious moral dilemmas, and thus underline the difficulty of achieving agreement about what counts as a fact. Would funding the Social Security system require taking funds from a younger generation, or would moderate changes alleviate the problem? Does the Second Amendment guarantee private ownership of unregistered firearms, or is it intended only to ensure the maintenance of a functional militia? Are tuition rates going up because of the greed of university administrators and faculty, or are the increases a legitimate consequence of maintaining high standards in our educational institutions? Is online privacy to be protected at the cost of national security? To raise concerns about the difficulty of establishing what is true in the political realm is not, however, to suggest that actual facts do not exist or that the truthfulness of a claim cannot be ascertained.

These observations about the political arena raise important questions about the ethics of public advocacy. Such concerns arise in everyday settings as well. Here is one example.

> Many parents worry that some vaccines may cause autism and other neuro-logical disorders in children. Han hosts a radio talk-show at his university that is competing with local commercial stations for listeners. He is aware that encouraging the public concern about vaccines—a popular and contro-versial topic—will increase his listenership. He is also aware that a vast amount of scientific data suggests that vaccines are safe, and that the real danger lies in people failing to have their children vaccinated. Han has read that much of the concern about vaccines can be traced to a paper published in 1998, which has now been repudiated by the journal that published it. In addition, the author's medical license has been revoked. Nevertheless, he has seen the results of a recent survey of parents that found that more than one in four agreed with the statement, "some vaccines do cause autism in otherwise healthy children." Should he appeal to his listeners' lingering fears in a bid for higher ratings, or set the record straight regarding vaccines?

ARGUMENTATION, ADVOCACY, AND ETHICS

In the first three chapters we considered the nature, structure, and contexts of arguments, along with a method for analyzing arguments. This chapter addresses a different kind of issue—the ethical obligations that arise any time we engage in argumentation with others.

Why is it important to discuss the ethics of advocacy and argumentation? Argumentation makes many of us uncomfortable because we know that its usual goal is persuasion—that the exchange of reasoned views is intended to bring about a change of views. Few facts more clearly define who we are than how we think, the opinions we hold, so it's not surprising that we often feel a little defensive when we realize someone is trying to influence our thinking. Some communication theorists have even suggested that efforts to persuade are a kind of aggression.[1] Whether or not we view persuasion as violence, we can agree that trying to influence another person's decisions is an activity with a clear moral dimension. Thus, ethical questions arise the moment argumentation begins.

It is hard for many of us to admit that the goal of argumentation is often to shape another person's thinking, so we find ourselves saying things such as, "I'm not trying to persuade you; I just want to tell you what I think." Maybe we imagine such claims excuse us from the responsibilities of ethical argument. When we do acknowledge our intent to change thoughts by arguments, most of us recognize that we should not attempt this without some regard for the other person. The question arises: How can we ensure that our argumentation is morally grounded?

A tentative framework for the ethics of advocacy arises from a consideration of the people—the advocate and the audience—who come together in a setting where arguments are advanced and heard. Both advocates and audience members have ethical responsibilities, although we often think only of the advocate's.

As an ethical advocate, I should seek to:

- Accurately represent my own views.
- Regard audience members, including opponents, as reasoning people.
- Present good evidence and sound reasoning on the topic under discussion.

As an audience member I also incur some basic ethical responsibilities. I am obliged to:

- Listen carefully and critically to the advocate's case.
- Allow other members of the audience to hear and assess the case as well.
- Make an informed decision or response when necessary.

This chapter explores several approaches to the ethics of advocacy, with particular attention to an approach rooted in the concept of **virtues,** *personal qualities that assist us in making ethically good choices.* First, however, let's consider the challenge of developing an ethics of advocacy that is adaptable to our diverse social setting, in which various moral viewpoints are present. Discovering an ethical perspective that is widely acceptable is crucially important to the goal of improving public discourse.

ARGUMENT ETHICS AND SOCIAL PLURALISM

Our contemporary diversity of values and beliefs makes the challenges facing the argument ethicist difficult to negotiate, but also renders the ethical practice of advocacy imperative. **Pluralism** is a term that is widely used to refer to *the variety of moral and ethical perspectives present in contemporary societies.* For example, one participant in a discussion about euthanasia may hold a firm religious conviction that we should never take another's life; a second embraces a personal philosophy that mercy at times outweighs a regard for preserving life; a third has been raised in a cultural community that teaches that decisions about life and death should be entirely a matter of individual choice. Can any ethical perspective hope to bridge all three views? Perhaps, but finding that approach will take some work and thought.

As we saw in Chapter 1, the potential for argumentation to manage disagreement without violence or coercion has rendered it invaluable in free societies. The value of argument, however, depends on advocates' willingness to argue within ethical boundaries. In a political debate, for instance, if a politician lies about the content of a proposed spending bill, the audience will find it difficult, at best, to render a reasoned decision about whether the bill deserves support.

Opponents in controversies may pursue their arguments ethically, but from radically different moral perspectives. For example, a Palestinian advocate may argue, without any distortion of available evidence, that Israeli policies make it difficult for Palestinians to find jobs; while an Israeli advocate may argue, from equally reliable evidence, that those same policies are necessary to maintain security. In many prolonged public debates, ethical advocates can be found arguing on different sides of almost all issues about which reasonable people can disagree.

> The value of argument depends on advocates' willingness to argue within ethical boundaries.

The controversy that characterizes much public argumentation in a pluralistic society is not a bad quality in and of itself. Indeed, the two-sidedness of controversial argument secures many of argumentation's benefits. Among these benefits are:

1. Disagreements are aired.
2. Ideas are tested.
3. Positions are refined.

In the contemporary context any workable approach to argumentation ethics must be acceptable to people who disagree about the very bases of morality itself. Citizens of the same country, the same city, the same neighborhood may inhabit vastly different communities in terms of the values, culture, and beliefs that shape their senses of what is right and good. Thus, an ethics of advocacy rooted in a single moral orientation is likely to garner only limited acceptance. For example, the parents of children in one high school may include Muslims, Christians, Jews, Hindus, and people with no religious affiliation. The same group of parents may include political liberals, conservatives, and moderates. Civil discussion of an issue such as the school's sex education curriculum will require mutual respect for these differences among all participants to that discussion.

SOME APPROACHES TO ARGUMENT ETHICS

Various ethical models have been proposed as guides to ethical discourse in a pluralistic society. A leading communication ethicist, Richard Johannesen, has identified several perspectives from which an ethic of human communication may be developed.[2] An overview of these perspectives should help us familiarize ourselves with various approaches to advocacy ethics.

Political perspectives are *ethical perspectives that rely on the essential values of a political system for their criteria of ethical assessment.* One possibility for an ethics of argumentation is to derive principles from the values embodied in a political view such as democracy or a political document such as the United States Constitution. For instance, the right of freedom of speech would constitute an ethical value. Thus, actions that enhance freedom of speech are considered ethical. Allowing all sides to a debate equal time to express their views and a venue in which to state those views are examples of actions that enhance freedom of speech and which are encouraged as ethical according to this perspective. Actions that inhibit freedom of speech, such as intentionally disrupting a setting in which an advocate is presenting an argument, would be inconsistent with a value for free speech.

Human nature perspectives are *ethical perspectives that develop around one or more essential qualities of human nature.*[3] If we define human nature according to a criterion such as reason—in other words, that it is essentially human to reason—an ethics of argument might be based on the right of every advocate to exercise reason on any given issue. An ethical action would enhance the audience's capacity to exercise reason, for example, providing adequate evidence for making a rational decision. It would be unethical, from this perspective, to prevent an audience from having access to evidence that is crucial to rational decision-making.

Some people have suggested that the essence of human nature is found in our tendency to seek to persuade one another. Thus, any action that prevented the exercise of an ability to persuade would be unethical. The idea behind this perspective is that ethical communication enhances our humanity.

Dialogic perspectives are *ethical perspectives that elevate efforts to preserve the two-sidedness of public discourse.* In this view, attitudes that nurture dialogue, such as genuineness and empathy, are valued in public discourse. For instance, a political candidate arguing against gay marriage might, nevertheless, express concern for those affected by a decision not to allow such marriages. Such a decision encourages the two-sidedness of debate.

Does this mean that an ethical advocate under the dialogic approach forgoes his or her convictions? Johannesen replies that the ethical advocate "does not forego his or her own convictions and views, but strives to understand those of others and avoids imposing his or her own on others."[4] "Monologic" communication, the opposite of dialogic communication, is marked by self-centeredness, deceptiveness, and other qualities that prevent dialogue. In a dialogic perspective, monologic communication is considered unethical.

Situational perspectives are *ethical perspectives that identify ethical consider-ations or principles inherent to each unique communication setting.* The situational approach minimizes "criteria from broad political, human nature, dialogical, or religious perspectives" and avoids "absolute and universal standards."[5] The situational ethicist seeks to appreciate the nuances of each argument setting and each issue being debated. This perspective allows the possibility of tailoring ethical standards to debates, from serious social issues such as racial discrimination to those addressing more focused and less morally weighty topics such as whether to participate in social media sites.

John Merrill, a journalism professor, points out a potential problem inherent in the situational approach. He comments that "if every case is different, if every situation demands a different standard, if there are not absolutes in ethics, then we should scrap the whole subject . . . and simply be satisfied that each person run his life by his whims or 'considerations' which may change from situation to situation."[6] The situational approach does recognize that the topics we debate in a free society bring into play a range of values, from our deepest moral commitments to mere preferences or matters of taste. Can a single ethical standard possibly be appropriate to all such situations?

Each of these four perspectives offers some guidance in our search for an ethical practice of argument. You may find one of them especially attractive and wish to develop some of your own thinking about ethical argumentation around that perspec-tive. The following section addresses another possibility for an ethic of advocacy in a pluralistic society, one that draws on an approach that has attracted attention from ethicists over the past several decades.

VIRTUES IN ARGUMENTATION

The ancient Greek philosopher Aristotle discussed human virtues as providing a basis for ethics. He located the foundation of ethical behavior in the individual's character rather than in external considerations such as moral rules. Recently, the relationship between virtues and ethics has again become a topic of intense discussion among scholars. Can an ethical system based on human virtues or character qualities provide a helpful alternative to the approaches outlined above, one that more effectively addresses the condition of moral pluralism?

The idea of virtues focuses attention on moral and practical qualities of individual people, especially those qualities that promote or improve the wide range of beneficial practices essential to a thriving society.[7] Thus, while virtue ethics place emphasis on the individual's character, they do so as a step toward creating a functioning society.

Virtues include not only moral and intellectual commitments, but physical abilities and skills as well. For example, a virtuoso musical performer has a deep understanding of and commitment to music, as well as a set of remarkable physical skills. An outstanding athlete can display a moral commitment to fair play as well as the physical quality of agility. Similarly, a great surgeon would likely possess the moral virtue of empathy for the patient and the physical and intellectual skills required to perform a successful surgery.

The conduct of academic research, a practice common to universities and colleges, is carried out by both students and faculty. The set of virtues that promote the practice of academic research might include such moral qualities as intellectual humility, a desire to discover the truth, and honesty in presenting discoveries. Practical virtues that enhance academic research might include perseverance in spite of fatigue, diligence, and the ability to maintain focus when faced with distractions.

The cluster of virtues connected with practicing law would differ somewhat from those we associate with academic research, but there would be some overlap as well. The practice of law is improved when an attorney lives out the virtues of regard for justice, knowledge of the law, and the ability to reason clearly in public. Notice that in each case, virtues are associated with a human endeavor: music, athletics, medicine, research, law. These virtues enhance the ethical practice of the endeavor in question.

One ethicist, Gilbert Meilaender, has written that interest in virtue ethics "suggests a widespread dissatisfaction with an understanding of the moral life that emphasizes duties, obligations, troubling moral dilemmas, and borderline cases."[8] By contrast, the study of virtue ethics emphasizes "the habits of behavior that make us who we are" as human beings living in complex and varied social structures.[9] Here the word, "habit" does not refer to an automatic response, but to a determined and practiced effort to do what a particular set of circumstances requires as an ethically good response. A virtues approach to ethics does not emphasize rules of conduct, but rather the personal qualities required to enhance beneficial activity.

Virtues guide us to act morally in public and private settings, in part by focusing our attention on the important moral features of a situation. Ethicist Amélie O. Rorty writes that "virtues form interpretations of situations; they focus the person's attention and define what is salient, placing other concerns in the background." She adds that "to act well, and to do so reliably, a person must perceive and interpret situations appropriately, and do so reliably."[10] Virtues assist us in this process of making practical choices reliably and ethically.

Our specific concern here is the ethical conduct of argumentation and advocacy. Argumentation, like medicine or music, is one of those beneficial endeavors that constitute our social lives, so it would be worthwhile to identify the virtues that will improve the practice of advocacy and argument. **Argument virtues** are *those moral qualities and skills that help people think and act morally in an argumentative situation, and thus pursue argumentation in a manner that promotes and improves its practice.* The moral qualities of an ethical advocate would also assist our perceptions of and responses to the ethical issues that an argumentative situation raises. What, then, are some of those virtues that are particularly relevant to improving the social practice we call argumentation?

Most people, when they think about public argument and advocacy, would say the most important virtue is **honesty,** *a commitment not to willingly mislead, and generally a regard for what is or what we take to be true.* Philosopher Caroline Simon writes that honesty may be the most essential virtue in communicating with others.[11] She defines honesty as "truthfulness," which reveals itself as "an aversion to misrepresenting one's opinion."[12] Honesty in argument includes qualities such as candor or openness, as well as an unwillingness to mislead or to conceal facts.

Simon adds, however, that honesty alone is not enough to ensure ethical communication.[13] Before we explore some of the other virtues that enhance the practice

FIGURE 4.1 Functions of Virtues in Argument

Virtues:
1. Form interpretations of situations
2. Focus attention on salient facts

of argumentation, let's consider some of the common marks of *dis*honesty that can hinder or undermine the public practice of argument. Dishonesty in argument or advocacy can take various forms, including:

- Advancing conclusions or reasons we know to be false.
- Suggesting a false conclusion without stating it directly.
- Twisting or distorting evidence to create a false impression of what the evidence proves.
- Using evidence that we know to be inferior to other available evidence.
- Alluding to nonexistent evidence.
- Intentionally using old evidence that has been replaced by better evidence.
- Using sources of information we know to be unreliable.
- Presenting, as our own, ideas or evidence that originated with someone else (plagiarism).
- Concealing available evidence so it is not available to people involved in making a decision.

This is not an exhaustive list of dishonest behavior in argumentation, but it does suggest some of the most common forms that an advocate's failure to live out the virtue of honesty may take. In some difficult or questionable situations, you may only be able to decide what is honest by asking yourself whether you would be comfortable with your audience knowing exactly what you had done in inventing, presenting, and documenting your argument.

Courage is also necessary to the ethical practice of argumentation, as communication theorist Ronald Arnett suggests.[14] Arnett defines courage as a determination to avoid "easy answers" to the difficult questions that advocates often face. He writes that simply "to listen to another's position" as well as "to question another's decision" can require "a good dose of courage."[15] Courage in argumentation does require such a determined willingness to listen and to question, that is, to practice the basic components of free speech. But courage also requires something more.

Courage in argument is *a willingness to accept the risks associated with open advocacy of one's position, even when that position is unpopular or dangerous.* It takes courage to speak up against a prevailing injustice, as Martin Luther King Jr. did during the civil rights movement. It also requires courage to point out that a factory is dumping waste directly into a local river, or to challenge a city council's decision to cut funding to a local women's center. Sometimes it takes courage just to say what others are not willing or able to say. Without courage, our storehouse of ideas is limited to those already accepted.

> Without courage, our storehouse of ideas is limited to those already accepted.

FIGURE 4.2 Some Virtues in Argument

Virtues in argument include:
- Honesty
- Courage
- Cooperation
- Respect for persons
- Regard for contexts

What additional virtues contribute to the sound practice of argumentation? Argumentation is a process that requires the virtue of **cooperation** if good decisions are to be reached and controversial issues resolved. We can define the virtue of cooperation as *a willingness to engage the argumentative process so that a rational resolution of the issues can be achieved.* A virtues approach to argument ethics would suggest that we must strive to cooperate in the argumentative process, even when we disagree sharply with our opponent's views. Cooperation involves a commitment to make the best case possible for our own views, but it also requires us to both listen to and seek to address the opposing arguments.

Because argumentation is a social activity, **respect for persons,** *a regard for others as reasoning persons,* is another virtue of ethical argumentation. By our participation in argument, we affirm a value for people as both givers and hearers of reasons. This respect for persons should also be extended to those with whom we sharply disagree. If we do not consider our opponents' positions to be reasonable, we can still see them as people capable of reasoning. Failing to maintain this regard for others as reasoners can result in dismissiveness, verbal abuse, and on occasion violence—all of which undermine the argumentative process.

Participants in the argumentative process should strive to demonstrate regard for their opponents as reasoners, even in the face of uncomfortable or unfriendly arguments. Ethical argumentation involves a sincere commitment to developing our own arguments in a way that shows we view others as intelligent, reasoning, and reasonable people. This means, among other things, that we will seek out the best available evidence while recognizing that interpretations of evidence vary. We should avoid tactics that circumvent reason or that otherwise suggest that we do not view the other person as capable of forming reasonable opinions. Making excessive use of emotional appeals, employing arguments you know to be weak, or seeking to intimidate an opponent would all be ethically suspect in argument.

So far we have discussed honesty, courage, cooperation, and respect for persons as virtues of an ethical advocate. Each of these virtues focuses on a person—either the individual making an argument or the intended audience for that argument. But what about the settings in which arguments are made and heard?

In thinking about argument ethics it is easy to overlook the physical places, organized events, and human relationships that provide the contexts in which argumentation occurs. Without a commitment to creating and preserving **argumentative contexts,** however—*the spaces, venues, and relationships in which arguments are made and heard*—argumentation does not flourish as a beneficial social practice. Argumentative contexts must be kept open and inviting for the presentation of arguments, which requires attention not just to maintaining physical spaces but also to human relationships and even to the issue of time. Ethical advocates will practice a fifth virtue, **regard for contexts,** which we can define as *a willingness to create and preserve space for argumentation to occur, cultivate the relationships in which it occurs, and allow the argumentative process to continue as long as necessary to ensure reasonable resolution of issues.*

Argumentative contexts—whether spaces or relationships—can be undermined in various ways. Failing to let advocates make their arguments by creating noise or other disturbances during a debate, disrupting or destroying a physical space set aside for the purpose of airing views, and using insults and derogatory labels that demean a participant would all be examples. Of course, such actions can also demonstrate a failure of respect for persons, even a lack of courage, if they are done out of fear of an inability to answer the arguments that would have been advanced.

CHAPTER REVIEW

We live in a pluralistic society, in which a wide variety of different values and beliefs are represented. This fact poses a challenge for a contemporary ethics of advocacy. Ethical systems for conducting argumentation have tended to look to political values such as justice, to the essential value of all human beings, to attitudes that promote or inhibit dialogue, or to the special requirements of each particular argumentative situation.

This chapter has urged a virtues approach to argument ethics, an approach rooted in the individual advocate's character and behavior, as a solution to the ethical challenges that pluralism poses. Virtues of ethical advocacy include honesty, courage, cooperation, respect for persons, and regard for the contexts in which arguments are made and heard. If these virtues accurately describe an advocate engaged in the ethical practice of argument, improving public discourse will mean living out these virtues when we develop and present our own arguments.

EXERCISES

A.   Provide an instance of argumentation that you have read or heard about that you consider to be unethical. Explain why you came to this conclusion. Did the individual advancing the argument fail to exhibit a virtue mentioned in this chapter? Should some other principle or virtue of argument ethics be added to those already discussed?

B.   Develop your thoughts on argument ethics by answering the following questions:

1. For you, what are the most fundamental ethical obligations of individuals presenting or hearing arguments?

2. For you, what constitutes an obvious violation of argumentative ethics?

3. When was the last time you believed you were hearing an unethically presented argument? What qualities of the argument or how it was presented struck you as unethical?

4. Identify four or five values that might garner wide agreement in our own pluralistic society. (A likely example would be the value of freedom of speech.)

5. In what practical ways might an advocate develop the virtues discussed in this chapter as a matter of personal character?

C. Review the discussion of the virtues of an ethical advocate. In light of these virtues, what ethical issues, if any, do the following scenarios raise for you?

1. Protesters at a University of California campus forced the cancellation of an invited speech by a conservative advocate of administrative policies. The protests became so heated that police feared violence. Some protesters even blocked access to the site of the speech. A university spokesperson said publicly that she did not agree with the protesters, and that universities should be places where all views—even repellent ones—should be heard and critically evaluated.

2. Members of a group that opposes abortion are distributing materials urging alternatives to women entering an abortion clinic. No physical action is taking place to obstruct entrance to the clinic.

3. During a campaign speech, a candidate for national political office calls another candidate's moral character into question, based on the second candidate's alleged misuse of campaign funds. The second candidate is not present to respond.

4. A proponent of euthanasia has been asked to write an editorial in support of the practice for a news magazine. He believes euthanasia is morally justified in some cases. He also believes that one argument in particular, which he has developed and used several times in public, is both sound and highly persuasive, even to opponents of euthanasia. He decides to show a draft of the editorial to a trusted friend who teaches logic. The friend points out a technical problem in his argument that he had not noticed before. However, the euthanasia advocate believes that his audience would not be able to spot the logical problem in the argument.

D. Think of an example of a movie, documentary, television program, or song that you feel has a persuasive message. Employing the virtues of advocacy discussed in this chapter, write a one-page paper in which you evaluate your example from an ethical perspective. For example, was courage in advocacy displayed? Honesty? Was the audience treated with regard as reasoning people?

ENDNOTES

[1]See, for example, Sally Michael Gearhart, "The Womanization of Rhetoric," *Women's Studies Quarterly* 2 (1979), 195–201.

[2]Richard L. Johannesen, Kathleen Valde, and Karen Whedbee, *Ethics in Human Communication,* 6th ed. (Prospect Heights, Ill.: Waveland, 2008), Ch. 2–6. See also Ronald C. Arnett, "The Practical Philosophy of Communication Ethics and Free Speech as the Foundation for Speech Communication," *Communication Quarterly* 38 (Summer 1990), 208–217.

[3]Johannesen, et al., 41.

[4]Johannesen, et al., 21.

[5]Johannesen, et al., 35–36.

[6]Quoted in Johannesen, et al., 79, from John C. Merrill, *The Imperative of Freedom* (New York: Hastings, 1974), 170–173.

[7]Richard L. Johannesen, "Virtue Ethics, Character, and Political Communication," in *Ethical Dimensions of Political Communication,* ed. Robert E. Denton (New York: Praeger, 1991), 69–90. See also Stanley Hauerwas, *A Community of Character* (Notre Dame, Ind.: University of Notre Dame Press, 1981). This approach probably begins with Aristotle's *Nichomachean Ethics,* trans. Martin Oswald (Indianapolis: Bobbs-Merrill, 1975).

[8]Gilbert Meilaender, "Virtue in Contemporary Religious Thought," in *Virtue: Public and Private,* ed. R. J. Neuhaus. (Grand Rapids, Mich.: Eerdmans, 1986), 7.

[9]Meilaender, 7–8.

[10]Amélie O. Rorty, "Virtues and Their Vicissitudes," in *Midwest Studies in Philosophy,* Vol. XIII (Notre Dame, Ind.: University of Notre Dame Press, 1988), 136–148, 137.

[11]Caroline J. Simon, "Verbal Virtues," *Michigan Academician* 23 (1991), 335–343.

[12]Simon, 341.

[13]Simon, 341.

[14]Ronald C. Arnett, "The Practical Philosophy of Communication Ethics," *Communication Quarterly* 38 (Summer 1990), 208–217, 215.

[15]Arnett, 215.

RECOMMENDED WEBSITES

FactCheck.org

www.factcheck.org

FactCheck.org, a project of the Annenberg Public Policy Center, "aims to reduce the level of deception and confusion in U.S. politics" by monitoring the "factual accuracy of what is said by major U.S. political players." (FactCheck.Org Mission Statement)

Here is a link to a helpful discussion of how to spot fake news, provided by Factcheck.org: http://www.factcheck.org/2016/11/how-to-spot-fake-news

PolitiFact.com

www.politifact.com

PolitiFact, a service of the *Tampa Bay Times,* rates politicians according to the truthfulness of their public claims. The site has been awarded a Pulitzer Prize.

Institute of Communication Ethics

http://www.communicationethics.net/home/index.php

This site explores the question of communication ethics, providing additional insights into the potential and challenges of the topic.

5 Reasonable Arguments, Reasonable People

Hear the other side.
St. Augustine of Hippo (354–430)
Theologian

I'll not listen to reason . . . .
Reason always means what someone else has got to say.
Elizabeth Gaskell (1810–1865)
British novelist, in Cranford

KEY TERMS

acceptance	linguistic consistency	support
consideration	rebuttal	valid argument
	refutation	validity
	repudiation	

There's been a lot of talk about a post-truth political climate, raising obvious questions about how the public can know whom to trust. Jeffrey Rosen of the National Constitutional Center has said:

> If we really do live in a post-fact society and if we're so much in our filter bubbles and echo chambers that citizens can't converge around a common understanding of facts, then we can't sustain the public reason and civil discourse, which includes constitutional discourse that Madison thought was necessary for the republic to survive.[1]

If Rosen is right, then democracy itself is threatened by the careless treatment of facts and truth in our political culture. Reasoning without facts, or in the presence of unreliable evidence, is precarious. Having some guidance regarding how to sort out fact from mere assertion is, then, critical to our individual and private reasoning processes. Rosen's concerns suggest a larger question: What qualities render an argument reasonable?

Just as there are reasonable and unreasonable arguments, so there are reasonable and unreasonable ways of presenting and discussing arguments. Because the human element is always a component in the argumentative process, we should add another question to complete the picture of reasonable advocacy: What qualities characterize a reasonable advocate?

Chapter 4 considered ethical advocacy as a step toward responsible argument and improving our public discourse. This chapter focuses on two additional basic components of rational public discourse—reasonable arguments and reasonable people. When we combine these two concepts with our understanding of ethical advocacy, we begin to see a more complete picture of rational and responsible public discourse.

What does the expression, "That's reasonable," actually mean? The statement may be simply self-referential, meaning "That argument makes sense *to me*" or "I agree with that argument." Usually, however, we are also making an objective evaluative statement about the quality of the argument *as* an argument. Similarly, when developing our own arguments, we usually want them to be reasonable in some testable way.

What, then, are the criteria of a reasonable argument, and how can these criteria be applied to specific arguments?

REASONABLE ARGUMENTS

The objective requirements of a reasonable argument are that (1) it advances good reasons, (2) its structure is sound, and (3) the definitions of its key terms are clear and consistent. These three criteria are also referred to as support, validity, and linguistic consistency. A reasonable argument satisfies all three criteria, while an unreasonable argument violates one or more of them. Let's look at each criterion briefly here. Subsequent chapters will explore them in greater detail.

Support

As noted above, the first criterion of a reasonable argument is **support**, *the strength and accuracy of the argument's evidence.* For an argument to be sound or reasonable, its evidence must be in good order. For example, suppose we read this argument in an editorial:

> A study recently published in the journal *Neurology* has found that mental activity from early in life, not just in one's older years, reduces the risk of cognitive decline late in life. The study involved 294 individuals over the age of 55. Cognitive decline was 15 percent slower for people who were mentally active throughout life than for people who were less so. Participants were asked about their activities as children, and the responses suggest that cognitive activity even in childhood plays a role in protecting the brain from patterns of memory loss and deteriorating mental agility later in life.[2]

Applying the criterion of support to this argument, we might ask whether the evidence provides us with good reasons for accepting the conclusion advanced. Certain questions about accuracy come to mind. For instance, do I have any way of checking these figures, or must I simply trust the source of the argument? Questions must also be asked about the sources of the evidence. We want to be assured that the source cited—in this case, the journal *Neurology*—is reliable in what it reports, and that it is not sharply at odds with other credible sources. We might also ask whether 294 participants is a large enough group to support the conclusion.

Specific tests and sources of evidence will be explored in subsequent chapters. For now we should simply note that reasonable arguments provide evidence for their claims that is accurate and that is derived from reliable sources. When an argument fails to provide sound evidence or derives evidence from questionable sources, we likely are encountering an unreasonable argument.

Validity

The criterion of support is not difficult to grasp because we are accustomed to thinking about evidence. Less familiar, however, is the concept of an argument's underlying logical structure, the pattern of reasoning that connects—or perhaps only appears to connect—reasons to a conclusion. When we look at an argument from this structural perspective, we are testing its validity. **Validity** refers to *a solid internal structure that allows for reliable connections between evidence and conclusions in an argument.* A **valid argument** is *an argument whose structure connects its reasons to its conclusions in a reliable manner.*

An example may be helpful at this point. As we noted earlier, the basic units of argument are a connective—a belief, value, or generalization—and a reason rooted in observation, which we termed evidence. When these two kinds of reasons are combined in a valid manner, they lead to a conclusion. For example:

> **Connective:** Members of the union have full medical coverage. (generalization)
>
> **Evidence:** Kelly is a member of the union.
>
> **Conclusion:** Therefore, Kelly must have full medical coverage.

In this argument the connective and evidence are related in such a way that if they are true, the conclusion is said to "follow"—to be justified or reasonable, based on its reasons. As you can see, Kelly is simply a specific case of the general principle being applied. Unless there are other facts about his case that we don't know (Toulmin's "rebuttal"), the conclusion should be trustworthy. The argument is valid: its reasons are arranged in such a way as to lead reliably to its conclusion.

So what does an *in*valid argument look like, one whose structure renders it unreasonable? Consider this example:

> **Connective:** All members of the union have full medical coverage.
>
> **Evidence:** Kelly has full medical coverage.
>
> **Conclusion:** Therefore, Kelly must be a member of the union.

While this argument sounds a lot like the one above it, it is invalid—its structure does not allow us to draw this conclusion from these reasons. Why not? The general claim or connective states that all members of the union have medical coverage, but notice that this is not the same as saying that *only* members of the union have this coverage. Kelly might have purchased coverage independently, obtained it through an employer, or gained coverage under a family member's policy. This argument is flawed, not in its reasons (the reasons may be true to fact) but rather in its form or structure. Validity or sound structure is the second criterion of a reasonable argument.

Linguistic Consistency

It might seem as if checking an argument's support and its structure would be sufficient for determining whether it was sound. However, there is another factor that is often hidden from view, but that is just as important to check. The third criterion of a reasonable argument is its **linguistic consistency,** *the clarity of the argument's language and its use of terms in the same way throughout the argument.* The criterion of linguistic consistency also implies that where there is potential for misunderstanding an important term, an advocate is responsible for clarifying its meaning for the audience. Once a definition has been introduced—whether stated or only implied—the advocate is obliged to maintain that definition throughout the argument.

The following humorous example shows how an obvious shift in the meaning of a key term can cause problems in an argument that otherwise is sound (if we can be a little generous):

> Nothing is better than a good education, but a cheese sandwich is better than nothing. It follows that a cheese sandwich is better than a good education.

What's the problem here? The term "nothing" fails the test of linguistic consistency. We can demonstrate this fact by looking at the two different definitions of "nothing" conveyed in the argument. In the first instance it means "not anything one can obtain in life." In the second instance it takes on quite a different meaning, "not anything at all." If we take the second sense of "nothing" and try to substitute it for the first use of "nothing," we get a nonsensical statement: "Not having anything at all is better than a good education." A few devout adherents to a rigorous monastic tradition might agree with this statement, but not many of the rest of us would.

Let's consider a more serious example. Suppose a public relations executive makes the argument at a press conference that her company CEO's belief about a change in the market is "true":

> This is something the CEO takes to be true because it is based on facts he has available to him. Although outside sources have contradicted this belief, saying his views are not true because not grounded in fact, he accepts it to be true because it is something he has believed for a long time. We are confident that the facts will bear out the truthfulness of this belief.

It appears that the term "true" has two different meanings in this brief example. In the first sentence, "true" is defined as:

1. Based in facts.

But in its second use, "true" is apparently defined as:

2. Something believed for a long time.

Though the two meanings may be related, they are not the same. As a result, the conclusion that someone holds a true belief is thrown into doubt. In this statement a key term receives two different meanings, which are potentially confused with one another.

To review, when evaluating an argument we have to consider three basic factors—support, validity, and linguistic consistency. As advocates and as critics we should keep the following questions in mind:

1. Does the argument exhibit sound *support* for its conclusion?

2. Is the argument structurally sound or *valid*?

3. Does the argument demonstrate *linguistic consistency?*

If the argument fails one or more of these tests, we are not obliged to accept it as reasonable. It is important to remember that an argument is not necessarily reasonable because we agree with it, nor is it necessarily unreasonable because we disagree with it. To label an argument reasonable or unreasonable should reveal more than our own inclinations or biases: the question of an argument's reasonableness is best resolved using reliable criteria of evaluation. Subsequent chapters will explore the issues of support, validity, and linguistic consistency in more detail.

The last chapter examined the ethics of advocacy as one component in constructive public discourse. In this chapter we have been examining the three basic criteria of reasonable arguments with the same goal in mind—improving public

FIGURE 5.1 Qualities of a Reasonable Argument

A reasonable argument exhibits:

- *Support:* Its evidence is in good order; its claims are truthful and accurate.
- *Validity:* It is constructed in a way that permits dependable movement from its reasons to its conclusion.
- *Linguistic consistency:* Its key terms are defined clearly and consistently throughout.

---

argumentation. A final crucial component of beneficial public discourse is the issue of how we should conduct ourselves when arguments are advanced. That is, we need to ask what the qualities of a reasonable person are.

REASONABLE PEOPLE

Developing arguments that satisfy the three criteria outlined in the previous section is one important aspect of productive public discourse. However, we also need to consider the qualities that are implied when we say someone is a reasonable person.

When we make such a claim—which we all do at one time or another—what traits are we attributing to that person? Do we simply mean that the individual strikes us as mannerly, or seems to think as we do? What criteria define a reasonable person? Being reasonable does not mean avoiding disagreements, though it may have some bearing on how we manage disagreements.

Engaging the argumentative process in a reasonable manner should be a commitment undertaken by all parties involved. There are many instances in which one side's best efforts to proceed in a reasonable fashion in a dispute are met with an obstinate refusal on the other side to engage the issues, answer arguments, or provide evidence for claims. *If argumentation is actually to achieve beneficial working agreements, all advocates must commit themselves to engaging in the argumentation process in a reasonable manner.* This commitment reflects the virtue of cooperation discussed in Chapter 4.

Most of us consider ourselves to be reasonable people most of the time, though virtually everyone will admit to being unreasonable at least some of the time. Moreover, we all find some other people to be reasonable or unreasonable. Take a minute and think of the most reasonable and the most unreasonable people you know. What qualities lead you to label them as reasonable or unreasonable? Though we will not likely achieve consensus on such a difficult issue, people who earn the label "reasonable" tend to exhibit three characteristics. When these characteristics are apparent in public settings, the quality of public discourse tends to improve.

1. Reasonable people are willing to provide other people with their reasons, that is, to communicate about how they think. For example, Jeff and his roommate Franklin are talking when Franklin mentions a recent local election in which the city's mayor was returned to office for a third term. Jeff reacts to the election results by saying, "This is so stupid! How can the people of this town be so dense! That guy is an idiot! I can't believe they elected him again!" Franklin asks Jeff why he thinks the mayor should not have been reelected. Jeff responds, "It's so stupid, that's why! It's just ridiculous!"

Feeling that the conversation is going nowhere, Franklin heads down the hall to Steve's room. Steve also disagrees with the election outcome, but when Franklin asks why, he responds by giving his reasons. "Mayor Alexander refused to sign a citizen-backed funding measure that would have provided the city with a new library. His only reason was that local businesses opposed the idea because it raised taxes. He came out against the school bond issue for the same reason. Then, last month he prohibited a rock concert in the park to raise money for disaster relief because local residents said it would be too loud. I mean, he's out of touch—Alexander only attended four of twelve city board meetings last year."

Jeff refused to present his reasons for objecting to the mayor's reelection, but Steve was willing to tell Franklin what he was thinking. Such a willingness to communicate one's reasons indicates a propensity to "think things through." It also signals a willingness to engage in the cooperative activity of reasoning with others. A willingness to "reason out loud" also may exhibit a value for open discussion of ideas and issues as the best way of improving communication, enhancing social life, and discovering solutions to difficult social problems. A willingness to communicate your reasons to others is not by itself a complete description of a reasonable individual, however. This quality must be balanced with a willingness to listen to the reasoning of others, which brings us to a second quality of reasonable people.

2. Reasonable people are willing to listen carefully, to consider what other people have to say. Sarah and her friend Lee disagree about abortion: Sarah is pro-choice, while Lee is pro-life. They both also have strong feelings on the subject, but even though they can't see eye-to-eye, they have agreed to hear one another out. "Let's do this," suggests Lee. "You tell me what you think, and I will only interrupt if I don't understand something you said. Then, you do the same for me." It took more than an hour to set out their reasons and to answer each other's questions, but at the end of the process they were still friends and each had a better understanding of the other's views.

Expressing respect for the reasoning of other people involves listening to their arguments and evaluating those arguments thoughtfully. This is not to say that all arguments are created equal; however, reasonable people are not threatened at the prospect of hearing an argument that challenges their own views. Reasonable people are open to the give and take of argumentation.

3. Reasonable people are willing to search for the best reasons and conclusions available through the interactive process of argumentation. For example:

Ben has approached his boss with an idea for marketing a new dental care product the firm has just developed. Ben wants to use social media to market the product to a younger demographic. The boss's first response is discouraging—she doesn't think the idea will work because most of the company's customers are over fifty. "These consumers still respond best to magazine and television ads," she says, "but if you can show me that the idea could work, I might let you give it a trial run on a limited basis." Ben spends the next week researching social media marketing of dental and health care products to younger consumers, then shows the boss some data he has found that support his idea. "Social media marketing of dental and health care products is most successful with younger consumers, especially those under thirty," he says, "more successful than magazine and television advertising. And although this demographic is not the largest part of our market, my research shows that it is the fastest growing part." The boss is impressed with

FIGURE 5.2 Qualities of a Reasonable Person

> **Reasonable people are:**
> - Willing to communicate their reasons to others.
> - Willing to consider what others have to say.
> - Willing to search for the best reasons and conclusions available.

Ben's research and open to new ideas. She gives Ben permission to pilot a social media marketing scheme for the new product.

The boss responded to Ben's idea in a reasonable way. She did not close off the possibility of a new piece of evidence coming to light, of a new idea working as well or better than an old one. A reasonable person is open to new ideas and evidence even when they come from an opponent or might require altering a cherished belief. Reasonable people are committed to the mutual, interactive search for facts and truths that will lead to better judgments and decisions. This search for the best reasons and conclusions is the principal goal of argumentation.

Does all this mean that reasonable people have no settled convictions, no strong beliefs? Actually, the thinking of reasonable people is often characterized by a solid core of firm, rational commitments. Your political views may be liberal, moderate, or conservative; you may have strong religious convictions or no religious commitments; you may believe that humans make their own choices or that behaviors are caused by external factors. You may hold any number of strong views and be a reasonable person. Reasonable people are marked more by an attitude toward reasoning with others than by their individual views. They are open to argument and to considering new evidence. They are also willing to engage in debate, within the constraints of their core beliefs and a basic regard for other people as givers and hearers of reasons.

When we are firmly convinced that a view we hold is correct—for example, that capital punishment is immoral or that gun control is a bad idea—we might have difficulty seeing that those who disagree can have any reasonable basis for doing so. Seldom, however, are all of the reasonable arguments on a single side in a controversy. Reasonable people may disagree on nearly any topic, and to say that people who disagree with us are unreasonable is simplistic.

A recent study conducted jointly by researchers at George Washington University and UCLA suggests that the use of logical appeals in advertisements actually triggers a higher degree of brain activity and more potential counter-arguments than does the use of visual imagery to persuade. To the claim that a reasonable person seeks good reasons and conclusions, therefore, we might add that a message based on reasoning rather than images alone encourages us to be more reasonable in our responses.[3]

RESPONDING TO ARGUMENTS

British social psychologist Michael Billig points out in his book, *Arguing and Thinking*, that "no matter how sophisticated the science of persuasion becomes, there will always be the possibility of counterargument." He refers to the impossibility of creating a perfect persuasive approach as "Quintilian's uncertainty principle," for the famous Roman teacher of rhetoric who originally noted that human beings can always imagine a response to any argument. Because of this innate human ability, Billig says, no argument or appeal will ever guarantee success in persuasion.[4]

Billig's assertion that no perfect science of persuasion can be developed is reassuring. But if he is right, why do we so often find ourselves falling prey to bad arguments, unreasonable appeals, and deceptive persuasive tactics? Perhaps it is because we are not aware of the range of possibilities open to us when we are listening to or reading arguments. This section considers five possibilities for responding to the arguments we read and hear every day: acceptance, consideration, rebuttal, refutation, and repudiation.

Acceptance is *the agreement to accept the argument as presented; that is, to find it persuasive, or at least lacking in any major flaw.* When hearing or reading an argument advanced by a politician whom you support, you may be inclined to offer little or no objection or scrutiny. In many cases we already accept an advocate's point of view on a topic; or maybe we are just willing to agree that a particular conclusion is reasonable, based on the evidence presented. In accepting an argument, we may reinforce a view we already hold, or we may be persuaded to take on a new view or modify an earlier view.

One important reason for studying argumentation is to ensure that we do not accept an argument as sound when it is not. We may be most vulnerable to unreasonable arguments when they advocate something we already believe. Acceptance can mean that we are not apt to answer an argument with a counter-argument, but imagining a counter-argument is still a useful way of evaluating the argument. It is a good idea to test even an argument we are inclined to accept by asking about validity, support, and linguistic consistency. This involves a process of reasoning with ourselves, as honestly as possible.

We are most likely to accept an argument if it was developed by an advocate who shares our views. Suppose you belong to a group that advocates a peaceful solution to the conflict between Israel and Palestine. You invite a speaker to your campus who is an expert on the subject and whose views closely parallel those of your group members. As you listen to the speaker, you find yourself agreeing with most of what he has to say. You learn a few new things, pick up a new idea, and maybe leave with some new evidence, but your general response is to accept his argument as presented. You may not find yourself imagining a counter-argument and you don't leave feeling you need more time to think it all over, but you were already convinced of the speaker's views.

We all accept arguments we hear on some occasions, despite Quintilian's uncertainty principle. We also lower our rational defenses just a bit at times. We may not apply the criteria of support, validity, and linguistic consistency to arguments with which we agree, which leaves us open to the risks of failing to question our settled convictions.

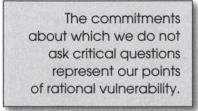
The commitments about which we do not ask critical questions represent our points of rational vulnerability.

The commitments about which we do not ask critical questions represent our points of rational vulnerability—the issues on which we are most likely to accept an unreasonable argument. Perhaps we have accepted an idea without carefully thinking it through, or maybe circumstances have changed enough that it is now time to reconsider our views. When you are inclined to accept an argument without critical examination, try applying Billig's suggestion—imagine a counter-argument. You may still agree, or you may discover that it is time to modify your thinking.

Consideration is *an agreement to think about the argument further, to withhold any final judgment about its quality for the time being.* Consideration is neither acceptance nor rejection, though either may follow consideration.

When an argument strikes us as at least potentially reasonable, when we see no obvious problems with its evidence, language, or structure, we usually find ourselves willing to consider the argument further. Nevertheless, we may not yet be convinced; we may feel we need more time to evaluate the argument.

Consideration is often a response to new evidence or to a new idea that seems important enough to warrant our attention. Perhaps your roommate has a religious idea that you have never thought seriously about before. She believes in reincarnation, the idea that souls move from one body to another following death. Thus, we each live many lives, not just one. Perhaps you have never thought about this idea and you are not sure you want to accept it. She presents some evidence, mainly testimony from people who say they remember having lived previous lives. You find this interesting, even somewhat persuasive. But you are not ready quite yet to accept the idea of reincarnation. You want more evidence and more time to think it over. This is the response of consideration.

The criteria of support, validity, and linguistic consistency should each play a role in the consideration process. For instance, you might want to ask whether the testimony seems reliable, a question regarding support. Moreover, even if the people providing the testimony were sincere in their belief that they had lived previous lives, would this be evidence that they had, in fact, done so? This question would raise issues of the structure of the argument: whether the reasons lead to the conclusion. Finally, it might be a good idea to get a precise definition of the term "reincarnation," and even to ask whether the term is defined in different ways by different authorities.

Rebuttal is *a counter-argument, a reasoned answer that addresses specific points made or evidence advanced in the original argument.* This is not to say that rebuttals must be good or successful replies, only that they are replies that themselves count as arguments. A rebuttal will include reasons and conclusions of its own. It may challenge an argument's structure, bring its evidence into question, advance different evidence, or question the original argument's definitions. For example:

> Sarah Chayes is a political commentator and an expert on military and security affairs. She has argued that US officials have diverted resources away from important safety and security concerns such as white-collar crime since the 9/11 attacks, while claiming to protect citizens from terrorism. Chayes offers a rebuttal to concentrating effort and resources on a single security concern—a terrorist attack: Lax security in other arenas—for example, maintaining our transportation infrastructure—has actually "made it easier for terrorists to achieve success." While seeking to combat the terrorist threat, "the intelligence community is neglecting other crucial phenomena." Moreover, by setting the goal of zero domestic terrorist attacks, officials have made success easier for terrorists. Finally, Chayes argues, public safety is not what these officials are protecting. "It is their own reputations."[5]

Refutation is *a thoroughly successful response to an argument, one that clearly demonstrates a damaging flaw to the satisfaction of a relatively objective listener or reader.* (Of course, the individual advancing the original argument may not acknowledge that he or she has been refuted.) Here is an example of an apparently successful refutation.

> It has been asserted that widespread voter fraud has involved large numbers of individuals voting on behalf of deceased citizens. Is there any truth to the claim? Some sources quoted a report by the Pew Charitable Trust as evidence of deceased individuals voting. The report states, however: "Approximately

24 million—one out of every eight—voter registrations in the United States are no longer valid or are significantly inaccurate." The report said nothing about voter fraud, but rather that voter registration systems need to be upgraded. Professor Lorraine Minnite of Rutgers University and author of *The Myth of Voter Fraud* states: "This issue of dead people voting is just not substantiated." Nearly all claims that votes were cast using the names of dead people are the result of clerical errors or as a result of people who voted legally, using absentee ballots, who later died. In South Carolina, the state election commission found that of 207 cases of alleged voter fraud using the names of deceased persons, 106 cases were clerical errors by poll managers; 56 cases resulted from a living person wrongly listed as deceased; 32 cases were erroneous entries indicating someone had voted who had not; 3 cases were absentee ballots issued to registered voters who had cast ballots and later died; and 10 cases could not be decided due to limited data. Researchers found that reports of fraud regarding deceased voters were "unfounded or greatly exaggerated."[6]

Repudiation is *dismissal of an argument without serious consideration.* Repudiation may take the form of a phrase such as "That's just ridiculous" or "That's crazy," perhaps followed by a brief statement of "obvious" reasons to the contrary. Repudiation may appear as a personal attack, such as "Well, I'd expect someone like Bill to say something like that." It can involve labeling the person or group making an argument—"That's just a fundamentalist talking" or "What do you expect from a liberal?" Repudiation may also take the form of laughter, silence, or some other nonverbal refusal to respond to the argument.

Because repudiation is a refusal to participate in the argumentative process, we may ask whether it is ever reasonable. Billig contends that repudiation by silence *is* reasonable in certain special cases, because answering some arguments attributes to them a status they don't deserve. He writes:

> The refusal to enter a debate can itself be a rhetorical strategy, based upon the recognition that the mere act of answering a question imparts legitimacy to the question. Thus, the serious historian would be well advised to refrain from discussing the reality of the Holocaust with the self-styled, anti-Semitic "experts," because to do so implies a legitimate controversy between two schools of thought.[7]

A commitment to improve public discourse requires a corresponding commitment to engage in the argumentative process in a reasonable and serious fashion. Consequently, we can identify uncritical acceptance, a refusal to enter dialogue, or even a weak rebuttal as unreasonable responses to arguments. As we have seen, acceptance, consideration, and rebuttal offer potentially reasonable responses to arguments. Repudiation is a reasonable response only when an argument clearly has no merit and deserves neither consideration nor response.

Argumentation is an interactive and cooperative process that involves socially complex, ongoing, mental, and verbal activity. Reasonable people may disagree about what constitutes a reasonable argument, as any survey of the positions on a public controversy reveals. Though our own attitudes and actions occasionally are based on unreasonable arguments, we should aim to base belief, action, and debate on the most reasonable arguments we can discover. This is the obligation of all parties to argumentation, and one source of agreement and cooperation that should accompany all responsible argumentation.

CHAPTER REVIEW

One goal in presenting our own arguments and evaluating others' reasoning is to improve the overall quality of public discourse. Any sound or reasonable argument meets the three criteria of support, validity, and linguistic consistency. Support is a concern for the quality of an argument's evidence. Validity reminds us that a reasonable argument makes reliable connections between its evidence and its conclusion. Linguistic consistency is clarity and consistency of definitions in an argument.

The quality of public discussion also depends on how advocates present and respond to arguments. Characteristics of reasonable people include willingness to let others know what they think, to hear others' opinions, and to search for the best evidence and conclusions possible.

We have a range of options for responding to arguments that we hear or read. Among these are acceptance, consideration, rebuttal, refutation, and repudiation.

EXERCISES

A. Think of an argument you have read or heard recently that struck you as particularly unreasonable. Try to identify exactly what seemed unreasonable to you. In which of the five ways discussed in this chapter did you respond to this argument?

B. What is your opinion of Michael Billig's assertion that it is wrong to answer those who question the historicity of the Holocaust? Do you agree that an argument should not be answered in some cases? Why or why not?

C. Would you classify the following examples as rebuttal or refutation? Explain your answer.

1. Governor Rick Snyder of Michigan backs a proposed new $300 million stadium for the Detroit Red Wings on the argument that such a resource would bring needed revenues into downtown Detroit. This idea would make sense if it weren't for the fact that it has already been tried and has failed. New stadiums built in the '80s and '90s in Detroit did not generate significant revenue for downtown businesses. People came to the games, then got into their cars and drove home.

2. Prior to the 2003 invasion of Iraq, some politicians suggested that opposing the invasion was unpatriotic because it meant opposing the president of the United States. Political columnist E. J. Dionne rejected that reasoning. If that were the case, Dionne argued, "then Abraham Lincoln was an unpatriotic appeaser for opposing the Mexican War as a young congressman in the 1840s."[8]

3. Evidence from a mass grave in northern Afghanistan suggests the fate of several hundred Taliban fighters captured by a US-backed warlord, the leader of the Northern Alliance. How did the hundreds of men in enormous graves die after their capture in the city of Konduz in November 2001? Leaders of the militia to which the men surrendered say the prisoners were not mistreated, though they said some likely died of wounds received in combat or while trying to escape. An investigating team from Physicians for Human Rights, however, has examined a number of the bodies at the site, and concludes that this could not be the case. Team members concluded that, given the complete absence of evidence of other causes of death, the men in the mass graves died of suffocation. This claim is consistent with reports of eyewitnesses that the prisoners were transported hundreds of miles in airtight steel shipping containers. Surviving Taliban corroborate this account, saying that hundreds if not thousands of their comrades died in transit to a remote prison. Exhumed bodies from the mass graves reveal no bullet wounds. It is also clear from autopsies that these men, who were between the ages of seventeen and thirty-nine, did not starve to death and were not beaten.[9]

D. Think of a friend, relative, or acquaintance whom you consider to be particularly reasonable. Describe the qualities of this individual that lead you to this conclusion.

ENDNOTES

[1]Jeffrey Rosen, interview by Terry Gross, *Fresh Air,* aired on National Public Radio, February 1, 2017, http://www.npr.org/2017/02/01/512851970/if-confirmed-would-neil-gorsuch-rule -contrary-to-trumps-policies.

[2]Robert S. Wilson, Patricia A. Boyle, Lei Yu, Lisa L. Barnes, Julie A. Schneider, and David A. Bennett, "Life-span Cognitive Activity, Neuropathologic Burden, and Cognitive Aging," *Neurology* online edition, July 3, 2013, http://www.neurology.org/content/early/2013/07/03 /WNL.0b013e31829c5e8a.abstract.

[3]Mark Wheeler, "Buyer Beware: Advertising May Seduce Your Brain," UCLA Newsroom, September 20, 2011, http://newsroom.ucla.edu/portal/ucla/buyer-beware-advertising-may -seduce-215473.aspx.

[4]Michael Billig, *Arguing and Thinking* (Cambridge, U.K.: Cambridge University Press, 1996).

[5]Sara Chayes, "Blinded by the War on Terrorism," *Los Angeles Times,* July 27, 2013, http://www .latimes.com/news/opinion/commentary/la-oe-chayes-terrorism-20130728,0,4319811.story.

[6]Robert Farley, "Trump's Bogus Voter Fraud Claims," *FactCheck.Org,* October 19, 2016, http://www.factcheck.org/2016/10/trumps-bogus-voter-fraud-claims.

[7]Billig, 252.

[8]E. J. Dionne Jr., "Patriotic Liberalism," Workingforchange, February 28, 2003, http://www .workingforchange.com/printitem.cfm?itemid=14574.

[9]"Chronology of PHR Activities and Investigations Concerning the Mass Graves at Dashte-e-Laile near Shebarghan, Afghanistan," Physicians for Human Rights, http://physiciansforhumanrights. org/library/chronology-of-phr-actions-and.html (Accessed September 6, 2010).

RECOMMENDED WEBSITES

Conflict Research Consortium

Guy Burgess and Heidi Burgess

conflict.colorado.edu

This website on civility in public discussions suggests standards for improving public discourse that parallel and supplement standards suggested in this chapter.

ProPublica

www.propublica.org

Our discussion of a reasonable person brings to mind the idea of the informed citizen. ProPublica is an investigative journalism organization founded to bring stories with "moral force" to the voting public.

III

Support:
The Content of
Arguments

6 Evaluating Evidence

> Alternative facts are not facts. They're falsehoods!
> *Chuck Todd (1972–)*
> *United States journalist*

> Everyone is entitled to his own opinion, but not his own facts.
> *attributed to*
> *Daniel Patrick Moynihan (1927–2003)*
> *United States senator*

KEY TERMS

accessibility	credibility	qualify the source
adequacy	external consistency	recency
	internal consistency	relevance

You are shopping with a friend. She points out that, though we think of the food supply as largely safe, foodborne illnesses such as E. coli and salmonella are a serious health threat to people in the United States. You are skeptical and respond that you have never gotten sick after eating something purchased at a grocery store or in a restaurant.

Not to be so easily dissuaded from her point, your friend notes that she just read in a reputable news source that a new study at Ohio State University found that foodborne illnesses cost the United States $152 billion annually in health care and other costs, and that seventy-six million people get sick from something they eat every year. "That's about one in four of us," she says. "You might have gotten sick from infected food and not even known the source. The government should do more to protect consumers."

You, however, are leery of excessive government intervention in our lives, and tell her so. She then adds, "What if I told you that more than five thousand people die every year in the United States because the government doesn't require inspections of all foods before they go to market?" "OK," you say, "those are pretty high numbers. Maybe you're right that we need stricter rules about food safety." What changed your mind was the subject of this chapter—evidence.

Chapter 5 introduced support as one criterion of reasonable arguments. To reiterate, support is the strength of the argument's evidence, the truthfulness or accuracy of the claims the argument advances to bolster its conclusion. Evidence can be derived from various sources, including personal experience, testimony, experiment, record-keeping, expert opinion, images and physical objects, and other forms of direct or indirect observation. This chapter focuses on several general criteria for evaluating evidence and its sources. These criteria are widely accepted as the marks of good evidence.

As we will see, evidence is often *interpreted* through a framework of personal and cultural values. What counts as sound or reasonable evidence may vary dramatically from one person to another, from one cultural setting to another. People holding different values may understand and interpret the same piece of evidence in quite different ways. Therefore, before we consider how to evaluate evidence and its sources, let us review the intimate relationship between evidence and personal values.

EVIDENCE AND VALUES

Though evidence usually originates in experience—either our own or someone else's—we always view it through the lenses of our personal values. Let's look at an example that demonstrates how the same evidence can lead to strikingly different interpretations.

> Recently a research team at Oregon Health and Science University successfully replaced a disease-bearing gene in the mitochondrial DNA of one female donor with a normal gene from a second female donor. The resulting embryo—which now had three parents—no longer carried the disease-bearing gene. However, this genetic therapy was unusual in that it altered germline DNA, meaning that if the embryo were to grow into a mature human being and reproduce, the genetic repair could be transferred to subsequent generations.[1]

Suppose we take this report on a scientific development as a piece of evidence: germline changes to human DNA have now occurred in a lab. What do we conclude from this evidence? This development was immediately hailed by some within the scientific community as a breakthrough that would open the way for vast medical advances. Others in the scientific and ethics communities have condemned the research as morally suspect, however, because it crossed the boundary separating the activity of "scientific research" from the activity of "altering human life in the laboratory."

> Evidence leads us to conclusions along the pathways of our personal or community value commitments.

These two conflicting responses to the new DNA development represent radically different interpretations of the same evidence. As this example suggests, evidence leads us to conclusions along the pathways of our personal or community value commitments. For some, the values for scientific progress and unfettered intellectual enterprise become the most important commitments in deciding the merits of this research. For others, values regarding the nature of life and the ethical limits of science prevail.

Let's return briefly to the scenario that opens this chapter. If your personal values motivate you to place a high priority on safety, your friend's advice might be highly persuasive. You would be less inclined to find your friend's evidence about the safety of the food supply persuasive if, for example, your values direct you to be suspicious of government regulation of business. Again, we often interpret evidence—in this case the research and profit record of a large company—according to the values we consider most important.

In addition to recognizing how our values inform our interpretation of evidence, we need some general criteria for testing the reliability of the evidence used to build our arguments and make the decisions that shape our lives. Evidence that does not stand up to these basic tests probably will not provide a sound foundation for our thinking. What are the general tests of evidence?

GENERAL TESTS OF EVIDENCE

Seven general tests may be applied to different kinds of evidence: accessibility, credibility, internal consistency, external consistency, recency, relevance, and adequacy. Employed together, these tests offer us a means of assessing whether an argument provides sufficient support for considering or accepting its claims.

Accessibility:
Is the Evidence Available?

The first test of evidence is also the most basic. The test of **accessibility** involves asking about *the availability of evidence for examination.*

Sometimes an audience is willing to accept an argument without personally examining the actual evidence. In such cases a simple allusion to well-known or readily accepted evidence may be sufficient. For instance, a speaker arguing for more funding for AIDS research states:

> As has often been reported, over a million people in the United States live with HIV infection.

The statistic has been widely and frequently reported. If we did doubt this claim, however, we might ask the advocate to either provide the evidence itself or point us to an accessible source, such as the website of the Centers for Disease Control and Prevention (www.cdc.gov).

Inaccessible evidence is a serious problem when we are not sure about the reliability of a claim and have no way of examining the evidence on which it is based. In such cases we are under no obligation to accept either the evidence or the claim it supports. Suppose you read the following argument:

> It is now a certainty that we have been visited by extraterrestrial beings. The government has secret records that report more than five thousand un-explained UFO encounters in the United States alone over the past fifty years.

The person advancing this argument claims the existence of secret government documents that provide evidence to support a controversial claim, but these documents are not accessible for you to examine. In this case, to accept the evidence is to trust the credibility of the advocate alone, a risky venture.

In some cases, good evidence is both physically available *and* technically inaccessible. This situation arises when evidence is too complex to decipher without special expertise. For example, an orthopedic surgeon shows you X-rays of your knee. To the doctor, these images provide clear evidence for concluding that you have a torn ligament. You may not see what the doctor sees, but you may still have good reason to accept the doctor's word that the evidence can be interpreted to mean a torn ligament. In such cases, the test of accessibility may have to be set aside in favor of trusting an expert's interpretation of the available evidence. Even in such cases, though, you may choose to consult a second expert if you are not satisfied that you have been given a good interpretation of the evidence. If your audience is not likely to accept your claim readily or if the evidence is not well known, full citation of the source of evidence is important.

Credibility:
Is the Source of the Evidence Reliable?

As you might expect, the best evidence is derived from sources that have **credibility,** *a reputation for accuracy and reliability.* (Chapter 7 discusses specific methods for locating and evaluating particular types of sources, such as books or the internet.) There are two generally applicable standards of source credibility.

1. Does the source have a reputation for accuracy? No published or online source enjoys a universally good reputation for the accuracy of what it records or reports, but some are widely recognized as usually reliable. Major newspapers and news magazines such as *The New York Times* and *Time;* the publications of well-regarded professional organizations, such as the American Medical Association; carefully reviewed periodicals, such as *Nature;* books published by university presses; and websites established by universities, research foundations, and government agencies are just a few examples of sources that enjoy good reputations for accuracy. The next chapter covers the topic of source credibility in greater detail.

2. Does the source possess appropriate credentials? This criterion focuses on the education and expertise of persons cited as authorities on a topic. Only individuals with extensive education and experience in a particular area are typically regarded as reliable sources of evidence when expertise is required.

Expertise is not transferable from one domain of study to another. For example, a famous physicist offering an opinion on the historical accuracy of a religious text should not be considered to be speaking as an expert.

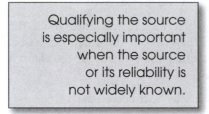

Qualifying the source is especially important when the source or its reliability is not widely known.

If an audience may not recognize either the reputation of a published source or the qualifications of an expert source, you will need to **qualify the source,** *state the source's credentials or give reasons for its credibility.* Qualifying the source is especially important when the source or its reliability is not widely known. For example, in a classroom speech about euthanasia, Sara qualified the source because the expert she cited was not well known outside his field:

> We might think that because euthanasia has not received much press coverage lately that it no longer represents a major controversy, but the issue is not likely to go away any time soon. Some experts predict a long and difficult struggle lies ahead. Dr. Arthur Caplan, a medical ethicist at the University of Pennsylvania, states that the current controversy "is merely the first round in what is going to be a long and heated debate on the issue."[2]

Because Professor Caplan was not known to most of her audience, Sara decided to qualify the source by briefly stating Caplan's qualifications for commenting on the future of the euthanasia controversy. If there is any question about whether one of your sources will be accepted as credible, you should qualify the source by providing the appropriate credentials.

Similarly, you should explain the nature or function of organizations with which your audience may be unfamiliar. It is not necessary to explain the function of the Central Intelligence Agency (CIA) to most audiences or to explain that the *Washington Post* is a major US newspaper, but if you were to cite the National Center for Public Policy Research it would be important to clarify that this organization is a conservative think tank in Washington, DC.

When you are in doubt as to whether to qualify a source, it is better to err on the side of telling people something they might already know than to leave them uncertain about a source's credentials. In the following example, notice that a distinction is made between the journalist reporting on a new study and the authors of the study themselves. Although the journalist plays an important role in relating a new set of findings to the public, he himself is not the expert being cited:

> CBS News reported that children of military parents are at increased risk from a range of maladies, including emotional and behavioral problems. CBS correspondent Ryan Jaslow cites a new report from the American Academy of Pediatrics, published in the journal *Pediatrics*. Jaslow writes, "Children of military parents may endure parental deployments of up to eighteen months. Pediatricians need to be aware of physical and psychological effects on children of such lengthy deployments. Effects include anxiety, depression and withdrawal." He quotes pediatrician Dr. Ben Siegel as saying, "By under-standing the military family and the stressful experiences of parental wartime deployment, all pediatricians, both active duty and civilian, and other health care providers, can be the 'front line' in caring for U.S. military children and their families. Pediatricians play a critical role in identifying how well or poorly a child or family responds to a major stressor such as an extended deployment, and can provide the necessary education and support, including referral to a mental health professional when needed."[3]

Internal Consistency: Does the Evidence Contradict Itself?

At a press conference, a reporter asked a US diplomat about rumors that the United States might be planning a military action against a country accused of developing nuclear weapons. The diplomat responded:

> This notion that the United States is prepared to launch a military attack against any foreign country to disrupt a nuclear weapons program is simply ridiculous. Having said that, we must insist that we are not ruling out any options in our efforts to prevent the development of nuclear weapons by countries who threaten us or our allies.

The diplomat's apparent contradiction brings us to our second general test of evidence—**internal consistency,** *the requirement that evidence and sources must not contradict themselves.* The reporter believed that the diplomat's answer involved a contradiction. Why is it "ridiculous" to think that the United States is prepared to launch a military attack to stop a nuclear weapons program when no option has been ruled out?

Internally inconsistent evidence is self-refuting: it casts doubt on the advocate's case and weakens the credibility of the source from which the evidence was drawn. Internal inconsistency might seem so obvious that it would be easily identified and resolved before an advocate went public with the evidence, but this is not always the case. For example, government officials and heads of corporations may make contradictory claims under the pressure of public scrutiny.

A major mobile phone service provider has been accused of providing the government with information on client phone records that it held in its massive electronic storage facilities. The company denied that it was aiding the government agency, however, and said publicly that the low-level employee involved in releasing the data was acting independently. Later in the investigation, however, a senior manager at the company indicated he was fully aware the government collection of cell phone data was taking place.

Internal consistency is one criterion of good evidence. We should read and listen carefully for contradictions or inconsistencies in evidence we are asked to accept. The same rule should apply to evidence we use in our own arguments.

External Consistency: Does the Evidence Contradict Other Evidence?

The quote opening this chapter that is attributed to the late Senator Daniel Patrick Moynihan suggests we should be suspicious when an advocate's "facts" are not widely regarded as true. Point well taken—claims regarding any body of evidence ought to be carefully scrutinized. In political and scientific controversies, however, the opinions of qualified sources may vary. Such variety is often evident in the writing of history and in assessments of famous individuals and their accomplishments. For example, Ayn Rand was a famous twentieth-century author who penned such bestselling novels as *The Fountainhead* and *Atlas Shrugged,* but authorities disagree about her skills as a writer and her contributions as a thinker. Editorialist Cathy Young has this to say about the divided evaluations:

> Followers of her philosophy, Objectivism, regard her as the greatest thinker to have graced this earth since Aristotle and the greatest writer of all time. Mainstream intellectuals tend to dismiss her as a writer of glorified pulp and a pseudo-philosophical quack with an appeal for impressionable teens.[4]

Such differences among experts occur; nevertheless, the best evidence usually meets the test of **external consistency,** *the requirement that evidence must not be sharply at odds with either the majority of evidence from other sources or with the best evidence from other sources.* The test of external inconsistency is a check against evidence that seems to contradict or ignore broad agreements among experts, settled judgments, and well-established facts or scientific findings. Sound evidence usually will not run contrary to what the majority of the most informed voices have to say.

The test of external consistency can sometimes be applied to controversies involving cultural or religious traditions or long-standing, tested, ethical positions. In some communities, external consistency with previous teaching or moral commitments on a topic is an important matter. When facing pressure from social change, for example, religious organizations might appeal to their own earlier teachings on issues such as homosexuality, the structure of the family, or the role of women within the organization.

A classic example of evidence that is at odds with both the majority and the best available evidence is found in some recent arguments, by groups in both Europe and the United States, that the Nazi Holocaust either did not occur or was not nearly as serious as has been reported. These groups advance evidence that contradicts massive physical and testimonial evidence to the contrary, the best available historical evidence on the Holocaust, and the broad consensus of expert opinion.

When the test of external consistency shows us that evidence contradicts the best or the majority of other evidence that is available to us, it is important to stop and take a closer look at the evidence and perhaps to do additional research. If we still decide to accept the externally inconsistent evidence, this decision should be carefully informed.

Conspiracy Theories and the Test of External Consistency

We hear a lot of talk about conspiracy theories—explanations for well-known events that involve hidden forces manipulating history in unseen ways. These theories run counter to most or the best available evidence. In other words, a conspiracy theory is actually an argument that violates the test of external consistency. Famous conspiracy theories include the allegation that the US moon landings were faked, that the Mafia was behind the assassination of President John F. Kennedy, and that a secret cabal controls world banks and governments.

If a conspiracy theory is convincing because good evidence is being ignored or suppressed, then it would seem that the antidote to conspiratorial thinking would be to provide good evidence to the contrary. Surprisingly, this may not be the case. Journalist Alex Koppleman has pointed out that good evidence usually fails to convince a true believer in a conspiracy theory, partly because a financial or behavioral commitment to a theory dramatically increases one's resistance to change.

Koppleman quotes Chip Berlet, a journalist and scholar who studies conspiracy theories. Berlet states: "As soon as you criticize a conspiracy theory, you become part of the conspiracy." Social psychologist Evan Harrington writes that the "whole appeal" of conspiracy theories is that one now possesses information that is "secret or special." We all have a strong tendency to want to know something that is hidden from others, and this tendency works against accepting evidence to the contrary. Moreover, inconvenient evidence can be forced to support the conspiracy narrative. As a result, conspiracy theories and those who believe them may have some built-in psychological defenses against the test of external consistency.[5]

Recency:
Is the Evidence Up to Date?

With evidence that might be affected by advances in research, another important consideration is **recency,** *the requirement that the evidence be up to date and not superseded by more timely evidence.* What is considered good evidence on some topics today may be worthless as evidence in a few years, perhaps even in a few months. In fields of study such as medicine, energy, and biotechnology, new evidence comes to light constantly. For example, the advent of CRISPR technology, which replaces genes within organisms, with potential applications to medicine and other fields, changed the entire field of genetics almost instantly when it was introduced to labs in 2015. In some political controversies, changes in a nation's or a region's political mood can render the best evidence antiquated almost overnight. Thus, advocates should ask whether their evidence is recent enough to be relevant.

Some evidence that is not clearly out of date may still be old enough to raise questions about its timeliness. Such questions can affect your credibility with an audience, so it is worth the effort to search for more recent evidence, particularly when research on a topic has been in the news recently and so is widely known. For example, suppose a speaker on the topic of capital punishment uses the following evidence:

> The August 26, 1991, edition of *The Nation* reports that between 1979 and 1990, federal courts corrected constitutional violations in 40 percent of the cases in which state courts were ready to proceed with executions. Thus, capital punishment is often unconstitutionally applied and should be abolished.

This evidence, while interesting, is also dated—that is, it fails the test of recency. Research on the constitutionality of capital punishment is ongoing. More recent evidence would likely be more persuasive to audiences. In fact, updated figures are available that actually strengthen the speaker's claim.

When facts are certain to change over time, the recency of evidence is a major concern. Here is an example of using evidence that is not recent enough to account accurately for a rapidly changing problem. In an editorial on the problem of solid waste disposal, a student writes:

> Solid waste is one of the major threats facing our society. In 1989, when the severity of the problem began coming to light, *Newsweek* reported that "Americans collectively toss out 160 million tons [of garbage] each year— enough to spread 30 stories high over 1,000 football fields . . . ."[6]

The evidence is made vivid by the use of comparison and points to a serious problem, but it is too old to reflect accurately the problem audiences face today. Is the situation worsening or improving?

This evidence might still be useful, however, if the student added more recent evidence that revealed a trend. For example, she might add the following information:

> The Environmental Protection Agency reported that people in the United States disposed of 229 million tons of solid waste in 2001 and 236 million tons in 2003. The solid waste figure for 2007 stood at 254 million tons. These figures have risen steadily since 1960, when Americans threw out 88 million tons of waste, a fraction of the 2014 figure of more than 258 million tons.[7]

Not all reliable evidence has to bear a recent date. Some ideas are not considered outdated even though they have been believed for a long time. Some geological evidence gathered more than a hundred years ago, for example, is still accepted as reliable by geologists. Arguments about human nature may draw on reliable evidence as old as the ancient philosophers. The ideas about democratic government expressed in the United States Constitution, a document written more than two centuries ago, are still considered relevant. Nevertheless, confirming older findings and ideas with more recent information can lend credibility to the evidence. In testing the recency of evidence we need to ask whether the issue at hand requires the most recent evidence available.

Relevance:
Does the Evidence Bear on the Conclusion?

Evidence that is accessible, internally and externally consistent, and recent must also be clearly related to the conclusion it is advanced to support. The test of **relevance** asks *whether the evidence advanced has any bearing on the argument's conclusion.*

Let's consider an example. Science writer Jeff Wheelwright has claimed that Finland is becoming "a sort of DNA laboratory for mankind." As support for his claim, he advances the following facts:

FIGURE 6.1 Tests of Evidence

These tests assess the evidence in an argument:
1. Accessibility
2. Credibility
3. Internal consistency
4. External consistency
5. Recency
6. Relevance
7. Adequacy

> As research subjects the Finns are an agreeable lot. When asked to participate in studies . . . three out of four will say yes. Access to clinical records is much easier in Finland than in the United States because the health care system is streamlined, centralized and computerized. Foreign collaborators may tap into the resources as well.[8]

Wheelwright's evidence is clearly related to his claim and, if true, provides reasonable support for that claim.

On the other hand, consider the relationship between evidence and conclusion in the following argument:

> Four out of five US citizens face unemployment, poverty, or reliance on welfare at some point in their lives. There is also a widening gap between rich and poor in this country. The wealthiest 1 percent of Americans control more wealth than the bottom 90 percent. Moreover, a recent survey of US attitudes revealed that pessimism has risen to its highest point in more than thirty years. These staggering statistics are signs of the disastrous failure of the current administration's economic policies in improving the lives of average people in the United States.

In this example, the evidence, while dramatic and perhaps true, has little or no bearing on the conclusion. No causal link is forged between the statistics and the claim about the present administration's economic policies. All that we are provided is a strong assertion following three alleged pieces of evidence. As support for the claim, we would need evidence about specific economic policies of the current administration and how these policies failed to help average Americans.

If we doubt the relevance of a piece of evidence to its conclusion, we may want to ask for clarification. In some instances, it may not be possible to directly question the person making the argument, and we are left to make the best judgment we can about relevance. Two questions can help us make a decision about the relevance of evidence to a claim:

1. What is the specific claim being advanced?
2. Does the evidence provided, if accurate, provide support for this claim?

If the claim advanced matches closely with what the evidence, viewed independently, seems to prove, then the test of relevance has likely been met. As we have already noted, values and other connectives will influence the conclusions people draw from a piece of evidence, but there are reasonable limits to how far a particular item of evidence can be stretched as support for a claim.

We can apply the test of relevance to our own arguments as well. This test should remind us to clarify the relationship between evidence and conclusions in our own arguments. It is easy to assume—mistakenly—that a connection between evidence and conclusion that makes sense to you will make sense to your listeners.

Adequacy:
Is the Evidence Sufficient to Support Its Claim?

The six tests discussed to this point are helpful in making general evaluations of evidence, but it is still a matter of personal judgment whether evidence that has passed most or all of these tests is actually convincing. A summary test asks us *whether the evidence presented, when taken together, is sufficient to support its claim.* We can call this the test of **adequacy.**

Imagine that you were not convinced that there was a serious wealth and income gap between the richest and the poorest US citizens. What would it take to convince you? Perhaps a single strong piece of evidence would be sufficient. For example, you read that the wealthiest three hundred households control more wealth than the bottom 90 percent of all households combined. Then you hear in a class that the richest 20 percent of households owns 95 percent of the nation's financial assets—wealth other than real estate—leaving 80 percent of citizens to divide up the remaining 5 percent of those assets. You are slowly becoming convinced when you see a graph in a major news source that shows that in the past thirty years the wealthiest 1 percent of people in the United States have seen their income grow by 281 percent and the top fifth by 90 percent, while the poorest fifth of US citizens have seen their incomes grow by only 16 percent in the same period. Perhaps this last piece of evidence has convinced you—there is a serious wealth and income gap between rich and poor in the United States. At this point the accumulated evidence has achieved adequacy for you.

How much evidence is enough? That can depend on several factors, but one that nearly always comes into play is the seriousness of the question being decided. For example, if I am asked to risk my own or someone else's life on the basis of the evidence before me, I should require the evidence to be both good and plentiful. We face such a situation when sitting on a jury, hearing arguments in a case in which the accused might receive a death sentence. Deciding whether to accept a job offer that would require moving to a different state is also a serious decision, though not as serious as whether an accused person is guilty or innocent of murder. A request to sign a petition to allow a local restaurant to serve wine may require less evidence to support it.

The more serious an issue is, the more reasonable it is to require that more and better evidence be provided. What we regard as gravely serious or clearly trivial may reflect our personal values; still, reasonably assessing the adequacy of evidence requires placing a claim somewhere on that continuum.

The test of adequacy is a summary test that requires us to consider *all* the criteria just discussed—accessibility, internal consistency, external consistency, recency, and relevance. Adequacy is achieved when the quantity and quality of the entire range of evidence advanced to support a claim satisfy these criteria, while at the same time being commensurate with the seriousness of the claim. One way of applying the test of adequacy is to ask whether an objective and reasonable person would be willing to accept a claim solely on the basis of the evidence presented. If we can answer this

FIGURE 6.2 Visual Images as Evidence

E.C. Stebinger photo
Courtesy of GNP Archives

Lisa McKeon photo
USGS

question yes, then we have further reason for believing that the evidence for a specific claim is adequate.

EVALUATING VISUAL EVIDENCE

The tests we have been discussing are designed with traditional types of evidence in mind, usually presented in written or spoken form. Images, however, play an increasingly important role as evidence in public discourse, often in combination with more conventional types of evidence. The tests discussed to this point in the chapter—especially recency, accessibility, and external consistency—can also be applied to images, though we want to ask additional questions that focus on special qualities of the image as evidence.

First, an image—such as the before and after pictures of a melting glacier presented as evidence of global warming (see Figure 6.2)—should present a typical case rather than an extraordinary one. Thus we should ask whether the image is characteristic of the situation or event being discussed. Such images can lend powerful support to a case by rendering a problem serious and clearly evident. These images leave little doubt that, at least in this region, temperatures are steadily rising. As the images are from a government source, they will strike most viewers as credible.

Second, given the ease with which perspective can be manipulated in setting up a photograph, and images themselves digitally altered, we will also want to ask whether an image presented as evidence has been artificially changed to create a false impression.

Third, in most cases it is also important to ask whether an image is supported by other types of evidence, such as statistics or testimony. That is to say, visual evidence often corroborates other forms of evidence.

Fourth, images can have a powerful emotional impact on audiences. We can introduce another example of visual evidence to illustrate these third and fourth tests.

FIGURE 6.3 Visual Evidence and Impact

Image courtesy Ad Council and United States Forest Service

Statistics suggest that only about 37 percent of African-American children between the ages of 6 and 12 experienced outdoor recreation in 2011, compared with 67 percent of Caucasian children. These are startling statistics, but they do not convey the limitless possibilities and vast potential that a child experiences in a visit to a natural environment, such as a forest. Figure 6.3 is an example of visual evidence that captures the emotional content of these possibilities in a way in which the statistics alone never could. The image thus also enhances the statistical evidence.

It is helpful to ask whether an image is persuasive because of its tendency to support the point being argued or because of its emotional force alone. Emotional force is not in itself inappropriate for public discourse, but persuasion based on emotional content alone is not an adequate way to build a strong case.

INTERPRETING EVIDENCE

As we have already noted, most evidence does not speak for itself. We must interpret the evidence we hear or read, that is, determine what it means and what conclusions it might support. We should also help audiences interpret the evidence we advance to support our own claims.

Some evidence is relatively easy to understand and requires little interpretation. Interpretation becomes particularly important when:

- Evidence is technical or difficult to understand.
- Evidence might be understood in several ways.
- Implications of the evidence are not readily appreciated.

One common mistake advocates make in presenting their evidence is to assume that its implications are clear to an audience. Helping an audience to understand how a piece of evidence supports a claim is crucial to constructing a good case. Of course, interpretations can themselves be argumentative. That is, an interpretation may advance only one among many possible understandings of the evidence. Consequently, an advocate may need to interpret both for clarity and for the sake of supporting a particular claim.

FIGURE 6.4 Interpreting Statistics for Clarity

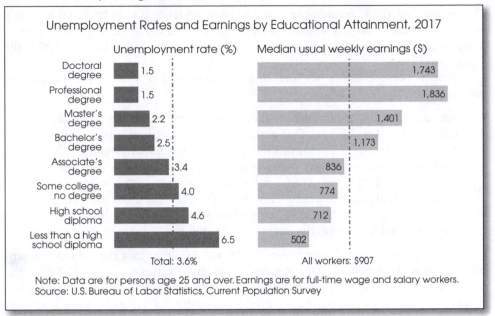

Note: Data are for persons age 25 and over. Earnings are for full-time wage and salary workers.
Source: U.S. Bureau of Labor Statistics, Current Population Survey

Interpreting for Clarity

Clarifying the significance of a piece of evidence for an audience is helpful in crafting a strong argument. When the evidence is highly technical, interpretation for clarity can be essential to an audience's understanding of the evidence.

One common technique for interpreting evidence for clarity is simply to convert it to a visual form. With statistical evidence, this can be accomplished simply by representing the evidence in the form of a graph or chart. For example, interpreting the statistical relationships among unemployment, earnings, and education would be difficult for an audience if it was simply hearing a description of those statistics. Figure 6.4 is a relatively simple bar graph that interprets the statistics for clarity.

Another common technique for clarifying an interpretation is by means of a comparison to something familiar. Here is an example:

> Most of us assume that beaches are natural formations that last indefinitely, but recent studies by the US Geological Survey and several universities have shown that beaches gain and lose sand every year. Some beaches disappear entirely with time as the sand is lost to erosion or to rising water levels. This loss can create problems: many beaches perform crucial functions such as preventing wave damage to shorelines. Some vital beaches along the Mississippi River are actually maintained by pumping sand from an inland source.
>
> To understand the implications of the recent research on beaches, think of these natural formations as being less like mountains than like wetlands or forests—fragile, constantly changing, and needing our protection in order to perform their natural functions.

In this example, comparing beaches to wetlands and forests helps the audience understand how to interpret the evidence about beach erosion and maintenance.

Interpreting to Support a Conclusion

As we have noted, the meaning or significance of evidence is not always immediately apparent. When advanced without interpretation, some evidence may not appear to support its claim. In such cases, you need to provide an interpretation that makes the connection clear.

Here is some evidence without an interpretation that shows its connection to its claim:

> You are attending a conference where medical specialists are reporting on the health of US children. One authority on psychiatric disorders states: "A new medical survey has revealed that minority children are significantly less likely to be diagnosed with attention deficit hyperactivity disorder (ADHD) than are white children. ADHD is the most common and one of the most serious mental health issues for children in the US. That being said, Hispanic children's diagnosis rates are 50 percent lower and the rates for black children are 70 percent lower than the rates for white children."

Here is some evidence of an apparent problem, but what does the evidence mean? Does it mean that minority children are less likely to suffer from ADHD? That the condition is overdiagnosed in white children? Are there consequences to such a finding? The evidence must be interpreted in order for an audience outside the medical profession to know what it represents.

The authority continues by explaining that actual rates of ADHD are the same from one group to another, and that the lower rates of diagnosis in minority children mean these children often are not getting necessary medical attention and are not receiving the same level of screening for mental health issues as are white children. Thus, the lower rates of diagnosis mean that many cases of ADHD are simply being missed in minority children. This is one interpretation of the evidence.

Does this failure of diagnosis have any serious consequences? The speaker continues her presentation by noting that unaddressed ADHD dramatically affects educational and occupational success later in life, and is even strongly correlated with likelihood of incarceration. Finally, she says, early detection and treatment are crucial to correcting the disorder. As it turns out, these interpretations of the findings about undiagnosed ADHD are crucial to the audience's correct understanding of this evidence.

CHAPTER REVIEW

The strength of an argument depends directly on the quality of its evidence. This chapter has discussed seven general tests of evidence that help in evaluating whether evidence provides good support for its claim. These seven tests are accessibility, credibility, internal consistency, external consistency, recency, relevance, and adequacy. Sound evidence should satisfy each of these criteria.

When employing visual evidence, it is important to ask whether the image presents a typical case and whether it may have been altered. We should also ask whether other evidence supports the visual evidence and whether the image is persuasive only because of its emotional impact.

The chapter has also considered interpretation of evidence. Some interpretations clarify the meaning of the evidence. Other interpretations demonstrate the connection between evidence and a conclusion. Interpretation of evidence is important whether we are hearing an argument or developing an argument of our own, as evidence does not speak for itself.

EXERCISES

A.   Using the basic tests discussed in this chapter, evaluate each of the following examples as evidence. Where do you spot specific problems with the evidence? Which examples seem to provide the best evidence?

1. Details about the Air Force's new X-37B space plane are so secret that even pilots and top military brass are unaware of the new craft's negative ion–detecting altimeter, plasma-fueled jet pulse engines that can run continuously for two years without refueling, revolutionary navigation system that is keyed directly to the Earth's magnetic fields, and microwave monitoring of pilots' brain waves.

2. It is actually beneficial to your dental health to eat chocolate every day! Recent studies at a major research laboratory have corroborated earlier research proving that regular chocolate consumption prevented dental cavities as effectively as regular tooth brushing.

3. "About 17% of kids and teens in the U.S. are now considered obese," according to the Centers for Disease Control and Prevention. *The New England Journal of Medicine* has reported recently that this situation leads to more cases of type 2 diabetes in children.[9]

4. Every year five times as many US citizens die of infections they acquire during a hospitalization than do Canadians—more than seventy thousand Americans as contrasted to fewer than nine thousand Canadians. We should note that Canada also has a socialized medical system, while the United States retains a health-for-profit model. The dramatic disparity in the number of deaths from hospital-acquired infections clearly indicates that it is time for the US to join the rest of the world and turn the administration of our medical system over to the government.

5. State official with oversight responsibilities for executions: "Although I am not actually familiar with the regulations regarding required medical training for correctional officers attending an execution, I am certain that they have medical training—at least a year or two, but I don't know for sure."

6. "The widely cited statistic that one in three women ages 35 to 39 will not be pregnant after a year of trying, for instance, is based on an article published in 2004 in the journal *Human Reproduction*. Rarely mentioned is the source of the data: French birth records from 1670 to 1830. The chance of remaining childless—30 percent—was also calculated based on historical populations. In other words, millions of women are being told when to get pregnant based on statistics from a time before electricity, antibiotics, or fertility treatment."[10]

B.   Explain how the test of external consistency plays a role in the following examples.

1. A senator's press secretary insists that, despite claims to the contrary by the FBI, the senator's own former staff members, and international diplomats associated with the case, a foreign government did not intervene to influence the senator's vote for a major trade bill that favored the country in question.

2. Executives at large search engines and social networking organizations claimed to have been unaware the government was gathering personal information from their computers, but security experts countered that large-scale data mining could not have taken place without corporate knowledge, indeed, cooperation. While it is possible the executives themselves were unaware of efforts to spy on private citizens, some employees had to have known. Indeed, so complex and powerful are the security measures that companies such as Google and Facebook employ, it would not be possible for an outside entity to collect, let alone decipher, sensitive personal data on users of these services without inside assistance.

ENDNOTES

[1] Rebecca Taylor, "Scientists in Oregon Create Embryos with Three Genetic Parents," LifeNews.com, October 25, 2012, http://www.lifenews.com/2012/10/25/scientists-in-oregon -create-embryos-with-three-genetic-parents.

[2] G. Jeffrey MacDonald, "New Orleans Arrests Spark 'Mercy Killing' Debate," *Christian Science Monitor* online edition, August 1, 2006, http://www.csmonitor.com/2006/0721/p01s02 -ussc.html.

[3] Ryan Jaslow, "Pediatricians Warned Children of Military Personnel Face Mental Health Risks," CBS News, May 27, 2013, http://www.cbsnews.com/news/pediatricians-warned-children-of -military-personnel-face-mental-health-risks.

[4] Cathy Young, "Ayn Rand at 100," *Reason,* March 2005, 24.

[5] Alex Koppleman, "Why the Stories about Obama's Birth Certificate Will Never Die," *Salon,* December 5, 2008, http://www.salon.com/2008/12/05/birth_certificate.

[6] Melinda Beck, "Buried Alive," *Newsweek,* November 27, 1989, 67.

[7] Environmental Protection Agency, "Municipal Solid Waste: Basic Facts," http://www.epa.gov /msw/facts/htm. Reported by Keep America Beautiful, http://www.kab.org/aboutus.asp?id=35 &rid=56 (Accessed October 1, 2006).

[8] Jeff Wheelwright, "Finland's Fascinating Genes," *Discover,* April 2005, 54.

[9] Karen Kaplan, "Type 2 Diabetes, Once Considered a Disease for Adults, is Increasingly Common in Tweens and Teens," *Los Angeles Times,* April 14, 2017, http://www.latimes.com/science /sciencenow/la-sci-sn-diabetes-youth-rising-20170413-htmlstory.html.

[10] Jean Twenge, "How Long Can You Wait to Have a Baby?" *The Atlantic,* July/August 2013, http://www.theatlantic.com/magazine/archive/2013/07/how-long-can-you-wait-to-have-a -baby/309374.

RECOMMENDED WEBSITES

PolitiFact.com
www.politifact.com

FactCheck.org
www.factcheck.org

Several excellent web sites have made it easy to check the accuracy of evidence advanced in political controversies. The *Tampa Bay Times* maintains its Pulitzer Prize–winning site PolitiFact.com for this purpose. The Annenberg Public Policy center provides the FactCheck.org site.

7 Locating and Evaluating Sources of Evidence

> Nothing in all the world is more dangerous than sincere ignorance,
> than conscientious stupidity.
> *Martin Luther King Jr. (1929–1968)*
> *United States Civil Rights leader*

> We expect more from technology and less from each other.
> *Sherry Turkle (1948–)*
> *United States scholar of science, technology, and society*

KEY TERMS

digital literacy

editorial process

news and commentary
  publications

popular magazines

refereed

scholarly journals

special-interest periodicals

You are doing research for a persuasive speech on the causes and health effects of childhood obesity. In the course of your research you entered the words "childhood obesity" into an internet search engine and came up with links to the National Institutes for Health; an article titled, "F as in Fat: How Obesity Policies Are Failing in America," posted by an organization called Trust for America's Health; a summer camp for overweight children; and a site selling weight loss supplements for teenagers. You have also listened to several podcasts on the epidemic of childhood obesity in the United States, interviewed a professor in the biology department of your university, spoken briefly with a pediatrician you know personally, and read a web page on nutrition provided by a fast food chain. The reference librarian at your school helped you locate a recent study of the health effects of childhood obesity, published in the latest issue of *The Journal of the American Academy of Pediatrics*. While visiting relatives one weekend you watched a documentary on the topic and read a news magazine's cover story titled "Why Are America's Kids Getting Fatter?" A friend has also sent you a link to a news report that includes a story on the causes of childhood obesity.

Having taken some information from each of these sources, you are ready to write your speech. How should you evaluate the relative merits of the range of sources you have discovered on your topic?

One advantage of living in a technologically advanced democracy is that access to information is virtually limitless. For the same reason, however, the problem of evaluating sources of evidence is more complex than ever before. This chapter considers the major sources of evidence available for speeches and papers, as well as the basic steps to determine which sources are most reliable for providing your arguments with adequate, sound support.

SOURCES OF EVIDENCE

When considering sources of evidence, it is important to ask whether the source is appropriate to the topic being investigated and whether the source is reliable. Other considerations can include the source's intended audience, pressures on the source that may affect treatment of a topic, and the source's political perspective.

Evaluating the propriety and reliability of sources can be a challenging task for a variety of reasons, not the least of which is that one person's credible and balanced

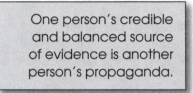

One person's credible and balanced source of evidence is another person's propaganda.

source of evidence is another person's propaganda. For instance, you may find the Brookings Institution's reports to be among the most reliable sources of evidence on United States domestic and foreign policy, while a friend views these publications as politically liberal misinformation. She finds publications of the Cato Institute, a libertarian source, more reliable. The fact that attitudes toward sources of evidence vary widely, however, does not imply that we are without resources for evaluating them. Let's take a closer look at some of the most common sources of evidence and some ways of evaluating each.

Periodicals

We have available to us today a staggering array of periodicals—both print and online versions—ranging from scholarly publications to supermarket tabloids. Sometimes we are uncertain about the quality of a particular periodical, perhaps especially about its quality as a source of evidence. When reading a periodical, whether print or online versions, we should ask ourselves about the type of publication it is and about the perspectives of its owners, editors, and writers.

We can begin with **scholarly journals,** *periodicals that feature essays and studies by experts, scholars, and researchers who are qualified to conduct research in their own fields.* Scholarly journals are published by professional and academic organizations with the purpose of reporting on original research or experimentation. Examples include the *Journal of the American Medical Association, Psychological Bulletin,* and *Critical Studies in Mass Media.* Summary versions of many such periodicals are available online for readers who are not intimidated by technical language and topics. For example, the *Journal of the American Medical Association* online version can be found at www.jama.ama-assn.org. The digital storage service JSTOR provides access to nearly two thousand academic journals and is available through most college and university libraries. JSTOR archives many journals, including some that have been discontinued; books; historical documents; and other primary sources.

One reason that scholarly journals are considered among the most reliable sources of evidence is that the articles they present are **refereed,** that is, *reviewed by two or more qualified readers before publication.* The **editorial process** is a *careful review of submitted research reports that provides an important check on the quality of research published in a periodical.* When the editor of a scholarly journal receives a manuscript to consider for publication, she or he will send it out to selected professionals qualified to judge whether the essay or study constitutes original and reliable research. Only after the referees and the editor are satisfied that the research reported in the manuscript has achieved the standards set by the discipline will it be published in the journal.

The principal audience for scholarly publications consists of specialists in the discipline. The language often is academic and technical. When you draw evidence from a scholarly journal, it may be necessary to interpret the evidence for your audience. Still, scholarly journals can be valuable sources of information to the diligent nonexpert.

Political considerations can affect what is published in scholarly journals. For instance, an article reflecting an ardently capitalistic economic approach that offends a socialist journal editor or referee is less likely to get published in that journal than in some others. Manuscript reviewers for a liberal law journal that publishes research on the Supreme Court might reject an article that speaks favorably about the opinions of conservative justices.

Even scientific journals can reflect political or theoretical biases in the articles they publish. An editor may decide not to publish an otherwise excellent piece of research that tends to confirm the views of the "enemy camp," a school of thought with which the editor disagrees. This caution about political perspectives and theoretical preferences is not intended to challenge the reliability of scholarly journals, but only to make you aware that even these highly reliable publications can reveal political and ideological biases.

Another type of source worth considering for your research is **special-interest periodicals,** *periodicals that focus on specific topics but are written for wider audiences than scholarly journals are.* Examples include *Psychology Today* (www.psychologytoday.com), *Entertainment Weekly* (www.ew.com), and *Wired* (www.wired.com). Special-interest publications are usually attractively presented, illustrated with numerous photos and other visual features. Online versions of these periodicals include links to a wide range of sources on related topics. For example, the online version of *Wired* provides numerous resources for readers interested in technological news.

The stories and reports in special-interest periodicals are written by journalists and other writers with special training in a relevant field of knowledge. These authors often base their stories on interviews with experts, recent books, scholarly journals, government reports, and the publications of research institutions. Special-interest publications can provide sound evidence and have the distinct advantage of being accessible to many readers. Many of their readers are well educated, so the language may be moderately technical and the writing is of a high quality.

News and commentary publications are *periodicals that specialize in reporting news and presenting informed editorial opinions.* Examples include print news magazines such as *Time* (www.time.com), newspapers such as the *New York Times* (www.nytimes.com) and the *Chicago Tribune* (www.chicagotribune.com), political commentary publications such as the *New Republic* (www.tnr.com) and the *National Review* (www.nationalreview.com), and an ever-increasing number of online sources of news and discussion of current issues such as *Slate Magazine* (www.slate.com). All major news and commentary sources have online presences, and it is as easy to access an international source of news as a domestic source. Among the sources of Asian news is Channel Newsasia (www.channelnewsasia.com). African news and commentary is available at News Africa (www.newsafrica.net). Arabic news is available at Arabicnews.com (www.arabicnews.com) and Arab World News (www.arabworldnews.com). European news sources include the International Herald Tribune European online edition (www.iht.com/pages/europe) and BBC (www.bbc.co.uk). For Latin American sources of news, try Zona Latina (www.zonalatina.com) or Latin American Newsletters (www.latinnews.com).

The reporters, editors, and other writers on the staffs of news and commentary publications may draw on personal observation and interviews with experts, as well as information gathered from wire services, scholarly publications, government institutions, and a variety of other sources. They may provide good background on controversial topics. Their editorial pages can provide you with good examples of arguments on important issues. In some instances these publications also may serve as sources of statistical or testimonial evidence.

Another type of publication is **popular magazines,** *periodicals intended to provide pleasure reading and advice on a range of personal and professional issues.* Examples include *Glamour; People;* and online sources such as Oprah.com, the internet version of *O, The Oprah Magazine.* These glossy magazines feature numerous graphics and advertisements, as well as advice and updates on issues from health to home decorating. Stories and reports in popular magazines are usually written by magazine staff and freelance writers, and occasionally by well-known people who may or may not have expertise in the appropriate field. Some articles in these magazines may be edited versions of longer articles that appeared in other publications. Popular magazines are aimed at a general audience and do not assume a high level of education. The language is simple; articles often are short and shallow, brief and lacking detail. For these reasons popular magazines are not typically good sources of information for academic research.

Special-interest publications, news and commentary periodicals, and popular magazines are published by commercial publishers to provide information, to make a profit, and occasionally to advocate a particular political perspective. You should bear in mind this last point, particularly when you consult these periodicals. The individuals and groups who own and edit popular publications, like most of the rest of us, have a political point of view.

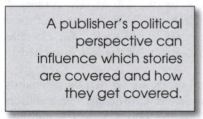

A publisher's political perspective can influence which stories are covered and how they get covered.

A publisher's political perspective can have a great deal of influence on which stories are covered and how they get covered. For instance, Rupert Murdoch, the politically conservative Australian media magnate, owns the British newspapers *News of the World, The London Times,* and *The Sunday Times,* as well as US newspapers *The New York Post* and *The Wall Street Journal.* In fact, through his company News Corp., Murdoch has full or partial ownership of more than fifty newspapers and magazines.

Books

Books are another important source of evidence for developing an argumentative case. As any trip to a large bookstore or university library reveals, tens of thousands of titles are available to readers, including many different types of books—ranging from scholarly university publications to popular novels.

When you are evaluating a book as a source of evidence, here are some questions to ask.

1. Who wrote the book? The author's credentials or qualifications to write a book on the particular subject are important to ascertain and evaluate. You might ask about the author's experience, education, or position. Some books contain brief descriptive notes on the author. Most credible authors cite other leading authorities writing in the same field on related topics. An online search may reveal an author's accomplishments, educational background, other publications, and even organizational memberships. All these aspects of an author's credentials can help you determine whether the author is a reliable authority on the subject you are investigating.

Background information can also provide clues about an author's perspective or biases. Authors' underlying assumptions, preferences, or prejudices may color their presentations or interpretations of information. Author bias becomes a problem when important evidence is ignored or misinterpreted to support a predetermined point of view. For example, books about a religious movement written by a member of that movement might not treat historical doubts about the religion's origins very seriously. Harder to identify are the biases of a scientist or social scientist toward or against a particular theory, set of data, or opponent in the field. Members of the general reading public are usually unaware of debates that, for example, divide members of the psychology discipline over the causes and treatment of mental illness. Reference librarians may be able to point you to additional sources of information on an author, which can help you make judgments about how qualified or objective the author is likely to be. When using a book as a source of evidence, be sure to qualify the author by citing credentials.

2. *When was the book published?* Just as good evidence should be recent, good books should reflect current information in a field. As noted in Chapter 6, up-to-date sources are especially important in continually changing fields such as the sciences and social sciences. Determining the recency of a book is usually as simple as checking the publication date. With a book that has been reprinted, look for the earliest date listed for its *original* publication. Because of the time that elapses between research and writing a book and its actual publication—often a year or more—books, even those in digital format, usually are not as current as recently published articles in periodicals. Check for the date of original publication when citing an electronically formatted book.

3. *Who is the book's publisher?* University press publications typically represent reliable scholarship by individuals who are recognized as scholars and authorities. Many legitimate publishing houses are not widely known (examples include Routledge or Peter Lang), yet produce highly reliable works. Ask the reference librarian about publishers whose names you don't recognize. When a publisher handles only works that advance a particular point of view, or when a press is operated by an advocacy organization, the source should be used with some caution. The same is true of so called "vanity presses," businesses that will publish anyone's work provided the author pays for publication. You should also be skeptical of publications by organizations known to hold extreme views and of any publication that does not clearly identify a publisher.

4. *For what audience is the book written?* The more general and less educated the intended audience is, the simpler a book's treatment of its subject is likely to be. It may still be a reliable source, but the evidence it presents may not give you a thorough and sophisticated picture of the topic. As is the case with periodicals, books written for an educated audience usually provide the most detailed and best-researched evidence. The style of writing, thoroughness, and type of evidence advanced can all be indicators of a book's reliability as a source of evidence.

5. *What method of obtaining data or conducting research did the author use?* You may want to determine whether the book seems to have been researched carefully or instead relies on anecdotes, rumors, assumptions, and secondhand reports. Check to see whether the writer did the major research reported or relied strictly on others' research. Statistics, testimony, and other data should be documented. Reliable books tell the reader where quotations and statistics come from. Check to see whether the book has an index and a bibliography: these features often indicate a thorough and scholarly approach to a topic.

6. *What do others think of the book?* To find an answer to this question, check to see whether the book is mentioned in other books on the same topic. Reviews of many books are published in the *Book Review Digest, Publishers Weekly,* and *The Library Journal.* Electronic or paper copies of such regular publications are often available through university and college libraries. Book reviews are also available online through Amazon.com (www.amazon.com) and many other sources. Though it is not always easy to discover what knowledgeable people think of a new book, sources of information on recent publications are widely available and relatively easy to come by.

Television

Documentary programs such as *60 Minutes,* interview programs such as *Charlie Rose,* investigative reporting shows such as *Dateline,* and political reporting programs such as *The Situation Room with Wolf Blitzer* can be sources of reliable evidence. Because they are primarily commercial in nature, however, these shows must be made attractive to a large audience. Commercial pressure can affect both the accuracy and depth of the information that hosts and guests provide. Moreover, these shows must compete successfully with other television fare, such as situation comedies and sports programming. Thus, for example, interviewers may "lead" their guests or focus on sensational topics, such as family conflict or workplace problems.

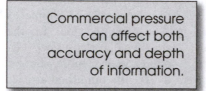
Commercial pressure can affect both accuracy and depth of information.

Television documentaries can be a source of interesting and reliable information, in part because networks often have other than purely commercial reasons for providing documentaries. The Museum of Television Broadcasting notes that documentaries have various functions. They provide "prestige" for advertisers, focus attention on important issues, create "a record of the human experience and the natural world," and provide a means of "artistic and social expression."[1] Thus, the success of documentaries may not be tied directly to ratings and advertising.

Television documentary programming on networks that specialize in this form—such as The History Channel and the Public Broadcasting Service—often provides useful, thoroughly researched information. As a result, these programs can sometimes be good sources of evidence. Even such generally reliable sources can be subject to pressure from donors and sponsoring organizations, however, and the analysis that commercial network documentary programs provide is sometimes too brief for adequate analysis of complex social problems such as drug abuse or illegal immigration.

Many popular documentary movies have appeared in theaters in recent years, including Michael Moore's *Where to Invade Next* (2015) and Morgan Spurlock's *The Greatest Movie Ever Sold* (2011). These movies have in some cases proven to be extremely popular (Moore's earlier film, *Fahrenheit 9/11* (2004), earned $228 million and sold more than three million DVDs) and are often cited as sources of evidence. However, they typically reflect a political bias that is so strong as to affect the accuracy of what they report. Any evidence from these and similar productions, such as Bill Maher's *Religulous* or Ben Stein's *Expelled,* should be corroborated by referring to other sources.

Interviews

One highly reliable and often overlooked source of evidence is a face-to-face interview with an expert on your research topic or with someone who is directly affected by policies related to your topic. Such interviews can generate evidence and background information, as well as involving you, the researcher, more directly in the lives of people who "live" the controversy. The faculty members of colleges and universities are often experts in their fields of study and can also direct you to other sources of potential interviews. Online searches may also reveal the recognized experts on a topic, who may respond to telephone and email inquiries. Increasingly, experts are interviewed in classroom settings by means of Skype and other technologies.

When you contact someone for an interview, always identify yourself and the purpose of your contact. If you are arranging a face-to-face interview, ask for an appointment and be punctual in keeping it. When preparing for an interview, do some background reading about the topic of the interview, as well as the views, experiences, and credentials of the individual whom you will interview. In addition, be sure to work out ahead of time the questions you intend to ask. Phrase the questions so they allow you to obtain the information you are seeking. Try to avoid questions that elicit simple yes or no responses, as well as leading questions that begin, "Don't you think that . . . ?" Prepare questions that will structure the conversation along helpful lines and let the interviewee talk.

When you employ the information gained in an interview to develop a case, be sure to qualify the source by mentioning appropriate credentials and experience, and inform your audience that you conducted the interview. Carefully review what was said and decide which statements are most useful to you.

The Internet

Today the internet is often the first place we turn when searching for evidence on virtually any topic, so we need to know not just how to use the internet for research, but also how to evaluate websites.

The internet is a vast and easily accessible storehouse of information. Indeed, it represents the largest collection of human knowledge ever assembled. Search engines such as Google make it relatively easy to locate material in this extensive data labyrinth. Google responds to 3.5 billion searches every day, a mind-boggling number. Still, the internet is an extensive warehouse of both reliable and unreliable material, necessitating a careful and critical approach. Among its 650 million websites are extraordinarily valuable sources of information and also much useless, inaccurate content.

Nearly all organizations, legitimate or otherwise, have internet presences. The Mayo Clinic, the FBI, the state of California, Greenpeace, the Democratic Party, the Sci-Fi Channel, and millions of other organizations have well-developed websites. Essentially every questionable or disreputable organization is present on the internet, so it is crucial to be attentive and critically aware when employing evidence from online sources. Developing skill in distinguishing between credible and questionable websites is an important aspect of developing **digital literacy**—*the capacity to skillfully navigate and employ online sources.*

Many scholarly journals, government publications, and other important materials are available online. For instance, a summary of current medical research can be found on the website Medical News Today (www.medicalnewstoday.com). The US Government makes a wide variety of information available online. For example, government-approved information on medical issues is available on the Surgeon General's website (www.surgeongeneral.gov).

Internet archives such as Project MUSE (http://muse.jhu.edu/search) provide links to the full texts of articles from hundreds of journals and newspapers, thus offering virtual encyclopedias of information on topics from the latest medical research to developments in the entertainment industry. Other sites such as TownHall.com (www.townhall.com), Truthout (www.truthout.org), RealClearPolitics.com, and Politico (www.politico.com) archive the works of dozens of editorial columnists. As mentioned earlier, news organizations also have their own websites. Reuters (today.reuters.com/news/home.aspx) is an example.

Though the internet can be a valuable research tool, evaluating internet sources can be difficult for several reasons, including the sheer number of websites available and the fact that many sites have been created by individuals or organizations to promote a point of view, occasionally with little regard for accuracy. We often know little or nothing about those responsible for creating a particular website. Moreover, many websites do not undergo the traditional editorial process that is typical for most books and virtually all articles in scholarly journals.

How do we know when we are exploring a reliable website on the internet? Here are a few pointers that, over the past several years, have become part of a standard set of criteria for evaluating web-based sources of information.

Evaluating Internet Sites

Language and Content

Among the first markers of a reliable website is its language and appearance. In nearly all cases, credible websites reflect a serious, moderate tone in the language and visual elements used to connect with their audiences. Such sources are not given to extreme statements, extreme language, extreme positions on controversial topics, or sensational images. Measured, grammatical, and well-written prose characterizes responsible and professional organizations that offer balanced and reliable information. The nature of a website's prose is, of course, a matter of judgment on the reader's part. Nevertheless, the difference between an extreme, careless approach to writing and a careful, professional approach is usually evident to a discerning reader. Similarly, reliable sources typically employ appropriate visual elements that send a serious message regarding their mission. For an example of language and visual elements that suggest a reliable source, visit the website of the Library of Congress (www.loc.gov/index.html).

In addition to language, we can consider a website's content. A trustworthy web page will usually be consistent with other responsible sources of information. This is the test of external consistency applied to a source. You should ask whether the site tends to contradict other reputable sources reporting on the same topic or issue. For instance, a site that argues that the United States moon landings were faked, The Faked Apollo Landings!!! (www.ufos-aliens.co.uk/cosmicapollo.html), presents interpretations that fly in the face of established evidence, ranging from the direct experience of living astronauts to the records of reputable government agencies.

Creator of the Site

Millions of organizations and individuals have created websites. There are currently about eight hundred million active websites. You may even have your own site or web page. Ease of participation is one of the internet's great attractions, but searching for evidence in this vast array of offerings poses some problems, not the least of which is determining which sites are reliable. It is important to ascertain what group or individual is responsible for a particular site.

Reliable internet sources are assembled by credible organizations or individuals. For example, the United Nations, *National Geographic,* and the United States Department of State are all recognized sources when it comes to information on global issues. The Mayo Clinic, the Cleveland Clinic, the American Medical Association, WebMD, and the Centers for Disease Control are widely acknowledged sources for information on medical issues. Social trends are tracked by organizations such as the Gallup Poll, the Kaiser Family Foundation, and the MacArthur Foundation. If you have a question about whether a source is recognized as reliable, ask a faculty member or reference librarian.

> Reliable internet sources are assembled by credible organizations or individuals.

Established professional, government, and research organizations have developed websites with a great deal of reliable information that can be useful when you are preparing a case. A few examples include:

The American Medical Association: www.ama-assn.org

The Federal Bureau of Investigation: www.fbi.gov

The Kaiser Family Foundation: www.kff.com

The Smithsonian Institution: www.si.edu

The National Aeronautics and Space Administration: www.nasa.gov

Other organizations' sites, however, may pose special problems as sources of evidence. For example, we may not know whether an organization is politically neutral or biased. Lobbying organizations such as the National Rifle Association (www.nra.org) or Greenpeace (www.greenpeace.org) have political agendas that influence how information is presented and interpreted on their websites. This does not mean that information provided on such sites is unreliable. It does mean that you should identify the organization sponsoring the site you are using, assess the organization's credibility and political stance, and determine what biases might influence its presentation of information. When possible, consult sites created by organizations with opposing views. The same criteria that applied to source credibility apply here— does the source have appropriate qualifications to speak with authority on this topic?

Podcasts

Podcasts are digital audio and video files that can be downloaded into a mobile device. As the use of mobile devices becomes increasingly common, podcasts are enjoying increasing popularity: one in five people in the United States over the age of twelve say they have listened to at least one podcast in the past month. In 2016, requests for podcast downloads stood at more than three billion a year, double the number of requests in 2012.

> Podcasts, a highly democratic information and opinion medium, require careful evaluation.

Podcasts influence opinion, and thus should be considered a source of evidence. Nearly thirty thousand deal with political issues and other topics of public interest. They are created by so-called legacy organizations such as the *New York Times,* as well as by individuals with few resources and little or no public reputation. They are thus a highly democratic information and opinion medium, but for that reason require careful evaluation.

Evaluating a podcast involves several of the same criteria that we have discussed with regard to other sources. First, it is important to know who is creating the podcast, what the purposes are, and whether the source has connections to political or special-interest organizations. Second, we should ask whether the creator of the podcast is generally considered a reliable source of information, or perhaps has a reputation for sensationalism and hyperbole. Evaluating the creator's reliability also involves knowing about credentials such as education, occupational experience, and other expertise.

A third factor to consider in evaluating a podcast as a source of evidence is whether the podcast itself is regularly updated and tends to incorporate recent information. Finally, as podcasts often report on findings from other organizations, we should ask whether the podcast's sources are themselves reliable and accurate.[2]

ASCERTAINING A SOURCE'S POLITICAL PERSPECTIVE

When evaluating sources of evidence, whether digital or traditional, reliability is not the only consideration. Even when you cite otherwise reliable sources, it is important to ascertain their political perspectives. Some sources advocate a point of view when they appear to be reporting events as they are. A critical reader or listener must also be aware of the influence of political perspective on the presentation and interpretation of evidence. Though ascertaining the political perspective of a source is not always easy, the following are some clues to look for, in the form of questions.

1. What assumptions seem to be at work? It can be helpful to ask what an author or an organization takes for granted. For example, what conclusions and evidence are treated as worthy of acceptance without examination? Conversely, what evidence and conclusions are taken as worthy of repudiation, or rejection without consideration? For instance, does the source suggest that almost any policy change is preferable to a new tax or that the federal government should be limited in its power? If so, you may be reading a politically conservative source. Does the source seem to assume that other uses of government money are more urgent than defense spending? If so, the source may be politically liberal.

2. Imagine the event in question being reported in a different way. Let's consider an example. When the Israeli government sends troops into Palestinian neighborhoods, some sources will report that Israel is controlling a Palestinian rebellion. These sources may be expressing a preference for Israel's point of view. Other publications will report the same action as an Israeli government crackdown on legitimate Palestinian dissent, and thus reflect their sympathy with the Palestinians affected. Checking the reporting of an event in more than one publication, especially a foreign source as well as a US publication, can reveal biases in reporting. An evident bias does not by itself disqualify a source of evidence, but it is a factor to be aware of in your choice of evidence.

3. Consider the source's reputation and purpose. Some periodicals have a well-known editorial bias. For example, the *National Review* is widely recognized as a politically conservative journal, as is *Forbes. The New Republic* represents a politically liberal point of view, as does *The Progressive.* Some publications, blogs, and websites exist solely to advance a particular perspective on an issue, but may not indicate that purpose openly. It may be necessary to do some research on a group in order to discover its agenda.

4. *How are groups described or treated?* For instance, what is the view of homeless people or the unemployed? Are they portrayed as victims of political decisions or as people who lack initiative? Are immigrants discussed as welcome additions to our population who deserve our assistance—or as threats to the economy and to US citizens seeking scarce jobs? Political commentator E. J. Dionne has written of changing attitudes toward gay marriage: more and more people in the United States, he says, reject the idea that gay people are "social revolutionaries looking to alter the nature of marriage." Instead, "they are seen as simply wanting to be part of an institution that is already open to their straight fellow citizens."[3] Dionne's measured language and respectful references suggest a supportive attitude toward gay people and same-sex marriage. In another example, conservative writer Ann Coulter refers to the National Rifle Association as "America's oldest civil rights organization" in one of her columns. This unusual classification of the conservative National Rifle Association suggests her favorable view of the organization, and something about her political views as well.[4]

5. *What style and language are used?* As noted earlier in our discussion of websites, a source's language and style can indicate political perspective. Is the style emotional or inflammatory? What phrases are repeated? Are emotionally loaded terms such as "censorship," "murder," or "political repression" used? Are labels such as "Communists," "abortionists," "bleeding hearts," "right-wing fanatics," or "fundamentalists" used to describe groups? A writer's attempt to discredit a group by labeling is often a clue to that writer's political orientation. Notice how language choice conveys as much as the content of Charles Krauthammer's assertions in his syndicated column regarding climate change: He labels the claim that climate change is a result of careless human activity, "human sin with pollution of carbon." This view, he comments, is the "oldest superstition . . . . It was in the Old Testament. It's in the rain dance of Native Americans. If you sin, the skies will not cooperate."[5]

Though these five clues to political perspective are not always reliable, they often provide some sense of the writer's or speaker's point of view, which can help you evaluate the source as a source of evidence.

CHAPTER REVIEW

It is helpful to have ways to evaluate the reliability of sources of evidence, such as books, periodicals, television programs, interviews, websites, and podcasts. Knowing how to spot the political perspective of a source, including its biases, prejudices, and preferences, is another means of assessing the source's general trustworthiness when you choose evidence.

EXERCISES

A.   Compare the coverage of a major event or controversy by two US news magazines. Is one publication more conservative or liberal in its coverage of the story than is the other? What evidence did you find of a political perspective?

B.   Compare the coverage of the two periodicals in exercise A to that offered by some alternative press publication—for example, *The Progressive, Mother Jones,* or *The Utne Reader*—on the same topic. What differences do you see between the coverage in these publications and the coverage in the mainstream publications?

C.   Locate an editorial or news report on a similar or related topic in a newspaper or news magazine originating in another country. Examples, in addition to sources mentioned in this chapter, include the French newspaper *Le Monde* and the British newspaper *The Guardian.* You might also consult a newspaper whose audience is made up of members of a particular ethnic or language group, such as *The Arab Times.* What differences in emphasis and coverage do you notice when you compare these with United States sources?

ENDNOTES

[1] The Museum of Broadcast Communication Archives, http://www.museum.tv/archives/etv/D/htmlD/documentary/documentary (Accessed September 29, 2006).

[2] Nancy Vogt, *Pew Research Center: Journalism and Media,* "State of the News Media 2016: Podcasting: Fact Sheet," p. 16, June 15, 2016, http://www.journalism.org/2016/06/15/podcasting-fact-sheet.

[3] E. J. Dionne, "Can Same-Sex Couples Help Save Marriage?" *Washington Post,* July 31, 2013, http://www.washingtonpost.com/opinions/ej-dionne-can-same-sex-couples-help-save-the-family/2013/07/31/a814a0fc-f9ef-11e2-a369-d1954abcb7e3_story.html.

[4] Ann Coulter, "The Left's Continuing War on Women," *Ann Coulter Official Home Page,* March 27, 2013, http://www.anncoulter.com/columns/2013-03-27.html.

[5] "Krauthammer: Global Warming 'Oldest Superstition Around,' 'The Rain Dance of Native Americans,'" *Real Clear Politics Video,* May 6, 2014, http://www.realclearpolitics.com/video/2014/05/06/krauthammer_global_warming_the_oldest_superstition_around_the_rain_dance_of_native_americans.html.

RECOMMENDED WEBSITES

The University of California, Berkeley, Library
www.lib.berkeley.edu/evaluating-resources

The Cornell University Library
www.library.cornell.edu/olinuris/ref/research/webeval.html

Online Writing Lab
Purdue University Owl

owl.english.purdue.edu/owl/resource/747/08

This website, provided by the Purdue University Online Writing Lab, provides an overview for citing internet sources.

9 Tips on Conducting Great Interviews
www.forbes.com/sites/shelisrael/2012/04/14/8-tips-on-conducting-great-interviews

Shel Israel, a technology writer for Forbes magazine, is an experienced interviewer who has distilled years of experience in this essay.

8 Using Statistics as Evidence

There's a world of difference between truth and facts.
Facts can obscure truth.
Maya Angelou (1928–2014)
United States poet

Minds are like parachutes—they only function when they are open.
Attributed to James Dewar (1842–1923)
Scottish physicist

KEY TERMS

extent of the generalization

fallacy of hasty generalization

finding

generalizations from a sample

mean

median

mode

population

property

random sample

representative

sample

sample size

sampling

statistics

stratified sample

variation

We often read statistical reports such as the following:

There are 300 million privately owned firearms in the United States, roughly one gun for every person in the nation. About one-third of US citizens own guns. Alaska has the highest rate of gun ownership, with 61.7 percent of its residents owning firearms. Guns were responsible for more than 15,500 deaths in the United States in 2017.

Such numerical information now confronts us at every turn. A defining characteristic of the present cultural scene is an abundance of statistical data. Information about life sciences, for example, now doubles every year. Data are now being accumulated so rapidly, resulting in quantities so vast, that a new phrase has been coined to describe the phenomenon: Big Data. Big Data are likely to affect nearly every aspect of life over the coming decades, from how we practice law and medicine to how we teach nontechnical subjects such as composition and art history. The mechanisms and implications of Big Data are largely beyond our reach and understanding as citizens, but a basic understanding of the methods by which data are collected helps us understand the sources and uses of Big Data.

This chapter considers the important question of evidence derived from statistics, particularly as those statistics appear in news sources and other public discourse. Chapter 6 introduced seven general tests of evidence and the interpretation of evidence. Chapter 7 covered several sources of evidence and ways of evaluating such sources. This chapter develops specific tests for evaluating one of the most common types of evidence in public discourse. It also explores various sources of statistics, the methods used to develop survey statistics, and the question of interpreting statistics.

We live in a world of statistics. In a single issue of a daily newspaper, for example, we may read that people in the United States consume an average of twenty-two teaspoons of sugar each day, that 57 percent of people responding to a survey believe the military budget should be cut, that nine thousand people were killed in accidents caused by drunk drivers last year, or that the national uninsured rate fell to 10.9 percent at the end of 2016, compared to 17.3 percent in 2013.

Statistics are *numerical evidence from records, studies, reports, surveys, polls, and the like.* Some statistics are simple reports derived from record-keeping, such as birth records for a particular county. Other statistics commonly encountered in public discourse are generalizations from sampling, such as polls concerning political attitudes.

As with all evidence, it is important to ask basic evaluative questions before accepting statistics as sound. Two fundamental questions should be asked of any statistic:

1. Is the statistic from a reliable source?

2. Has the statistic been interpreted correctly?

Both these questions can be difficult to answer from the standpoint of the typical reader or listener. For example, we hear a speaker assert:

> Nearly 1,200,000 people in the United States are infected with HIV, and another 400,000 have AIDS. The American Cancer Society reports that there are 40,000 new HIV infections each year in the United States. Of these, 70 percent are in men, 30 percent in women. Clearly we are not doing enough to educate people about AIDS.

How were these figures arrived at? Were records kept of every instance of HIV infection, or is this generalization based on a sample? Have the figures been correctly interpreted as providing support for a particular claim?

Often we have little knowledge of how any specific statistic we read in the news was arrived at. Questions of interpretation can also be complex. Opinion varies widely from one audience to another as to the reliability of a particular statistic. For instance, the organizers of a demonstration in Washington, DC, might estimate that more than 500,000 people had gathered, but government or media industry sources might estimate the crowd at fewer than 250,000. A disagreement is likely to ensue over which statistic is more accurate, largely because assessments of the event's success hinge on the number of people in attendance.

Here is another example, this time inviting a debate over how to interpret a set of figures: National Oceanic and Atmospheric Administration records indicate that 2012 was one degree Fahrenheit warmer than 1998, previously the hottest year on record, and 2013 tied with 2003 as the fourth warmest year on record. The past nine years rank in the top twenty-five hottest on record. The warmest year on record was 2016. Hurricane formation has increased by 100 percent since 1900.

From these and similar statistics, advocates draw two radically different conclusions. Environmentalists conclude that human-generated global warming, resulting from increased levels of atmospheric CO_2, is a serious and growing threat to our survival. People who advocate continued development of fossil fuel sources counter that these increases are the result of natural fluctuations in the earth's temperature, and are nothing to be concerned about. A "heated" debate between the two camps continues, with a question of how to interpret weather statistics at its very center.

These examples illustrate that statistical evidence, though often highly persuasive, can also carry with it certain difficulties of interpretation and understanding. Knowing the basic vocabulary and general tests of statistics can help us assess both the reliability and the interpretation of statistics when they appear as evidence. Let's begin with statistics derived from record-keeping.

RECORD-KEEPING

Some statistical evidence is relatively straightforward—for example, the reports of medical record-keeping agencies. The National Institutes for Health and the Centers for Disease Control report that the number of people in the United States with tuberculosis fell from 84,000 in 1953 to 22,000 in 1983, rose again to the 1953 level by 1991, then fell to 14,511 in 2004. By 2006 the number had dropped to 13,800 active cases; in 2015, it reached a record low of 9,563 cases. These statistics reflect the number of cases of tuberculosis that doctors and hospitals reported to the NIH and CDC. Statistics such as these are usually highly reliable estimates. While some cases undoubtedly go undetected, doctors have been required to report cases of tuberculosis for more than fifty years. These statistics allow comparisons that help government agencies detect trends and suggest policy changes to limit the spread of disease.

Statistics on countable phenomena such as traffic deaths, infant mortality rates, and people applying for unemployment compensation often are derived from record-keeping. Generally reliable statistical information on such matters is available from a variety of government agencies, such as the Centers for Disease Control and the National Institutes of Health, as well as private foundations such as the Kaiser Family Foundation.

When we accept reports of record-keeping agencies, we are trusting the credibility of the agency itself as well as the accuracy of any secondary source that has reported the data. Any time we use statistics as evidence, the general tests of evidence discussed in Chapter 6 come into play. For instance, we usually want to ask whether the statistic is generally consistent with other statistics available on the topic. In the following example, the test of external consistency has been applied to the statistic:

> We usually want to ask whether the statistic is consistent with other statistics available on the topic.

> Japanese car companies such as Mitsubishi, Honda, and Toyota like to point out that they are now US companies that make 55% of their total automobile output in the United States.

A news writer reporting on the auto industry responds:

> However, even the Japanese cars with the largest number of American-made components only use about 70% of the car's total parts, compared to 90% in

many American cars. And, a professor of the history of automobile manufacturing at the University of Dayton reports that only about 10% of the profits of Japanese auto companies go to U.S. investors, compared to 90% of the profits from American car companies.[1]

The reliability of sources is also relevant when evaluating statistics of any type. The University of Michigan—a leading research institution—would be considered a reliable source for the statistics in the previous example. The same would be true of statistics from the US Army and its own record-keeping about, for example, decreased recruitment of new soldiers in 2007, and a resurgence of those numbers to 107 percent of recruitment goals in 2012. In 2015 the Army reached 100 percent of its goal of recruiting fifty-nine thousand new soldiers. Such figures are used to adjust goals and perhaps to improve recruiting practices.

When an organization is generally recognized as reputable, when outside investigators have access to reported records, and when there is no obvious reason that the records might have been misreported, statistics can usually be considered reliable.

Not all statistics derived from record-keeping are reliable, however. Some organizations, with a stake in public perceptions of their activities or influence,

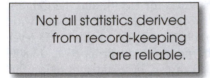

Not all statistics derived from record-keeping are reliable.

deliberately misreport records and do not allow outside review. For example, some special interest organizations are known for exaggerating their membership numbers. A few charity organizations have been caught underreporting donations. It is important to ask whether the organization reporting the statistic is considered trustworthy and whether it would have any reason to falsify its records.

Not all unreliable record-keeping is the result of an intentional effort to mislead the public. Records of crimes, for instance, may be faulty because a large number of crimes are not reported. Similarly, many cases of disease go undiagnosed and thus never become part of official medical records. Unemployment statistics tend to report only those people who are actively looking for work. Consequently, it is important to evaluate statistics derived from record-keeping critically, just as we would any other type of evidence.

Finally, we should avoid jumping to conclusions about causes when examining statistics. Figures like those on tuberculosis or army recruiting do not by themselves establish the *causes* of events. These statistics do not tell us, for instance, whether the decrease in reported tuberculosis cases is a result of increased workplace screening, higher rates of immunizations, better treatment protocols, or a variety of factors. Similarly, the army's improved recruiting statistics might be incorporated into a broader case about the possible impact of the recession, but we would have to object if a speaker claimed, on the basis of these statistics alone, that the recession *caused* the army's higher recruiting numbers. (Attributing cause will be discussed in more detail in Chapter 15.)

SAMPLING AND GENERALIZATION

Much statistical evidence is derived by a technique called sampling. For example, a recent study suggests that interest in starting a business is vibrant among young people in the Middle East and North Africa. A sample of young people across the region's countries revealed that "a median 27% of young Arabs who were not already business owners said they intended to start a business in the next 12 months."[2]

This statistic was not derived from record-keeping, which would be impractical for gathering such data.

Sampling is *statistically selecting and observing members of a group or population who are taken to be representative of the rest of the group.* It comes into play when it is not possible or practical to count or examine every individual instance of an event or attitude. For instance, we might read:

> In a random telephone survey of 2,500 registered voters, 53 percent expressed a favorable attitude toward the current administration's economic policies and 43 percent expressed dissatisfaction with the president's policies. Thus, a majority of voting citizens still supports this administration's economic policies.

Statistics such as these do not reflect what *all* members of the population think. Rather, they reflect what *some* members of the population think. The researchers conducting the survey generalize from the opinions of a carefully selected sample of the group to the opinions of the entire group.

Generalizations from a sample are *claims that take as their evidence a sample drawn from a population, and advance a conclusion about members of the entire population.* The so-called inductive leap—an inferential movement beyond an argument's evidence—is part of every generalization. To know whether this leap is reasonable in a given case, we can identify the elements and apply several tests of generalizations to those elements. These elements include the sample itself, a finding about the sample, the population from which it was drawn, the property that was transferred from the sample to the population, and the extent of the generalization.

The sample, sample size, and finding are present in what we will term the evidence statement of the generalization. The **sample** supporting a generalization consists of *the members of a group actually observed or consulted during the sampling process.* In many statistical generalizations the sample is clearly stated, as in the example about the 2,500 registered voters who were interviewed by telephone. The **sample size** is simply *the number of members in the sample:* in this case, 2,500. The **finding** is *what was observed about members of the sample.* In our example the finding is communicated in the statement, "53 percent expressed a favorable attitude toward the current administration's economic policies, and 43 percent expressed dissatisfaction with the president's policies."

What we will term the generalization statement will usually express a population, a property, and an extent of the generalization. The **population** is *the group or class to which the generalization is meant to apply.* The sample should be of the same group, or population, to which the generalization is applied, though this is not always the case. In the example above, the generalizing statement is: "Thus, a majority of voting citizens still supports this administration's economic policies." The group these researchers *intend* as their population is "voting citizens," but they actually drew their sample from "registered voters." Because not all registered voters actually vote, the two groups are not the same. This discrepancy creates a weakness in the generalization—the group sampled and the group generalized about overlap, but are not identical. Generalizations often fail to define their population adequately.

Generalizations also involve a **property,** *a quality projected from the sample to the population.* In the example above, the property is expressed as the property of "supporting this administration's economic policies."

We also can identify the **extent of the generalization,** *the portion of the population that is said to exhibit the particular property.* In our example the extent is expressed as "a majority of voting citizens." The portion of the sample in which the property is observed and the extent of the generalization should correspond closely.

Let's take another look at our example, identifying the elements discussed to this point:

> **Evidence statement:** In a random telephone survey of 2,500 registered voters, 53 percent expressed a favorable attitude toward the current administration's economic policies and 43 percent expressed dissatisfaction with the president's policies.

The evidence statement includes:
> **Sample:** 2,500 registered voters
> **Sample size:** 2,500
> **Finding:** 53 percent expressed a favorable attitude toward the current administration's economic policies and 43 percent expressed dissatisfaction with the president's policies.

> **Generalizing statement:** Thus, a majority of voting citizens supports this administration's economic policies.

The generalizing statement includes:
> **Property:** supporting the administration's economic policies
> **Population:** voting citizens
> **Extent:** a majority

Representativeness of Samples

The underlying assumption that allows an inference, from the observation of a sample to a generalization about an entire population, is that the sample is **representative,** that it *accurately reflects the presence of a particular quality in the entire population.* This assumption is the connective that links the evidence of the sample to the conclusion that expresses the generalization. The assumption of representativeness usually is unstated, but it is present in all generalizations. The soundness of a generalization depends on whether we find the sample to be representative of the population from which it was drawn.

Three important criteria for assessing the representativeness of a sample are the size, stratification, and randomness of the sample.

Size of the Sample

A sample must be large enough to reveal accurately the variations present in a diverse population, but no larger than is necessary to represent the population accurately. How many subjects are enough to provide an accurate picture of the larger group from which the sample was drawn? That question belongs to the discipline of statistics; a thorough answer is beyond the scope of this text. Nevertheless, several foundational concepts related to sample size can be introduced here.

Sufficient sample size depends on many factors, two of the more important being:

1. Size of the population.
2. Degree of variation within the population.

*Relevant differences among members in a population—the degree to which members of a population vary in ways that may be relevant to the quality being tested in a generalization—*are referred to as **variation.** The pencils in a case of mechanical pencils, all manufactured by the same facility during the same week of production, probably will not vary much from one pencil to the next. Thus, the observation that two mechanical pencils from a case worked well may be a large enough sample to support the generalization, "The pencils in this case work well." Human populations, however, vary a great deal more in attitudes on political, social, and religious issues. For example, the first ten people you meet in Chicago may favor strong environmental protection legislation, but that sample is not large enough to support the generalization, "Residents of Chicago favor strong environmental protection legislation." Chicago has a lot of people, and they are not similar enough in their political views for such a small sample to support a generalization about them all. The **fallacy of hasty generalization** is *a generalization based on a sample that is too small to support it.* As a population becomes more varied, the size of a sample relative to a population has to increase if the sample is to be representative.

Wouldn't interviewing a large number of people always be best? Actually, in many cases it would not. Because interviewing subjects is time-consuming and expensive, researchers try to establish the smallest number of individuals necessary to account adequately for all the variation in a population. Further, the more people who are interviewed, the more occasions we have for error in collecting and entering the data.

These concerns are especially relevant when researchers contact subjects directly, as in telephone and face-to-face surveying. Some sampling regarding attitudes and behaviors is done by email, so a substantial increase in the number of subjects is possible without a significant increase in cost. Nevertheless, researchers still try to identify the smallest number of subjects for the study that will ensure that the sample accurately represents the population. Careful sampling technique makes it possible to develop highly reliable generalizations about attitudes in large human populations from samples slightly larger than a thousand subjects. Indeed, increases in the accuracy of generalizations about attitudes are negligible in samples over a thousand, even when populations are large.

For instance, a recent sample of eleven hundred licensed drivers revealed that "roughly a third of American motorists say cell phone use by fellow drivers is their main annoyance on the road." The study goes on to state that the finding was that 31 percent of those surveyed reported cell phone use by other drivers to be their primary source of annoyance on the road. The study had a margin of error of only three percentage points, which means that while 31 percent of the sample reported this attitude toward cell phone use, researchers were confident that between 28 percent and 34 percent of the total population of US drivers have this same property.[3] Thus, the extent employed in the generalization is "roughly a third."

Important to achieving a representative sample are procedures known as stratification and randomness.

Stratification of the Sample

To be representative, a sample must reflect the diverse elements within a population, particularly when the population reflects a high degree of variation—that is, when its members represent subpopulations whose views may vary. A **stratified sample** is *a sample that adequately reflects the various groups that introduce variation within the population.*

Imagine that you wish to ascertain attitudes toward a proposed nuclear power facility to be built within thirty miles of the city. The population in any city consists of a variety of subgroups, whose attitudes toward the facility are likely to vary. These groups might include unemployed people, retired people, families with young children, people at various income levels, men, women, ethnic and cultural minorities, political liberals, moderates, and conservatives.

Pollsters will seek to stratify this population so as to interview the smallest number of people who will account accurately for the attitudes of members of these subpopulations. Suppose that approximately one in thirty members of the population in the city are white working women who have moderate incomes and young children, and who identify themselves as political liberals. Approximately one in every thirty people in the sample should be a member of this subpopulation.

A similar procedure would be followed in identifying other relevant subpopulations. For instance, pollsters will also seek to identify subgroups whose opinions would be likely to vary from those of politically liberal, white, working women with young children. Thus, the subgroup of retired people living on fixed incomes might also be identified as reflecting variation of opinion regarding the proposed power plant.

When stratification is done accurately—that is, in a way that reflects relevant differences in the population—the process assists researchers in finding the smallest sample necessary to account for the significant variation present in the population.

Randomness of the Sample

A well-stratified sample of sufficient size may still not represent a population accurately. Extraneous factors may influence the selection of the sample, in ways that affect subjects' responses to a question. For example, if an interviewee is acquainted personally with an interviewer, the interviewee's responses may be less forthcoming than otherwise would be the case. Samples may also be affected by biases in selection. To guard against these possibilities, researchers seek a "random" sample of each subpopulation. A **random sample** is *a sample in which every member of a given population had an equal chance of being selected for the sample.* For example, in sampling randomly from the subpopulation of white working women who have moderate incomes and young children, and who identify themselves as political liberals, the researcher must try to ensure—to the extent possible—that every member of this group has the same opportunity to be included in the sample group. The goal of a random sample is to avoid bias in the sample.

When researchers attend carefully to stratification and randomness in sampling, the sample is more likely to be representative. For instance, in a survey of attitudes about the quality of a city's public schools, a sample that drew too heavily upon people living in neighborhoods where the schools enjoyed a strong academic reputation would likely overrepresent favorable attitudes toward public schools. A well-stratified sample would represent, in numbers proportional to the actual population, people living in districts with stronger and weaker schools. A random sample drawn from these stratified groups would further reduce the risk of sampling error and result in a representative sample.

INTERPRETING STATISTICS

You are probably already aware that most statistical evidence is subject to various interpretations. In fact, the same numbers can even be advanced to prove contradictory claims. Consider the following example:

> Nearly 80 percent of the job losses in the current recession are of jobs held by men. Some conservative pundits have argued that this statistic means women's gains in the workplace are hurting men. However, this is apparently not an accurate interpretation of the data. Women represent only 25 percent of full-time workers, and many available positions remain divided by gender. Many women compete with women for clerical, nursing, elementary-school

teaching, and receptionist positions, while many men compete with men in areas such as construction and factory work. Consequently, women's gains at work do not equal men's losses.

In this example, conservative commentators interpreted a statistic to support the claim that women's gains in the workplace hurt men. A respondent, however, interpreted the same statistic to argue that women's job gains do not hurt men. Which interpreter is accurate? The answer to that question might depend upon a variety of factors, including projections about future job gains by women and whether gender division is likely to continue in the job market. Nevertheless, a few basic statistical concepts can assist us in interpreting numerical evidence.

Means, Modes, Medians, and Misleading Statistics

Averages are among the most important findings of studies that involve sampling from a population. Different ways of defining "average," however, can lead to different conclusions. Let's consider the following example from a local newspaper about the incomes of people in a community:

> Our survey of 500 employed residents of the county, about 1 percent of the total working population, indicates that the mean income for a working person in the county is between $25,000 and $29,999 annually, in keeping with the national average of $26,000.

The example mentions "the mean." **Mean** is another word for *the arithmetical average, the sum of a set of figures divided by the number of figures in the set.* In this example, the mean is determined by dividing the sum of the sample members' incomes by the number of those surveyed—in this case, 500.

Sometimes, however, a mean can be misleading, especially when "average" is taken to be synonymous with "typical" or "usual." However, it has been said that means are made up of extremes. The mean income figure reported in the example seems to indicate that residents of the county are doing well financially, but that may not be the case. We need to take a closer look at the actual figures that produced this mean figure. Employing income ranges rather than actual income figures, the survey showed the following approximate distribution of incomes:

$8,000–9,999	105
10,000–14,999	217
15,000–19,999	26
20,000–24,999	16
25,000–29,999	11
30,000–39,999	23
40,000–59,999	15
60,000–74,999	54
75,000–100,000	31
over 100,000	2

It is just as important to consider the interpretation given to any statistic used as evidence as it is to think about the accuracy of the statistic itself. Looking at these statistics, we can see that the generalization from the mean is misleading. The **mode**—*the most frequently occurring observation or response in a sample*—turns out to be between $10,000 and $14,999 annually. In other words, most people in the

FIGURE 8.1 Definitions: Mean, Mode, and Median

> **Mean:** The sum of a set of figures divided by the number of figures in the set; the arithmetical average.
>
> **Mode:** The most frequently occurring observation or response in a sample.
>
> **Median:** The figure that exactly divides the top half from the bottom half in a range of figures.

community make much less than the reported mean of $25,000 to $29,999. The mode reveals a central tendency in these figures that the mean does not show.

More important, the mean does not reveal much about the actual distribution of incomes in the county. The median income might tell us more about that. The **median** is *the figure that exactly divides the top half from the bottom half in a range of figures.* From these figures, we can easily see that well over half the people surveyed, 322 or 64.4 percent, earn less than $15,000 annually; they earn about $10,000 to $22,000 less than people described in the mean. Few people in the survey—11, or 2.2 percent—actually earn incomes in the mean category. The mean or arithmetical average income in this example is not a typical or usual income.

Moreover, the survey results reveal that much of the community's income is concentrated in a relatively small band of high earners. A few people—87, or about 17.4 percent of the sample, earn over $60,000. Almost four times as many people earn less than $15,000. The approximate combined income for those 87 people is 50 percent to 100 percent more than the combined incomes of the 322 people who make less than $15,000.

Similarly, the combined income of the 217 people in the second-lowest earning group is the same as the combined income of the 31 people in the second-highest earning group. Thus, though seven times as many people are in the $10,000 to $14,999 range, their combined income is no more than that of the 31 in the $75,000 to $100,000 range. In other words, although the mean income suggests a prosperous community, these additional statistics suggest a striking financial stratification!

Although the *mean* income in the county is between $25,000 and $29,999, this figure says little about the financial situation of the county's workers and certainly does not tell us what a "typical" income in the county is. A typical income in this county—revealed more clearly in the *median* (more than 250 people make less than $15,000) and *mode* (the 217 people making $10,000 to $14,999)—is well below the reported national average of $26,000. The original newspaper report suggested something rather different—that income levels in the county were relatively high. The paper's survey results, however, actually reveal a county in which a few people earn relatively high salaries and a lot of people make very little.

Judging from these examples, we should interpret statistics with caution. Whenever possible, we should look at the actual figures from which generalizations are derived. If the actual figures are not available, the mean, median, and mode may be revealing. We should be cautious about accepting means reported on their own.

Now let's look again at an earlier example of a generalization:

> In a random telephone survey of 2,500 registered voters, 53 percent expressed a favorable attitude toward the current administration's economic policies, while 43 percent expressed dissatisfaction with the president's policies. Thus, a majority of voting citizens supports this administration's economic policies.

Suppose that this survey included the following items, each of which received the number of responses indicated:

Which response best represents your reaction to the following statement?

In general, I support the current administration's economic policies.

1. Strongly agree   535
2. Agree   790
3. No opinion   99
4. Disagree   210
5. Strongly disagree   866

The results of the survey show that 53 percent of the subjects, or 1,325 people, responded that number 1 or number 2 best represented their reaction to the statement, thus indicating that they agreed with the current administration's economic policies. The generalization as we have it, then, may be statistically accurate. But have the statistics been interpreted accurately? A few basic concepts regarding statistical averages and related concerns can help us answer this question.

A closer look at these figures might reveal important information. The actual responses of those surveyed tell us more than just how a majority responded. For instance, we can see that the mode in this survey was number 5, the 866 people who marked "strongly disagree." Only 535 people said they "strongly agree." One immediate interpretation of the figures, then, is that people who disagree with the survey statement tend to have stronger opinions than do the people who agree with it. This is an important observation because people who express strong opinions in political polls tend to take actions—such as voting.

The actual responses reveal two other interesting points. Notice that a relatively small number of people had no opinion about the statement. This fact could indicate a sharp division within the voting public on this issue, with few people being undecided. Notice also that when response 4 is added to response 5, 43 percent of respondents express some level of disagreement with the claim to which they were asked to respond.

The original claim that "a majority of voters support the current administration's economic policies" may be a statistically correct report of the results of the survey, but it may not be a particularly enlightening interpretation, or one that would lead to accurate predictions about voting behavior. The figures reveal a sharply divided public, with stronger sentiments among those who disagree with the statement in the survey. Opposition to the administration's economic policies may be stronger than the summary suggests, and may affect the election in ways that the initial interpretation did not predict.

Interpreting for Prediction

Statistics are frequently interpreted as supporting predictions. For example:

Of 1,370 undergraduates surveyed at California State University campuses, 62 percent said they voted for the Democratic candidate for governor in the last election and 58 percent said they backed the Democratic candidate for Congress. Thus, the liberalism that has marked the voting habits of Californians in the past election can be expected to continue over the next several decades, as these students mature and move into the political mainstream.

Predictions often involve the assumption that what is true of a population now will also be true of it in the future. This assumption can be risky, given that attitudes change over time. Establishing that things will be the same in the future as they are now is more difficult than simply describing what is true of a group now. To defend the prediction about students' future voting habits, we must suppose that these students' political attitudes are not likely to change much. Someone might counter that voting habits change as people mature, however, so what is true now of the population of students is not likely to be true of them in the future. Because we recognize that political thinking and voting behavior often change as we age, the prediction is less than certain in this argument.

Statistically based predictions are more easily justified when they concern phenomena that do not change over time, or when changes are regular or incremental. For example:

> Measurements taken along the fault line indicate that the two plates move in opposite directions at a rate of .87 inches per year. This rate of movement has resulted in one major earthquake in the vicinity every 100 to 150 years. Geological evidence indicates that the last major quake along this fault occurred approximately 100 years ago, so scientists predict a major quake some time in the next 50 years.

Interpreting for Clarity and Impact

Statistics benefit from interpretation for clarity or to reveal their significance. Numbers by themselves often do not say much to an audience. For example, if I assert that the cigarette industry in the United States spends more than $13 billion on advertising every year, it may sound as if the industry spent a lot of money. Still, the magnitude of the figure may be hard to grasp immediately, so I might consider interpreting the statistic for clarity and impact:

> In 2016, tobacco companies spent more than $9 billion marketing their products in the United States. That translates to $25 million each day, or about $1 million every hour.

The astronomical amount spent on advertising cigarettes is easier to apprehend now that the original figure has been broken down into more manageable numbers. This is one method of interpreting statistics for an audience. When a statistic is central to an argument, interpretation for clarity can be crucial to the persuasive impact.

Large numbers in economic reports are notoriously difficult to take in at a glance. If I read that our combined national debt is $17 trillion, I can't imagine what that number means. When a reporter interprets it as meaning "each person in this country personally owes $53,382 toward the national debt," the number suddenly is understandable. This particular interpretation dramatically increases the personal significance of an otherwise incomprehensible number.

Another method of interpreting statistics for clarity and impact is to use a comparison. Suppose you read the following statistic in an editorial: "If employment of women matched that of men in the United States, the nation's gross domestic product would increase by 5 percent." On its own, the statistic is hard to interpret. Is this a major increase or inconsequential? A simple comparison can help audiences to interpret the statistic. For example: "An increase of 5 percent would add $750 billion to the gross domestic product, or about five times the annual budget of the state of California."

CHAPTER REVIEW

Statistics are among the most frequently encountered types of evidence. Statistics are derived from record-keeping reports and sampling. The reliability of statistics derived from record-keeping depends on the credibility of the agency or organization that collects and manages the records. Statistics derived from record-keeping do not in themselves establish the causes of particular figures rising or falling.

The accuracy of generalization from a sample depends on the representativeness of the sample. The tests of sample size, stratification, and randomness are important to assessing representativeness.

Statistics are often presented in public discourse as means, medians, or modes. A mean is a statistical average; a median is the middle number in a set of findings; while a mode is the most common figure.

Statistical evidence often requires interpretation for clarity or impact, or to support a prediction. Two common methods of interpretation are breaking large numbers down to more manageable figures, and comparing obscure statistics to more familiar numbers.

EXERCISES

A. For each of the following generalizations, identify (a) the sample, (b) the finding, (c) the population, (d) the property, and (e) the extent.

1. A telephone survey of 500 Democrats who voted in the last election indicated that 75 would now vote for a Republican candidate. Thus, at least 15 percent of Democrats will switch to the Republican Party in the next election.

2. Most Americans oppose continued United States military involvement in the Middle East. A recent poll of 250 people living in or around Chicago revealed that 63 percent of those surveyed oppose such involvement.

3. A survey commissioned by the American Bar Association Young Lawyers' Division asked a random sample of over 3,000 attorneys to rate their level of job satisfaction. A surprising 25 percent said they were either somewhat or very dissatisfied with their work. Thus, a substantial minority of attorneys is not happy with having chosen a career in the law.

4. An Associated Press/Ipsos poll surveyed 1,000 adult Americans. The poll found that 70 percent of those surveyed were worried about the federal deficit. However, the same poll also found that only 35 percent of those surveyed were willing to make a personal financial sacrifice to balance the budget. Thus, a sweeping majority is concerned about the deficit, while a minority of people is willing to adjust lifestyles to make a difference. (Note: There are two findings, two extents, and two properties in this example.)

5. A survey of California residents indicates that a vast majority are unhappy with the state's current direction. In a survey of 1,500 registered voters, 80 percent responded with "agree" or "strongly agree" to the statement: California is on the wrong track.

B. In the following examples, differentiate between the statistical evidence and any conclusions based on those statistics.

1. Following a right to life rally in Washington, DC, the United States Parks Department estimated the number of people in attendance at 200,000. Organizers of the march estimated the number at 500,000 and charged the Parks

Department with capitulating to pressure from the media and the pro-choice movement to underestimate the numbers.

2. The figures just in for April show that new home sales dropped 9.5 percent to an annual rate of 894,000. In March, economists had projected an annual new home sales rate of 988,000. This is the biggest decline in percentage since 1997. The figures, combined with a higher jobless rate and the drop in the stock market, may point to a significant downturn in the economy. Government economists argue, however, that despite the apparent decline, new home sales are actually up 0.6 percent when compared to the projection of 889,000 in April. These economists maintain that we should not be alarmed by a single number.

3. During the first quarter of this year, business investment in equipment purchases, computer equipment included, decreased at an annual rate of 2.6 percent. Business equipment purchases also declined the last quarter of last year. We have to consider these drops to be the "canary in the mine" for our economy. Businesses aren't investing in equipment, so they must be projecting a stagnant economy.

4. Historical studies show that 15,000 people have been executed in the United States in the last 300 years. This statistic gives us a strong reason to believe that the human race is self-destructive.

5. The latest census data reveal that, for the first time since census figures have been recorded, the non-Hispanic white population in California dropped below 50 percent of the state's total population. This fact accounts for a well-funded lobbying organization's inability to get popular support for a proposal banning bilingual education in public schools.

ENDNOTES

[1]Jennifer Lawinski, "Some American Cars Are Foreign-Owned, but Made in the U.S.A.," Fox News, December 10, 2008, http://www.foxnews.com/story/0,2933,465005,00.html.

[2]Steve Crabtree, "Entrepreneurial Goals Common among Young in Arab States," Gallup Polls, February 26, 2010, http://www.gallup.com/poll/126113/Entrepreneurial-Goals-Common -Among-Young-Arab-States.aspx.

[3]Ken Thomas, "Poll: Drivers Feel Less Safe on the Road," *Detroit News,* July 7, 2005.

RECOMMENDED WEBSITES

Gallup

www.gallup.com

Gallup is a leading polling service. The website offers a wealth of information about developing reliable generalizations from carefully selected samples.

NORC at the University of Chicago

www.norc.org

Another major polling institution is the National Opinion Research Center, located at the University of Chicago. This reputable organization investigates a wide range of political and social attitudes and behaviors.

9 Using Testimony as Evidence

Truth is not merely what we are thinking,
but also why, to whom and under what circumstances we say it.
Václav Havel (1936–2011)
Czech playwright and politician

We don't see things as they are, we see things as we are.
Anaïs Nin (1903–1977)
French author

KEY TERMS

biased testimony

concurrent testimony

expert testimony

lay testimony

reluctant testimony

testimony

unbiased testimony

A recent proposal to allow cell phone use on airlines met with stiff opposition from both consumers and lawmakers. "Keeping phone conversations private on commercial flights may not be enshrined in the Constitution," said Senator Lamar Alexander of Tennessee, "but it is certainly enshrined in common sense." Alexander backed a bill that would ban cell phone use on commercial flights. "This legislation is about avoiding something nobody wants: nearly 2 million passengers a day, hurtling through space, trapped in 17-inch-wide seats, yapping their innermost thoughts."[1] The senator's testimony was employed to support one perspective in a controversy.

Testimony is *personal report of direct experience, expression of personal opinion, or judgment based on expert knowledge.* It is an essential source of information about the world, because any one person's experience and knowledge are necessarily limited. We seek and value testimony in situations in which our own experience does not allow us direct knowledge or when our own knowledge is inadequate.

TYPES OF TESTIMONY

Testimony is often divided into two broad categories: lay testimony and expert testimony.

Lay Testimony

Lay testimony is *a report of personal observation, experience, or opinion on a topic not requiring special expertise.* Such testimony may be used as evidence when the issue at hand does not require evidence from expert sources. Statements from members of the general public regarding the state of the economy are examples of lay testimony that might be advanced as evidence in an argument. Another example of lay testimony is a witness to a crime testifying in court.

Here is an example of effective use of lay testimony, by a victim of autism describing his experience living with what he calls his "damaged" brain: "It's prevented me from making a living or ever having a girlfriend. It's given me bad fine motor coordination problems where I can hardly write."[2]

Lay testimony can also help explain motives or account for new trends. For example, there has been increased interest in fertility clinics among women in their late twenties and thirties. Researchers seeking to understand this new trend interviewed women who had visited one of the clinics. One woman said, "I wanted to separate my desire to have kids with my timing to be with someone." The fertility clinic "helped relieve the pressure" she was feeling about pregnancy and relationships. "You want to have children with the right person," she commented.[3]

Lay testimony is sound evidence when we want to understand public opinion or personal motivation. It can also be useful in establishing the causes of events where eyewitnesses were present. This is one reason for the great popularity of Twitter and other social media that allow for immediate dispersal of eyewitness reports. Tweets regarding developing events such as protests and statements by public officials are now a valuable source of the evidence of lay testimony.

The Limits of Lay Testimony

Lay testimony does, however, have limits as evidence. It should not be used where technical knowledge is important to resolving an issue. Such situations require the testimony of qualified experts.

Testimony about technical or specialized topics should be viewed with some suspicion when it comes from people who are not qualified as experts in the appropriate field. For example, televangelist Pat Robertson may claim expertise in several areas, but he is not a climate scientist. Thus, he is a lay witness when it comes to global warming. He has suggested that because there are no sport utility vehicles or oil refineries on Mars, global warming on earth is a hoax. Referring to measurements revealing slight planetary warming on Mars, Robertson commented: "How many SUVs, how many oil refineries are there on Mars? And yet, it's the relationship to the sun that is affecting the climate on Mars."

> Lay testimony should not be used where technical knowledge is important.

Meteorologists have dismissed the idea that global warming could be the result of solar radiation, however. "The small measured changes in solar output and variations from one decade to the next are only on the order of a fraction of a percent," Michael Mann, a climate scientist from Penn State University has explained. While Robertson is entitled to his views on global warming, he is not an expert on the topic. His statements may hold authority for his many viewers, but should be treated with skepticism. Mann's comments, however, bring us to the topic of expert testimony.[4]

Expert Testimony

Expert testimony is *the judgment or opinion of a qualified specialist in a discipline about matters relevant to that discipline.* The opinion of an economist on the state of the economy, testimony from a successful director on the artistic components of a popular film, and the opinion of a cardiologist on the benefits for the heart of taking aspirin are all examples of expert testimony that might be advanced as evidence in an argument. To be reliable, expert testimony must be used to support conclusions on topics within the specialist's area of training.

In the following example, author Jason Koebler employs expert testimony to support his case regarding the rise of artificial intelligence (AI) in the arena of law. He notes that AI legal assistants—robolawyers—will manage a wide range of legal matters:

> Roland Vogl, the executive director of the Stanford Program in Law, Science and Technology, says bots will become the main entry point into the legal system: "Every legal aid group has to turn people away because there isn't time to process all of the cases . . . . Lawyers will only get involved when it's really necessary," he says.[5]

Expert testimony can also be a useful way to sum up the significance of a problem. For example, Dan Clawson and Naomi Gerstel, authors of *Caring for Our Children: Child Care in Europe and the United States,* sum up their work on the US child care system by saying that our current system represents "a fragmentary patchwork both at the level of the individual child and at the level of the overall system."[6]

Expert testimony is helpful as support when you are proposing a solution to a problem. Here is an example of expert testimony on a radical solution to global warning. The expert's credentials are provided to establish his credibility to testify on this topic.

> Russian scientist Yuri Israel, who heads the Global Climate and Ecology Institute, has proposed an unusual solution to a difficult environmental issue: intentionally burning huge amounts of sulfur in the upper atmosphere so as to "create a reflective layer that would lower the heating effect of solar radiation." His hope is that this dramatic action would prevent further global warming. Israel thinks we could use aircraft fuel enriched with sulfur and that the solution would cause "very little pollution."[7]

Special Tests of Expert Testimony

When we evaluate expert testimony, the greatest concern is the expert's qualification to testify. In some cases an individual's expertise is generally recognized; in others, expertise might have to be established before an audience will accept the expert testimony as credible. You can usually do that by stating the expert's credentials, such as training, positions held, publications, and awards. It is also important to qualify the source if any question exists about whether the audience will recognize that expert.

Testimony from an expert should be limited to questions germane to the expert's field of expertise. Expertise cannot be transferred from one arena to another. If a widely regarded psychologist hosting a national radio talk show offers his opinions on political issues, for example, his testimony about politics should be classified as lay.

Combining Testimony with Statistical Evidence

In building an argumentative case, writers and speakers often combine expert and lay testimony. Expert testimony secures a point by providing the opinion of someone who has carefully studied a situation, while lay testimony helps clarify how a problem affects ordinary people. The strongest cases make use of a variety of evidence, and thus often incorporate statistical evidence with testimony. Let's look at an example.

> The *Los Angeles Times* reported on a study showing a connection between hours spent watching television and increased risks of death from heart disease and other ailments. The study, published in *Circulation,* a journal of the American Heart Association, involved more than 8,800 men and women. Researchers found a strong connection between TV hours and increased risk of death from cardiovascular disease, even "among people who had a

healthy weight and exercised." In order to bolster the study's impact, reporter Jeannine Stein sought the expert testimony of medical professionals. Among them was Dr. Prediman K. Shah, director of the cardiology division of the Cedars-Sinai Heart Institute, who said that unused muscles trigger dangerous changes in our bodies. "If your activity is slowing down, you metabolize cholesterol less and synthesize it more," he said.[8]

Biased, Reluctant, and Unbiased Testimony

In evaluating testimony, it is important to determine the sources' relationships to the events or people that are the subjects of their testimony. In this respect, most testimony falls into one of three categories: biased, unbiased, or reluctant.

Biased testimony, sometimes called "interested testimony," is *testimony from individuals who stand to gain if what they say is accepted.* A biased witness has an interest or a stake in whether his or her testimony is taken to be reliable. For example, a defendant stands to gain if his denial of committing a crime is accepted as true, so his testimony is biased. Similarly, a company that advertises that its light bulbs are "the best on the market" is also an interested witness regarding the quality of its own light bulbs.

The designations "interested" and "biased" testimony do not by themselves mean that the testimony is unreliable, though they do mean that the testimony should be viewed with some suspicion and accepted only after careful efforts at verification. We should ask of any testimony, expert or lay, whether the individuals testifying will benefit from their testimony being accepted as true.

Conversely, witnesses may stand to lose something—money, freedom, reputation— if their testimony is accepted. For example, if my testimony about a coworker means that I may be socially ostracized, I stand to lose if it is accepted as true. *Testimony from sources who will lose something as a result of their testimony* is called **reluctant testimony.** Reluctant testimony is not necessarily reliable, but there is a strong presumption that it is true. We tend to assume that people do not readily testify against their own self-interest.

Finally, *testimony from individuals who will neither gain nor lose if their testimony is accepted as true* is called **unbiased testimony.** If an accountant is called as an expert witness and testifies that the financial records of an individual on trial for fraud do not indicate any suspicious activity, we would assume that the accountant has nothing to gain or lose if the testimony is accepted as true. If, however, we were to discover that the accountant is related to the defendant, we would have to consider any testimony offered as biased or interested. For example, health researcher Robert Green appeared to be offering unbiased testimony about how genetic testing may affect the insurance industry. Commenting on whether people are more likely to purchase long-term health insurance if they discover they carry a gene associated with Alzheimer's disease, he replied: "It would be a natural thing that people might consider if they find out that they are at an increased risk for Alzheimer's disease." Indeed, people are five times more likely to purchase such insurance when they find they carry such a gene.[9]

When evaluating lay or expert testimony, we should first determine whether the source is biased. If a source is likely to be biased, we should accept the testimony only with caution, if at all. Unbiased and reluctant sources can be accepted with fewer reservations, though the accuracy of their testimony should still be assessed by a comparison to known facts where possible.

Any one of these three types of testimony may be independent—meaning that it is from a single source—or concurrent. **Concurrent testimony** is *testimony that is* *consistent with other available sources of testimony on the topic.* Though concurrent testimony is not always more reliable than uncorroborated testimony from an individual, an audience usually presumes that testimony is less reliable when it conflicts with other testimony. When testimony conflicts, we must determine what the majority of testimony tends to indicate.

As noted in our discussion of external consistency in Chapter 6, sound expert testimony is usually consistent with the views of other specialists in the field. It is almost always possible to find an expert to support a point of view. If many other experts in the area contradict the testimony of an authority, however, that person's testimony is called into question. Concurrence tends to strengthen the credibility of both expert and lay testimony.

GUIDELINES FOR USING TESTIMONY AS EVIDENCE

Following are some guidelines for using testimony as evidence in your own arguments.

1. Quote sources accurately. If you paraphrase, always indicate clearly that you are doing so. Have the original source ready in case someone asks you to produce it.

2. Identify your sources. Let your audience know whom you are quoting and where you found the testimony.

3. Use credible sources. Whether you are using expert or lay testimony, make sure your sources are well qualified and have appropriate credentials.

4. Qualify the source. If any doubt exists about the source's credibility, state the source's credentials as an expert or establish the credibility of ordinary sources.

5. Use biased sources with caution. A biased source may be unreliable. Audiences will be suspicious of sources they know to be biased.

6. Be brief. A brief quotation that makes the point is better than a long quotation that requires interpretation or otherwise makes more demands on an audience.

CHAPTER REVIEW

Testimony can come either from lay witnesses or from experts. Testimony may be biased, reluctant, or unbiased, depending on whether the people testifying have an interest in the issue at hand, and depending on the depth and type of their involvement. When evaluating testimony, we should consider the expert's qualifications to testify, as well as the consistency of witnesses with one another and with other evidence.

EXERCISES

A.   Which of the following are examples of expert testimony and which of lay testimony? When is concurrent testimony being advanced? Indicate whether the sources should be considered biased, unbiased, or reluctant.

   1. "The increasing use of active sonar by militaries around the world threatens the survival of numerous marine species, including entire populations of whales and porpoises," according to Frederick O'Reagan, president of the International Fund for Animal Welfare, an animal rights organization that has been heavily involved with efforts to protect sea mammals from the effects of marine technology.[10]

2. A local high school has had problems with students getting sick during classes. Some teachers suspect that a newly installed insulation material may be causing the symptoms, which include headaches, nausea, and coughing. After sampling the air in the classrooms, two environmental toxicologists hired by the school board, with the consent of the teachers' union, testify that "the insulation in the school building is safe and could not be causing the sicknesses."

3. You testify in court that a recently deceased eccentric millionaire signed a note leaving you $6 million after you helped him to change a flat tire that had stranded him in a Nevada desert.

4. Three independent handwriting experts, called by the court and not associated with clients on either side of the case, testify in court that a recently deceased eccentric millionaire signed a note leaving you $6 million.

5. Daniel Freeman of the Institute of Psychiatry at University College London says that the number of paranoid people is increasing every year. Freeman states that one in four members of the general public has paranoid thoughts on a regular basis. "These days, we daren't let our children play outside. We're suspicious of strangers. Security cameras are everywhere."[11]

6. Several followers of a faith healer testify that they have seen him heal people with terminal illnesses.

7. A recent report from ACT indicated that "only about half of this year's high school students have the reading skills they need to succeed in college, and even fewer are prepared for college-level science and math courses." Richard L. Ferguson, chief executive of ACT, said: "It is very likely that hundreds of thousands of [high school] students will have a disconnect between their plans for college and the cold reality of their preparation for college."[12]

8. Professor Noel Sharkey of the University of Sheffield's Department of Computer Science will speak to a group of international leaders in May. His topic is the increasing use of fully autonomous weapons in battle. The so-called "killer robots" are redefining warfare and introducing new risks to civilian populations. "If we do not put an end to this trend for automating warfare . . . ," he says, "we could face a very bleak future where machines are delegated with the decision to kill humans."[13]

9. A widely respected reporter for a major newspaper writes an editorial column critical of the paper's decision to install a caller ID phone system that allows the paper to identify all callers to the newspaper and thus, according to the reporter, "compromises reporting by violating the crucial principle of source anonymity."

10. Richard Schmidt, a psychologist who works as an auto industry consultant, is an expert on human motor skills. Schmidt argues that the problem of sudden acceleration is typically caused by drivers: "When the driver says they have their foot on the brake, they are . . . wrong. The human motor system is not perfect, and it doesn't always do what it is told."[14]

ENDNOTES

[1]Cecilia Kang and Ashley Halsey III, "US Considers Cellphones on Flights but No Calls," *The Washington Post: Technology,* December 12, 2013, http://www.washingtonpost.com/business /technology/us-considers-cell-phones-on-flights-but-no-calls/2013/12/12/17b171ec-635e-11e3 -aa81-e1dab1360323_story.html.

[2]Jon Hamilton, "Shortage of Brain Tissue Hinders Autism Research," *National Public Radio Health News,* February 4, 2013, http://www.npr.org/blogs/health/2013/02/04/170835708/shortage-of -brain-tissue-sets-autism-research-back.

[3]Shari Roan, "Mother Load Deferred," *Concord* (N.H.) *Monitor,* August 14, 2005, http://www .concordmonitor.com/apps/pbcs.dll/article?AID=/20050814/REPOSITORY/508140390/1022 /LIVING02.

[4]David Edward, "Pat Robertson: Global Warming a Hoax because No SUVs on Mars," *The Raw Story,* April 17, 2012, http://www.rawstory.com/rs/2012/04/17/pat-robertson-global-warming -a-hoax-because-no-suvs-on-mars.

[5]Jason Koebler, "Rise of the Robolawyers," *The Atlantic,* April 2017, 27.

[6]Quoted in "US Child Care Seriously Lags behind that of Europe," *American Sociological Association News,* November 18, 2002, http://www2.asanet.org/media/childcare.html.

[7]Mosnews (Russian news source), November 30, 2005, http://www.mosnews.com/news/2005/11/30.

[8]Quoted in Jeannine Stein, "Watching TV Shortens Life Span, Study Finds," *Los Angeles Times,* January 12, 2010.

[9]David Schultz, "It's Legal for Some Insurers to Discriminate Based on Genes," January 17, 2013, National Public Radio, http://www.npr.org/blogs/health/2013/01/17/169634045/some-types-of -insurance-can-discriminate-based-on-genes.

[10]"European Parliament Calls for Halt to High Intensity Naval Sonar Use," Natural Resource Defense Fund, October 2004, http://www.nrdc.org/media/pressreleases/041028a.asp.

[11]Quoted in Rosie Mestel, "Paranoid? Me? Who Said So?" *Los Angeles Times,* October 21, 2008, http://latimesblogs.latimes.com/booster_shots/2008/10/paranoid-me-who.html.

[12]Quoted in Tamar Lewin, "Many Going to College Aren't Ready, Report Finds," *The New York Times,* August 17, 2005.

[13]"Robotics Experts to Debate 'Killer Robots' Policies at UN," May 13, 2014, *Kurzweil Accelerating Intelligence,* http://www.kurzweilai.net/robotics-experts-to-debate-killer-robots-policies-at -un#!prettyPhoto.

[14]Quoted in Ken Bensinger and Ralph Vartabedian, "Data Point to Toyota's Throttles, Not Floor Mats," *Los Angeles Times,* November 29, 2009, http://mobile.latimes.com/inf/infomo?view =webarticle&feed:a=latimes_1min&feed:c=nationnews&feed:i=50753295&nopaging=1.

RECOMMENDED WEBSITE

Federal Rules of Evidence

Cornell University Law School

www.law.cornell.edu/rules/fre

The Cornell University Law School provides this page as a review of federal rules of evidence and its admissibility during a trial. Articles VI through VIII address questions of testimony, and are worth reading through to see how testimonial evidence is treated in courtroom settings.

IV

Validity:
The Structure of
Arguments

10

Validity in Conditional and Enumeration Arguments

"Contrariwise," continued Tweedledee, "if it was so, it might be;
if it were so, it would be; but as it isn't, it ain't. That's logic."
Lewis Carroll (1832–1898)
British mathematician and author

There are two kinds of people in this world—
those who believe there are two kinds of people, and those who don't.
Robert Benchley (1889–1945)
United States humorist

KEY TERMS

antecedent

argument from direction

conditional argument

conditional statement

consequent

dilemma

disjunctive argument

enumeration argument

exclusive disjuncts

false dilemma

inclusive disjuncts

modus ponens

modus tollens

necessary condition

premise

slippery slope argument

sufficient condition

You are having a conversation with a friend who considers herself a misunderstood artist. "I learned in my art history class today," she says, "that all of the great geniuses of the art world have been misunderstood. And," she adds, "I know that I am misunderstood, so I am beginning to think that I am a genius. What do you think?" You now find yourself in an awkward position, for even if your friend *is* a genius, she cannot arrive at that conclusion based on the reasons she was using. Why not? The problem with her reasoning brings us to the concept of validity, the first of three general criteria of reasonable arguments. Though her two reasons may be true—that great artistic geniuses tend to be misunderstood, and that she is misunderstood—the conclusion that she is a genius simply doesn't follow.

Chapter 5 introduced validity as a concern for the structure or form of an argument, the connections between reasons and conclusions. In this chapter we will examine the form underlying two of the more common types of reasoning, which we will call conditional and enumerative. We will consider the rules of validity for each of these widely used approaches to reasoning. Along the way we will also look at a few special types of arguments that employ these structures.

VALIDITY IN CONDITIONAL REASONING

A **conditional argument** is *an argument built around an "if-then" statement or an equivalent.* Another common term for such an argument is "hypothetical syllogism."

We will refer to *the if-then statement in a conditional argument* as the **conditional statement.** We sometimes use the term **premises** for *the reasons in conditional arguments, as well as in the enumerative and categorical arguments* discussed in this chapter and the next. Evaluating the validity of a conditional argument is not difficult, but it does require familiarity with the components of these arguments. Consider this common conditional statement:

If you study hard, then you will succeed in college.

The conditional statement has two parts—a clause following "if" and a clause following "then." *The "if" clause in a conditional statement* is called the **antecedent.** The term "antecedent" simply means "that which comes before." The antecedent in the example is:

If you study hard,

The "then" clause in a conditional statement is called the **consequent,** *an event that follows from or is a result of another event.* The consequent in the example is:

then you will succeed in college.

All conditional statements have these two parts—an antecedent and a consequent. Here is another example of a conditional statement:

If the rains are delayed in that region of the country, then the crops will fail.

Testing Validity in a Conditional Argument

Notice that a conditional statement by itself is not a complete argument. To make a conditional statement part of a complete argument, it must be accompanied by another reason that tells us something about its antecedent or its consequent. If this second reason claims that part of the statement is or will be true, the reason is said to *affirm* that clause. Let's add a second reason to the conditional statement above that affirms part of the statement:

If the rains had been delayed in that region of the country, then the crops would have failed.

The rains were delayed.

This second reason affirms the first half, or antecedent, of the conditional statement. That is, it says the first half of the statement is true.

Once we have this second reason in place, it is easy to see what the conclusion of the argument should be:

If the rains had been delayed in that region of the country, then the crops would have failed.

The rains were delayed.

Thus, the crops failed.

If the second reason claims that one clause of the conditional statement is or will be false, it is said to deny that clause. We can add a second reason that denies one part of the same conditional statement:

FIGURE 10.1 Structure of a Conditional Argument

A conditional argument has three components:
1. Conditional statement
   antecedent   *consequent*
   If . . . ,   then . . . .
2. Second reason
3. Conclusion

> If the rains had been delayed in that region of the country, then the crops would have failed.
>
> The crops did not fail.

As before, once this second reason is in place it is easy to discover the argument's conclusion:

> If the rains had been delayed in that region of the country, then the crops would have failed.
>
> The crops did not fail.
>
> Thus, the rains were not delayed in that region of the country.

A conditional argument proceeds in one of these two basic ways—by affirming or denying one half of its conditional statement.

In order to become more familiar with this idea of affirming and denying parts of the conditional statement, let's look at another example. The following argument affirms the antecedent of the conditional statement with which we started the chapter. Here is the same conditional statement again, this time with its antecedent and consequent marked:

> **conditional statement**
>
> *antecedent*   *consequent*
> If you study hard, then you will succeed in college.

Now we will add a second reason that affirms the antecedent of the conditional statement.

> **second reason**
> And you are studying hard.

At this point we are ready to add the conclusion that follows from these two reasons:

> **conclusion**
> So, you will succeed.

Notice that the second reason, "And you are studying hard," refers back to, or repeats, the language of the antecedent, "If you study hard." Notice also that this second reason affirms the antecedent: it says it is true. This is the first type of valid conditional argument, one that affirms the antecedent. The first rule for valid conditional arguments is:

1. Affirming the antecedent creates a valid conditional argument. This method of reasoning is traditionally called ***modus ponens*** (meaning "*mode that affirms*").

Let's alter the example we started with a bit in order to discover the second way of constructing a valid conditional argument:

> If you study hard, then you will succeed in college. But you are not succeeding in college, so you are not studying hard.

Notice that in this example the second reason refers back to, or repeats, the language of the consequent of the conditional statement. Notice also that this argument's second reason does not affirm the consequent. Rather, it denies the consequent, or says it is *not* true. This is the second type of valid conditional argument, and we can express its form in this rule:

2. Denying the consequent creates a valid conditional argument. This method is traditionally called ***modus tollens*** (meaning "*mode that denies*").

To review, the two rules of validity for a conditional argument are that the argument must either:

1. Affirm the antecedent

or

2. Deny the consequent

Remember that these rules are applied to the second reason in the argument, not to its conclusion.

These two rules have to do only with the validity of the argument: its form or structure as it moves from reasons to conclusion. The rules of validity tell us nothing, for example, about whether the argument exhibits support, that is, has adequate evidence. Testing the argument's form does not tell us whether it is true that studying hard results in success in college—though we often hear that it does, and most people assume some connection between the two events. Again, validity is a concern for an argument's form, while support is a concern for its content.

To this point we have established that affirming the antecedent and denying the consequent will both produce valid conditional arguments. Just as there are two forms of valid conditional arguments, there are two faulty or fallacious ways of constructing a conditional argument. As you may have guessed, these faulty forms are the reverse of the valid forms.

Affirming the antecedent resulted in a valid conditional argument, but *denying the antecedent* results in a faulty conditional argument. Let's look at an example of this error in validity. Here is the conditional statement we started with:

conditional statement

antecedent   *consequent*

If you study hard, then you will succeed in college.

Now, rather than affirming the antecedent in the second reason, let's deny it, that is, say it is not true:

second reason

You are *not* studying hard.

Denying this reason results in the following conclusion:

conclusion

So you will *not* succeed in college.

This argument is invalid, even though it may look reasonable. Why is a conditional argument that denies its antecedent invalid? To answer this question, we need to take another look at the conditional statement we started with.

> If you study hard, then you will succeed in college.

Notice what this conditional statement says and does not say. It says that studying hard leads to success in college, but it does *not* say that studying hard is the *only way* to succeed in college. In other words, the statement does not rule out the possibility that someone might succeed on the basis of sheer talent without hard work. As a result, this statement does not allow the conclusion that, because someone is not studying hard, they will not succeed in college.

Another invalid argument starts with the same conditional statement:

> If you study hard, then you will succeed in college.

Then, it adds this second reason:

> You are succeeding.

And it draws this conclusion:

> So, you must be studying hard.

This argument is not valid. It is said to affirm its consequent, which will not result in a sound connection between the reasons and the conclusion. The conditional statement does not say that studying hard is the *only* way to succeed. It simply states that studying hard will certainly lead to success.

Maintaining Consistent Wording

Chapter 5 discusses linguistic consistency as a criterion of reasonable arguments. As in other kinds of arguments, the wording must remain consistent throughout a conditional argument or a false conclusion might be drawn from what appears to be a valid argument.

An example will help to illustrate how this problem of inconsistent wording can be hard to detect. Notice the slight shift of wording as we move from the conditional statement to the conclusion in the following argument:

> If evolution occurred, then God is not required for life to exist.
>
> Evolution did occur.
>
> So God does not exist.

This change in wording actually affects the argument's substance; that is, it significantly alters the meaning of a key phrase. The conditional statement in this example states if evolution occurred, this fact would eliminate the requirement for God to bring life into existence. It does not, however, state that if evolution occurred, this fact would disprove God's existence. In fact, the conditional statement does not say anything about whether God exists. The conclusion, however, shifts the wording to this second and stronger claim, which was not conveyed in the original conditional statement's consequent.

With consistent phrasing, our example argument would look like this:

> If evolution occurred, then God is not required for life to exist.
>
> Evolution did occur.
>
> So God is not required for life to exist.

Recall, again, that deciding that an argument is valid does not tell us anything about whether the argument's reasons are true.

Negative Conditions

Conditional statements can set up negative relationships between events, as well as positive relationships. Let's consider an example of a conditional statement that sets up negative conditions:

If you do *not* study hard, then you will *not* succeed in college.

The rules of validity still apply to such negatively phrased arguments. Affirming the antecedent of the conditional statement, for example, yields the following valid argument:

conditional statement

antecedent   *consequent*

If you do *not* study hard, then you will *not* succeed in college.

second reason

You are *not* studying hard.

conclusion

So you will *not* succeed in college.

Notice that affirming the antecedent in the second reason results in the negative statement: "You are *not* studying hard." This is because we are affirming, or saying that it is true, that you did *not* study.

What about denying the consequent of a negatively phrased conditional statement, our other valid procedure? Here is what the argument looks like with the consequent denied:

conditional statement

antecedent   *consequent*

If you do *not* study hard, then you will *not* succeed in college.

second reason

You *are* succeeding in college.

conclusion

So you must be studying hard.

Notice that in this example, which is a valid argument, *denying* a negative statement results in the *positive* assertion: "You are succeeding in college."

Special Cases of Negative Conditionals

There are a few special cases of conditional statements. We often set up a conditional statement using the word "unless" in place of the phrase "if not." Whatever follows the word "unless" in a conditional statement must be treated as the antecedent, even though it may come as the second part of the conditional statement. Consider the following conditional statement as an example:

consequent   *antecedent*

You will *not* succeed *unless* you study hard.

This statement should be read as saying:

> *antecedent*   *consequent*
> If you do *not* study hard, then you will *not* succeed.

The word "unless" affects only the antecedent of the conditional statement, rendering it negative. It does not have any effect on the consequent.

Another phrase, though, "only if," makes both the antecedent and the consequent negative. It must be read as if it means "if not . . . then not." The phrase "only if" affects both the antecedent and the consequent: it renders both the antecedent and the consequent negative. Here is an example:

> *consequent*   *antecedent*
> You will succeed in college *only if* you study hard.

This is the same statement as:

> *antecedent*   *consequent*
> If you do *not* study hard, then you will *not* succeed.

Notice that the antecedent is still the phrase that follows the word "if." It will help in testing the argument's validity to move the antecedent, the "if not" phrase, to the beginning of the conditional statement where it belongs.

Here is another example of a conditional statement that uses the phrase "only if":

> *consequent*
> A cure for Alzheimer's will be developed
>
> *antecedent*
> *only if* we put serious funding behind the research effort.

This statement should be translated into the statement:

> *antecedent*
> If we do *not* put serious funding behind the research effort,
>
> *consequent*
> then a cure for Alzheimer's will *not* be developed.

Notice that "only if" affects both the antecedent and the consequent. Remember that the clause following "if" is always the antecedent, whether it appears first or last in the statement.

Necessary and Sufficient Conditions

As we have seen, conditional statements express a causal relationship between two events. Such relationships are sometimes described as being either "sufficient" or "necessary" conditions.

A **sufficient condition** is *a condition that will bring about another event*. In the following example, the antecedent is a sufficient condition for the consequent:

If that animal is a whale, then it is a mammal.

This conditional statement says that being a whale is a sufficient condition for being a mammal. If "being a whale" is the case, then "being a mammal" also must be the case.

The antecedents of positively phrased conditional statements identify sufficient conditions for the events described in their consequents. Here are some additional examples of conditional statements whose antecedents set up sufficient conditions for the events described in their consequents:

> If Jenn was a member of the military, then she is eligible for financial aid.
>
> If the Tigers win their last game this season, then they will be in the playoffs.
>
> If the temperature rises another ten degrees, then we will be faced with a life-threatening weather emergency.

Now, what about the necessary condition relationship? A **necessary condition** is *a condition without which another event cannot occur.* Negatively phrased conditional statements identify necessary conditions. So, for example:

> If it is *not* a mammal, then it is *not* a whale.
>
> It is not a mammal.
>
> So it is not a whale.

This conditional argument says that being a mammal is a necessary condition for being a whale. That is, in the absence of the quality of being a mammal, we will also expect the absence of the quality of being a whale. More conditions must be in place before we would call a mammal a whale, but without this quality—being a mammal— an animal will not be identified as a whale.

Here are some other conditional statements that set up necessary conditions in their antecedents for the events described in their consequents. Notice that these statements only make claims about something that will not occur if the antecedent condition is not fulfilled:

> If Fran is not a certified technician, he cannot join the maintenance team.
>
> If the new tax measure is not passed, the community pool will not open on time.
>
> If the stock market does not recover, we will not move ahead with the merger.

Conditional reasoning is common in all areas of public and private discussion. It occurs virtually any time that we are reasoning about causes and effects, that is, when we are thinking about which events will bring about other events.

The Argument from Direction: A Special Case of Conditional Reasoning

The basic structure of a conditional argument is apparent in several specific types of argument that are common to public discourse. One of these is the **argument from direction,** *an argument that strings together two or more conditional statements to predict a remote result from a first step.* The rules of validity for arguments from direction are the same as the rules for simple conditional arguments.

Here is an example of the argument from direction:

> If you cut taxes by 1 or 2 percent on low income–housing developers during the current building surge, you cut their incentive of a federal tax credit for producing low-income housing. If these developers lose interest in the tax credit, they will move on to more profitable projects, leaving thousands of units unfinished that are already started. Therefore, it is important not to cut taxes on these developers in the middle of a building boom.

The conclusion of this argument from direction urges that the first step in the progression not be taken. *An argument from direction urging that the first step in a progression not be taken* is called a **slippery slope argument.**

You have likely noticed that the argument from direction actually advances a series of linked conditional arguments. Thus, these arguments have the form:

If A occurs then B will occur.

If B occurs then C will occur.

C is undesirable.

Therefore, to avoid C we should not allow A.

The argument from direction, then, involves a series of conditional claims, each of which can be tested. Each link in the conditional chain might be assessed for validity, though in most cases these arguments proceed by affirming the antecedents of each conditional link. The process is valid, though we still want to ensure that the events predicted are likely to occur. We must ask whether the conditional claims are true, as well as whether the argument is valid.

Here is another direction argument that has been part of the public debate over assisted suicide:

Allowing states to assist with the suicides of desperate patients could lead to a situation in which nonterminal patients legally choose suicide, and eventually to patients who simply suffer from mental stress opting to end their lives with a doctor's assistance.

Rewritten as two conditional claims, the argument looks like this:

1. If states are allowed to continue to assist with the suicides of desperate patients, then nonterminal patients will be able to legally choose suicide.

2. If nonterminal patients can legally choose suicide, then patients who simply suffer from mental stress eventually may opt to end their lives with the assistance of a doctor.

If these claims are true (which they may not be), once the first condition is satisfied, the others are expected to follow. Thus, in conditional arguments, as in other arguments, we must ask about both the accuracy of the claims and about the validity of the argument.

Now that we have covered the basic components in conditional validity, we can consider validity in a second very common type of reasoning—enumerative reasoning.

VALIDITY IN ENUMERATIVE REASONING

Federal Aviation Administration officials were seeking to discover the cause of a recent airliner crash. Witnesses on the ground reported hearing an explosion prior to the airplane's crash. The flight recorder seemed to confirm this possibility. The FAA officials began with what seemed the three most likely causes: an engine malfunction, the accidental explosion of a substance onboard the plane, and a terrorist's bomb. Examination of the airliner's engines showed no evidence of explosion or malfunction. Moreover, the plane was not carrying explosive substances, according to cargo records. Therefore, investigators concluded that a bomb was the most likely cause of the airplane's destruction.

The FAA officials were employing a method of reasoning called enumeration. An **enumeration argument** is *an argument that sets out alternative explanations or options and then follows a process of elimination.* Enumeration is common when alternative solutions to a problem are being considered or when one of several actions is being urged. As we will see in Chapter 15, enumeration arguments are also used when the causes of events are being sought.

Let's take a closer look at the structure of enumeration arguments. The argument above has the form:

> A or B or C.
>
> Not A and not B.
>
> Therefore, C.

Here is an example of enumerative structure in an argument about managing asteroids that threaten the Earth:

> Experts are now calling for a plan to deal with the threat of asteroids hurtling toward Earth. Plans advanced to this point include nuclear weapons detonated near the asteroid, ion propulsion vehicles that would capture the asteroid and redirect its course, and lasers fired from satellites that would destroy the asteroid. Advanced ion propulsion technology is years, if not decades, away, and satellite-mounted lasers do not at this point have sufficient range and force to destroy a large asteroid. This leaves the nuclear option, which requires a year's notice to launch and intercept the threatening asteroid with a nuclear-tipped projectile.

Testing Validity in Enumeration Arguments

Valid enumeration arguments typically proceed by eliminating or "denying" possibilities until one or none is left. Invalid enumeration arguments tend to affirm possibilities in their reasons and to move to denying options in their conclusion. For instance, a mechanic tells a customer:

> Your car's electrical problem is caused by a bad battery, or a bad starter, or a short in the ignition. We found a short in the ignition, so you should be okay now.

Well, as the customer discovered, the mechanic was wrong in his reasoning. The car had *both* a short *and* a bad starter. Affirming options in an enumeration argument is invalid because this approach does not account for the possibility that other enumerated alternatives may still be active options.

Here is an example of a valid enumeration argument. Notice that it proceeds by denying alternatives, and concludes with an affirmation.

> The administration has three options for responding to the latest aggressions in the Middle East—air strikes, cruise missile attacks, and troops on the ground. Cruise missile strikes are unlikely because they do not show sufficient resolve and involve too little actual risk. Troop deployments, on the other hand, are too risky, as they could involve direct fighting between US troops and already deployed Russian forces. So, the most likely response is air strikes against selected targets.

Testing the Enumerated Options

Enumeration arguments have a built-in potential for misuse because they allow the advocate to establish two important points for the audience. First, the advocate establishes how many options the audience faces. Second, the advocate determines which of these options is acceptable. Because these arguments potentially give the advocate a measure of control over an audience's decision-making, it is important to point out that the options in any enumeration argument must be tested by asking two questions. These questions, then, also suggest possible rebuttals of enumerative arguments.

The first of these questions is:

1. Have all the plausible options been identified? Note that the test says "all *plausible* options." Advocates are not responsible to account for every conceivable or far-fetched alternative, only those that are reasonable possibilities.

For example, in trying to determine the cause of a sudden downturn in the economy, economists will consider possibilities such as a rise in unemployment, rumors about an increase in interest rates, or consumer confidence being shaken by a terrorist act. However, if someone were to suggest that the cause was astrological, that the stars were improperly aligned, it would not be reasonable to ask economists to seriously consider this option.

The test of asking whether all plausible options have been eliminated suggests a possible rebuttal for an enumeration argument. We can always identify a previously unidentified, yet plausible option. For instance, perhaps a recent natural disaster has had a dramatic effect on consumer confidence.

The second question we should ask of the options in an enumerative argument is:

2. Have all rejected options been convincingly eliminated? If an option that an advocate treats as eliminated is actually still viable, the conclusion of an enumeration argument is suspect. In the example above regarding the economy, perhaps the possibility that consumer confidence was shaken by rumors of an interest rate increase was not carefully eliminated as a possible cause of the economic slowdown. If so, one strategy of rebuttal is to point out that this possible cause is still a reasonable option for consideration.

Disjunctives and Dilemmas

Two closely related types of enumeration argument deserve special attention, both because they are so common in public discourse and because they can easily be confused with one another.

Disjunctives

A **disjunctive argument** is *an argument that presents limited options: two enumerated alternatives, or disjuncts, often marked by an "either/or" statement.* Because of their simplicity and clarity, disjunctive arguments provide an appealing, and thus very common, form of enumerative reasoning.

Here is a brief example of a disjunctive argument derived from a medical diagnosis.

> The symptoms you are describing might be caused by either an allergy to milk or by low levels of thyroid hormone. The lab reports indicate that your thyroxin levels are slightly below normal. Therefore, we are going to proceed with a prescription for synthetic thyroxin and cancel the test for milk allergies.

A disjunctive statement is made up of two disjuncts. In our example, they are:

1. Either you have a milk allergy.
2. Or you have low levels of thyroxin.

This example is of a pair of **inclusive disjuncts,** *two alternatives that might both be true at the same time.* While it would seem reasonable to assume that the patient is not suffering from *both* maladies, it is possible that he is. Affirming that the problem is low levels of thyroxin does not rule out the possibility of a concurrent milk allergy. Thus, the only valid procedure is to deny one of the two options before affirming the other one in the conclusion. This last statement implies that affirming one disjunct and denying the other in the conclusion is *not* valid. As we have seen, the truthfulness of one option in a disjunctive argument does not rule out the possibility of the other; they both might be true.

In a valid disjunctive argument, the structure of the argument ensures that if the reasons are true, the conclusion follows from those reasons. As with other enumeration arguments, the disjuncts must account for all the plausible options and the rejected disjunct must be eliminated convincingly.

The other major category of disjunction is **exclusive disjuncts,** that is, *two alternatives that cannot both be true at the same time.* For example,

> NCAA regulations stipulate equal spending on men's and women's sports programs. Our athletic budget is currently at its maximum limit as established by the board of trustees, so a decision to add a men's lacrosse team would mean eliminating women's volleyball. Unfortunately, we can't support both teams. We have decided to continue the women's volleyball program, and therefore we will not add men's lacrosse to the school's athletic program.

This example involves exclusive disjuncts—the presence of one of the enumerated options means the absence of the other. In such cases, affirming a disjunct is valid. Notice also that this example does not employ the words "either" and "or," though they are implied: either men's lacrosse or women's volleyball, but not both.

Dilemmas

A **dilemma** is simply *a strategy of argument that forces a choice between limited and undesirable options.* Dilemmas often employ disjunctive structures. The economist John Kenneth Galbraith's humorous definition of politics, in a letter he wrote to President John F. Kennedy, provides a good example. Politics, Galbraith wrote, "consists in choosing between the disastrous and the unpalatable."[1] Because the unpalatable is preferable to the disastrous, it is the obvious path.

The dilemma argument is often used when an audience may be reluctant to accept an option being advocated. A speaker or writer in such a circumstance may develop a dilemma to press the audience toward a difficult choice. Here is an example of a speaker advocating nuclear power before an audience that has reservations about the idea. A dilemma is employed to set nuclear power against a less desirable alternative.

> The options we face are nuclear power or dramatic climate change. I know some of you are uncomfortable with the nuclear power option because of problems such as nuclear waste storage. But when you get some idea of the dangers of climate change, you will realize that it is a much worse option than nuclear energy.

A dilemma argument that uses artificially limited options to mislead an audience is called the fallacy of **false dilemma.** Here is an example:

> One side or the other is going to win in this conflict, whether or not we are pleased with either. Admittedly, both sides seem willing to disregard basic human rights. But we must back the one most likely to work for our interests in the region, and that means sending aid to the Democratic Front.

The speaker argues as if the audience faces only two options, but what about the third option of not helping either side? Or would it be possible to end the conflict through urging each side to negotiate? Notice how the speaker resolves the dilemma for the audience by suggesting which of the limited options they should select and why.

In some cases, dilemmas are employed to reveal the gravity of a situation, to make the point that no good options are available. For instance, a newscaster reflecting on a politician's recent actions states, "Either he's that dumb, or he really doesn't know the law. I'm not sure which is scarier." The point of the dilemma seems to be that there is no good way of explaining the politician's decision.

CHAPTER REVIEW

Validity is a concern for an argument's form or structure—the relationships of reasons to other reasons, and of reasons to conclusions. When reasons in an argument are connected properly to one another and to their conclusion, the argument is valid.

Validity must take account of the type of argument being advanced. Two common forms of deductive reasoning are conditional and enumeration arguments.

Conditional arguments employ an "if-then" statement or some equivalent. The "if" clause expresses the antecedent. The "then" clause expresses the consequent. A valid conditional argument affirms the antecedent in the second reason or denies the consequent.

The chapter also discussed necessary and sufficient conditions. Necessary conditions are conditions without which some other event will not occur. Sufficient conditions are conditions under which some other event will occur.

Enumeration arguments set out alternative accounts of an event or action, then eliminate alternatives until one or none is left. The disjunctive argument, one type of enumeration argument, operates on the basis of an "either-or" reason that sets out alternative causes or possibilities. When all the alternatives have been set out, a valid disjunctive argument denies one of its disjuncts and affirms the other in its conclusion. Dilemmas are strategies of argument that advance undesirable disjuncts. The goal of a dilemma is to force a choice between these undesirable alternatives. Dilemmas often employ disjunctive structures.

EXERCISES

A. For each of the following conditional arguments, indicate which statement serves as the conditional statement, which as the second reason, and which as the conclusion. Put the conditional statement in its "if-then" form if necessary. State whether the argument affirms or denies its antecedent or consequent. Indicate whether the argument is valid or invalid.

> **1.** If our administrators were well trained, then our schools would be among the best. Our schools are not among the best, so our administrators must not be well trained.

2. Local government will not improve unless people get involved. People are getting more involved, so I'm sure we'll see improvements.

3. The government said it would intervene only if problems arose in the region. Problems arose, so the government intervened.

4. If this is a genuine Picasso, it will exhibit his careful attention to form. It does exhibit such careful attention to form, so it must be a genuine work of the master.

5. We know that when food supplies are short in the southern part of a country, the residents flee to the north. Food supplies now are quite short in the south, so we can expect a crush of refugees to the north within the month.

B.   Each example in this exercise is a dilemma, an enumeration argument, or an argument from direction. Identify the type of argument advanced in each of the following.

1. Giving loans to Third World countries leaves them with a crippling debt that they can never pay off. The effort to pay off interest on the debt leads to further borrowing and deeper debt. The lending nations are left with bad debts. Their economies suffer as a result. Thus, it would be better not to make loans to Third World countries.

2. A nation's value system can be derived from one of three sources: a common religion, a general culture, or a unifying statement of citizen rights. The United States has not had a common religion for a long time and we no longer can claim to have a culture common to most of our citizens. Thus, the Constitution remains our only source for common, unifying values.

3. It is not abortion itself that I oppose but, rather, the principle it introduces. It legitimizes the notion that a society can terminate unwanted human life. This principle, once accepted, can be extended and applied to a wide variety of potentially "unwanted" human life. The aged, the terminally ill, the handicapped—in another time, perhaps even members of a despised race or religious faith—all these people are at risk.

4. It costs $32,000 a year to keep a prisoner in prison, and $4,000 to manage the same prisoner on probation. Thus, though releasing criminals is unpopular with voters, it is more cost-effective than simply keeping them in prison for long periods of time.

5. Macroevolution—evolution from one species to another—has never been observed, nor has it been produced by natural mutations, nor by induced mutations. Macroevolution, therefore, is not scientifically verifiable.

6. Due to the controversy surrounding the crowd size for events held on the National Mall in Washington, DC, the National Park Service—the government agency that oversees all activities on the Mall—has stated that it will no longer provide estimates of crowd size. Opponents of the decision have responded that the only way to resolve ongoing conflicts over crowd size is for the Park Service to supply accurate numbers of those attending large events. Methods of crowd estimation are now so accurate as to be beyond dispute—except for purely political reasons. So, it is time for the Park Service to resume crowd estimation, and time for political organizations to stop disputing these estimates for their own ends.

C. Are the following disjunctive arguments valid? Explain your answers, making reference to the disjuncts as either inclusive or exclusive.

1. Either Jones will have his contract renewed or he will look for a new job. He is looking for a new job, so his contract must not have been renewed.

2. Either Ms. Garcia has forgotten the rules or she is deliberately trying to usurp the committee's authority. She is fully aware of what the rules require in these cases, so this is a deliberate attempt to circumvent the committee.

3. The planet's rings are formed of either rock or ice, and cannot be formed of both substances at the same time. We have no way of testing for ice using spectrography, but we can test for rock. Using this test we have discovered that the rings do consist of rock, so they must not be made up of ice.

4. Because of the size of the city's financial burden, the only possibilities for avoiding bankruptcy are to reduce retiree benefits or to cut back on emergency services. We have decided that cutting retiree benefits is not fair to the thousands of retirees affected, so emergency services will be cut.

D. Each of the following exhibits the same problem of enumerative reasoning discussed in this chapter. Identify the problem and explain how each argument might be answered.

1. Either we decide what the future of our nation will be by enacting strict immigration laws, or illegal immigration will decide that future for us.

2. Will you sign our petition supporting animal rights, or are you in favor of abusing animals?

ENDNOTES

[1]John Kenneth Galbraith, "Letter to President Kennedy, March 2, 1962," in *Ambassador's Journal: A Personal Account of the Kennedy Years* (Boston: Houghton Mifflin, 1969).

RECOMMENDED WEBSITE

ChangingMinds.org

Dave Straker

http://changingminds.org/disciplines/argument/syllogisms/conditional
_syllogism.htm

http://changingminds.org/disciplines/argument/syllogisms/disjunctive
_syllogism.htm

http://changingminds.org/disciplines/argument/fallacies/false_dilemma.htm

This extensive web site discusses many of the techniques used to achieve persuasion and influence. These links are to discussions of several topics discussed in this chapter—conditional arguments, disjunctive arguments, and false dilemmas.

11 Validity in Categorical Arguments

All men are mortal.
Socrates is a man.
Therefore, Socrates is mortal.
Aristotle (384–322 BCE)
Greek philosopher

All opinions are not equal. Some are a very great deal more robust,
sophisticated and well supported in logic and argument than others.
Douglas Adams (1952–2001)
British humorist and writer

KEY TERMS

categorical argument

categorical statement

conversion

convertible statement

distributed term

end term

enthymeme

middle term

particular affirmative statement

particular negative statement

predicate term

subject term

term

universal affirmative statement

universal negative statement

The development of artificial intelligence in computers is raising some intriguing ethical issues. For example, if a computer becomes self-aware, does it then have rights? Those who answer yes to this question employ categorical reasoning, the type of reasoning discussed in this chapter:

A computer with artificial intelligence may become self-aware.

Any self-aware entity has certain basic rights.

So, computers with artificial intelligence will have rights.

A **categorical argument** (sometimes called a "categorical syllogism") is *an argument composed of three categorical statements—two statements that are its reasons, or premises, and one that is its conclusion.* A **categorical statement** is *a statement that establishes a relationship between two categories, or classes, of objects.*

This chapter explores the validity or structure of such arguments. We will consider some ways in which categorical arguments can be presented in a valid form, and also some of the structural problems that can develop as we create categorical arguments.

Let's take a closer look at how a categorical argument you might encounter in everyday discourse is constructed. Consider the following example:

> All the history teachers at City High School are tenured. Ben is a history teacher at City High School. Therefore, Ben is tenured.

Recall our earlier distinction between inductive and deductive arguments. The argument above, like all categorical arguments, is deductive. That means that if the reasons in this argument are true and if the argument is valid, the conclusion *necessarily* follows from the reasons. This particular argument is valid as it stands: its conclusion must be true if its reasons are true.

But not all arguments that have the form of a categorical argument are valid. Can you spot the mistake in reasoning in the following letter to the editor of a newspaper?

> Dear Editor:
> Your paper reported that all three members of the newly appointed Latin American trade negotiation team had financial ties to the same South American bank. It is also well known that the members of the team are members of the same political party. It seems fair to conclude that other members of the political party in question are being influenced by a foreign financial entity.

Embedded in this letter is the following invalid categorical argument:

> All members of the negotiating team are people with financial ties to a particular bank.
>
> All members of the negotiating team are members of the same political party.
>
> Thus,
>
> All members of the political party in question are people with financial ties to a particular bank.

Something is wrong with the structure of this argument. Even if its reasons are true, this argument's conclusion does not follow in a logical way from those reasons. The argument's structure is the same as the structure of the following argument:

> All the men in the van are over forty.
>
> All the men in the van are bearded.
>
> Thus,
>
> All bearded men are over forty.

These arguments exhibit a problem of validity or structure. The structural problem is obvious in the second example, but some technical understanding can help you discover similar problems when they are less obvious.

Statements in categorical arguments are of four basic types. The categorical statements we have been dealing with so far in this chapter have all been of the same type—the universal affirmative type. They are called **universal affirmative statements** because they are *statements that make a positive claim about every member of a particular category.* A statement about a category with only one member, such as the statement, "Bill is a real patriot," is also treated as a universal affirmative statement. We will use the abbreviation **UA** to mark universal affirmative statements. Later in the chapter we will consider three other types of statements that have a categorical form and show up in categorical arguments. First, though, let us explore the concept of "terms" and how they function in categorical arguments.

TERMS AND THEIR DISTRIBUTION

Each of the three statements in a categorical argument contains two terms. A **term** is *a noun or noun phrase that represents a category of objects in a categorical statement.* A term may be either a single word, such as "men," or a phrase that names a category, such as "men in the van." Terms such as "human beings," "softball players," or "hybrid cars," or phrases such as "the members of that band," "employees who work the night shift," and "former Soviet Republics" might be used as terms in a categorical statement. *The first term in a categorical statement, the subject or principal focus of the argument,* is called the **subject term.** *The second term in a categorical statement, the term that attributes or denies a quality to the members of the category represented in the subject term,* is called the **predicate term.** Here is a simple example of a categorical argument with the subject and predicate terms labeled:

> subject term   predicate term
> All / voters in the election / are / citizens of the country /. **UA**

> subject term   predicate term
> All / citizens of the country / are / persons eligible for jury duty /. **UA**

Thus

> subject term   predicate term
> The / voters in the election / are / persons eligible for jury duty /. **UA**

Notice that one term in this argument—"citizens of the country"—appears in each reason but not in the conclusion. In any categorical argument *the term that appears in both reasons and not in the conclusion* is called the **middle term.**

The other two terms—"voters in the election" and "persons eligible for jury duty"—are called the **end terms,** which are *the two terms that appear once in a reason and once in the conclusion of a categorical argument.* The role of the end terms is to connect the reasons to the conclusion in a categorical argument.

The middle term is supposed to connect two reasons to each other in a categorical argument. It can do this only when it is properly distributed. A **distributed term** is *a term that, in a statement, refers to every member of the category of objects it represents.* Consider, for example, the following statement:

> subject term   predicate term
> All / the players on the team / are / students at the school /.

The term "players on the team" is said to be distributed because it refers to every member of the category that the term names or represents—all the players on the team. The term "students at the school" is said to be undistributed because it does not refer to all the students at the school, but only to some of them; that is, the statement refers only to some members of the category that the undistributed term represents.

Universal affirmative statements always distribute their subject terms and never distribute their predicate terms. We will use the abbreviation **D** to mark a distributed term in a statement. When a term is undistributed, we will use the abbreviation **U** to mark it.

Let's take another look at an earlier example and mark the distributions of the terms in all three statements: the two reasons and the conclusion.

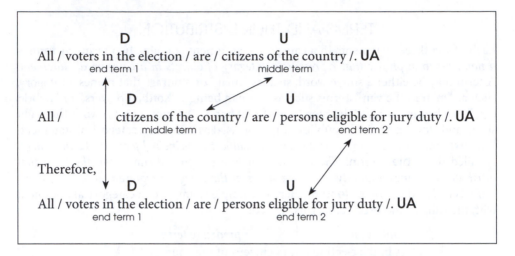

Distribution in Other Types of Statements

So far our discussion of categorical validity has focused on arguments made up of universal affirmative statements, that is, statements having the form "All A are B." Categorical arguments, however, can consist of other types of statements. Each of these four types of categorical statements has its own unique pattern of distribution, that is, its own distinct way of distributing its terms. The four general types of categorical statements, with the distribution of their terms marked, are:

	subject		*predicate*	
	D		**U**	
1. Universal affirmative:	All A	are	B.	**UA**

The subject term is distributed but the predicate term is undistributed.
            (Example: All birds are warm-blooded.)

	D		**D**	
2. Universal negative:	No A	are	B.	**UN**

Both the subject term and the predicate term are distributed.
            (Example: No birds are cold-blooded.)

	U		**U**	
3. Particular affirmative:	Some A	are	B.	**PA**

Both the subject term and the predicate term are undistributed.
            (Example: Some birds are flightless.)

	U		**D**	
4. Particular negative:	Some A	are not	B.	**PN**

The predicate term is distributed but the subject term is undistributed.
            (Example: Some birds are not songbirds.)

Notice that each of these statements distributes its subject and predicate terms in a way unique to that type of statement. These patterns of distribution do not change.

For instance, all universal negative statements have two distributed terms regardless of where the statement appears in an argument.

While we are on the subject, let's note that two rules govern whether a term is distributed in a categorical statement. If you study the examples above you will notice that:

1. The subject terms of both kinds of universal statements (universal affirmatives and universal negatives) are distributed.

2. The predicate terms of both kinds of negative statements (universal and particular negatives) are distributed.

Distribution applies whether we are making universal affirmative statements or either kind of negative statement. For instance, I might say, "All the cars in the company parking lot are cars covered with snow." Although I *do* intend to say something about every car in the company lot, I am *not* saying anything about all the cars in every parking lot in the city. Thus, the phrase or term, "cars in the company parking lot" is distributed, but the term "cars covered with snow" is not distributed. It is the case that I am speaking about every car in the company parking lot; however, there may be thousands of cars covered with snow in *other* parking lots about which I am not making any claims. Although these other cars may be covered with snow, my statement does not "cover" them.

Now, notice that if I say, "None of the cars in the company parking lot is orange," I am once again talking—by exclusion this time—about every car in that particular lot: not one of those cars is orange. Thus, the term "cars in the company parking lot" is distributed. My statement also refers to all orange cars—it says that not any of them (that is, no orange car) is in that particular lot. Strictly speaking, I am saying, "No car in the company parking lot is among *all* the orange cars that exist." In this case, then, the subject term ("cars in the company parking lot") and the predicate term ("orange cars") are both distributed. Each phrase or "term" refers to an entire category of objects—cars in the lot, and all orange cars.

Let's add one more statement to our discussion: "Some cars in the company parking lot are not blue." In this case, the term "cars in the company parking lot" is *not* distributed as it does not refer to all the cars parked there. However, the statement *does* refer to all blue cars. That is, none of the cars in the category that includes all blue cars is among some of the cars in the lot. So, in an odd way the term "blue cars" is distributed across the entire category of blue cars. I am actually saying, "Some of the cars in the company parking lot are not any members of the category that includes all blue cars."

Categorical arguments can contain statements other than universal affirmatives. That is, they may mix the different kinds of statements. Consider this argument, which combines three different types of categorical statements:

         U   U

Some / migratory birds / are / herbivorous birds /. **PA**

         D   D

No / herbivorous birds / are / birds of prey /. **UN**

Therefore

         U   D

Some / migratory birds / are not / birds of prey /. **PN**

Can you identify the middle term and end terms in this argument?

The first reason or premise in this argument is a **particular affirmative statement** (**PA**), *a claim that attributes a specified quality to only some members of a category*: "Some A (migratory birds) are B (herbivorous birds)."

The second premise or reason is a **universal negative statement** (**UN**), *a claim that denies a specified quality to every member of a category*: "No B (herbivorous birds) are C (birds of prey)."

The conclusion is a **particular negative statement** (**PN**), *a claim that denies that some members of a category possess a specified quality.* It has the form "Some A (migratory birds) are not C (birds of prey)."

Recall that a term is said to be distributed if its statement refers to every member of the category of objects that the term describes. That is why the only distributed terms are the subject terms of universal statements (universal affirmatives and universal negatives) and the predicate terms of negative statements (universal and particular negatives). Notice that the predicate of a negative statement is saying something about every member of the category. Thus, the statement:

>   **D**   **D**
> No / horses / are / reptiles /.

Is saying this:

> No member of the category "horses" is a member of the category "reptiles."

The statement completely excludes all members of one category (horses) from all members of another (reptiles). In this way, any negative statement—a universal negative or a particular negative statement—is making a claim about *all* members of its predicate category.

Notice that in the following particular affirmative statement, the members of the categories mentioned are *not* referred to in their totality:

>   **U**   **U**
> Some / boats / are / wooden objects /.

The statement does not refer to all boats, nor does it refer to all wooden objects. Thus, it has no distributed terms. It contains neither the subject of a universal statement, nor the predicate of a negative statement.

Conversion

With an understanding of distribution, we can switch the subject and predicate of a universal negative statement and find a logically equivalent statement. Thus,

>   **D**   **D**
> No / horses / are / reptiles /.

makes the same claim as the statement

>   **D**   **D**
> No / reptiles / are / horses /.

The process of switching a statement's subject and predicate terms in order to create an equivalent statement is called **conversion**. A **convertible statement** is *a statement in which the subject and predicate terms of a statement are distributed similarly.*

The other convertible statement is the particular affirmative, which has two undistributed terms. Thus, the statement

U   **U**

Some / ships / are / white /.

makes the same claim as the statement

U   **U**

Some / white objects / are / ships /.

In a universal negative statement, both terms are distributed. In a particular affirmative statement, neither the subject nor the predicate is distributed. Thus, we can say that when the distribution of subject and predicate terms in a statement is the same, the statement is convertible.

CATEGORICAL ARGUMENTS: RULES OF VALIDITY

These observations about the distribution of terms in the four different types of categorical statements lead us to the first rule of validity for categorical arguments. It has to do with the crucial middle term, the term that occurs in both reasons and thus links them to each other:

1. The middle term in a valid categorical argument must be distributed exactly once. Notice that this rule says that the middle term must be distributed once, but it also says that the middle term cannot be distributed twice. That's the reason for the phrase, "exactly once."

What if the middle term is distributed twice? Let's look at an example where this occurs:

I have noticed that environmental activists are political liberals. Moreover, these same environmental activists oppose new businesses in the area. It's pretty clear, then, that political liberals oppose new businesses.

Here we have the categorical argument:

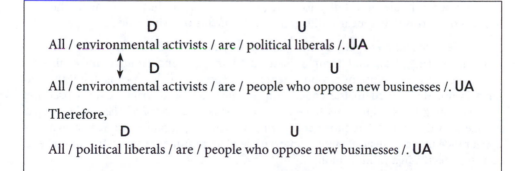

In this argument, the middle term—"environmental activists"—is distributed both times it appears. As a result, the term does not make any particular connection between the predicates of the first two statements. This argument is the same as affirming that:

All dogs are mammals.

All dogs are carnivores.

Therefore,

All mammals are carnivores.

Here's an example of an argument that distributes its middle term in the proper way, making a connection between its two reasons:

> All people with a rational fear of persecution in their home countries qualify as political refugees. All the people now arriving from Sudan have a rational fear of persecution. Hence, they all qualify as political refugees.

This argument contains the following categorical reasoning:

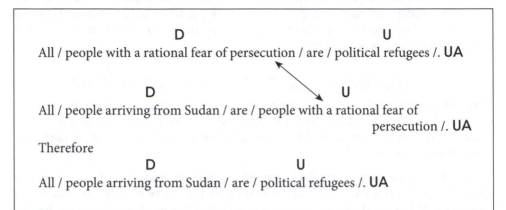

The middle term in this argument, "persons with a rational fear of persecution" is distributed in the proper way—exactly once. The argument passes the first test of validity. (Whether the reasons are accurate in what they assert is another question. Again, validity is only a test of an argument's form, not of the truthfulness or accuracy of its reasons.)

Two additional rules of validity must come into play before we can know that a categorical argument is valid. These two rules require us to look not just at reasons, but also at the conclusion.

The second rule of validity for categorical arguments has to do with the end terms—the terms that appear in the argument's conclusion. That rule is:

2. Neither end term may be distributed only once in its two appearances. This rule means that if an end term is distributed in the conclusion, it must also be distributed in the premise or reason where it first appears. It also means that if the end term is not distributed in the conclusion, it must not be distributed in a premise. Because categorical arguments have two end terms, *this test must be applied twice.* Notice also that the test requires comparing a term's appearance in a reason with its appearance in a conclusion. Here is an example of an argument that distributes its end terms correctly, in a valid fashion:

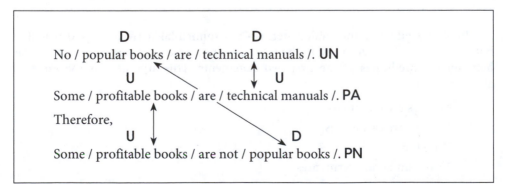

FIGURE 11.1 Validity of Categorical Arguments

> **To evaluate the validity of categorical arguments, it is important to know:**
> 1. The four types of categorical statements.
> 2. The two rules of distribution.
> 3. The three rules of validity.

In this argument the end terms are "profitable books" and "popular books." End terms are always the two terms in the conclusion. Notice that the term "profitable books" is never distributed in the argument, so it is not distributed "only once." Notice also that the term "popular books" is distributed twice, so in a different way it is also not distributed "only once."

In this example we can see that this second rule of validity must be applied twice—once to each end term. We can also see that there are two different ways to satisfy the rule—by not distributing an end term at all, or by distributing it twice.

We have one more rule to consider for categorical arguments. That rule has to do with negative statements, including the statement that is the conclusion. It is:

*3. **The number of negative premises in the argument must equal the number of negative conclusions.***[1] This rule means that when a categorical argument has a negative reason it must also have a negative conclusion in order to be valid.

Let's look at our previous example again, this time noticing that it has one negative reason and a negative conclusion:

           D   D
No / popular books / are / technical manuals /. **UN** (negative reason)

           U   U
Some / technical manuals / are / profitable books /. **PA**

Therefore,

           U   D
Some / profitable books / are not / popular books /. **PN** (negative conclusion)

This argument satisfies the third rule of validity because it has an equal number of negative reasons and conclusions. That is, it has one negative reason and one negative conclusion. Of course, the other possibility for satisfying this rule is for an argument to have no negative statements at all. In this way its number of negative reasons (zero) would equal its number of negative conclusions (zero). (A valid argument never has two negative reasons, because nothing can be concluded from two negative reasons.)

For a categorical argument to be valid—for its structure to be sound and reliable—it must pass all three of these tests. Remember that showing that an argument is valid does not by itself establish that an argument is reasonable. In addition to being valid, a reasonable argument must also meet the test of support, which means it must provide sound reasons. A reasonable argument must also exhibit linguistic consistency, that is, its definitions of key terms should be clear and consistent.

Applying the Rules of Validity

Here is an example of a categorical argument with all its terms marked according to the rules of distribution:

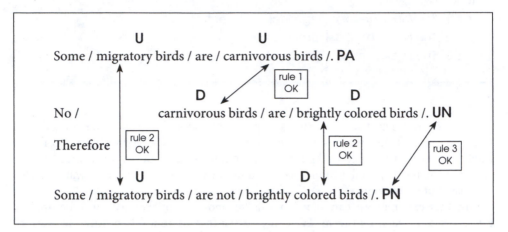

Let's test the validity of this argument, using all three rules. Applying the first test, we see that the middle term—"carnivorous birds"—is distributed exactly once. It is distributed in the second reason as the subject of a universal negative statement. So far, so good—the first rule of validity has been satisfied. We have marked the term as OK.

As for the second test—neither end term may be distributed only once—the end term "brightly colored birds" is distributed in both of its positions, and so is not distributed "only once." This end term is distributed properly. We must apply the rule to both end terms, however. The second end term—"migratory birds"—is not distributed in either of its appearances: it is not distributed at all. Thus, it also is not distributed "only once," so it adheres to the second rule. Both terms are OK.

Finally, let's apply rule three. The argument has one negative premise and one negative conclusion. It does not break the third rule, because the number of negative premises equals the number of negative conclusions.

This argument is valid, as it passes all three tests.

Using the same terms, let's modify the example to read:

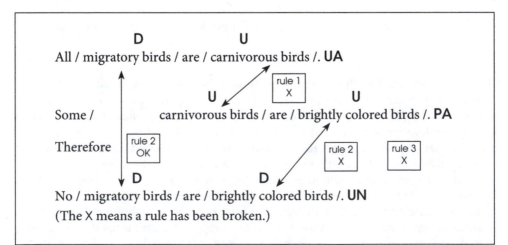

This syllogism is not valid. The middle term—"carnivorous birds"—is not distributed in either premise, and therefore does not make a connection between the two reasons or premises. No link is ever forged between the end term category "migratory birds" and the other end term category "brightly colored birds" through the crucial middle term, "carnivorous birds," because "carnivorous birds" is never used to refer to all the objects in its category. As a result, no conclusion can be drawn from combining these two reasons.

Now, let's apply the second test. One of the end terms—"migratory birds"—is properly distributed, thus making a potential link between the first reason and the conclusion, but the other end term—"brightly colored birds"—is not. "Brightly colored birds" is distributed only once. As a result, the term does not create a link between the second reason and the conclusion.

Finally, let's apply rule three. That rule states that the number of negative reasons must equal the number of negative conclusions. There is no negative reason in this argument, but there is a negative conclusion. Thus, the third rule of validity is broken, as well.

Abbreviated Categorical Arguments

Categorical reasoning has been of interest to people who study arguments from ancient times to the present. The Greek philosopher Aristotle dealt extensively with the topic as early as the fourth century BCE. In one of his books, titled simply *Rhetoric,* Aristotle drew attention to the fact that many categorical arguments presented in public settings are shortened, or missing a basic component. He referred to such *truncated, or abbreviated, categorical arguments, missing one or more of the basic components, such as a reason or a conclusion,* as **enthymemes**. Aristotle's concept of the enthymeme remains a helpful way of understanding how categorical arguments actually function in our public discourse.

To illustrate how enthymemes work, let's look at an example of a categorical argument that has a missing reason. Imagine that an English teacher makes the following argument at a conference of English teachers:

> The novels of Arthur C. Clarke involve only male protagonists. Thus, his novels are not appropriate to the modern high school English classroom.

Typically, listeners mentally "fill in" the missing reason in an enthymeme, as you did if this shortened categorical argument made sense to you. Because of this interaction between a speaker's statement and the listener's mind, enthymemes can boost the listener's involvement in producing the meaning of the argument.

Enthymemes develop quickly in public discourse, which makes it crucial to assess the strength of their reasons, including those that you, the listener, have supplied.

The first statement in this argument, one of its reasons, is a universal affirmative statement:

> The novels of Arthur C. Clarke involve only male protagonists.

The second statement is the argument's conclusion, a universal negative statement:

> Thus, his novels are not appropriate to the modern high school English classroom.

Though this argument is perfectly understandable, a reason is missing. The missing reason, which the listeners fill in, is some version of another universal negative statement:

No novels involving only male protagonists are appropriate to the modern English classroom.

Thus, the complete categorical argument or syllogism looks like this:

The novels of Arthur C. Clarke involve only male protagonists. **UA**

[No novels involving only male protagonists are appropriate to the modern English classroom.] **UN**

Thus

[Clarke's] novels are not appropriate to the modern high school English classroom. **UN**

Setting out an enthymeme or abbreviated categorical argument in complete form is one step toward evaluating the strength of the argument.

Finding Missing Statements

In the preceding example of an enthymeme, it is relatively easy to identify the missing reason. In some abbreviated categorical arguments, however, it is not immediately apparent what reason has been left unstated.

It may have occurred to you already that when we have any two of the three statements in a valid categorical argument—two reasons, or a reason and the conclusion—we can always find the missing statement by applying the three rules of validity. (If we are working with an abbreviated *in*valid argument, it will not be possible to find a statement that adequately completes the argument.) For example, here is a valid categorical argument with a missing reason:

No passengers on the flight are suspects in the jewel theft.

Because

All passengers on the flight are people cleared by the FBI.

The first step in finding the missing reason in this shortened categorical argument would be to standardize the argument and mark the distribution of terms. To do that, we must first decide whether we are dealing with two reasons, or with a reason and a conclusion. In our example, the indicator "because" suggests we are reading a reason and a conclusion. Standardized and with the distribution of its terms marked, the argument looks like this:

Because

               D   **U**

All / passengers on the flight / are / people cleared by the FBI /. **UA**

[Missing reason.]

Thus,

               D   **D**

No / passengers on the flight / are / suspects in the jewel theft /. **UN**

Now it is easy to see that the end terms of the argument are "passengers on the flight" and "suspects in the jewel theft." The middle term must be "cleared by the FBI," because it is in a reason, but not in the conclusion. Notice also that "people on the flight" has been used twice in the argument, so it cannot be used again. It will not appear in the missing reason because each term is used only twice in a categorical argument.

The next step is to identify the two terms that must be used again in the argument and to decide how they would have to be distributed. The terms that must appear in the missing reason are "suspects in the jewel theft" and "people cleared by the FBI." In addition, we know that "people cleared by the FBI," as the middle term, will have to be distributed the next time it is used. The first rule of validity for categorical arguments states that the middle term must be distributed exactly once, and "people cleared by the FBI" has not yet been distributed in the argument.

Looking now at "passengers on the flight," we can see that it must also be distributed in the missing reason. The second rule states that neither end term may be distributed only once. "Passengers on the flight" has been distributed once already, so it must be distributed again the next time it appears in the argument.

Finally, the conclusion of this argument is a negative statement, but the reason we have is not. The third rule states that the number of negative reasons must equal the number of negative conclusions, so our missing reason must be a negative statement.

Our only option, then, is the universal negative statement:

> **D**   **D**
> No / people cleared by the FBI / are / suspects in the jewel theft /. **UN**

Placing this statement into the argument, we get the following valid categorical syllogism:

> **D**   **U**
> All / passengers on the flight / are / people cleared by the FBI /.

> **D**   **D**
> No / people cleared by the FBI / are / suspects in the jewel theft /.

Thus

> **D**   **D**
> No / passengers on the flight / are / suspects in the jewel theft /.

A similar process can be followed to find a missing statement in any valid categorical argument. If it is not possible to find a workable missing statement that completes the argument, we must conclude that the argument is not a valid one.

CHAPTER REVIEW

Categorical arguments express the relationships among three classes, or categories, of objects. To be valid, a categorical argument must exhibit three qualities. First, it must make a connection between the two reasons through the middle term. This connection is made when the middle term is distributed exactly once. Second, its end terms—which connect reasons to the conclusion—may not be distributed only once. Third, the number of negative premises must equal the number of negative conclusions.

Categorical arguments often appear in public debate in the incomplete form that Aristotle called the enthymeme. By applying the rules of validity, we can supply the missing elements in an enthymeme so that we actually understand what a speaker or writer is asking us to accept and whether the argument is valid.

Validity is a concern for the form or structure of an argument. The validity of an argument and the truthfulness of its statements are separate considerations.

EXERCISES

A. For each of the following categorical arguments, identify each statement as one of the four standard forms, for example, as a universal affirmative. Identify the middle terms and end terms in each statement. Using **D** and **U**, mark the distribution of each term. Applying the three rules of validity for categorical arguments, indicate whether each argument is valid or invalid.

1. All tour guides are polite.

   All tour-bus drivers are polite.

   Therefore

   All tour-bus drivers are tour guides.

2. All New Englanders are explorers.

   No explorers are cautious.

   Therefore

   No New Englanders are cautious.

3. All company employees are well trained.

   Some well-trained people are not competent.

   Thus

   Some company employees are not competent.

4. All members of the Civic Party are political opportunists.

   All political opportunists are members of the Central Committee.

   So

   All members of the Central Committee are members of the Civic Party.

5. All poems by Poe are poems that use iambic pentameter.

   No poems in this collection use iambic pentameter.

   Thus

   No poems in this collection are poems by Poe.

B. Put the following arguments into standard form and mark the distribution of terms. Find the missing statement by applying the rules of validity.

1. None of the men who rented the car were bald, though some men who rented the truck were bald.

2. Several members of the bargaining team are retired teachers, though all members of the bargaining team are members of the teachers' union.

3. The actors in that play could not have been graduates of the theatre program, because none of them came to the defense of the director.

4. All the papers in the Twain Collection belong to the Twain estate, and all the items belonging to the Twain estate are currently being sold at auction.

ENDNOTES

[1]This formulation of the rules for categorical syllogisms follows Monroe Beardsley, *Thinking Straight: Principles of Reasoning for Readers and Writers,* 4th ed. (Englewood Cliffs, N.J.: Prentice-Hall, 1975), 61. Beardsley credits Wesley C. Salmon, *Logic,* 2nd ed. (Englewood Cliffs, N.J.: Prentice-Hall, 1973), 53.

RECOMMENDED WEBSITES

Categorical Syllogisms

Jennifer Mundale

pegasus.cc.ucf.edu/~jmundale/Categorical%20Syllogisms-online.htm

This description of categorical syllogisms, by philosophy professor Jennifer Mundale, provides a more traditional treatment than the one offered in this chapter. The discussion may give you a greater appreciation for this history of categorical syllogisms, as well as for the complexity that lies just below the surface of this form of reasoning.

The Subject of Logic: "Syllogisms"

Stanford Encyclopedia of Philosophy

http://plato.stanford.edu/entries/aristotle-logic/#SubLogSyl

V

Linguistic Consistency: Language in Argument

12 Definition in Argument

It is the business of thought to define things, to find the boundaries;
thought, indeed, is a ceaseless process of definition.
Vance Palmer (1885–1959)
Australian poet

The best definition is the most convenient one.
C. S. Lewis (1898–1963)
Anglo-Irish literary critic

KEY TERMS

argumentative
   definition

circular definition

common usage

define

definition report

distinction without
   a difference

etymology

euphemism

labeling

original intent

paradigm case

reclassification

Though you may not think of yourself as famous, a judge might consider you to be a public figure in certain instances. The law makes a distinction between a private citizen and a "public figure." A public figure is defined as anyone who is widely known or who has made widely publicized statements as part of a controversy. Otherwise you are a private citizen—or are you? The distinction between public figure and private citizen has major implications for lawsuits about invasion of privacy and defamation. For example, if the court categorizes you as a public figure, the standard of proof for arguing defamation of character is higher—not only do you have to prove that an assault on your reputation occurred, but that the insult was actually *intended* to cause you harm.

So, are you a public figure? You might be. The category of public figure can be divided into more specific categories, such as "limited purpose public figure" and "involuntary public figure." A limited purpose public figure is widely known because she or he made statements in a limited but public context, such as during a public controversy about animal rights. In other contexts, the same individual might not be a public figure. An involuntary public figure is well known, but only accidentally; for example, because of making statements to the media after an accident. As a result, others might make harshly critical claims about your actions or statements, and those criticisms might be protected by law.[1]

Definitions are crucial to every area of public reasoning. An automobile manufacturer argued that a recent action was not a "recall" but rather a "voluntary company-authorized maintenance." The distinction is important to the company because the term "recall" implies that a part was faulty; "voluntary maintenance" does not. Similarly, political commentator John Leo points out that "Democrats warn of 'global warming'; Republicans talk calmly about 'climate change.'"[2] Other terms being "hotly" contested today include "marriage," "torture," "person," and "socialized."

To **define** is to *advance a meaning for a word or to classify an object, person, or act.* Though we often take definitions for granted, no activity is more crucial to the outcome of an argument than defining key terms. Whoever controls the definitions in a debate controls the debate itself. In Chapter 5 we learned that linguistic consistency—defining terms clearly and in the same way throughout an argument—is one of the three general criteria of reasonable arguments. This chapter discusses the types and uses of definition in argument, as well as questions to ask about the definitions you use in your own arguments or encounter in others' arguments.

> Whoever controls the definitions in a debate controls the debate itself.

DEFINITION REPORTS: DEFINING FOR CLARITY AND EMPHASIS

Definition has a variety of functions in writing and speaking. One of the most common is to clarify the meaning of an important term. For example, we are all familiar with the term "World Wide Web," and we probably assume that popular search engines have access to all of its content. However, this is not the case. The term "deep web" has been advanced to describe the numerous World Wide Web sites that are not available to familiar search engines. This definition of "deep web" is an example of a **definition report,** *a noncontroversial definition that all parties to a debate agree upon, or that states a generally accepted or agreed upon meaning.* When there is agreement that a term carries a stated meaning, or when a term is defined simply to clarify or emphasize its meaning, we are encountering a definition report. Definition reports do not themselves elicit controversy because all concerned parties agree to the definition advanced.

Definitions drawn from dictionaries and other authoritative sources are typically definition reports used to clarify a term's meaning. For example:

> Astronomy websites define "gravitational lensing" as the bending of light by the gravitational field of a massive cosmic object, such as a large galaxy. Thus, a massive galaxy in the cosmic foreground will bend light from a more distant galaxy or quasar, thus providing evidence of the distant object's existence.

Definition reports may also be used to establish that all parties involved in a discussion or controversy agree that a term carries a particular meaning. Thus, in a case involving a charge of libel, both sides may agree at the outset that the term "libel" means to injure someone's reputation by printing false allegations. Definition reports may also reveal new developments, drawing attention to important changes taking place. For example:

> The rise of international internet banking has created the need for a new term—financial tech, or fintech. This new term has also revealed a new world financial order, one that will be important to shaping the financial future. The country that is leading the way in fintech, the one with the most developed approach to internet banking? China.

In other circumstances, definition reports are used to establish the meaning of a technical term for an audience unfamiliar with the terminology of a particular industry or field of study. For example, scientists now realize that we have at least as many cells in our bodies that do *not* carry our DNA as we have cells that *do*. These are nonhuman cells—mostly bacteria—some of which perform important functions and actually help us to maintain health. As evidence of their presence and function grew, the term "microbiome" was coined to describe all the nonhuman cells that live in our bodies. The microbiome is now the subject of intense study.

ARGUMENTATIVE DEFINITIONS

Some definitions advanced in arguments do more than simply clarify the meaning of a term. An **argumentative definition** is *a definition employed strategically to categorize an object or event so as to support a particular conclusion to an argument.*

An argumentative definition may be surprising or controversial. Thus, President Franklin Roosevelt once opened a speech to the Daughters of the American Revolution with the unexpected words, "Welcome, fellow immigrants!" Roosevelt was defining the members of his audience as "immigrants," though they might have preferred to see themselves as "established members of United States society."

Argumentative definitions are more common than we might think in our public discourse. The meanings of terms such as "marriage" and "person" are regularly contested. Actions are defined in the course of controversy as well. For instance, a politician might defend an allegedly illegal act of concealing documents from the public by arguing, "I wasn't breaking the law; I was simply acting in the interest of national security." By defining or categorizing the act in question as "acting in the interest of national security" rather than as "breaking the law," the politician seeks to establish a different understanding of his actions.

Here is another example of how a dispute over definitions might appear in a public controversy:

> The wall dividing Israel and the Palestinian territories is just that, a security wall intended to keep terrorists out of Israel so as to protect its citizens from harm. And, in fact, it has functioned that way.

In response, an opponent argues for a different definition:

> The so-called security wall is actually a fence erected as part of an Israeli land grab. It is serving to expand Israeli territory by taking territory away from Palestinians.

While an individual advancing an argumentative definition may sincerely believe it is accurate and well supported, such a definition is not merely a report of a widely accepted meaning. Argumentative definitions are strategic in that they are advanced to support debatable contentions.

Argumentative Definitions and Categorical Reasoning

Definition is closely related to the topic of categorical validity discussed in Chapter 11, because definitions establish categories into which a person, an idea, or an action is placed to support a conclusion. In the following argument, the crucial term "parent" is defined to support the argument's conclusion that a couple who are not a child's biological parents should be granted custody:

A child's parents are those who nurture and care for that child, who look out for the child's best interests, who love the child. Though they are not her biological parents, the Walkers have visited Sara, brought her gifts, and shown consistent concern for her well-being. Thus, the Walkers, not the Smiths, are Sara's parents and therefore should be granted custody of her.

Argumentative definitions often incorporate criteria that reflect beliefs, values, or assumptions. The above definition of "parent" is not widely accepted. Instead, "parent" is defined to support the particular conclusion being advanced. The definition establishes the criteria for being parents as: (a) those who nurture and care for the child, (b) those who look out for the child's best interests, and (c) those who love the child. Because the Walkers satisfy these criteria, they are called Sara's parents. The argument concludes that because parents are entitled to custody of their children, the Walkers are entitled to custody of Sara.

As this example suggests, the reasoning behind argumentative definitions typically involves three steps:

1. A category (for example, "parent") is defined by setting out criteria.
2. A person, an object, or an act is placed in the category on the basis of its having satisfied the criteria.
3. The new member is asserted to have other qualities of the members of that category.

Argumentative definitions thus operate in much the same way that categorical arguments do. Indeed, categorical validity is the basis of definitional reasoning. Notice how this process of categorization works in the following argumentative definition of assisted suicide:

Assisted suicide is murder, because it is the intentional taking of an innocent and irreplaceable human life.

The defined term typically forges a connection between the two reasons. As in many definitional arguments, one reason is left unstated in this example because it is assumed that the audience will understand that it is implied. We can supply the missing reason and set the argument out as a complete deduction:

Assisted suicide is the intentional taking of an innocent and irreplaceable human life.

[Taking an innocent and irreplaceable human life is murder.]

Assisted suicide is murder.

In this form the close relationship between argumentative definition and categorical reasoning is clear.

STRATEGIES OF DEFINITION

Three specific uses of argumentative definition are so common to public discourse as to require special consideration. Any of these strategies of definition can be used to subtly suggest a meaning without directly stating it. We will refer to these three approaches as euphemism, reclassification, and labeling.

Euphemism

Euphemisms are *less objectionable and often less accurate terms exchanged for harsh, condemning, or emotionally charged terms.* For example, many politicians want to cut social safety net programs, but rarely use the term "cut." Because the programs are so popular with voters, politicians use terms such as "overhaul," "revamp," and "fix" to mask their real goal—which is to cut. Euphemisms, quite common in political discourse, should be recognized for what they are—a kind of argumentative definition.

Anne Soukhanov of *The Atlantic Monthly* writes of an intriguing euphemism that has been used in some United States newspapers: "food insecurity." She calls this term "a euphemism for malnutrition and hunger, or the fear of them," among older citizens. She adds that Hugh Rawson, in *A Dictionary of Euphemisms & Other Doubletalk,* says that euphemisms are a culture's "outward and visible signs of our inward anxieties, conflicts, fears, and shames."[3]

Because terms shape our perceptions, we can imagine a euphemism as an effort to move perceptions of an object, person, or action down a scale of severity. To reject a euphemism, then, is to attempt to reverse this process. Thus, the police might refer to road blocks to randomly check for compliance with a mandatory seat belt law as "spot-checking for safety compliance." This term is intended to reduce negative public reaction to the practice, which drivers experience as a nuisance and perhaps as an unwarranted search. A local resident who opposes the practice argues that "spot-checking" is a euphemism for "invasion of privacy." She rejects what she takes to be a euphemism and attempts to move the practice of random checks higher up a scale of severity. We can visualize the use of euphemism in this way:

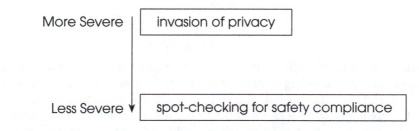

EUPHEMISM

More Severe   invasion of privacy

Less Severe   spot-checking for safety compliance

Some euphemisms may be understood as instances of the broader category of reclassification, the second strategy of definition we will consider.

Reclassification

Following more than a thousand reports of children swallowing the magnetic nickel-plated beads called Buckyballs, the manufacturer was threatened with a suit by a consumer group. The consumer complaint alleged that Buckyballs were being sold as toys, and thus often given to children to play with. The manufacturer responded that Buckyballs were never intended to be sold as a "toy," but rather as an "adult desktop gift item."[4]

Reclassification, involves *strategic placement of an object, person, or idea under a new heading.* Consider the following argument:

> The current term-limit restrictions were promoted as citizen empowerment laws, but they are really lobbyist empowerment laws. Voters are forced to rapidly expel from office the very people they influenced in the political process—the legislators. The result is that every four years a bunch of political beginners gets thrown into a world of moneyed lobbyists who can easily manipulate them.

In this example, "term limit restrictions" are reclassified from "citizen empowerment laws" to "lobbyist empowerment laws."

Another example of reclassification occurred in an interview with NBA player Stephen Jackson, who rejected the NBA commissioner's argument that the NBA's ban on casual clothing during press conferences was simply a "dress code." "It's one thing to enforce a dress code," said Jackson, "and it's another thing if you're attacking cultures."[5] Jackson reclassified the ban on casual clothing as "attacking cultures," thus rejecting as inaccurate the "dress code" definition used to justify the ban.

To visualize reclassification, and to distinguish it from euphemism, we might imagine a horizontal rather than a vertical movement of an object, action, or person from one category to another. For example, a physician wants a patient to undergo an expensive and somewhat painful procedure to remove a suspicious-looking section of skin from her forehead. The procedure is normally referred to as "preventive elective surgery." Sensing the patient's reluctance to move forward with the procedure, the physician suggests thinking of the operation as an "outpatient procedure" that will reduce the chances of more serious problems and procedures later on. Thus, we can imagine reclassification as a horizontal movement from one category to another:

RECLASSIFICATION

| preventive elective surgery | ⟶ | outpatient procedure |

Labeling

Labeling is *characterizing a person, group, idea, or institution by introducing a suggestive name or term.* Labeling is often used in place of an actual argument. Notice how labels such as "fake news" or "hoax" tend to obscure the actual issues. As a result, the advocate seems to be relieved of the responsibility of advancing or responding to an argument. Similarly, a military action might be labeled "irresponsible adventurism." A minority business assistance program might be dismissed as "the same old racial politics." Again, a label substitutes for an actual argument against the idea or action.

Labels are common in the political arena. Terms such as "tax-and-spend liberals," "red-necked conservatives," "neofascists" and dozens of others are employed to characterize the motives and agendas of political interest groups. Labeling is a definitional strategy that should be challenged *when it is used to obscure complex issues and circumvent real arguments.*

> Labeling should be challenged when it is used to obscure complex issues and circumvent real arguments.

Labeling can also be used responsibly to create a new category by inventing a name for an action, group, or policy. This more positive use of labeling provides audiences with a vivid image of an abstract idea. For example, Mark Tercek, head of the environmental advocacy group known as the Nature Conservancy, has referred to crucial natural structures such as beaches and wetlands as "natural infrastructure," thus grouping and labeling the underlying support networks that sustain natural balances. Because audiences are already familiar with the idea of commercial infrastructure, such as roads and electrical systems, they can more readily imagine a biological system by bringing Tercek's term to mind.

FIGURE 12.1 Uses of Definitions

Definitions may be used to:
- Clarify meaning (definition reports)
- Suggest conclusions (argumentative definitions)
- Deflect meaning (euphemisms)
- Facilitate defense or accusation (reclassification)
- Obscure issues (labeling)

EVALUATING DEFINITIONS

Because definitions are so important to persuasive writing and speaking, we should not employ or accept a definition without knowing which type it is. A definition report typically will not be the source of controversy. It will be widely acknowledged as accurate and will not tend to give an advantage to one side in a controversy. By contrast, an argumentative definition of terms, objects, or acts is usually controversial and does tend to assist the case of one side in a debate. If we encounter an argumentative definition, we should determine whether it involves euphemism, reclassification, or labeling. In evaluating any definition employed in public discourse or in our own writing, we can ask three additional questions.

1. Is the definition circular? A **circular definition,** which may be either a mistake or a deceptive tactic, is *a definition of a term by reference only to factors inherent in or strongly implied by the definition itself.* A circular definition eventually brings us back around to the initial term, phrase, or criteria being defined.

Notice how most of the following definitions of the term "endangered species" reflect circularity:

1. An endangered species is a group of animals that is dwindling in numbers and may go extinct soon.

2. An endangered species is a species threatened with extinction.

3. An endangered species is a species that is in danger of becoming extinct.

4. An endangered species is a species considered to be in imminent danger of extinction.

5. An endangered species is one in immediate danger of becoming extinct, and a species is extinct when no living member exists.

Now consider the following definition from an organization called Ecoagricultural Partners:

6. "An endangered species is a species whose population has declined by 50 percent over the past ten years or three generations, whichever is longer, and for which the causes of the reduction are not demonstrably reversible or not clearly understood, may not have ceased, or could recur."[6]

What makes this definition different from the first five? It is the fact that the definition does not simply repeat the idea of endangerment by giving it a new name—extinction. Instead, this definition provides the reader with a means of understanding what endangerment of a species means. If "endangerment" means "likely extinction," then presumably "likely extinction" means "endangerment." But what have we learned through this definition? The sixth definition does not simply provide us with a more or less apparent synonym; it takes us *outside* the term to criteria that help us understand the term itself.

The name "circular definition" suggests an unproductive process. Starting with an undefined term, a definition is suggested that is either strongly implied in the original term, or that simply provides us with an unhelpful synonym that leaves us with the same definitional question we started with.

2. Does the definition make a distinction without showing a difference? All definitions seek to differentiate. Typically, one category of objects or ideas is differentiated from another. For example, to define the category "octopus" as "a predatory, eight-armed, solitary mollusk" is to differentiate the octopus from other marine animals, but also from other mollusks, and even from other mollusks with tentacles—say, the cuttlefish. If we were interested in separating certain types of octopus from others, further definitions would be necessary. A useful definition must, then, identify differences.

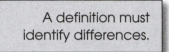
A definition must identify differences.

An apparent definition, however, may make a **distinction without a difference**, *a definition that suggests that a category exists, without adequately explaining how objects in this category differ from objects in similar categories.* Such a definition must be considered inadequate—it is essentially not a definition at all, but an effort to create the false sense that a new category has been identified. Imagine that someone approaches you in an airport, asking you to add your name to a list of people who support a measure to reduce noise from the airport in surrounding neighborhoods. You tell the individual, "I don't sign petitions." The response is, "It's not a petition." You ask, "Then, what is it?" The other person replies, "It's a registry of citizen support." Since this last statement comes close to being a definition of a petition, you would be justified in dismissing the statement as making a distinction without a difference.

The following example reflects a challenge to a distinction without an apparent difference:

> What is the distinction between "news" and "satire"? Shows such as *The Daily Show* and *The Late Show* actually report news and even provide insightful analysis of current events. They just do it in a humorous way.

3. Did the definition originate in an appropriate source? What counts as the best source of a definition depends on context. Are legal documents being interpreted, such that definitions must be consistent with legal sources, the intent of the law, or the intent of the framers of the law? Is the setting a political campaign, in which standard usage may be an appropriate source of definitions? Good definitions fit the argumentative context as well as the issue being resolved.

SOURCES OF DEFINITIONS

Some sources of definitions are better suited to certain contexts and issues than are others. Five standard sources are common usage, etymology, a paradigm case, original intent, and authority.

Common Usage

Common usage, *the meaning of a term in everyday language,* is one source of definitions. For example, in common usage "parent" usually refers to the biological or adoptive relationship of one person to another, with overtones of responsibility for care and legal guardianship. Definitions from common usage are appropriate in many contexts, particularly when we want to know what a word meant to someone who read it in a newspaper article or heard it in a speech or conversation. When a candidate makes a campaign promise, it is fair for listeners to define the terms of the promise on the basis of their common usage.

Let's look at an example:

> Mr. Wren has admitted threatening the clerk with a can of mace, but did he thereby commit a crime using a handgun? He certainly did, if we understand a handgun to be a hand-held object that emits a projectile capable of causing significant physical harm.

One possible response to this definition of "handgun" is to suggest that in common usage "handgun" refers to a hand-held weapon emitting a solid projectile at a velocity fast enough to do physical harm. Under this common definition of the term, a can of mace would not be considered a gun or a handgun. If the law were written to deter the use of handguns in crimes, a definition from common usage would fit the issue being resolved. Notice, though, that the common usage definition we just introduced—a weapon emitting a solid projectile at a velocity fast enough to do physical harm—tends to advance the case of the defense, and thus is also an argumentative definition.

Etymology

The *origin of a word*, its **etymology,** is appropriate to some controversies. Brief etymologies often can be found in dictionary entries before the definition itself is presented. *The Oxford English Dictionary,* Dictionary.com, and several other dictionaries provide extensive etymological information on English words.

A college career-planning counselor used an etymological definition to argue that documents originating in her office should substitute the word "vocation" for the word "occupation." Because "vocation" is derived from the Latin term *vocare,* meaning "to call," she hoped the change would encourage students to think of their future occupations as "callings" rather than merely as jobs.

Etymology doesn't always help in defending a definition, though. In a debate over the role of a university, one advocate defined the term from etymology as coming from the Latin term *universitas,* which this advocate took to mean "universal," or covering all topics of study. He went on to argue that universities should offer courses in virtually any topic, as their mission is to offer "universal" education. A respondent, apparently coming closer to the term's derivation, countered that *universitas* refers to "the whole" or to the community of scholars and students that makes up a university. This respondent argued that the word holds no implications for the curriculum of the university but, rather, suggests its constitution as a learning community. For a "university" to limit its curriculum, then, is not inconsistent with the term's etymology.

Paradigm Case

A "good example," a **paradigm case,** is *a representative example of the term or category in question; a typical member that defines the entire category.* For example, the press periodically reports on how historians and political scientists have "rated" presidents. Suppose you are arguing that Bill Clinton was a good president and someone asks you to define a "good president." You might define the category by referring to a paradigm case such as Harry Truman. Your argument probably will identify the qualities in

Truman that made him a good president, such as poise under pressure, decisiveness, leadership, and vision.

Original Intent

Original intent, *the meaning of a word or phrase in its original context, or what the initial definer of a term meant by it,* is particularly important in some cases in which a document or law is being interpreted. Interpretations of the United States Constitution often turn on questions of the original intent of those who authored the document. For example, in the long and continuing debate over how to interpret the Second Amendment to the Constitution, which makes the famous statement about "the right of the people to keep and bear arms," much has been said about what the framers meant by the term "militia." Did the framers intend something like the National Guard, or did they mean something closer to a militia of all adult citizens? When a term is defined for the purpose of research, we may also classify such definitions as arising from original intent:

> We studied schools located by busy roads to determine whether children at these schools suffer higher levels of asthma. A "busy road" was defined as a road that carries 30,000 cars daily, or 10,000 cars and at least 500 trucks. Trucks emit 57 times the amount of dangerous particulates that cars do.

Authority

Various authorities may be consulted for definitions. Individuals' expert knowledge might qualify them to advance definitions of terms within their specific fields of expertise. In the debate over assisted suicide, for example, a physician might be consulted for an authoritative definition of the adjective "terminal" when applied to a patient's situation. Does the term mean death will occur eventually, or does it mean death is imminent? Works such as dictionaries, lexicons, and concordances might also be considered authoritative for definitions. The *Diagnostic and Statistical Manual of Mental Disorders,* for example, is a key source of authoritative definitions in the fields of psychology and psychiatry; it might be consulted for definitions of terms such as "borderline personality disorder."[7]

CHAPTER REVIEW

How terms are defined is critical to argument. A definition that has an agreed-upon meaning is called a definition report. These definitions are not controversial. Argumentative definitions, however, may be introduced into a controversy to support a claim or advance a case. The meanings of key terms should be a matter of agreement among disagreeing parties. Meanings must also remain consistent throughout an argument to arrive at conclusions reasonably.

One strategy of argumentative definition involves substituting innocuous terms, euphemisms, for potentially offensive terms. Another tactic is reclassification, or redefining an action or idea to assist in accusation or defense. Labeling is a strategy of definition employed for the purpose of dismissing or condemning an individual or group, rather than addressing the argument. In evaluating a definition, we should also consider whether it is circular, makes a distinction without a difference, or originates in an inappropriate source.

Definitions can be derived in a number of ways. The most appropriate way is to derive definitions from the argumentative context. Among the common sources of definitions are common usage, etymology, paradigm case, original intent, and authority.

EXERCISES

A. Identify the strategies of definition—euphemism, reclassification, or labeling—employed in the following.

1. Because of high revenues generated by advertising, you can buy a year's subscription of a magazine online for $5. That's less than the newsstand price for one print issue of the same magazine, which runs around $7.95. This practice is ruining the magazine publishing industry, turning magazines into glossy advertising-delivery systems. To buy a year's subscription for $5 is not a bargain; it should be considered a crime!

2. Why shouldn't college athletes be paid, and paid well? After all, they are primarily entertainers, and entertainers are paid well.

3. A fetus cannot think, choose, or envision a future. Thus, a fetus is potentially a person but not a full person. As merely a potential person, a fetus does not have the rights of a full person.

4. An advertisement reads: Metrofund debt solutions—it's not a loan, it's a way out of debt.

5. Techniques such as sleep deprivation and exposure to extreme heat or cold are not torture, but aggressive interrogation techniques.

6. The president avoided the use of the term "mistake," preferring instead to call his errors in judgment "miscalculations."

7. Sugar is a type of poison, which is clear when we see its effects on the health of children and adults.

8. My client did leak classified material to WikiLeaks, but this does not make him a traitor. He is a whistleblower.

B. Identify the source of definition suggested in each of the following examples. Provide a possible response that might appeal to a different source of definition, or that questions how the definition is interpreted.

1. I opposed amnesty for war criminals, as the word amnesty comes from the Latin word *amnestia,* which means to forget. We should never forget the terrible things that were done in the region.

2. State law governing public education defines bullying as aggressive and unwanted behavior directed by one student at another, where there also exists a power imbalance such as age, size, or social status. The case before us is not a case of bullying, because the alleged victim is bigger than the alleged bully.

3. Everybody knows that marriage is a public bond between a man and a woman, so same-sex marriage violates even common sense understanding of marriage.

4. The best way to understand great art is to experience it directly. When you are listening to a Beethoven symphony or looking at a painting by Rembrandt, you know you are in the presence of great art.

5. The founders of this club defined "a member in good standing" as a "gentleman of good standing in the community who has paid his dues and who adheres to the values set out in the club's constitution." The terms "gentleman" and "his" make it clear that they had a male-only membership in mind. Thus, the club's bylaws restrict membership to men.

C. Which specific approach to evaluating definitions is being employed in this example? Explain your answer.

> We are being urged to buy US-made cars to help revive the economy, but what does "US-made" mean when we are talking about cars? Is Ford a US Car? The Ford Fusion is built in Mexico. How about Chevrolet? The Chevrolet Camaro and Impala are made in Canada. On the other hand, the Honda Accord and Toyota Camry are assembled here in the United States. It can be very difficult to make the distinction between US and foreign.

D. Identify the places in the following example where argumentative definition and definition report are used.

> Despite assurances from Google about free access to digital books, Google Search represents a monopoly on orphaned books—books that are out of print but still under copyright. Google will effectively own the rights to all such books.

ENDNOTES

[1]"Limited Purpose Public Figure," *FindLaw Legal Dictionary,* http://dictionary.findlaw.com /definition/limited-purpose-public-figure.html.

[2]John Leo, "Double Trouble Speak," *U.S. News and World Report,* July 4, 2005, 30.

[3]Anne Soukhanov, "Word Watch," *Atlantic Monthly,* April 1994, 135.

[4]Ilya Marritz, "Safety Group Sues Buckyballs Founder in Product Recall Case," *National Public Radio,* January 10, 2014, http://www.npr.org/2014/01/10/261271856/safety-commission-sues -buckyballs-founder-in-product-recall-case.

[5]Marc Stein, "Pacers' Jackson Calls Ban on Chain's 'Racist Statement,'" http://www.ESPN.com, October 20, 2005.

[6]Ecoagricultural Partners, http://www.ecoagriculture.org/page.php?id=65&name=Glossary (Accessed November 2, 2010).

[7]*Diagnostic and Statistical Manual of Mental Disorders,* 4th ed. (Washington, D.C.: American Psychiatric Association, 2000), http://www.psychiatryonline.com/resourceTOC.aspx ?resourceID=1.

RECOMMENDED WEBSITES

Academic Phrasebank

Manchester University

www.phrasebank.manchester.ac.uk/writing-definitions

Manchester University in England provides this description of definitions and how they work.

Dictionary.com

dictionary.reference.com

An online dictionary that provides definitions, etymologies, and examples of word usage, Dictionary.com is an excellent and convenient source of definition reports. It includes extensive information on word origins, as well as help with distinguishing the meanings of words that sound and look alike.

Thesaurus.com

thesaurus.com

Thesaurus.com provides valuable assistance with synonyms and antonyms.

13 Ambiguity, Equivocation, and Other Language Considerations

Time flies like an arrow. Fruit flies like a banana.
Groucho Marx (1890–1977)
United States comedian

Always be sincere, even if you don't mean it.
Harry Truman (1884–1972)
United States president

KEY TERMS
ambiguity

equivocation
mixed metaphor
redundancy

semantic ambiguity
syntactic ambiguity

In a highly controversial decision known as *Citizens United,* the Supreme Court ruled that corporations have free speech rights similar to those of individual citizens. Thus, the Court reasoned, it is wrong to place limits on corporate campaign contributions, as such limits would constitute a violation of First Amendment rights. Critics of the decision noted that the term "person" played a crucial and potentially misleading role in the decision and in subsequent public debate.

In common usage, a "person" is an individual human being with rights. In legal circles, however, there is a long tradition of talking about corporations as "persons," enjoying legal protections and rights similar to those of an individual. Should corporations as "persons" be viewed as entities with rights similar to those of an individual person? The *Washington Post* responded to the decision with an editorial arguing that "nothing in the First Amendment dictates that corporations must be treated identically to people."[1]

This example brings us back to the issue of linguistic consistency in arguments. Linguistic consistency, you will recall, is the requirement that all key terms in an argument maintain the same clear, unchanging definition throughout the argument. The following sections examine ambiguity and equivocation as sources of inconsistent definitions. We will also discuss several other common problems of language in argument.

AMBIGUITY

You hear a radio interview with the author of a new book on pet psychiatry, cleverly titled *Pets on the Couch.* The title's humor derives from an intentional ambiguity: household pets often avail themselves of the comfort of a living room couch, causing their owners a bit of frustration. It's a familiar and somewhat friendly image: the family pet on the couch. However, "the couch" is also shorthand for a psychiatric evaluation, bringing to mind the image of a therapist with a notepad listening dispassionately to a patient. The word "couch" is ambiguous in this title; that is, it brings to mind two images at once—the familiar living room couch and the unexpected image of the pet on the psychiatrist's couch. Only the subtitle resolves the ambiguity: *Neurotic Dogs, Compulsive Cats, Anxious Birds, and the New Science of Animal Psychiatry.* The author is Nicholas Dodman, a veterinarian.[2]

More than one meaning of a word or phrase in a single context is called **ambiguity.** Ambiguity in a key term can be demonstrated by rephrasing the term or phrase to reveal its possible multiple meanings. The ambiguous term itself should not be used in the rephrasing; otherwise the ambiguity will persist.

Suppose the following statement appears in an argument:

Christians believe in a personal God.

The key term, "personal," is ambiguous in this statement. Someone hearing this claim might take it to mean that:

Meaning 1: Christians believe that God exists as a person, that is, as a being with attributes such as will and motive.

Another listener might think the expression means that:

Meaning 2: Christians believe that God relates to people individually.

Yet another listener might assign this meaning:

Meaning 3: Christians believe that individuals determine God's nature as they see fit.

The ambiguity can be resolved by rephrasing the statement to reveal the possible meanings of "personal" in this context, as we have done here, and then asking which meaning was intended.

Ambiguity can develop for several reasons. **Semantic ambiguity** is *the ambiguity that occurs when a word or phrase carries more than one meaning in a particular context.* For example, the following headline illustrates semantic ambiguity:

Auto executive recalls cars with reclining seats.

The term "recalls" can mean either that the executive "remembers" such cars, or that she is "ordering them returned to the company for repairs."

Syntactic ambiguity is *the ambiguity that occurs when the structure or grammar of a sentence renders the meaning of a word or phrase uncertain.* The meaning of the ambiguous term or phrase does not change, but its grammatical function or specific application is unclear. For instance:

Campus police were ordered to stop drinking after midnight.

The phrase, "stop drinking," does not change meaning in this sentence—it means to put an end to the consumption of alcohol. But are the campus police to stop consuming alcohol themselves, or, as is more likely, are they to keep students from consuming alcohol?

EQUIVOCATION

Ambiguity is similar to **equivocation,** *changing meaning of a key term in the course of an argument.* When a key term is equivocal in an argument, the argument cannot satisfy the criterion of linguistic consistency.

To illustrate this point, let's consider several closely related meanings of the word, "popular." This word comes originally from the Latin word for people, *populus*. Its most basic meaning is "having to do with the people." By a slight modification, it has also come to mean "generally accepted." We see both meanings in the following statement: "It is a popular idea that people in the United States elect their presidents by a popular vote." As close as these meanings are, we could not quite substitute one for the other in this sentence; the meanings remain distinct.

The term "popular" has additional meanings. Notice that one nuance of the term "popular" in its first use in the sentence above—"widely accepted"—is "not quite true." Thus, we might hear someone say, "It is a popular belief that Columbus was the first European to visit the Americas, but Nordic explorers were here long before him."

The term "popular" can also mean "enjoyed or appreciated by many people," as in "popular music." From this fourth meaning we get an additional one—something that is popular in this sense may also be superficial, the sort of thing that might be enjoyed by large audiences but that lacks any real artistic or intellectual merit. For example, "The Harry Potter books and movies are popular entertainment, but they do not measure up to the standards of truly great literature or cinema." In this sentence the term "popular" may mean either "widely enjoyed" or "shallow."

Here is an example of how equivocation can affect everyday argument:

> The idea of a public health-care reform bill has proved very popular in recent months, but health-care reform is a serious and complex issue. It calls us to move beyond popular solutions to a carefully studied plan for the future of our entire system of delivering health services.

Equivocation in a key term is exploited here to dismiss certain health-care reform solutions. Two different uses of "popular" are evident, but the term is treated as if it has only a single meaning. In this way a repudiation of solutions that might merit careful attention is subtly suggested.

When we suspect that equivocation is a problem, it is helpful to point out that multiple meanings of a term are at work in an argument. For example:

Meaning 1: Widely accepted or supported.

Meaning 2: Superficial or shallow.

Because the two meanings cannot be substituted for one another in the argument, the term "popular" is equivocal here. As with ambiguity, we should be on the alert for equivocation in arguments that we read or hear. It is also important to avoid equivocating in our own writing and speaking.

As this example illustrates, the method of identifying and resolving equivocation is similar to that used with ambiguity. By finding a synonymous word or phrase for the equivocal term in each of its appearances, we can show that the synonyms are different and are not interchangeable in the argument.

Equivocation can also be intentionally exploited to create confusion about meanings. The term "interrogation" has been the source of some controversy because of the various meanings

> Equivocation can be intentionally exploited to create confusion about meanings.

that can be assigned to it. Though the term itself might simply mean "to question," it can also refer to aggressive efforts to extract information from a suspect. Some concern has been raised that in certain government documents it might be used to refer to techniques that might be better described as "torture." The meaning of the term might even shift within a single document.

OTHER LANGUAGE CONSIDERATIONS

Occasionally we hear or read a sentence that strikes us as odd, though we may not be sure why. For instance, a speaker says, "Child abuse is a widespread, uncontrollable crime that is difficult to enforce." This individual probably meant to say, "Child abuse is a widespread, uncontrollable crime, and the laws prohibiting it are difficult to enforce," but it didn't come out that way. The flaw in this sentence might have been identified and solved if the writer had asked: Does the sentence say what I want it to say? A different problem with language occurs in the following sentence:

Predicting is difficult, especially about the future.

Let's consider four additional common errors in writing and speaking that might confuse or distract an audience as we conclude this chapter.

Redundancy

Baseball legend Yogi Berra, when asked about an unusual occurrence during a game, famously replied, "It was like déjà vu all over again." Berra's comment is humorous because of his use of **redundancy,** or *unnecessary repetition of an idea or term.* The notion of déjà vu means that an event seems to be occurring for a second time, that is, all over again.

While Berra's redundancy was probably intentional, unintended redundancy is a common error in composition. For example, a police spokesperson states, "It took us a while to get to the security video because there was so much extensive damage to the building." The idea of extensive damage is stated twice here, in the phrase "extensive damage" and in the phrase "so much." What this speaker meant to say was, "It took us a while to get to the security video because there was so much damage to the building." or "because there was extensive damage to the building." Repetition can be helpful in securing or clarifying a point, but unintentionally redundant language can distract an audience.

Mixed Metaphor

You have probably heard or read a statement that is a **mixed metaphor,** that is, *a linguistic combination of images that do not belong together.* For instance, a candidate wished to point out that his opponent in a debate was not free of racial prejudice. "While he accuses others of prejudice," the candidate remarked, "he is himself the kind of guy who just can't seem to wake up and smell the coffee right in his own backyard." Here a metaphor for becoming alert to obvious problems—to "wake up and smell the coffee"—is combined with a metaphor for addressing issues close to home, that is, "in your own backyard." The two phrases introduce different pictures, however, and thus a clash develops that can be distracting to readers or listeners—and perhaps embarrassing to a speaker.

Another example of mixed metaphor comes from a Congressional leader expressing dissatisfaction with a new health-care bill: "Some have tried to pin a rose on this bill to make it sound like a solution to our health-care problems." Pinning a rose on something might make it *look* better, but it won't *sound* any different. The metaphors of sight and sound have been mixed.

Choosing the Wrong Word

"I know it sounds like an old touché, but the cream always rises to the top." That the cream always rises to the top is not a touché; it is a cliché. "Touché" means "touch" in

French; it indicates that a point has been scored in a fencing match. It clearly is not the word this speaker wanted. Though the two words sound similar, they have completely different meanings.

Sometimes a writer or speaker may choose the wrong form of the right word, as in this example: "Criminals who break the same law repeatable should be punished so they can never commit the crime again." Here the word "repeatedly" was intended, not "repeatable."

The problems that can arise from selecting the wrong word are also illustrated in the following example:

His accolades have made him a leading expert.

The word this speaker was looking for was probably "credentials" or "experience," but not accolades—which means "praise" or "commendation."

Sometimes the problem is linked to similar spelling of words that have different meanings, as in this sentence: "Today many people are quite weary of much that they are asked to read." Perhaps they are, but the writer apparently intended "wary" rather than "weary." We often hear speakers affirm that someone "contacted" a virus, when they mean to say that the person "contracted" a virus.

As these examples suggest, selecting the wrong word creates a humorous contradiction that undermines the speaker's point and credibility.

Misusing a Common Expression

A speaker, answering a question about a practical problem in his proposal, said: "We will burn that bridge when we come to it." That could be counterproductive. The expression he wanted was "We'll cross that bridge when we come to it," meaning we will deal with problems as they arise. The other expression that became confused with the correct one, undoubtedly because of their common use of the bridge metaphor, was "Don't burn your bridges behind you," a warning not to cut off your means of escape from a situation. The latter expression is sometimes altered to achieve the opposite meaning: "Burn your bridges" means "don't allow yourself a way to back out of a commitment."

In most cases correcting this problem is as simple as checking to see whether an expression sounds right or makes sense. Is someone making money hand over foot or hand over fist?

CHAPTER REVIEW

The rule of linguistic consistency states that key terms in an argument must be clearly and consistently defined. Two common problems of definition in arguments are ambiguity and equivocation. Each problem involves multiple meanings of a key term in a single context or in different contexts. Ambiguous terms have more than one possible meaning in a single context. The problem of ambiguity may be caused by semantic or syntactic concerns. Equivocal terms change meaning as they are used more than once.

Using language well also means paying close attention to what we are saying. In writing arguments we should try to avoid some common errors that can render our arguments less effective: redundancy, mixed metaphors, using the wrong word, or misusing a common expression.

EXERCISES

A. For the following examples, identify the term or phrase that is ambiguous. What are the possible meanings in each case?

1. I walked across campus to hear the bacteria talk.

2. Marine Corps Stamps Out Wednesday.

3. Perplexed by the disappearance of his sister, Vincent stood at the edge of the lake and thought, "Phyllis is at the bottom of this!"

4. Woman Decapitated in Freak Accident before Attending Lecture.

5. Culinary Columnist Advises Cooking Party Guests.

6. Princeton Freshman Wants QB Shot.

7. Scientists to Count Kangaroo Rats from Outer Space.

8. Free Pony Rides Threatened Here.

9. The shady dealings at the fertilizer factory finally got to Hal. "This whole business stinks," he said.

10. Campus police were requested to kick the fraternity members off the roof of the library.

B. Identify the equivocal term or phrase in each of the following examples. Provide in your own words the two different meanings the equivocal word conveys.

1. Some people say that homosexuality is acceptable because it is natural to some individuals. However, I don't find that homosexual behavior is exhibited in nature, that is, in other animals. So how can people say it's natural?

2. The Marines have a new recruiting slogan, "A commitment to something greater than themselves." I just don't agree. There is nothing of greater value than the individual human being.

3. Everyone knows that a fact is something that can be proven, something grounded in reliable evidence, that is, more than simply a rumor. Although I can't prove this particular allegation is a fact, it is more convincing to me than a rumor—and I guess I'm willing to call something this convincing a fact.

4. I read a study that claimed that chimpanzees are more evolved than human beings, but I don't see how this can be. After all, if chimps were more evolved than we are, wouldn't they be doing these studies on us?

5. Persons have rights, including the right to free speech. The Supreme Court has ruled that corporations are persons, so corporations have constitutionally protected rights just like all citizens of this country do.

6. The senator alleged that her Senate office phones had been illegally tapped by the FBI; later she suggested that by "tapped" she meant she had been under surveillance of some kind by some government agency. She has since stated that by "her office phones" she meant the office phones, her personal phones, and her and her staff's computers. She has further clarified that she actually meant "surveillance" to include routine monitoring that the FBI carries out on all calls to foreign officials. So, the initial claim should now be understood to mean that the senator believes some communication between her office and foreign governments, by her or her staff, had been routinely monitored by the FBI or some related organization—a common and perfectly legal occurrence.

C.   Explain the response to an equivocal term that is employed in this example.

What does socialized medicine mean? "Socialized" carries a negative connotation for many people in the United States, and yet can mean simply that the government is involved with the financial backing of medical care. The term can also mean a particular political philosophy which opposes private ownership and sees a central government as responsible for the entire economy. By exploiting this double meaning, the opponents of government-backed medical care can make it appear to be associated with communism or Marxism.

D.   Identify the specific language problem in each of the following statements.

1. This class is suitable for the beginner through advanced levels and everyone in between.

2. I have investigated the topic from one end of the political pole to the other.

3. Leaders on both sides refuse to work for compromise, hoping instead that war will lead to the inhalation of their enemies.

4. Health care is still a very difficult needle to thread, and a lot of people think the president was spiking the football a little too early yesterday when the new bill passed the House by a razor-thin margin.

5. He self-taught himself everything there was to know about navigation.

6. With the latest Supreme Court decision, we can finally take gay marriage off the table as a political football.

7. My research makes light of how these artists participate in the dominant ideology.

8. Our opponents have employed misleading language to make this disastrous situation sound good to the eyes of the American people.

E.   Each of the following sentences reflects a problem with a word. Which word causes the problem? Which word or words should have been used instead?

1. The biblical profits spoke the message in their own words.

2. He advanced a good argument, one that most people should easily except.

3. With the acception of only two books, all his novels are about women.

4. The audience was made up entirely of perspective student athletes.

5. During the ceremony to commemorate the five hundredth anniversary of Columbus's voyage, one of his ancestors gave a very memorable speech.

6. I chose to discuss weather the NEA should be abolished.

7. My uncle was involved in a very serious accident in which his foot was decapitated.

8. Justice can become a very ridged concept in some courtrooms.

9. I will try to explain how I derive at the conclusion that more gun control laws will not help control violence.

10. This passage eludes to the tremendous power of ancient Rome.

11. Lewis had a sorted past.

12. Exact statistics on the number of homeless people in the United States very greatly.

13. The new rules state that a doctor is not aloud to discuss his or her employment status with a patient.

F.   The following sentences contain errors of grammar, punctuation, or structure. Suggest how each sentence might be rewritten for greater clarity.

1. Cost overruns, which have become common in building nuclear power plants, have made this source of energy far less economical than was previously thought at its onset.

2. I wish to show how the *Webster* decision is not only morally but constitutionally correct, and overall is what the people of the United States are pushing for and have wanted a long time.

3. Cable television, with its preponderance of sound bites, has become the means by which many, perhaps, sadly obtain the bulk of their information.

4. The reaction was caused. By combining the two chemicals.

5. Values also were important because most of the athletes and their parents were looking for a school that values school first, then athletics, and I needed to express that in my speech that it is like that at my college.

ENDNOTES

[1] "The Supreme Court Removes Important Limits on Campaign Finance," *The Washington Post,* January 22, 2010, http://www.washingtonpost.com/wp-dyn/content/article/2010/01/21/AR2010012104482.html.

[2] Nicholas Dodman, *Pets on the Couch: Neurotic Dogs, Compulsive Cats, Anxious Birds, and the New Science of Animal Psychology* (New York: Atria, 2017).

RECOMMENDED WEBSITES

Editing Tips for Effective Writing

Walter McDougall and Tomoharu Nishino

www.sas.upenn.edu/irp/advising/thesis-writers/editing-tips-effective-writing

The University of Pennsylvania International Relations Program provides helpful suggestions for more effective language in your writing and speaking.

Notes on Ambiguity

Ernest Davis

http://cs.nyu.edu/faculty/davise/ai/ambiguity.html

For a more detailed system for identifying and categorizing sources of ambiguity, see this website provided by Professor Ernest Davis of New York University.

VI

Types and Tests
of Arguments

14 Analogies, Examples, Metonymy, and Narratives

> Metaphors are much more tenacious than facts.
> *Paul de Man (1919–1983)*
> *Belgian literary theorist*

> A woman without a man is like a fish without a bicycle.
> *Gloria Steinem (1934–)*
> *United States feminist writer*

KEY TERMS

a fortiori argument	conclusion relationship	judicial analogy
analogy	dangerous precedent	literal analogy
argument from example	emotional appeal	metaphor
	evidence case	metonymy
coherence	evidence relationship	rule of justice
conclusion case	fidelity	special pleading
	figurative analogy	worldview

Some scientists believe that human-like intelligence can be recreated in computers. Others disagree, arguing that computers will never be able to replicate the subtlety and complexity of human thought. The debate over artificial intelligence depends on whether researchers accept the comparison of the human brain to a computer. For those who understand the brain to operate much like computers, artificial intelligence is seen as a real possibility. However, for researchers who reject the comparison of the brain to a computer, artificial intelligence is seen as extremely unlikely. The debate continues. At its center is an argument discussed in this chapter—the analogy, or reasoning by comparison.

Analogies and a closely related argument, the argument from example, are among the most common arguments we encounter in public discourse. They are similar in that each uses a specific instance or case as evidence to support its conclusions. The analogy, however, draws a conclusion about the case from another similar case. The argument from example *generalizes* from one or a small number of cases to an entire class of objects or events. This chapter considers, as well, how these arguments can be evaluated. It will take up two additional methods of reasoning that lead an audience to visualize or imagine a situation, an event, or a solution to a problem: the metonym and the narrative argument.

ANALOGIES

A lobbyist for a national organization interested in firearms made the following argument to the school board of a major United States city:

> Students should be taught handgun safety in school. After all, cars are potentially lethal instruments, and we teach students how to drive safely in the public schools.

In this argument the lobbyist compared a familiar and generally accepted extracurricular educational goal, driver's education, with a less familiar extracurricular goal that he was advocating: firearms education.

Comparisons such as this, analogies, are among the most frequently encountered forms of argument. An **analogy** is *a comparison of something with which we are familiar to something with which we are less familiar, or about which we have some question.* Analogies often urge a conclusion about the unfamiliar case on the basis of what we know about the more familiar case. They can be highly effective arguments, though they also involve some built-in risks.

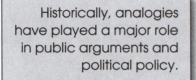

Historically, analogies have played a major role in public arguments and political policy.

Historically, analogies have played a major role in shaping public arguments and even political policy. In his campaign speech for the Illinois Senate on June 16, 1858, Abraham Lincoln used an analogy grounded in a biblical allusion to show the significance of the national political crisis over slavery:

> "A house divided against itself cannot stand." I believe this government cannot endure permanently half slave and half free. I do not expect the Union to be dissolved—I do not expect the house to fall—but I do expect it will cease to be divided. It will become all one thing, or all the other.

Lincoln's analogy of the union to a house (a family)—an allusion to a verse in the New Testament—shaped how many people in the US thought about the nation on the brink of the Civil War.

We will consider two basic types of analogies: literal and figurative.

Literal Analogies

The **literal analogy** is *a direct comparison between two allegedly similar items or cases.* Literal analogies play a variety of useful roles in developing arguments. They can clarify a meaning, explain a complex process, emphasize the extent of a problem, help to identify causes, or argue for fair treatment of a person or group.

Let's take a closer look at one way of employing an analogy. When used to clarify the meaning of an important term or concept, an analogy can help satisfy the test of linguistic consistency. For instance, the word "theory" elicits a great deal of controversy in the debate over evolution. David Quammen, writing in *National Geographic,* employs an analogy to clarify that "theory" does not always imply that an idea is untested or uncertain. The fact that evolution is a theory, Quammen explains, does not mean that evolution is "'just' a theory," any more than "relativity as described by Albert Einstein is 'just' a theory."[1] A "theory" in this sense means a widely accepted model supported by evidence, as Quammen's analogy makes clear.

A literal analogy might compare a person to a person, a city to a city, or a product to another similar product. Such an argument moves from an **evidence case,** *a familiar or widely established instance that is used as the basis for the argument,* to claims about a **conclusion case,** *an instance in the argument about which a claim is being advanced.* As you read the following example, try to identify the evidence case and the conclusion case:

> In their search for a nonaddictive opioid painkiller, scientists are looking to a common aquarium fish for help—the saber-toothed blenny. The blenny produces a venom that has dramatic pain-reducing properties in humans. Can such a solution work? It certainly wouldn't be the first time a medical fix has been discovered in the animal kingdom. Some common blood pressure drugs known as ACE inhibitors are a synthetic version of snake venom. This new painkiller from blennies is similar—it has a chemical structure that is easy to reproduce in the lab and it can pass quickly from the digestive tract to the blood stream.

What is the evidence case here? It is blood pressure medicine, a familiar case about which agreement exists. Thus, medicine serves as evidence in the argument. The potential for new painkillers, on the other hand, is the conclusion case. The argument seeks to establish the conclusion that new medicine may be derived from poisonous venoms.

Simple literal analogies—comparisons with no special or unusual qualities— reflect the following structure:

> **Evidence:** The evidence case is similar to the conclusion case in at least one important respect.
>
> **Connective:** The presence of some similarities between any two cases suggests the likelihood of other similarities.
>
> Thus,
>
> **Conclusion:** The conclusion case is also likely to be similar to the evidence case in other important respects.

When we are willing to accept that some similarities may suggest other similarities between the two cases being compared, we are judging the analogy to be a sound one. Because the evidence and the conclusion cases in an analogy are never actually identical, however, we should be cautious about employing an analogy as the sole support for a conclusion. Analogies are best used in combination with other kinds of arguments and evidence.

We are drawn to analogies as a way of rendering our ideas both understandable and persuasive. Nevertheless, it is important to test analogies to make sure they are reasonable.

Testing Literal Analogies

When someone argues from evident similarities, one possible option for rebuttal is to point to differences between the evidence and the conclusion cases. This response to a literal analogy is suggested by the question:

1. Are the cases being compared dissimilar in some critical respect? A critical dissimilarity is one that is relevant to the argument's conclusion. Here is an example of answering a literal analogy by applying the test of critical dissimilarity.

> There has been a great deal of public outcry over government bureaus such as the National Security Agency examining private email accounts. Some surveillance advocates point to a Supreme Court decision in the 1970s that allowed the Postal Service to examine the address on the outside of a mailed

envelope. They argue that what the NSA is currently doing is no different. However, the potential for invading the privacy of an email user by instantly examining a list of thousands of email addresses is vastly greater than was the slow and random process of physically examining the outside of a few dozen paper envelopes.

In this analogy, addresses on envelopes serve as the evidence case and email addresses as the conclusion case. A single important dissimilarity—the potential for examining a huge volume of email addresses in a short time—is said to counteract similarities between the evidence and conclusion cases in the original analogy. Looking for differences between the evidence and the conclusion cases is the first and most obvious means of testing a literal analogy.

There are other possibilities for testing literal analogies, however. Because analogies always involve presenting two allegedly comparable cases, a second possibility for testing analogies can be presented as the question:

2. Are the two cases presented accurately? If either the evidence or conclusion case in an analogy is presented inaccurately, the argument is weakened substantially. Applying this test to the example above, we would ask whether the situations with email and regular addresses were both described accurately. For example, does the NSA examine thousands of email addresses at a time? An analogy is reasonable only to the extent that its two cases are presented accurately, and persuasive only to the extent that the audience accepts both as accurate.

Analogies often can be answered by other comparisons that lead to quite different conclusions. Thus, a third test of analogies asks:

3. Is a better analogy available? One possibility for rebuttal when responding to a literal analogy is to advance a different comparison that strikes the audience as more appropriate. Thus, rather than comparing email addresses to addresses on paper envelopes, we might suggest comparing surveillance of email addresses to a similar method of collecting and examining cell phone numbers that have been called. Both these methods of surveillance can be carried out much more quickly than the physical examination of paper envelopes ever could have been in the past, and each provides a more accurate picture of a user's patterns of communication.

When we use this test, we are actually advancing a new analogy of our own that is subject to each of the tests just discussed. The process of argumentation involves continuing critical scrutiny of our own arguments as well as others' arguments.

Two Special Varieties of Literal Analogy

Though all literal analogies make comparisons between allegedly similar things, two special cases operate in ways that deserve particular consideration: the *a fortiori* argument and the judicial analogy.

A Fortiori Argument

The **a fortiori argument** is *a literal analogy that asserts that what is true of its evidence case is even more likely or even less likely to be true of its conclusion case.* (The term "a fortiori" means "from that which is stronger.") A critic of genetic enhancement makes the following *a fortiori* comparison to cosmetic surgery and Botox injections:

> Like cosmetic surgery, genetic enhancement employs medical means for nonmedical ends—ends unrelated to curing or preventing disease, or to repairing injury. But unlike cosmetic surgery, genetic enhancement is more than skin deep. If we are ambivalent about surgery or Botox injections for sagging chins and furrowed brows, we are all the more troubled by genetic

engineering for stronger bodies, sharper memories, greater intelligence, and happier moods.[2]

This advocate is arguing that if we are troubled by superficial medical treatments aimed only at physical enhancement, then we should be more troubled by advanced medical procedures with the same goal.

Here is another example of *a fortiori* reasoning:

> Silicon Valley invented a self-driving car. If they want to come up with effective measures to prevent abuse on Twitter they can certainly do it.

In this example, the evidence case is self-driving cars. The conclusion case is Twitter. The movement from evidence to conclusion case involves the *a fortiori* claim that inventing a self-driving car is a *more* difficult challenge than is fixing Twitter. The argument is that if Silicon Valley can solve the first challenge, it can certainly solve the second.

Judicial Analogy

The **judicial analogy** is *a literal analogy that insists on similar treatment for people, ideas, or institutions in similar circumstances.* The treatment that one person, idea, or institution has already received—the evidence case—is taken as the standard of just treatment for some other allegedly similar case—the conclusion case. In judicial analogies the evidence case is not simply compared to but *contrasted with* the conclusion case. Consider the following argument:

> We have instituted a range of laws to protect the rights of intelligent animals such as apes and dolphins. Many of our most capable computers and robots now exhibit similar levels of intelligence, and thus deserve similar protections against abuse.

Here is another judicial analogy, albeit a subtler one. On the topic of transgender access to bathrooms, an advocate states, "It's not about bathrooms, as it was never about drinking fountains." In this analogy, the evidence case is racial segregation. That issue was symbolized by segregated drinking fountains, but the real issue was always civil rights. Similarly, the argument over access to bathrooms—the conclusion case—is also about the larger issue of civil rights. As one case was resolved in favor of justice, so the argument goes, so should the other be.

These judicial analogies involve a widely accepted connective that has been called the **rule of justice,** *the idea that similar cases should be treated similarly.* In their book, *The New Rhetoric,* Chaïm Perelman and Lucie Olbrechts-Tyteca write that "the rule of justice requires giving identical treatment to beings or situations of the same kind."[3]

The judicial analogy, perhaps more than any other type of analogy, depends on establishing the close similarity of the cases being compared. The rule of justice demands that the cases be clearly similar in all relevant ways except the treatment they have received, so it is particularly important to ask whether a crucial dissimilarity exists between the cases being compared. For example, the university's athletic director might respond to an analogy comparing salaries of men's and women's basketball coaches by arguing that the men's coach is responsible for filling thirteen thousand seats in an arena for a game and bringing in one-third of the operating budget of the athletic program, whereas the women's coach has no such obligations. Thus, to the university they are not "similar cases."

A rebuttal to the judicial analogy might claim that a legitimate exception should be made in one or a limited number of cases. The term **special pleading** is sometimes applied to *the claim that an exception should be made to the rule or principle that would otherwise apply.* For example, military leaders do not like to make exceptions to rules regarding soldiers being assigned to combat duty, but exceptions are occasionally made on the basis of unusual family situations or health problems. Such a case might represent a legitimate instance of special pleading. Because of the potential for abuse inherent in special pleading, it is often referred to as the fallacy of special pleading. A typical response to special pleading is that it might establish a **dangerous precedent**, that is, *a basis for a series of undesirable exceptions for similarly exceptional cases.*

The rule of justice has a great deal of force in democratic societies. Certain rights, such as equal protection under the law, and some practices, such as allowing candidates equal time to present their views in the media, are grounded in a widely held acceptance of the rule of justice. When it can be clearly established that two cases are, in fact, similar, the rule of justice is a powerful principle. Judicial analogies are persuasive and have exerted unparalleled influence on our society recently, as exemplified by advocates of the women's movement, the civil rights movement, and more recently the gay rights movement. To be reasonable, these analogies must compare similar cases, present their evidence accurately, and not involve an illegitimate exception to the rule of justice.

Metaphors or Figurative Analogies

The analogies considered so far compare similar things. A **metaphor** or **figurative analogy** is *a comparison between things that are not of the same type, that come from different realms of experience.* Oceanographer David Doubilet, writing for *National Geographic,* provides the following brilliant metaphoric description of the exotic sea life inhabiting Lembeh Strait, off the coast of Indonesia:

> Think of a coral reef as Las Vegas: a glowing city of sexy fish slitting down boulevards of neon corals. Then imagine an undersea neighborhood that's more like the gritty desert beyond Vegas, where you run into quirky characters like the guy running the one-pump gas station, or the bar where people wait for aliens. That's Indonesia's Lembeh Strait.[4]

Metaphors often provide excellent means of describing or clarifying a situation, as Doubilet demonstrates. They can also help audiences visualize a situation or problem. As linguist George Lakoff and his coauthor Mark Johnson write, however, metaphors do much more than just illustrate: metaphors "structure our actions and thought."[5]

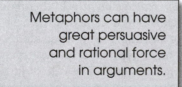

Metaphors can have great persuasive and rational force in arguments.

The metaphors we use to describe situations, people, and events shape how we understand our world. Consequently, they can have great persuasive and rational force in arguments. Lakoff and Johnson suggest, for instance, that we have many metaphorical ways of talking about love. Their examples include seeing love as a kind of magic ("She cast a spell over me") or as a kind of insanity ("I'm crazy about him"). We might even understand love as a kind of physical force ("They gravitated to each other immediately"). The metaphor to which we are most drawn will shape our view of our deepest feelings and commitments.[6]

Lakoff and Johnson emphasize the power of metaphors or figurative analogies to influence an audience's perceptions of a wide range of issues. Here are two other examples drawn from the history of psychology. In attempting to understand how the brain—a physical organ—produces the conscious experience we call thought, scientists through the centuries have often turned to metaphors. For instance, the eighteenth-century French psychologist Pierre Cabanis was famous for saying, "The brain secretes thought as the liver secretes bile." Similarly, the nineteenth-century Dutch physiologist Jakob Moleschott is alleged to have said, "The brain secretes thought as the kidney secretes urine." In these metaphors Cabanis and Moleschott compared things that are not alike—bile or urine and thought. Today, even though the brain *is* a physical organ, most people would agree that thought is something quite different from bile, but these scientists' metaphors proved quite powerful for a very long time.[7]

Are figurative analogies arguments? Some experts do not accept metaphoric comparisons as arguments, only as means of clarifying, illustrating, or making writing more appealing. Nevertheless, metaphors are often used in public discourse as a type of argument, or to bolster an argument. Because audiences frequently find them convincing—even more convincing at times than traditional forms of argument—we should have some understanding of their role as arguments. The persuasive power of the figurative analogy is related to its capacity to help audiences visualize a situation.

The following argument involves a common figurative analogy:

> Pornography is a cancer in our land. Like a cancer, it must be removed before it destroys our society.

This example involves an argument from figurative analogy. Does it actually prove anything, though? Before answering this question we have to recognize that, unlike literal analogies, figurative analogies do not compare characteristics between cases, but relationships between pairs of objects.

To clarify this point, let's imagine the argument in the example as two relationships between pairs of terms. The **evidence relationship** is *the familiar relationship pair that is used as support for the conclusion.* The **conclusion relationship** is *the relationship being urged in connection with the conclusion.* Our example, then, can be presented as the following relationships:

evidence relationship		*conclusion relationship*
Cancer is to the body	as	pornography is to the society.

What is the intended relationship between cancer and the body? The argument suggests that the relationship is one in which, if the former is not removed, it destroys the latter. What is affirmed, then, as the relationship between pornography and society? It is the same relationship as that between cancer and the body: destruction of one by the other if the latter is not removed. Thus, the conclusion is that pornography, like cancer, must be quickly removed from the "body" it infects. Unlike literal analogies, which move from case to case, figurative analogies move from one relationship to another relationship.

Figurative analogies suggest to our audiences how they should think about the subject under discussion. A carefully developed figurative analogy in the hands of a skilled writer can, for instance, shape a reader's view of the enterprise of science. This example is drawn from the philosopher Daniel Dennett:

> Through a microscope, the cutting edge of a beautifully sharpened ax looks like the Rocky Mountains, all jagged and irregular, but it is the dull heft of the steel behind the edge that gives the ax its power. Similarly, the cutting edge of science seen up close looks ragged and chaotic, a bunch of big egos engaging in shouting matches, their judgment distorted by jealousy, ambition and greed, but behind them, agreed upon by all disputants, is the massive routine weight of accumulated results, the facts that give science its power.[8]

FIGURE 14.1 Types of Analogies

Literal Analogies
- Simple literal
- *A fortiori*
- Judicial

These compare:

Evidence case   →   Conclusion case

Figurative Analogies (Metaphors)

These compare:

Evidence relationship   →   Conclusion relationship

Testing Figurative Analogies

Literal analogies and figurative analogies do not operate in exactly the same manner, so they are subject to different tests. We will use the "pornography as cancer" metaphor as our test case.

Because figurative analogies are used both as argument and as illustration, and because these two functions are easily confused, we must ask what role a specific figurative analogy is playing in a given argument. The first test of these analogies, then, is this:

1. Is the analogy advanced as illustration or as argument? For example, is the comparison of pornography to cancer advanced simply to illustrate what pornography is like, or is it offered as an argument against pornography? This analogy seems intended to do more than illustrate. It sounds as if it is being advanced to prove that pornography should be actively opposed. If the figurative analogy is advanced and understood as simply an illustration, we may be willing to accept it without careful scrutiny. The actual argument is somewhere else, not in the metaphor. If the figurative analogy is being advanced as an argument, however, it should be subjected to other tests.

Figurative analogies should not be used alone as arguments. Their nature as arguments that compare unlike things precludes this possibility. When a figurative analogy is advanced in the context of an argument, we need to ask:

2. Does the figurative analogy appear with other types of arguments? Rarely would we be willing to accept a metaphor as the sole support for a conclusion, but the line between illustration and argument is often blurred. Analogies can be highly persuasive by virtue of their ability to clarify; if we understand a point, we may think it has been proved.

When confronted with a persuasive metaphor we should be sure our judgment about the point in question is based on other types of arguments and evidence as well. In our example, we would not want to base a decision about how to regulate pornography on a single comparison to cancer.

We also should ask:

3. Are the relationships between the two pairs of terms in the figurative analogy, in fact, comparable? Similarity is what gives the figurative analogy value as illustration or argument. In order for a figurative analogy to have any impact, we must grasp the relationship between the two terms of the evidence relationship and accept a similar relationship between the two terms of the conclusion relationship.

The relationship between cancer and the body is one in which unchecked growth of the cancer eventually will destroy the life of the body. If we accept the analogy, we also accept that unchecked growth of pornography eventually will destroy a society. We also must accept that the presence of any pornography in society is as unacceptable as the presence of any cancer in the body. Further, we likely must accept that pornography grows like cancer—rapidly and inexorably. If we are inclined to reject any or all of these intended relational similarities, the figurative analogy fails this third test.

In responding to a figurative analogy, consider altering the analogy so as to support a different conclusion by exposing a different aspect of the compared relationship. We might argue that if our society has the cancer of pornography, it is certainly inoperable, and thus we must accept that fact, working not to "cure" ourselves but, rather, to control the cancer. Thus, rather than eradicate pornography, we should control or regulate it. Alternatively, we could extend the analogy to the point at which the conclusions it allows are absurd: If pornography is like cancer, it is a cancer people seek out and pay for. Shall we now expect that people will begin paying to be afflicted with cancer?

ARGUMENTS FROM EXAMPLE

Among the most astonishing success stories in the history of biotechnology is the sequencing of the human genome. The rapid decrease in the cost of genetic sequencing is often advanced as an example of how the costs of all medical biotechnologies are dropping. When the government's Human Genome Project was announced in 1990, the estimated cost to complete the sequencing of a single human genome was pegged at about $3 billion. By 2000 the cost had dropped to $300 million, still far beyond the range of even a wealthy consumer. By 2010, however, the cost of having your genome sequenced was down to $5,000, and only two years later to below $1,000. Today you can have the same work done for around $100. Can we generalize from this example that all health-related biotechnologies will exhibit a similarly precipitous drop in cost?

The argument from example, like the literal analogy, begins with a particular instance or case. However, an **argument from example** is *an argument that draws a conclusion about an entire class of objects or events based on a particular instance or a limited number of cases, rather than about a single member of a group.* Here's another instance of arguing from example:

> Hospital-acquired infections affect more than thirty million patients each year and result in ninety thousand deaths in the United States alone. We now know that simple procedural changes within hospitals can radically reduce these numbers. For example, the Mayo Clinic has reduced hospital-acquired infections by 30 percent simply by cleaning designated areas more frequently with a germicidal solution.[9]

The argument from example is employed when a single case or a small number of cases is considered sufficient to support a general claim. You can identify this type of argument because the example or examples will be named and a conclusion about an entire class of events, people, or objects then advanced. The argument from example is similar to the generalization from a statistical sample, except that it advances a single case or a limited number of cases as its evidence.

Returning to the Mayo Clinic example, the indicator "we now know" signals that the speaker thinks this case is sufficient to allow a conclusion about all similar procedural changes in hospitals. When we argue from example, we assert that a representative example or two are adequate to support a generalization to all similar instances. The connective assumption in the argument from example, therefore, is that the example is typical of the category.

In testing the argument from example, we should look first at this underlying assumption that connects the evidence to its conclusion. It is always important to ask of such an argument:

1. Is the example representative of the class from which it is drawn? In the example about the Mayo Clinic, we should consider other cases of similar procedural changes before generalizing. This case may not be typical of all hospitals; other examples might show different results.

A single, well-substantiated example can change the course of history, however. Doctors had long assumed that stomach ulcers were caused by stress, but Dr. Barry Marshall believed they were caused by bacteria. Because no one would support his research, in 1984 he ingested the suspected bacterium himself. "I drank it down very quickly, like a tequila shot," he said, in the process consuming several billion bacteria. (He later developed peptic ulcers.) Marshall says he drank the solution "out of sheer frustration," in an effort to prove his theory. Marshall's "single example—himself—changed all subsequent research on ulcers," writes reporter Rachel Sobel.[10] For his "gutsy" experiment, Marshall won the Nobel Prize in medicine.

Because an example argument rests on such a small number of cases, it is crucial that the example is true. A second test of example arguments asks:

2. Is the example reported accurately? An example is of no use if it can be shown to be not true to fact, or to be an exaggeration. In our example, the information about the Mayo Clinic is part of a publicized hospital study and is accurately reported. In other instances, however, the example may be exaggerated or important details left unreported.

In addition to testing examples according to the criteria of being both typical and factual, it is often possible to answer an example argument with a counter-example. Thus, we should always ask:

3. Is a counter-example available? While there is a downward line of cost when considering human genome sequencing, the same sort of analysis is not true of all other widely used medical technologies. For example, magnetic resonance imaging procedures have also come down in cost over the past several decades, but they now exhibit a wide price range that is governed by which part of the country you live in and which type of machine is used to perform the imaging. The machines themselves cost from $150,000 to more than $1.5 million, and the procedure ranges in price from $500 in some parts of the country to more than $5,000 in other locations. Big cities, especially on the East Coast, seem to be centers for high-cost magnetic resonance imaging, so medical technology costs in general may not be reflected in the simple downward line we can draw to describe genome sequencing.

METONYMY

A visualization approach frequently encountered in public discourse is related to the argument from example. Rather than one member of a group representing the entire group, **metonymy** is *the use of one object to represent another associated object, or of a single attribute to represent a complex object.* Like analogies, metonyms may be figurative. A British officer telling troops that, "Today we must defend the Crown," means that the soldiers must defend the Queen and all that the Queen represents—the United Kingdom. Here, an inanimate object—a queen's crown—represents an associated individual, but also a government and even a nation. Notice that this metonym is likely to have a greater emotional impact than would the statement, "We are fighting today because of decisions made by several of the Queen's military advisers, hawks in the House of Commons, and pressure from our allies."

Other metonyms are more literal. If the Secretary of State tells a group of reporters that "US tanks arrived in the Kurdish sector today," he is indicating only that the tanks themselves actually arrived in an area. His intended message, however, is that heavily armed US soldiers have arrived in the territory and are prepared to fight a battle. The metonym of the tanks thus becomes an abbreviated argument—it makes US purposes clear in a brief but effective way. This calculated use of metonymy strategically focuses the audience's attention on military force in a manner that differs from the statement, "Five United States Army officers and forty-five enlisted personnel arrived in the Kurdish section today."

Similarly, "angry shouts and fists greeted the security forces that tried to break up yesterday's protests in Sao Paulo," means the security forces encountered angry *people.* The statement has a very different meaning from "A crowd of people greeted the security forces that tried to break up yesterday's protests."

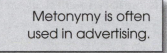

Metonymy is often used in advertising.

Metonymy is often used in advertising. For instance, a large discount store might run an advertisement in which a low-level employee is used to represent the company itself. The company wishes to be thought of as friendly and courteous, but these are not qualities the public usually associates with large companies. Thus, we read the following lines below a picture of a smiling middle-aged woman wearing a company shirt:

Bonnie W. *is* MegaCorp, and she cares about the people she works for—You!

A part of the company—Bonnie W.—stands for the whole company, leading to the generalization, "MegaCorp cares about you."

Metonymy is closely related to arguments that rely heavily or solely on visual images, a topic to be discussed in greater detail in Chapter 17.

NARRATIVE ARGUMENTS

A moment's reflection suggests that we are by nature storytellers. For reasons that have roots in our distant past, we seem naturally drawn to stories. Experienced public speakers know that if they want to attract the attention of an audience, it is as simple as saying, "Let me tell you a story." It has seriously been suggested that the name *homo narrans*—storytelling being—may be a more appropriate label for humans than is the traditional *homo sapiens,* or rational being. Consider just some of the many ways in which we encounter stories: in personal interactions, social media, novels, movies, and television programs, but also in video and online games, popular songs, and even in advertisements.

But stories are often intended as more than entertainment. They can be used to present arguments and influence audiences. Stories are highly persuasive. Many speeches, particularly those with autobiographical content, follow the form of a story. Candidates make extensive use of their personal narratives and other stories to shape public opinion of themselves. Understanding the basic elements of narrative argument can help us explore a wider range of arguments we discover embedded in the activity of storytelling.

Narrative Argument: Pros and Cons

Why would a writer or speaker choose to employ a story to convey a set of claims? Stories help listeners "see" how a set of ideas might work themselves out in the world of everyday life. Thus, narratives can be highly persuasive.

Second, narratives have the capacity to render an idea plausible by putting it directly into the audience's stream of experience. This effect seems to work in two ways simultaneously. First, the listener or viewer encounters a story as an account of the lives of other people, making judgments about characters and events. Second, at the same time, listeners project themselves into the story, identifying with characters and their predicaments. As a result, stories are a very personal and emotional method for presenting an argument. Stories thus have an inherent appeal to audiences that nonfiction prose often does not. As audience members relate personally to a story they hear or read, the narrative involves them more directly than does simply setting out reasons and conclusions.

A story's capacity to cause us to see a series of events cannot be separated from its capacity to affect us emotionally. What we see or vividly imagine engages our emotions. Whereas a speech or editorial affects us rationally and perhaps secondarily through our emotions, a story goes directly to our feelings about life and death, victory and failure, love and loss—issues about which we all experience strong affective responses. The impact of a story means that **emotional appeal**—*engaging the audience's emotions for the purpose of persuasion*—is a central concern of narratives. (Chapter 18 discusses emotional appeals in more depth.)

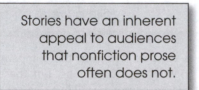

Stories have an inherent appeal to audiences that nonfiction prose often does not.

If stories are so powerfully persuasive, then why don't advocates use them exclusively, shaping all their arguments as narratives? Some advocates do rely heavily on stories, but narratives have built-in limitations as a method of presenting an argument. What, then, are the disadvantages of narrative argument?

The most obvious disadvantage of the narrative approach is the relative difficulty of presenting evidence. The "evidence" in a narrative comes in the form of the audience's capacity to believe that the story is authentic, that its predicaments, solutions, and characters are credible. Stories convince by a combination of visualizing a situation and forging an emotional connection with an audience, but some important information about an actual problem or proposal can seem awkward within the context of a story. For instance, a storyteller may portray boys acting aggressively, but is unlikely to have a character say, "I just read this really fascinating study in the *Journal of the American Medical Association.* It shows clearly that exposure to violent movies increases the violent actions of adolescent boys."

One foundational rule of good storytelling is, "Show, don't tell." Vivid portrayal is the key to successful stories; audiences will reject stories they find "preachy" or overly instructive. Still, well-constructed arguments require a certain degree of instruction—audiences need to have facts presented to them.

A second weakness of the narrative approach to argument is the loss of precision, detail, and comprehensive coverage in the presentation of a case. Because the elements of the story itself—plot, character development, scene, and mood—require the author's primary attention, a story may lack the details, nuances, and intricacies of a public controversy. Narratives portray a difficult situation, either as the broad strokes of events in a plot or simply as obstacles facing a protagonist. They do not usually portray the precise details of an important public crisis, a problem's historical development, new evidence that has come to light, or the arguments arrayed for and against various solutions. Because of these weaknesses in narrative argument, politicians, religious leaders, and other public figures often fashion their cases out of a mix of narratives and traditional arguments.

Protagonists, Values, and Worldviews

Stories are complex phenomena involving many components. Nevertheless, we can identify a few elements that are present in most narratives and crucial to their use in argumentative contexts. Identifying these elements is a first step toward understanding narrative as argument.

We will consider, first, the protagonist as a component in a story, then values, and finally worldview. If we suspect that a story is being presented with a persuasive intent—that it is advancing an argument—we should ask:

1. What does the protagonist believe in or strive for? The protagonist's motives and interests can provide a key to understanding the underlying claims of a narrative argument. We might boil this criterion down to the question: What does the protagonist want? Of course, we must also be alert to the fact that authors do not always write their own interests into their protagonists' interests. Some protagonists are clearly *not* speaking for the author, as is the case with Huckleberry Finn in Mark Twain's novel by the same name. Do we detect irony on the author's part? If, however, the protagonist emerges as an admirable figure, it is especially important to ask what he or she is pursuing.

For example, suppose the governor of a state wishes to promote voter support for public schools in advance of an important referendum. She sets out reasons regarding graduation rates, money to support teacher salaries, and the need for new school buildings, but she also incorporates a story—albeit a nonfiction story—to support her case. The story involves a child named Gary in a typical elementary school who has overcome various personal obstacles to succeed in school. Gary has a hearing impairment and grew up in an impoverished family, but he has not allowed these factors to prevent him from succeeding in school. In fact, Gary has recently won an award for his high score on a mathematics test. His teachers have written to the governor to tell her of Gary's determination and success. Gary has also written to the governor, urging her to tell people how important the schools are to thousands of children like him. The governor reads a passage from Gary's letter as part of her speech.

We can locate several important components in this protagonist's portrayal that contribute to the governor's case. First, the protagonist—the student—values both education and the public schools. Second, the protagonist personifies virtues, including hard work and determination. By building this story into her speech, the governor morally supports her claim that the public schools deserve voters' support. Third, the governor has forged a crucial emotional link with her audience. Notice that she has asked her audience to visualize an actual child, who now represents in an almost tangible way what the public schools mean emotionally to students.

It may have occurred to you that the governor's story functions as a type of argument from example; it advances what she hopes will be accepted as a typical case that represents many other students. Many stories used as part of an argument share a close relationship to the argument from example. As members of the audience, we see clearly what the protagonist desires (support for the public schools), and what values and virtues he represents (hard work, determination, love of education).

As this instance suggests, stories may have embedded within them an author's values and moral commitments. These values are persuasively conveyed to the audience through the story's capacity for visualization and emotional connection. Thus, a second question worth asking in the face of a narrative argument is:

2. What values inform the action in this story? One way of answering this question is to examine the values the admirable characters in the story advocate, choose, or represent. Do the attractive characters in the story seek freedom, self-determination, redemption, or victory over adversity? These may be the same things the author advocates through the narrative. A third question to ask of a narrative argument is:

3. What worldview emerges from this narrative? Often a story encapsulates *an entire system of interconnected assumptions and beliefs,* what we might term a **worldview.** Religions such as Christianity or Hinduism represent significant worldviews, but so does a comprehensive economic system such as capitalism or Marxism. A narrative's worldview is a moral system—often the author's own—within which a story's characters act and make decisions. Characters working against the protagonist may be found to reject the story's worldview, but are still bound by it.

Testing Narrative Arguments

We have been asking generally about the moral core of a narrative argument, the values, virtues, and beliefs it advocates. Of course, a narrative argument also has to be persuasive, so we need to ask what specific factors render a story not simply entertaining or instructive, but also persuasive to an audience. Two helpful criteria for evaluating a story's force as argument are coherence and fidelity.

The first, **coherence,** asks, *Do the components in this story create a meaningful and consistent whole?* In asking this question we are going inside the story to determine whether the action in the narrative is convincing on its own terms, whether it has a consistent internal logic. We might say that each narrative establishes its own set of rules by which its characters must abide. Whereas authors and other artists are not obliged to be perfectly consistent, a high degree of inconsistency renders a story implausible to an audience. For instance, if one of the story's main characters is suffering from a mental illness, the author has some obligation to understand the nature of that illness and to maintain some consistency in how the affected character behaves. In movies exploring a dangerously controlling individual, such as *The Master* (2012), *The Great Gatsby* (2013), or *The Founder* (2016)—the writer and director need to strive for a believable portrayal of the main character's personality. If the portrayal of control is compromised for the audience by a suggestion of empathy or altruism, the narrative's argument or message may be compromised as well.

The second test, **fidelity,** asks, *Does this story reflect what I know to be true about life experiences and human nature?* In asking about fidelity, we are essentially asking whether a narrative is true to life. Of course, numerous fictional stories are set in fantastic locations—distant planets, lost islands, the future—but even those stories can elicit in us a sense that the characters are acting as we would expect them to, that they are dealing with their circumstances as we or people we know would if faced with similar situations.

> In asking about fidelity, we ask whether a narrative is true to life.

A movie that many viewers felt violated the criterion of fidelity is *Star Trek: Into Darkness* (2013). Despite the presumably advanced technology of the future era in which it is set, many stealthy maneuvers go undetected by the movie's antagonists. Science fiction aficionados were quick to point out these rather conspicuous violations of technological progress. In this way the narrative failed to demonstrate fidelity: what we know about current technological advances was contradicted by implausible events in a more advanced technological future. By contrast, Matt Damon's character in *The Martian* (2015) struck audiences as reacting to his isolation on Mars in a believable manner. When a story violates fidelity, the force of any argument it might be advancing is weakened.[11]

CHAPTER REVIEW

Analogies are among the most frequently encountered arguments in public controversies. A literal analogy depends on establishing similarities between the things compared. Thus, it is susceptible to refutation by showing a critical dissimilarity between the evidence case and the conclusion case or relationships. Two special types of literal analogy are the *a fortiori* argument and the judicial analogy. When carefully employed, an analogy can be a persuasive and reasonable argument.

Figurative analogies, or metaphors, compare the *relationships* between two pairs of terms, with each pair drawn from a different realm of experience. Because they compare items that are not similar, some theorists question whether these arguments are ever reasonable. They are used as arguments, however, so we should understand how they work.

If a figurative analogy is advanced as an argument, not merely as an illustration, we should ask whether other arguments are advanced in support of the same point. We should also ask whether the relationships on each side of the analogy are, in fact, similar. Finally, even a good figurative analogy may be altered to support a contrary conclusion.

An argument by example bases a general conclusion on a particular case or example. Such an argument, however, does not move directly to a conclusion about a separate case, but rather draws a generalization about other members of the class from which the example is drawn. We should test an argument by example to ensure that the example is reported accurately, that it is not atypical, and that important counter-examples are not available.

Metonyms, like example arguments, use one object to represent an associated object. Careful use of metonymy can subtly shape how an audience understands a situation.

Finally, arguments may also be advanced in narrative form, so we need to recognize and be prepared to evaluate the persuasive and logical potential in the stories we see and hear.

EXERCISES

A.   State which type of literal analogy is developed in each of the following examples—simple, judicial, or *a fortiori*—along with the reasons for your identification. Identify the evidence case, conclusion case, and conclusion for each argument. Employing the tests of literal analogies, note any weaknesses that may be present in each comparison.

1. Just as bacteria in your stomach help you to digest food, bacteria in the soil help the soil to break down organic materials for plant nutrition.

2. When the first heart transplant was performed in the 1960s, there were loud protests from people who claimed that such a procedure was immoral. But everyone eventually got used to the idea and forgot the moral objections entirely. The same thing will happen when people see the practical results of cloning.

3. Leaders of industries that destroy the environment by their careless attitude toward pollution should be prosecuted for murder. They are murdering the Earth just as surely as a killer murders a human victim.

4. The Silicon Valley tech industries are living in an unrealistic bubble when it comes to future growth. Just look at housing prices. Over the past five years, growth in housing prices has exceeded those in New York by 65 percent. That's more of a gap than we saw at the height of the dotcom explosion of 2001–2002, when Silicon Valley housing prices exceeded New York prices by 58 percent.

5. High school principal to press: "I will not allow known gang members to come to school. The threat to my students is even greater than if a child came to school with measles. If a student is involved in a gang, I will simply say, 'You stay away from the school. You are considered a threat.'"

6. Men and women perform the same duties in other military settings, so allowing women in combat is only fair.

7. Thousands of people in the US struggle to locate adequate childcare. The government refuses to get involved, arguing that the system should remain privatized. Yet, Scandinavian countries have had nationalized childcare services since the 1970s without major problems arising and with adequate childcare available to everyone who wants it.

8. Some people are so dense as to question whether animals really experience pain under the rigors of experimentation. Wouldn't you experience pain if those experiments were performed on you?

9. You're asking whether we would be able to control the use of drugs if they were legalized. We can't even control the use of alcohol. How in the world are we supposed to be able to control the use of legalized drugs?

10. Business writer Rich Karlgaard notes, "One-third of Los Angeles residents now tell pollsters that they are sick of their city." Karlgaard attributes much of this unhappiness to the problems associated with illegal immigration. "What religion is to contemporary U.S. national politics—a bitter and hardening divide—illegal immigration is to California politics."[12]

B. Identify the example or examples advanced as evidence in each of the following arguments. What general conclusion is derived from each example? Employing the tests of example arguments, identify any potential weaknesses in the examples.

1. You can buy an Aston Martin Cygnet for around $40,000. Just be aware that you are not buying an Aston Martin at all, but a Toyota iQ. Sold as a Toyota product, the same car sells for around $20,000. This is not a rare occurrence, as car companies often change the identity of a less expensive car and then double or triple the price.

2. The oldest known use of zero as a placeholder in a numerical system is in Cambodia. A clear use of zero was discovered in a temple inscription dating from around 600 CE. Thus, the ancient residents of Southeast Asia had highly developed mathematical systems long before Europeans, who did not use zero until about 1100.

3. Retailers increasingly rely on sophisticated algorithms in setting prices. This requires that they hire economists who have skill in evaluating large data sets. Amazon currently has sixty full-time economists on its staff.

4. Sea captains can be trained to be conscientious about pollution. Korea already requires all captains to be educated in the international laws on dumping waste into the oceans. That requirement has made a major difference in the pollution-related activities of Korean ships.

5. California's new hands-free phone law shows that legislation banning handheld cell phone use while driving can be highly effective.

6. US foreign policy is shifting toward a less unified Europe, one reflecting the old model of independent and competing nations. The administration's support for nationalist candidates in France and England is clear evidence of this trend.

C. Differentiate the following analogy and example arguments. For the analogies, identify the evidence and conclusion cases. For the example arguments, identify the example itself and the general conclusion.

1. Israel and Sweden have long accepted gay men and women into their military service and have had few, if any, security problems as a result. Thus, gay men and women should not be viewed as a security risk in military organizations.

2. Social media outlets are wrestling with the question of which personal data deserve protection from commercial trading. They might get some help from laws governing buying and selling parts of the body. While we allow individuals to sell their hair, we don't allow them to legally sell their kidneys. This is because we see vital organs as constituting the person, and thus deserving protection. Similarly, personal data that we determine to constitute the person should be protected by law from being bought and sold.

3. Hewlett-Packard and Polaroid are companies that were started during the Great Depression. These cases suggest that times of economic hardship can also be times of great opportunity for savvy investors and entrepreneurs.

4. Airline pilots perform a task in which a single error can spell disaster, much like physicians. Pilots, much like doctors, must acquire knowledge that is constantly changing. Pilots, however, must requalify periodically to keep their licenses. Physicians can practice indefinitely without requalifying. Surely, requiring such requalification of doctors is just as important.

5. The waste of technology in the apparently pointless use of such sites as YouTube may actually have a purpose—the more instances of a new technology's use, the more likely that someone will discover a beneficial application for it. Science fiction writer Carrie Doctorow calls this approach "thinking like a dandelion." He writes "The disposition of each—or even most— of the seeds isn't the important thing, from a dandelion's point of view. The important thing is that *every crack in every pavement is filled with dandelions.* The dandelion doesn't want to nurse a single precious copy of itself. . . . The dandelion just wants to be sure that every single opportunity for reproduction is exploited."[13]

6. Age differences are insignificant to the success of a marriage. Why, I know a couple in which the wife is seventy-two and the husband is nineteen, and they are perfectly happy.

7. The Bureau of Alcohol, Tobacco, Firearms and Explosives conducted a sting operation in the San Francisco area aimed at slowing the illegal flow of guns into

California from Nevada gun shows. The agency netted more than one thousand illegally imported guns in a single operation. This proves that gun shows in one state can dramatically increase the number of weapons available in a neighboring state, a claim that gun rights groups deny.

8. According to Dr. Robert Massy of the Royal Astronomical Society, "galaxies form around black holes in the way that a pearl forms around grit."[14]

9. Caption on an anti-fur ad showing an animal's paw caught in a metal trap: "Get the feel of fur. Slam your hand in a car door!"

D. The following excerpts from famous speeches and essays suggest that figurative analogies have had a powerful impact in some important controversies. Identify the evidence relationship and conclusion relationship for each analogy.

1. *Context:* In February of 1860, Abraham Lincoln argued that the Democrats, his opponents, were making an utterly unreasonable claim concerning why voters should not elect a Republican to the presidency. A few months before the 1860 Republican National Convention, Lincoln visited New York, where he delivered the famous speech from which this figurative analogy is drawn. What is the picture presented in the evidence relationship? What is the exact relationship between the two people in the picture? To what groups did Lincoln compare these two people in his conclusion relationship?

> But you will not abide the election of a Republican President! In that supposed event, you say, you will destroy the Union; and then, you say, the great crime of having destroyed it will be upon us! That is cool. A highwayman holds a pistol to my ear, and mutters through his teeth "Stand and deliver, or I shall kill you, and then you will be a murderer!" To be sure, what the robber demanded of me—my money—was my own; and I had a clear right to keep it; but it was no more my own than my vote is my own; and the threat of death to me, to extort my money, and the threat of destruction to the Union, to extort my vote, can scarcely be distinguished in principle. (Abraham Lincoln, Cooper Union Address)

2. *Context:* Americans take for granted that their Constitution reflects good ideas about the governance of a democracy. When it was first proposed, however, the document elicited tremendous debate. James Madison, along with Alexander Hamilton and John Jay, argued vehemently for the Constitution in a series of pieces known collectively as *The Federalist Papers*. Madison developed a figurative analogy to urge adoption of the new Constitution that, he argued, might not be perfect but was clearly preferable to the Articles of Confederation. What two evidence relationships did he develop? What relationship is similar in each? What is the conclusion relationship?

> It is a matter both of wonder and regret that those who raise so many objections against the new Constitution should never call to mind the defects of that which is to be exchanged for it. It is not necessary that the former should be perfect: it is sufficient that the latter is more imperfect. No man would refuse to give brass for silver or gold because the latter had some alloy in it. No man would refuse to quit a shattered and tottering habitation for a firm and commodious building because the latter had not a porch to it, or because some of the rooms might be a little larger or smaller, or the ceiling a little higher or lower than his fancy would have planned them. (James Madison, *Federalist Paper 38*, January 1788)

3. *Context:* Demosthenes, perhaps the greatest orator of ancient Greece, urged the Athenian Senate to fight Philip of Macedon as if they had some idea about how to fight. To make his point, Demosthenes presented the following analogy, developed around the Athenians' fondness for watching boxing matches between untrained foreign captives and trained Athenian boxers. It's no secret who usually won these bouts, and why. What evidence relationship did he develop in this argument? What is the conclusion relationship? What is the ironic twist that gives the argument its own "punch"?

> The citizens of Athens, however possessed as they are of the greatest power of all in ships, fighting men, cavalry, and monetary resources, have never to this day made a right use of any of them. The war against Philip exactly resembles the methods of an untaught foreigner in the boxing ring. If he is hit, he hugs the place, and if you hit him somewhere else, there go his hands again. He has not learnt, and is not prepared, to defend himself or look to his front. So it is with the policy of Athens. If news comes of Philip in the Chersonese, an expedition there is voted; if it is Thermopylae, it is sent there. Wherever he goes, we hurry up and down at his instance, controlled by his strategy without any constructive military plan of our own, without foresight to anticipate news of what is happening or has happened. (Demosthenes, *Philippic I*, 351 BCE)

E.   Explain how metonym is employed in the following example.

> British Prime Minister Benjamin Disraeli (1804–1881) was asked, shortly after the publication of Darwin's *On the Origin of Species,* which side of the debate over evolution he supported. Disraeli responded, "I am for the angels, and against the apes."

F.   Think of a movie you have seen recently that you believe was arguing for a particular point of view. Write a brief analysis of the movie's coherence and fidelity as either contributing to or detracting from its persuasiveness. In addition, comment on the relationship between portrayal and point of view in the film.

ENDNOTES

[1] David Quammen, "Was Darwin Wrong?" *National Geographic,* November 2004, 4.

[2] Michael Sandel, "The Case against Perfection," *Atlantic Monthly,* April 2004, 51.

[3] Chaïm Perelman and L. Olbrechts-Tyteca, *The New Rhetoric,* trans. John Wilkinson and Purcell Weaver (Notre Dame, Ind.: University of Notre Dame Press, 1968), 218.

[4] David Doubilet, "Strange Terrain: Undersea Oddballs of Lembeh Strait," *National Geographic,* November 2005, 100.

[5] George Lakoff and Mark Johnson, *Metaphors We Live By* (Chicago: University of Chicago Press, 2003), 55.

[6] Lakoff and Johnson, 49.

[7] "Cognitive Science: From Brain to Mind," *Science Week,* http://scienceweek.com/2004/sa040903-4.htm.

[8] Daniel C. Dennett, *Breaking the Spell* (New York: Viking, 2006), 372.

[9] "Mayo Research: Intervention Drops Hospital Infection Rate by One-Third," EON: Enhanced Online News, March 10, 2010, http://eon.businesswire.com/portal/site/eon/permalink/?ndmViewId=news_view&newsId=20100319005029&newsLang=en.

[10] Rachel Sobel, "A Gutsy Gulp Changes Medicine," *U.S. News and World Report,* August 20, 2001, 59.

[11]For more information on narrative argument, see *The Subject in Story,* ed. Hans Ostrom and Wendy Bishop (Portsmouth, N.H.: Boynton/Cook, 2003) and Walter Fisher, *Human Communication as Narration* (Columbia, S.C.: University of South Carolina Press, 1989). Fisher provides a detailed discussion of coherence and fidelity in narrative.

[12]Rich Karlgaard, "California Leavin'," *Forbes,* May 23, 2005, 39.

[13]Adapted from Chris Anderson, "Waste is Good," *Wired* (July 2009), 72–77, 76.

[14]Pallab Ghosh, "Black Hole Confirmed in Milky Way," BBC Online, December 9, 2008, http://news.bbc/co.uk/2/hi/science/nature/7774287.stm.

RECOMMENDED WEBSITES

How to Write a Narrative Argument

Vivek Saxena, Demand Media

classroom.synonym.com/write-narrative-argument-4686.html

This website suggests a step-by-step process for constructing a narrative argument. It thus adds a compositional component to our discussion of analyzing narrative arguments.

Analogy (Rhetoric)

https://thoughtco.com/what-is-analogy-rhetoric-168909

This web page, created by English professor Richard Nordquist, provides helpful and interesting examples of various types of analogies.

15 Reasoning about Causes

Every theory is a self-fulfilling prophecy
that orders experience into the framework it provides.
Ruth Hubbard (1924–)
United States biologist

[W]hat is found in the effect was already in the cause.
Henri Bergson (1859–1941)
French philosopher

KEY TERMS

arguing from
   correlation alone

arguing from
   succession alone

argument from sign

causal agent

causal generalization

control group

correlated

fallible sign

falsifiable

hypothesis

infallible sign

observational study

post hoc fallacy

randomized study

rule of parsimony

sign

significant

succession

Survival rates for childhood cancer sufferers have risen significantly. Today, three out of every four children who develop cancer survive. There are currently more than 250,000 cancer survivors in the United States whose cancer was diagnosed when they were fifteen years old or younger, a statistic that represents a major medical triumph.

However, a recent study of childhood cancer survivors revealed that two out of every three of these survivors will develop significant health problems later in life, including heart and kidney disease, blindness, infertility, and paralysis. Researchers were faced with the vexing question as to why a great medical triumph was developing into a long-term medical crisis. Review of the clinical data on 10,397 survivors suggests that the causes of their perplexing medical problems could be traced back to the cancer cures themselves—massive doses of radiation and powerful, highly toxic medicines that did irreversible damage to organs and immune systems. "The individuals cured currently pay a large and unacceptable price for that," according to Dr. Harmon Eyre, medical director of the American Cancer Society.[1]

The scientist in the laboratory, the detective piecing together evidence to solve a crime, or investigators trying to determine the cause of an airplane accident are all seeking to find causes that will explain a set of observations. Though such investigations often are complex, the basic structure of the reasoning processes involved is relatively simple. Reasoning about causes is essential to daily life as well. When you are trying to decide why you didn't get a job or why your car insurance rates went up, you are engaged in causal reasoning.

This chapter considers the basic structure of causal arguments and identifies various tests that can be applied to this form of reasoning. The first section discusses explanatory statements called hypotheses and how they are formulated, supported, and tested. We also will see how analogies, as discussed in the last chapter, can be employed to establish cause. The second section considers the generalization process when it is used in combination with causal reasoning. We will consider several important tests of such causal generalizations.

ARGUMENTS ADVANCING HYPOTHESES

Physicist Brian Greene provides the following description of progress in scientific enquiry:

> Scientists put forward results, both theoretical and experimental. The results are debated by the community, sometimes they are discarded, sometimes they are modified, and sometimes they provide inspirational jumping-off points for new and more accurate ways of understanding the universe.[2]

Greene provides a good outline of the basic process of formulating, advancing, and testing hypotheses, or the "results" of scientific investigations. These "results" are, in fact, educated and often well-substantiated guesses as to what causes a particular event to occur. Greene underlines the importance of hypothesis reasoning to science, but the process of forming and testing hypotheses is crucial to a wide range of human endeavors, including business, politics, education, and even sports.

Let's look at a brief argument that involves this kind of causal reasoning:

> The ancient Nasca people of southern Peru created gigantic "geoglyphs," etchings in the dry, rocky soil of the Andes plateau that represented birds, spiders, and other natural objects. Archaeologists and scientists have long tried to discern the meaning or use of these land sculptures. One confusing element is that the shape of the sculptures is most clearly visible from the sky. Earlier hypotheses ranged from the mystical (the patterns were once thought to assist astrological observations) to the bizarre (one scholar actually surmised that the geoglyphs were created to be viewed from ancient hot air balloons). Recently, however, a joint Italian and German team has concluded that large rectangular stone platforms at critical viewing points in the sculptures are the key to understanding why they were originally created. These platforms are clearly altars for sacrifices to gods of the mountains and sky. The altars are placed at points in the sculptures where the gods could see the sacrifices being offered. Thus, it is now almost certain that these ancient geoglyphs were "prayer paths" to be walked as worshippers carried their sacrifices to altars in an effort to convince the gods to bring rain.

This argument advances a **hypothesis,** *an explanatory statement affirming that one or more events cause another event to occur.* The term "hypothesis" typically refers to a causal statement that is still being tested. It is a conjecture, based on available evidence, about a cause. As such, a hypothesis requires careful evaluation before it can be established as accurate.

Hypothesis arguments are advanced when the causes of an unexpected or unusual event are in question. In the example above, the first sentence expresses the unusual situation that requires an explanation: the presence of gigantic "geoglyphs" in the Andes plateau.

The Structure of Arguments Advancing Hypotheses

Hypotheses are advanced when an event is unusual enough to raise a question about its cause. The example about the unusual artifacts in Peru raises a question:

> **Question:** Why did the Nasca people create giant "geoglyphs" that are most visible from the sky?

An explanation, or hypothesis, is advanced to account for the unusual structures and thus answer the question:

> **Hypothesis:** These structures were created as prayer paths to aid worship practices.

This explanatory statement is the argument's hypothesis. It functions as the argument's conclusion.

Causal arguments of this type often advance evidence as additional support for the hypothesis. Thus, the following evidence might be advanced:

> **Support:** The altars that are part of the glyphs are placed at points where the gods could see the sacrifices being offered.

This statement offers support for the hypothesis.

To summarize, then, hypothesis arguments usually involve the following elements:

1. *Circumstances to be explained:* An event or phenomenon that requires a causal explanation.

2. *An implied question* raised by the circumstances: What caused this event to occur?

3. *The hypothesis itself:* A statement advancing an explanation of the event or answering the implied question.

4. *Supporting evidence:* Observations or other facts that support the hypothesis.

Developing a Hypothesis

The reasoning process by which hypotheses are developed is common to many problem-solving situations and scientific inquiry. The following example illustrates the general process:

> We were perplexed by how humpback whales were able to remember such long songs that change so frequently. We already knew that whale songs contain repeated phrases and sounds at predictable intervals. It occurred to us that perhaps, like humans, whales use rhymes to aid memory. If this were the case, longer songs, being harder to remember, would show more rhyming patterns. We tested this idea by counting the frequency of the repeated patterns in longer songs and comparing these to the frequency in shorter songs. Sure enough, the longer songs did show more repetitions, which tended to confirm our original thinking: whales use rhyming to remember their long, intricate, and constantly changing songs.

Whales were observed to remember long and complicated songs. This observation raised the question: How are they able to remember these songs? In seeking to answer this question, the first step of inquiry was:

1. Suggest a testable hypothesis. The hypothesis, which suggests a possible cause of the unexpected event, can be subjected to meaningful testing:

Whales use rhymes to aid memory.

The investigators used an analogy to human memory as an initial clue that their hypothesis was plausible. Still, the guess contained in the hypothesis had to be tested. This testing involved moving to the second step in the process of formulating hypotheses:

2. Generate the consequences of the hypothesis on the assumption of its accuracy. In this step we proceed as if the hypothesis is accurate, anticipating consequences that would be likely if this hypothesis were true. We ask, "If this hypothesis is accurate, what will we expect to find?" The answer to this question is:

If whales use rhymes to remember their songs, more repeated patterns will be present in longer songs than in shorter songs.

The third step in the process requires us to:

3. Compare actual observations to the generated consequences. Following this step, the investigators

tested this idea by counting the frequency of the repeated patterns in longer songs and comparing these to the frequency in shorter songs. Sure enough, the longer songs did show more repetitions, which tended to confirm our original thinking: Whales use rhyming to remember their long, intricate, and constantly changing songs.

After completing this stage in the process, we can proceed to the fourth step:

4. Accept, modify, or reject the hypothesis. The researchers in our example decided to accept their hypothesis without modifying it because of the close match between what they expected to find and what they actually observed.

A hypothesis should always be open to further testing, however. The scientists involved in our example have not actually proven this hypothesis to be true so much as they have failed to prove it false, though it has withstood one round of testing and so far stands as a reasonable explanation.

According to the famous philosopher Karl Popper, the only reasonable hypotheses are those that are potentially **falsifiable,** that is, *capable of being shown false.* The researchers' goal might be best understood as an effort to falsify the hypothesis— to prove it wrong. Had the researchers not discovered the more frequent use of repetition in the longer whale songs—a case of denying the consequent of the original conditional statement—they would have either modified the original hypothesis or rejected it altogether.

Evaluating a Hypothesis

A sound hypothesis argument should satisfy three criteria, suggested by three questions. The first of these is:

1. Does the hypothesis account adequately for the observation? This criterion is intended to filter out hypotheses that are clearly inadequate or insufficient because of their failure to explain some element in the observed circumstances.

As we have noted, hypotheses are advanced when the cause of some event is in doubt, so they always follow an observation that raises a question about cause. A reliable hypothesis will identify a **causal agent,** that is, *a testable element in the alleged cause that is capable of producing an observed effect.* The agent represents a clear link between cause and effect, and is crucial to a good hypothesis. Showing agency is an important component in addressing the criterion of adequacy.

An adequate hypothesis satisfies three conditions:

a. The hypothesis should account for all relevant elements in the observation.

b. The hypothesis should suggest a causal agent, a factor that actually could produce the observed effect.

c. The hypothesis should not rely on hidden or obscure causes that cannot be tested.

Let's look at an example of agency in a rather surprising hypothesis. The city of Oxnard, California, designated certain parts of the city as "gang injunction" areas, meaning that police consider these areas especially prone to gang activity. Citizens were even warned not to venture out alone in these areas.

An observant physician noted something unexpected in the gang injunction zones—an increased incidence of childhood asthma. *The Los Angeles Times* reported that "when Dr. Chris Landon looks at the boundaries of Oxnard's recently imposed gang injunction, he sees the outlines of a health crisis."

Landon argued that there was a connection between the zones and asthma. His hypothesis was that "the problems are linked," because there is a "reluctance by parents to let children go outdoors for fear of neighborhood violence." This hypothesis led the doctor to suggest a series of policy changes. "We need to increase outdoor activity, increase access to medical care and access to education," Landon said.

Was there any additional evidence to support his hypothesis? According to Dr. Rosalind J. Wright at Harvard Medical School, "[A] number of studies already point to a connection between exposure to violence and childhood psychological problems such as depression and anxiety, and there is ongoing work to examine the tie between high-crime communities and physical disease." Wright is coauthor of a study on asthma and urban violence published in the *American Journal of Public Health.*

Let's return to the question of agency: What is it about high crime areas that could cause physical problems such as asthma? Dr. Howard Spivak, director of the Center for Children at Tufts University and chairman of the Youth Violence Task Force for the American Academy of Pediatrics, states that "The impact of stress around violence and fear of violence must be taking their toll." The report goes on to explain, "People in high-crime areas may fail more often to keep medical appointments or follow prescribed exercise programs. And the fear of violence could lead parents to keep children indoors longer, lulling youngsters into a sedentary lifestyle that increases the risk of obesity or exposes asthma sufferers to mold and dust."[3] Spivak's statements are efforts to show agency in one alleged cause of childhood asthma—crime.

Other tests can also help us decide whether to accept a hypothesis. If we know that hypotheses similar to the one under consideration have been confirmed in similar cases, we have reason to believe that the hypothesis we are testing is accurate. We should not ignore what has already been proven in similar cases when searching for a reliable hypothesis. Thus, the second test looks for analogies to the present situation and asks the second question.

2. Have similar hypotheses been shown to be accurate in analogous cases? If we applied this test to the hypothesis regarding gang zones and asthma, our goal would be to locate similar links between respiratory disorders and high-crime areas of other cities. Researchers associated with the Harlem Children's Zone Asthma Initiative (HCZAI) have discovered that the rate of asthma in this urban area is a staggering 25.5 percent, twice the rate researchers expected to find, according to Dr. Benjamin Ortiz, Jr., of Columbia University. Dr. Mary E. Northridge, also of Columbia University, added that 56 percent of the children found to have asthma "have been to an emergency room in the last year because of their disease."

Has crime been shown to be a contributing factor in this analogous situation in the Harlem section of New York? The answer is apparently yes. The HCZAI suggests that fear of crime may cause people to close their doors and windows, trapping exhaust from furnaces and stoves. The same fear may keep people at home and away from doctors. We now have some confirmation for the original hypothesis using the test of analogous cases.[4]

Some events, we should note, are genuinely unique and may thus require unique hypotheses, for which no analogies exist. Experiments with super conducting materials, for example, have involved unique hypotheses. The creation of new elements in superconducting super colliders may be attended by similarly unprecedented causes. In cases of unique phenomena, the test of analogous cases may not be applicable. We need a third test:

3. Is an alternative hypothesis available that better explains the observed events? This test can be applied in one of two ways. We may:

a. Modify a good but incomplete hypothesis.
Or
b. Seek an entirely new hypothesis.

Let's look at an example of each approach.

a. *Modifying a good but incomplete hypothesis.* The Harlem researchers found that crime was only one of several factors causing childhood asthma. They also identified environmental factors such as exhaust from heavy trucks and buses, as well as pests such as cockroaches and rats that create allergens. The same study indicated that 31.9 percent of homes with an asthmatic child also had an adult who smoked, but only about 20 percent of homes with no asthmatic children had a smoker living there. Other studies have also linked adult smoking to childhood asthma.[5] A modified hypothesis must include these additional causal agents.

b. *Seeking a new hypothesis.* Coffee drinkers suffer a lower incidence of stroke. Researchers assumed that caffeine improved blood circulation in the brain and reduced blood clotting, thus making stroke less likely. However, that hypothesis had to be jettisoned when many doctors noted that decaffeinated coffee appeared to have the same stroke-reducing effect. A rigorous study confirmed that coffee of any kind reduces inflammation in blood vessels, thus preventing stroke. Caffeine played no causal role. In this case the original hypothesis about caffeine had to be rejected in light of new evidence.

When hypotheses compete, it is helpful to *look for the simplest or least complex causal explanation that still accounts for observed effects.* This approach is sometimes dubbed the **rule of parsimony.**

For example, following extensive design efforts and an aggressive marketing campaign, a car manufacturing company was at a loss to explain disappointing sales figures for a new fuel-efficient model. Executives advanced a complex hypothesis to explain why the new model was not selling: cautious consumers with too much debt, a weak economy, lower gas prices spurring a trend back toward larger vehicles, and competitors marketing similar models. However, sales personnel suggested a simpler explanation: the new car had been brought out in a limited number of colors, all of which were unpopular with potential buyers. A follow-up survey of customers confirmed the simpler explanation—color choice adversely affected sales.

ARGUMENTS FROM SIGN

Closely related to the hypothesis argument is the **argument from sign,** *an argument that reasons from an effect back to a cause.* This simplified version of hypothesis reasoning relies on well-established causal linkages that do not require the elaborate testing of the more rigorous hypothesis argument. A **sign** is *an effect of a well-known cause, one that allows us to reason back to the cause with some confidence.* If I am standing behind someone in the checkout line in a hardware store and notice that she is purchasing a container of drain opener, I conclude almost without noticing that she has a clogged drain at home. This relatively simple process of reasoning back to causes from their effects constitutes one of the most common forms of causal reasoning.

Consider for a minute how often we rely on sign reasoning. For example, the brake lights on the car in front of me on the freeway are illuminated, and I conclude the driver has applied the brakes. Unlike the customer with her container of drain opener, this sign has implications for me—I need to slow down to avoid a collision. Now imagine that you are sitting in class and a fire alarm sounds in the hallway. What do you conclude? For most people, their first conclusion is *not* that the building is on fire, but that the fire alarms are being tested. That's because we have much more frequently experienced a fire alarm being associated with the testing of the equipment than with an actual fire. Indeed, for most of us the sound of a fire alarm in a public building has never accompanied the occurrence of a serious fire. If we hear the fire alarm, notice a strong smell of smoke, notice in addition that people are running through the hallway outside the classroom, and hear approaching sirens, our conclusion is likely to be modified: this time there actually is a fire.

These two examples illustrate the difference between what have traditionally been termed infallible and fallible signs. An **infallible sign** is *an effect that virtually always and only accompanies a particular cause.* Thus, reasoning from sign to cause is almost automatic and highly reliable. In our example, the illuminating of brake lights functions for most drivers as an infallible sign of brakes being applied. That's because there are almost no other reasons we would see this phenomenon.

On the other hand, the fire alarm is a **fallible sign**—*an effect with more than one possible cause, though one cause is typical.* Ironically, the most common cause of fire alarms being sounded is the testing of an alarm system and the associated evacuation procedures. Whereas everyone knows this is not the purpose of fire alarms, it is their most common use—vacating buildings for practice. The actual reason for the alarm's existence is rather different, which is to prevent injury and death from fires. When

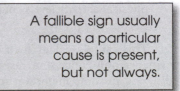

A fallible sign usually means a particular cause is present, but not always.

reasoning from a fallible sign, we consider probabilities: this sign *usually* means a particular cause is present, but not always.

How might sign reasoning be used in an argument? Imagine a work situation in which every morning the boss walks through an area where ten employees sit at desks. In your experience, the boss has always said "Good morning" to the employees. On this particular morning, however, he does not say good morning, but goes immediately to his office and shuts the door. The person at the next desk says to you, "Somebody is going to get fired." He then elaborates: "The boss has only walked through here without saying good morning on two previous occasions, and both times somebody got fired that day."

Here is an example of reasoning from fallible sign to cause—in this case a silent "fire alarm." If the only previous time that the boss has walked through the work area without saying good morning was a day on which someone was fired, then we at least know the basis of the sign reasoning. The two events—the boss's silence and a sudden employee dismissal—have been associated on at least two occasions in the past. Still, you might reply that there could be other reasons for the absence of a friendly good morning from the boss. Maybe he is concerned about a personal matter; or he has just learned that the head office is thinking of moving him to a different location; or he may have been distracted by something he was reading on the way to his office.

Again, sign reasoning is a routine kind of hypothesis formation we employ when faced with frequently occurring cause and effect pairs. As such, sign reasoning constitutes an important rational shortcut in a wide range of situations. Because we engage in sign reasoning almost without being aware of it, however, the process can mislead us as well. For instance, we see someone in a uniform and assume that she occupies a position of authority, but uniforms can deceive us as well. Another example of a rational shortcut is profiling. Law enforcement agencies have to train personnel *not* to reason from appearances back to likelihood of particular behavior. Thus, sign reasoning is crucial to everyday assessment of a variety of situations, but we also have to check that we are not allowing ourselves to be guided unthinkingly by our personal set of cause and effect connections.

ARGUMENTS FOR CAUSE BY ANALOGY

Analogies are another means to establish a causal claim. Such analogies not only show similarities between evidence and conclusion cases, but also focus on differences and try to explain the cause of the observed difference. Consider the following example:

> Recent reports from major medical centers reveal a rapid decline in the overall health of retired baby boomers when contrasted with members of this birth cohort who are still working. In particular, doctors have noted a spike in diabetes, obesity, and hypertension among retired boomers. Why would the two groups show such dramatic differences in overall health? Follow-up studies suggest that retired boomers dramatically decrease their level of physical exertion, including exercise, after retirement. Those still employed report considerably higher levels of physical activity. This difference in physical activity levels could easily explain the rise in diseases associated with a sedentary lifestyle.

This causal analogy focuses on dissimilarities as well as similarities between its evidence and conclusion cases. It explains why two otherwise similar situations are different in some important respect. A second dissimilarity is advanced as the cause of the original difference. The example advances similarities between retired and working baby boomers, using the contrast between the two cases to account for or explain further differences. The explanatory contrast is that working boomers are more physically active than retired boomers.

ARGUMENTS FOR CAUSE BY ENUMERATION

Chapter 10 introduced the concept of reasoning by enumeration, which is used frequently in searching for causes. Consider this surprising observation, reported in *Wired Magazine,* that demanded a causal explanation. Professor James Flynn discovered that "average IQ scores in every industrialized country on the planet had been increasing steadily for decades," despite the widely reported "dumbing-down of society." What was causing this phenomenon?

Flynn used the enumeration approach to search for an explanation. He decided to look at IQ scores, not as a report of intelligence at a moment in time, but as a phenomenon that evolved over a long period of time. This long-term view showed that IQ scores were steadily climbing, suggesting "that something in the environment . . . was driving the trend."

Though basic intelligence was long considered to be largely inherited, Flynn and his colleague William Dickens suggested a new hypothesis, that "a small difference in intelligence was magnified by environmental factors into a large difference." Using enumeration, Flynn and colleagues eliminated obvious potential causes such as poor schools and bad nutrition. Flynn's answer to the puzzle: technological advances have demanded that we become better at problem solving and spatial puzzles of the type used in some IQ tests. For instance, when you figure out how to use your new cell phone, you are improving your problem-solving ability. Video games may actually be the greatest "brain boosters" around. "Mastering visual puzzles is the whole point" of playing these games, Flynn pointed out. The so-called "Flynn Effect" is now well established.[6]

Recall from Chapter 10 that even valid enumeration arguments must pass two other tests. To be reasonable, they must:

1. *Set out all plausible options.* The test says *plausible;* the enumeration argument need not account for every conceivable alternative, only for those that are probable in some way.

2. *Eliminate options convincingly.* If an alternative that was treated as eliminated is still viable, the argument's conclusion is questionable.

These tests should also be applied to arguments seeking to establish cause by enumeration.

ARGUMENTS GENERALIZING ABOUT CAUSE

As we have been discussing them, arguments advancing hypotheses tend to account for a single event or set of related events. By contrast, the **causal generalization** is *an argument that affirms a causal relationship between two categories, or classes, of events.* We have been considering rising IQ scores in populations around the world. What about the opposite phenomenon in the office setting? A widely reported study of eleven hundred office workers "showed that excessive attentiveness to email messages was strongly correlated with a dramatic drop in IQ." Employees who checked their email frequently "showed a 10% drop in IQ." By comparison, a 4% decrease in IQ has been "associated with regular marijuana use." Workers in a control group who only checked email a few times a day showed no such drop in intelligence.[7]

In this example of a causal generalization, a causal link is suggested between excessive attention to email and a reduction in IQ. Like other generalizations, causal generalizations involve a sample and a population. However, in place of a property, these generalizations advance a cause-effect connection. The two causally related events in our example are:

Cause: Excessive attention to email

Effect: Reduction in IQ

The example mentions a **control group,** *a group, paralleling the experiment group, in which the suspected causal agent is withheld or eliminated.* In this case the control group consisted of workers whose attention to email was moderate or regulated. In such studies, researchers must try to ensure that the only significant difference between the groups being compared is the presence of a suspected causal factor in one group, usually called the "test group" or "experimental group." If a significant effect occurs in the experimental group, we have some basis for suspecting causation. Notice here the application of causal reasoning by analogy, as discussed earlier in this chapter. Control and experimental groups are assumed to be analogous to one another except for one critical dissimilarity: the presence of the variable or factor being tested in the control group.

Chapter 8 set out the tests of the representativeness of samples, which ask about the size, stratification, and randomness of the sample. The same tests must be applied to causal generalizations, as well, but assessing the *causal* claim in causal generalizations requires additional tests, some of which are similar to those for hypotheses.

1. Are the two events correlated? Events are **correlated** if they *occur together with regularity.* Figure 15.1 illustrates a direct correlation between a rise in temperature and a corresponding increase in CO_2 levels over a period of several decades. Temperature data for the graph are based on deviations in temperature from a long-term average. Events may also be indirectly correlated in a way that suggests a causal connection. That is, as the incidence of one event increases, the frequency of the other decreases. So, for example, regular cardiovascular exercise is indirectly correlated with high blood pressure. As cardiovascular exercise rates go up, average blood pressure tends to decrease. These two measures are thus indirectly correlated. Applying this test to the example, we have to confirm that excessive attention to email and reduction in IQ occurred together to a significant degree. **Significant,** as used here, means that the correlation *cannot be explained on the basis of chance or simple coincidence.*

Reasoning from Correlation Alone

The test of correlation suggests one of the most common errors in causal reasoning: **arguing from correlation alone,** or *attributing cause simply on the basis of events occurring or varying simultaneously.* Correlation by itself is not proof of causation. Let's consider an example.

> Sociologists have discovered a strong correlation between having fewer educational and monetary resources as a child, and a lower likelihood of divorce later in life. The correlation is not only significant, but persists even when differences such as race, religion, and age at marriage are controlled for.

It would be tempting to conclude from this correlation that growing up with fewer resources actually causes greater success at marriage. A growing body of evidence actually supports this correlation, but not the causal conclusion we are drawing from it. This case illustrates one of the problems associated with reasoning from correlation alone—it is easy to overlook a hidden or "lurking" variable that causes both correlated events.

FIGURE 15.1 Direct Correlation

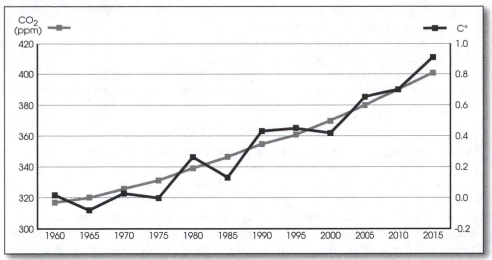

Temperature change from 1901–2000 baseline: NOAA National Centers for Environmental information, Climate at a Glance: Global Time Series, published March 2018, retrieved on April 4, 2018 from http://www.ncdc.noaa.gov/cag/ Atmospheric CO_2 : NOAA Earth System Research Laboratory and Scripps Institute of Oceanography, file created March 5, 2018.

In this example, the hidden variable is the number of siblings you grow up with. Having more siblings means fewer resources for you (and your siblings), as the family's resources have to be shared among more people. Moreover, having more siblings apparently helps children develop communication and conflict resolution skills that are important to successful marriages. Thus, a lurking variable—number of siblings— is the likely causal factor, both for fewer family resources and for more successful marriages.

A second problem is often associated with reasoning to cause from correlation alone. For example, physicians have long known that in autopsies, Alzheimer's Disease patients exhibit plaques that have formed on the surfaces of their brains. The correlation between the disease and the plaques was nearly perfect. It was reasonable to conclude, then, that these amyloid plaques caused the brain damage that we call Alzheimer's. Correlation meant causation, or did it?

Now researchers are exploring a new theory: that the amyloid plaques show up to protect the brain's nerve cells from other substances, called oligomers, that cause nerve cell damage. Thus, the plaques may be an effect of brain damage, rather than a cause. Correlation by itself does not tell us which way the "causal arrow" is pointing— which of two correlated events is cause and which is effect. Thus, we need other tests, in addition to correlation, before we can build a good case for causality.

The second test of the causal generalization asks:

2. Does the cause consistently precede the effect? This test, often referred to as the test of **succession,** seeks *assurance that the suspected cause consistently occurs before the alleged effect,* on the assumption that effects cannot precede their causes. In the example concerning workers distracted by office email, satisfying this test requires showing that excessive attention to email (the alleged cause) consistently *precedes* a reduction in IQ (the alleged effect) in the test group. If the lower IQ in the test group can be traced back to a time before members of the group started paying excessive attention to email, the causal claim is undermined.

FIGURE 15.2 Common Fallacies in Causal Generalizations

These are usually called fallacies:
- Arguing from correlation alone
- Arguing from succession alone (*post hoc* fallacy)

The *Post Hoc* Fallacy

Even though causes precede their effects, **arguing from succession alone,** *attributing cause simply on the basis of one event preceding another,* is risky. This mistake is so common that it has a special name: the **post hoc fallacy.** This term comes from the Latin expression, *post hoc ergo propter hoc,* which means "after this, therefore because of this." As with correlation, succession alone should not be taken as proof of causation. Baseball pitchers' and golfers' superstitious activities are based on this way of thinking: a certain movement preceded a good pitch or putt and so must have caused it. A similar mistake occurs in the following example:

> Handgun ownership in the county went up dramatically between June and September. Between November and March, the months immediately following this spike in gun purchases, the county's homicide rate fell to its lowest level in five years. This is just further proof that an armed citizenry can be effective in preventing crime.

Crime rates tend to drop during colder months, which may account for a drop in the homicide rate, but other factors may also be in play. Like reasoning from correlation alone, reasoning from succession alone can lead to problems, including failure to identify a potential common cause of both events, or suggesting a false causal relationship between two events that are only coincidentally related.

Here is another example:

> A year after the workplace smoking ban went into effect in bars and restaurants in California, tourism in the state boomed to record highs, generating $64.8 billion in travel spending and increasing state tourism revenues to a whopping 6 percent of the state's total revenues. Thus, the ban can be seen as a tremendous benefit to the tourism industry and all related businesses.

The ban alone, which may have played a role, is unlikely to have been the sole cause of the dramatic increase in tourism. The fact that the increase followed the ban does not actually prove a causal connection between the two events.

Correlation and succession together get us closer to justifying a causal generalization. When we see two events occurring together with some frequency and also see that one event always seems to precede the other, we can begin to make a case that one event causes the other. We still need to make a critical observation about the alleged cause, a factor common to all causal reasoning, however. The third test of the causal generalization asks:

3. Does the cause involve an agent that could act to bring about the effect? As with arguments involving hypotheses, this test asks whether a specific factor in the alleged cause could serve as agent—that is, could act to bring about the effect.

A recent study conducted in Bergen, Norway, observed the behaviors of five hundred boys involved in "aggressive sports," including karate, wrestling, and boxing. Researchers discovered that these boys were more often involved in fights and incidents of bullying than other boys were, and were significantly more likely to initiate violence towards others.

Were these boys more violent before they began to participate in the aggressive sports? The answer to this question was no. The researchers had now shown both correlation and succession for involvement with aggressive sports and violent behavior outside the sports setting.

What was it about the aggressive sport that was causing violent behavior? Researchers interviewed coaches and observed practices. They discovered that boys participating in aggressive sports were instructed to be more violent and were rewarded for violent behavior with praise, awards, and more playing time. Thus, the researchers suspected that the causal agent was psychological conditioning by coaches that encouraged violent attitudes and behaviors. These attitudes and behaviors were then transferred to settings in which they were not appropriate.[8]

Observational vs. Randomized Studies

It is important at this point to make a distinction between observational and randomized studies. **Observational studies** are *studies based on the examination of existing data sets in an effort to discover correlations.* They thus often result in causal claims on the basis of correlation alone, even in instances when no causal connection exists between the correlated events. Indeed, if researchers observe a sufficient number of sets of data for correlations, probability alone dictates that they will eventually discover correlations that appear to support causal claims. For example, a researcher may comb over existing data about diet and health, discovering in the process a correlation between eating citrus fruit and a reduced incidence of heart attacks. On the basis of such simple observation of correlation it would be hazardous to conclude that eating citrus fruit reduces heart disease.

Randomized studies, on the other hand, are *research studies intentionally designed from the outset to answer a single causal question.* As a result they are much less likely to result in erroneous causal claims than are observational studies. In randomized studies, researchers take care at the outset to satisfy the tests of size, randomness, and stratification that are discussed in Chapter 8. Thus, in a study of whether coffee consumption reduces the chances of developing Alzheimer's Disease in women, an effort would be made to select women randomly for the study, to account for other possible causal factors such as family history of the disease or regular exercise, to establish a control group of women who were not drinking coffee during the period of the study, and to stratify the sample so as to include members of various racial groups, socioeconomic groups, and perhaps even occupational groups. Such a study would also have to observe participants over a long period of time in order to determine whether there is any meaningful correlation.

CHAPTER REVIEW

Causal reasoning is crucial to personal and public discourse, and to endeavors such as science, commerce, and government. This chapter has considered several types of causal reasoning.

Arguments advancing hypotheses argue for a cause for a particular event or limited set of events. These arguments also suggest a method of inquiry for resolving questions about cause. First, a hypothesis is generated, along with its likely consequences if true. Then, these consequences are compared to actual observations, and the hypothesis is accepted, modified, or rejected accordingly. Two special methods of supporting a causal claim include using analogy and enumeration. Hypothesis arguments can be tested by asking about whether similar hypotheses have been shown to be accurate in analogous cases, whether they are adequate to explain an observation, and whether stronger alternative hypotheses are present.

The argument from sign is a means of reasoning back to a cause from the occurrence of a single supposed effect. Though a valuable rational shortcut, the argument from sign can also be misleading, as it is based on an assumed connection between one effect and its apparent cause.

Causal generalizations affirm a cause-and-effect relationship between two categories of event. Because they combine features of generalization arguments and hypothesis arguments, they should be tested like other generalization arguments. In addition, we should ask about the correlation and succession of cause-and-effect categories, as well as about the potential presence of a causal agent in the causal category.

Arguing from correlation or succession alone are common errors in causal reasoning. We should also ask whether claims in a causal generalization rest on an observational or randomized study.

EXERCISES

A. For each of the following hypothesis arguments, identify the observation(s) raising a causal question. Provide in your own words the causal question that arises out of the observation(s). Identify the hypothesis and, if present, any additional evidence advanced in its support.

1. Friday's accident was the first crash of the Air Force's newest stealth bomber. Surviving crew members say they observed a large flock of birds in the vicinity of the aircraft just before it crashed. It is speculated that the birds were sucked into the powerful engines of the bomber, causing it to crash.

2. Recent years have witnessed a dramatic increase in cancers of the large and small intestines in young people, with millennials showing a much higher incidence than baby boomers. Doctors are perplexed at this development and have searched for a cause. For now the best answer appears to be lifestyle choices. Intestinal cancers are linked to obesity, smoking, consuming alcohol, eating processed meat, and not consuming enough fiber. Each component in this lifestyle profile is also characteristic of millennials.

3. More than twenty whales beached themselves in the Canary Islands in 1989. Twelve more whales beached themselves along the coast of Greece in 1996. Similar incidents involving pilot whales have recently been reported in Oregon. In Hawaii more than two hundred bottlenose whales stranded themselves in 2005. Hundreds of pilot whales beached themselves in Antarctica in 2009. The whales showed strange symptoms such as internal bleeding and brain damage. The Navy had been testing deep-sea sonar devices in each of these areas prior to the beachings. That testing is the likely cause of these otherwise mysterious incidents. The 250-decibel sonar is so powerful that it can rupture blood vessels in the whales' brains, destroying their ability to navigate or killing them outright.

4. A woman in Nevada died as a result of a bacterial infection that was resistant to all known antibiotics. Doctors say this is a frightening sign that some bacteria have developed resistance to all pharmaceuticals—and the problem will only get worse. It seems that bacteria can "teach" other species of bacteria to be resistant by passing on small amounts of DNA that carry the code for resistance to antibiotics.

5. The United States will soon face a shortage of nearly ninety thousand doctors, mostly in family practice and primary care. Sixty million people in the US already live in regions experiencing a shortage of family physicians. Legislating mandatory medical care will not fix the doctor shortage: we will still face a medical crisis in this country. The primary cause of the current shortage of family practice physicians is the tendency of large teaching hospitals to encourage residents into lucrative and high-prestige specialties such as orthopedics and neurology. A review of recent medical school grads revealed that only 15 percent had selected family medicine as a specialty. Even fewer reported being encouraged to take this path through residency.

6. A new study by the Bureau of Labor Statistics indicates that by 2030, 38 percent of US jobs may be lost to automation. This is a higher percentage of at-risk jobs than in countries such as Japan, Germany, or Britain. Although jobs requiring less education are the most vulnerable to replacement by robots, the United States has a higher percentage of at-risk jobs even in arenas requiring education, such as finance and insurance.

7. After a decade of decline, traffic fatalities were up again in 2016. Traffic safety experts cite two causes: an improving economy and texting. The rising economy means cheaper fuel and thus more hours on the road by younger drivers. Drivers sixteen to nineteen years of age always post the highest traffic fatality rates. Texting means distracted drivers, the leading cause of accidents for the past six years.

8. US attitudes toward gay marriage have changed rapidly in this century, from a majority opposed in 2001 to a majority in favor in 2016. Why this dramatic shift in attitudes? There appear to be two reasons. First, most of us now realize that we know gay people personally. Second, most Americans now reject the idea of gay and lesbian people as revolutionaries seeking to effect broad social change.

9. Women leave the tech industries at twice the rate that men do. Why is this? The reasons are complex, but chief among them is the fact that industries whose foundational narratives elevate genius as an inborn quality create an atmosphere that is hostile to women. In our broader cultural narratives women are seldom celebrated as innate geniuses, and this bias works against them in the technology professions. At its root, the myth of the native-born genius is just that—a myth. Tech companies flourish for the same reasons as other successful companies—innovation, calculated risk, and team work. The story of the great genius is thus very misleading, as well as damaging to women.

B.   In the following examples, rival hypotheses are advanced to explain the same phenomenon. What are the alternative hypotheses in each case? How might they be tested to determine which is more reasonable?

1. Once the breadbasket of the Middle East, Iraq is rapidly turning into a dust bowl reminiscent of the plains states during our own Great Depression. Dust storms choke residents and deprive crops of sunlight. Different explanations for this stunning development are heard inside the country. To the average Iraqi the dust storms are the result of God's anger with the people of Iraq for ongoing violence and corruption. Agricultural experts studying the problem, however, note that two years of drought have followed years of warfare and resulting mismanagement of croplands. The nation no longer produces the large grain harvests it once did. For the first time Iraq will have to import 80 percent of its food this year. The damage to Iraq's land, water supplies, and agricultural production could take a decade or more to reverse.

2. Psychologists and counselors have noted a dramatic increase in the number of young people reporting feelings of jealousy in relationships. They speculated that fragmented families had led people in their teens and twenties to feel more threatened about intrusions on friendships and romantic relationships, but a recent study at the University of Guelph in Canada suggests a different cause. The study concluded that one of the unanticipated effects of the social networking site Facebook is to stir jealous feelings in its young users. Posts by those with whom they are romantically involved often suggest the existence of other relationships or interests. The result is that relationships often are undermined by feelings of suspicion and mistrust, and by a compulsive effort to attain more information.

3. What causes most cancers—lifestyle or bad luck? Despite the fact that we have been educating the public for decades about lifestyle changes to reduce cancer risk, more than 60 percent of adult cancers and all childhood cancers are tied to chance phenomena such as random genetic mutations. Every time a cell divides, several mutations occur. Although damage to DNA can be repaired by the cell, some inevitably goes undetected. Researchers have dubbed this the "bad luck theory" of cancer. Researchers acknowledge that up to 40 percent of cancers remain related to lifestyle choices such as smoking, but most causes would still be present in a perfect environment, free of known cancer causes such as sun exposure and smoking. The new theory challenges the standard environmental model of cancer.

4. The US explanation for dropping atomic bombs on the cities of Hiroshima and Nagasaki is that the action was needed to end the war and prevent the deaths of millions more Japanese citizens and soldiers on both sides. In Japanese textbooks the action is explained as America's effort to show the world that it would be willing to use nuclear weapons against its enemies—notably China and the Soviet Union—in the new era of the Cold War.

5. It is unclear why police officers in California are making fewer arrests in recent months. Some in law enforcement cite diminished manpower and changes in deployment strategies, but those trends started long ago and cannot account for the dramatic recent drop in arrests. It is more likely that officers have lost motivation in the face of increased scrutiny—from the public as well as their supervisors—and pressure from mayors who don't want their cities in the national media spotlight.

C. For the following causal analogies, identify the contrast advanced as cause and that advanced as effect.

1. Mills University and State University attract students from similar backgrounds. The entering freshmen at each institution have about the same SAT scores. Why do Mills students, then, always have an easier time landing good jobs after graduation? I think it is because of the extensive internship programs at Mills—something almost entirely lacking at State. Therefore, State should institute such internship programs.

2. Canada and the United States are both developed countries and in close proximity. Lower-income people in the US, however, are in worse health than poorer members of Canadian society. The only important difference between the two medical systems is that the US system is often unavailable to the poor and the unemployed.

3. By the end of the 1980s, more Vietnam veterans had committed suicide since the war ended than had died in the war. A 2013 study found Iraq War and Desert Storm veterans were more than twice as likely to commit suicide as civilians. Why is this? Most clinical psychologists now accept that the cause of the extraordinarily high suicide rate was PTSD, or post-traumatic stress disorder, a combination of depression and anxiety that results from extreme trauma. The widespread presence of this disorder in vets as compared with the general population was the only important difference between veterans and the rest of the adult population.

4. European and US teens report about the same level of sexual activity, but the pregnancy rate among European teens is much lower than among US teens. Comprehensive sex education for adolescents is mandatory in many European countries, including instruction in various forms of contraception. Comprehensive sex education is often unavailable to teens in the United States because of state and federal regulations. Experts believe the more thorough sex education in European schools contributes to a decrease in the teen pregnancy rate.

5. Middle-aged and less-educated white Americans are dying at younger ages over the past two decades, while members of racial minorities and well-educated whites have enjoyed increasing life spans during the same period. What accounts for the disparity in morbidity rates among these groups? Researchers point to drugs, alcohol abuse, and suicide as driving the trend for premature deaths among less-educated white Americans. These factors lead to what have been labeled "deaths of despair." Such deaths are concentrated in a demographic group that has borne the brunt of job loss due to automation and limited economic prospects.

D. In the following examples, identify the causal generalization being advanced. What factor is identified as cause? What is the supposed effect? State whether you see any potential problems in the causal reasoning in each example.

1. Research involving fifty-five mice specially bred to develop Alzheimer's Disease revealed that caffeine can be effective in restoring memory. Mice with Alzheimer's given the equivalent of five hundred milligrams of caffeine a day for eight weeks showed memory equivalent to normal mice. Mice with normal memories given the same amount of caffeine did not show any increase in memory. Thus, the chemical can work to restore lost memory but not to improve normal memory.

2. A study of more than 4,500 students in fifth through eighth grades found that children who watch R-rated movies, which often portray high levels of smoking, were fifteen times more likely to try smoking than were children whose parents limited them to G and PG movies.[9]

3. Two biologists at the University of Manitoba have demonstrated a striking correlation between practicing yoga and eating a healthy diet in a year-long study of 310 people. Some observers have speculated that, among yoga's other benefits, it stimulates an appetite for more wholesome foods.

4. A study involving seventy people found that a genetic mutation was common in subjects afflicted with Delayed Sleep Phase Disorder, or DSPD. People with this condition wake up later than normal, and also tend to go to bed later—their sleep patterns do not correspond to a 24-hour day. The genetic mutation was not found in the subjects who did not have DSPD. In addition, it is known that the gene in question plays an important role in establishing sleep rhythms.

E.   Explain how argument from sign is employed in the following examples. Which signs are taken as leading back to a likely cause? What is that cause?

1. While US and European interests are focused on the Middle East, Western nations need to be alert to the fact that China is rapidly developing as a major military power. In 2007 the People's Republic launched a missile that destroyed one of its own communication satellites, a remarkable technological achievement of which the Chinese did not inform other countries for two weeks. Satellite imagery has revealed an enormous underground naval base on the Chinese island of Hainan. The apparent purpose of this base is to launch naval operations in the Pacific. In January 2010 China conducted an advanced missile-defense test and in 2016 completed construction of a series of artificial islands in the South China Sea.

2. The planet GJ 1132b orbits the star GJ 1132, thirty-nine light-years away from Earth. The planet is one and a half times the size of Earth and, surprisingly, possesses an atmosphere. This is the first time scientists have detected an atmosphere around a planet close to Earth's size. How was the atmosphere, invisible to telescopes, detected? Astronomers measured the planet's radius using various wavelengths of light, and noticed that the planet appeared larger at some wavelengths than at others. This variation in apparent radius could only be due to a surrounding atmosphere.

3. Sales of large pickup trucks have risen by more than 20 percent in the past year. We know that pickup sales are a good indicator, not just that the building trades are rebounding, but that consumer confidence is also improving. When builders have plenty of work, they buy new pickups. Thus, improvement in the building trades means improved pickup sales. The building trades are themselves an excellent predictor of consumer confidence, so we can say that improved pickup sales are a reliable indicator of consumer confidence.

F.   In the following example, which test of causal generalization has been employed? Which other tests still need to be applied to establish cause?

For three years we interviewed prisoners who had been subjected to solitary confinement. We know that these prisoners are more likely to be incarcerated again upon their release than prisoners who never experience solitary confinement, but we don't know that solitary confinement is causal in this regard. It might be that the prisoners who are placed in isolation cells are already more likely to return to prison than are prisoners in the general population. Our task now is to discover whether something in the solitary confinement experience actually causes recidivism.

ENDNOTES

[1] Quoted in "Child Cancer Survivors Have Other Problems Later in Life," *USA Today* online edition, May 16, 2005, http:// www.usatoday.com/news/health/2005-05-16-children-cancer.

[2] Brian Greene, *The Elegant Universe: Superstrings, Hidden Dimensions, and the Quest for the Ultimate Theory* (New York: Vintage, 1999), 20.

[3] Quoted in Fred Alvarez, "Gang Ban May Make Breathing Easier," *Los Angeles Times,* July 26, 2004.

[4] Quoted in Dr. Mimi Zucker, "Childhood Asthma 'Epidemic' Reported in Harlem," *Respiratory Reviews,* July 2003, http://www.respiratoryreviews.com/jul03/rr_jul03_epidemic.htm.

[5] Zucker. The results of studies linking crime and childhood asthma have recently been corroborated. See Kamal Eldeirawi et al., "Association of Neighborhood Crime with Asthma and Asthma Morbidity among Mexican American Children in Chicago, Illinois," *Annals of Allergy, Asthma and Immunology* 117, no. 5, November 2016: 502–507.

[6]Stephen Johnson, "What's Behind the Surprising Rise in IQ?" *Wired Magazine,* May 2005, 100–105.

[7]Martin Wainwright, "Emails 'Pose Threat to IQ,'" *The Guardian Online: Technology,* April 22, 2005, http://www.technology.guardian.co.uk/online/news/0,12597,1465973,00.

[8]Lauren Aaronson, "Boys Who Box," *Psychology Today,* November/December 2005, http://www.psychologytoday.com/articles/pto-20051031-000007.

[9]"The Impact of Smoking in the Movies on Youth Smoking Levels," Campaign for Tobacco-Free Kids, http://www.tobaccofreekids.org/research/factsheets/pdf/0216.pdf (Accessed December 27, 2006).

RECOMMENDED WEBSITES

Definition: Causation

whatis.techtarget.com/definition/causation

This website features a definition of causation and a discussion of correlation and causation. The links take you to additional discussions of questions surrounding causality.

Causality

The Information Philosopher

www.informationphilosopher.com/freedom/causality.html

For a discussion of the concept of causality, see this website.

16 Moral and Practical Arguments

*That action is best, which procures the greatest happiness
for the greatest numbers.*
Francis Hutcheson (1694–1746)
Scottish philosopher

Food first, then morals.
Bertolt Brecht (1898–1956)
German playwright

KEY TERMS
arguing comparative advantages
argument from principle

argument from quality
argument from quantity
pragmatic argument

In some circles, there has been a good deal of interest in cloning a mammoth, thus reviving a long extinct species. One argument for proceeding with this idea is pragmatic in nature. If mammoths were reintroduced to the vast grassy plains of Siberia, for example, they might help reverse the effects of global warming, as well as related problems such as erosion and the loss of native plant species:

Mammoths could keep the region colder by eating dead grass, thus enabling the sun to reach spring grass, which has roots that prevent erosion. In addition, the gigantic beasts might increase available light to ground-level plants by pulling down trees, which absorb a lot of sunlight. Finally, by breaking the surface of insulating snow, they would allow freezing air to penetrate the soil. A single large herd of mammoths could dramatically alter the Siberian environment for the better.

Opponents of such "de-extinction" cloning, on the other hand, argue that tampering with the course of evolution is inherently dangerous, as we don't know the effects on other species of reintroducing extinct animals into the environment. Moreover, some argue that it is not morally justified to bring an extinct animal into an ecosystem for which it was not adapted for survival. The debate about de-extinction thus involves some of the types of arguments discussed in this chapter.

This chapter discusses four familiar arguments that develop around moral and practical concerns: pragmatic arguments, arguments from principle, arguments from quantity, and arguments from quality.

PRAGMATIC AND PRINCIPLE ARGUMENTS

The ubiquitous iPod has become the subject of public debate, largely because of the potential for hearing damage resulting from hours-long exposure to excessively loud music. The argument for regulating the sound levels possible in such devices tends to be practical in nature, suggesting that young listeners may damage their hearing with sound levels that can exceed a hundred decibels. The argument against regulation is often based on personal rights or responsibilities—the idea that people should be left to make their own choices about how loud their music can be. As this example suggests, arguments based on pragmatic consequences often are answered by arguments based on an appeal to a principle.

Let's consider these two arguments in more detail, starting with the pragmatic argument.

Pragmatic Arguments

The **pragmatic argument** is *an argument that recommends or discourages a course of action on the basis of its practical consequences.* Pragmatic arguments are common in debates over rules, regulations, and laws. For instance:

> Coal is yesterday's fuel. Mining and burning coal made sense in the nineteenth century, just like making tools from stones made sense in the Stone Age. However, coal is just not as cheap, efficient, or environmentally friendly as wind and solar power.

This argument for sustainable energy sources assumes that actions resulting in good consequences should be pursued or that actions resulting in bad consequences should be avoided. Notice that it also incorporates a literal analogy (discussed in Chapter 14).

The following is another example of the pragmatic argument:

> Genetically modified organisms (GMOs) are appealing for a variety of reasons. They create a huge new market for genetically enhanced products, bring down the cost of foods by eliminating the need for pesticides, and increase the amount of time an item, such as a tomato, can sit on a grocer's shelf without spoilage.

This argument affirms that something should be done because it has beneficial consequences, and in that way is pragmatic. That is, it suggests that genetic engineering of agricultural products leads to desirable results, and that these actions should therefore be pursued. The pragmatic argument is perhaps the most common argument we encounter when decisions are being made about which course of action to pursue.

Pragmatic arguments also may discourage action on the basis of bad consequences. For example:

> The dosage of the active ingredient in many sleeping pills is too high, leaving patients drowsy at work. In one study, workers taking a sleep aid were eight times more likely than other workers to fall asleep at work the next day. The dangers associated with a drowsy worker operating heavy machinery are evident to anyone who has worked in a factory or warehouse. Therefore, dosages of sleeping medicines should be more carefully regulated by the Food and Drug Administration.

This pragmatic argument takes as evidence the bad consequences of some sleeping aids and draws the conclusion that more stringent regulation of such drugs is needed. It moves from evidence to a policy conclusion, on the assumption that actions resulting in bad consequences should be avoided.

Testing Pragmatic Arguments

Because pragmatic arguments develop on the basis of suggested good or bad consequences, we can ask whether the stated consequences actually will develop from the action. The first test of the pragmatic argument asks:

1. Is the action in question likely to have the suggested consequences? Returning to our GMO example, we could challenge the assertion that genetically enhanced foods have significant advantages. Critics have countered that argument by claiming that genetically engineered foods carry no significant cost benefit to the consumer and are not nutritionally superior to other foods.

In our example concerning a method for reducing blood pressure, it would be important to consider whether patients will follow the four guidelines. A preventative procedure that patients don't follow will not have the predicted results. On the other hand, if we have good reason to believe that some sleep aids leave workers drowsy the following day, and that more careful regulation could solve the problem, then we might feel satisfied that the suggested action is reasonable.

The first test of pragmatic reasoning assesses whether the predicted consequences of an act are, in fact, probable. A second and related test considers unintended negative consequences of the action. It asks:

2. Will the proposed action have serious undesirable consequences? Rather than arguing against the specific benefits claimed for an action, it is possible to argue that the proposed policy actually carries with it serious undesirable consequences. Let's look at an example where this test of pragmatic reasoning was applied to a major government decision. For example:

> Solar energy facilities in the desert, such as the Ivanpah solar plant west of Las Vegas, reduce our dependence on fossil fuels and curb global warming. However, biologists estimate that six thousand birds die every year as they follow insects attracted to the facility's brilliantly luminous, four-hundred-foot-high, solar collecting towers. Moreover, environmentalists are concerned about the solar plant's destruction of pristine deserts in the Southwest, which are habitat for rare bird and reptile species, as well as for wildflowers and cacti.

Finally, pragmatic arguments often conceal or ignore a principle or value that is at stake if the suggested action is pursued. Thus, a third test of pragmatic arguments asks:

3. Does the proposed action violate an important principle? There has been a great deal of research recently on methods of genetically enhancing human beings. Suppose the physical and cognitive advantages of genetically enhanced humans were established to the satisfaction of a particular audience. It would still be possible to argue that such tinkering with basic genetic structures violates a moral, ethical, or religious principle. Drones provide another example:

> Drones are presenting us with an unprecedented regulation issue. On the one hand, they can provide many services, from delivery of products to surveillance. On the other hand, drones pose obvious challenges to principles such as privacy.

Many pragmatic arguments can be answered with appeals to a principle that the proposed action would violate.

Arguing Comparative Advantages

One way to respond to a pragmatic argument is by *arguing that an alternative course of action carries greater advantages than the proposed plan does*. This strategy is referred to as **arguing comparative advantages.** For example:

> There are twenty-nine thousand tons of radioactive, spent, nuclear fuel rods in temporary storage around the world. How should we dispose of them? Proposals range from simply burying the rods deep in the sea or inside the Earth's mantle, launching the rods into space, or dumping the rods in volcanoes. While volcanoes are abundant and spread throughout the world, the possibility of radioactive lava and ash from an eruption renders the volcanic option impractically dangerous; and at 2,400 degrees volcanoes are not hot enough to melt the fuel rods anyway. Launching nuclear waste into space, though an expensive proposition, would certainly get rid of it forever, and the cost of commercial rockets is dropping every year. However, the risks of such a project at the present time are enormous. Imagine a spaceship full of nuclear waste crashing into the Pacific Ocean on launch. Thus, the safest option at present appears to be burial in what are termed "deep final repositories," stable geologic formations deep in the sea or caves bored into mountains. While the nuclear waste would still be dangerous for centuries, we could store it safely until permanent disposal techniques are developed.

Using an enumerative structure, this approach considers each alternative on a pragmatic basis, recommending one option as clearly preferable to the others.

Arguments from Principle

The **argument from principle** *affirms that we should abide by values, principles, and duties, and avoid actions that violate the same.* For example:

> Mineral and petroleum companies have a moral obligation to clean up and repair the environmental damage caused by drilling and mining. For more than a century we have allowed these companies—especially when operating in underdeveloped countries—to operate as if environmental damage was the concern of local people or of the local government. It is time that this mind-set changes, and that these companies are held responsible for the environmental costs of their activities.

This argument affirms that an important moral principle—the obligation to clean up and repair environmental damage—is at stake in the debate over who is responsible for damage done at drilling and mining sites.

Arguments from principle may appeal to values, such as freedom, justice, or equality. They may also appeal to duties or obligations, such as the duty to care for one's family or the obligation to care for the environment. Some arguments from principle derive from rights, such as the right of free speech or the right to vote. Arguments from principle usually affirm that a moral directive is applicable in the situation at hand.

The source, content, and applicability of moral obligations may themselves be the subject of controversy, as in debates over AIDS and abortion. Public debate is frequently marked by disagreement over moral principles. It is also marked by disagreement over the application of moral principles to particular issues, as Michael Sandel, writing for *The Atlantic Monthly,* points out with regard to cloning:

Some say cloning is wrong because it violates the right to autonomy: by choosing a child's genetic makeup in advance, parents deny the child's right to an open future.[1]

The application of a law to the resolution of a dispute is a type of argument from principle. For example,

> Under the GINA (Genetic Information Nondiscrimination Act) guidelines, it is illegal to dismiss employees or deny them health insurance based on genetic information. Thus, the company's refusal to cover Mr. Randall because he carries genetic markers for bipolar disorder is a clear violation of federal law.

Arguments from principle are often powerful, because principles such as rights, values, and duties are crucial to life in a democratic society. These arguments, however, should still be tested to assess their soundness.

Testing the Argument from Principle

Questions usually attend the application of any principle to a particular situation. The most prominent question is usually whether the principle actually applies to the case being argued. The first test of the argument from principle asks:

1. Is the principle relevant to the issue under discussion? Many disagreements are rooted in differences over whether a moral principle exists and, if it does, how it applies in a particular case. For instance, do corporations have a moral obligation to repair environmental damage they cause? If so, how should it be applied in a case such as the BP oil spill in the Gulf of Mexico?

If we do agree that the principle in question is relevant to the issue at hand, the question arises as to whether the proposal being advanced represents a violation of the principle. The next test is:

2. Does the proposed action in fact violate the principle at issue? We looked at Michael Sandel's argument that cloning is wrong. He claimed that this practice, by "choosing a child's genetic makeup in advance," violated that individual's right to an "open future." Such arguments have been answered by critics who assert that the principle of choosing one's future is not violated by cloning:

> A cloned individual may have certain physical traits that are predetermined, but in some respects everyone goes through the normal process of reproduction. If you have a tall mother and a tall father, there is a good chance that you will also be tall. If we are talking about the loss of a right to autonomy— self determination—the cloned individual's life is no less autonomous than is the life of a twin. Just as twins make moral decisions that are independent of one another, so a cloned individual would have the freedom to make moral choices that differed from the donor of his or her DNA. Thus, the clone does not face a "closed" future.

Thus, the rebuttal states that the principle in question—the right to autonomy—is not violated by the proposed action of cloning.

In many cases, the response to an argument from principle is a pragmatic argument that affirms that following the principle in question is simply too costly, dangerous, or time-consuming. The respondent affirms that pragmatic considerations actually outweigh the principle in question or that another principle is more important. The test employed in those instances can be stated as:

3. Do other considerations outweigh this principle? Tension between pragmatic and principle considerations is common to public debates. It is evident, for example,

> Tension between pragmatic and principle considerations is common to public debates.

in the debate over whether a principled belief in abstinence from sex before marriage should be allowed to overwhelm the pragmatic goal of helping to prevent the spread of STDs by distributing condoms and discussing safe-sex practices at clinics. Advocates argue that the negative consequences of not allowing sex education and condom distribution are so devastating that they outweigh principled concerns regarding abstinence.

When Principles Clash

Arguments from principle are occasionally answered by advancing a rival principle that, it is argued, overrides the one being invoked. For example, in the debate over the safety of vaccines we have witnessed a clash of principles held by some parents and some doctors:

> Parents claim the right to refuse to provide vaccines for their children, on the basis of supposed health concerns. At the same time, doctors insist that they have the right—based on a concern for the safety of their other patients—to refuse service to parents who will not inoculate their children.

This clash of principles, common in both public and private settings, reminds us again of the central role that values play in argumentation. It is only through the clash of arguments, through a process of reasoning, that determinations are made as to which principle will prevail in a particular controversy. And despite legal decisions that place a law above personal convictions, people may hold tenaciously to their principles. Journalists have often chosen jail over violating source anonymity.

ARGUMENTS FROM QUANTITY AND QUALITY

You are watching a favorite television program when the following advertisement appears on the screen:

> Meet-Me Online has more than five million registered members, and has resulted in more than forty thousand happy couples!

The point of the ad is clear—Meet-Me Online is significant *because* of the sheer size of its membership. The large numbers of members and "happy couples" make this dating service significant and set it apart from other such services.

The ad introduces the argument from quantity—one member of another pair of arguments common in public and private discussion. Like pragmatic and principle arguments, arguments from quantity and quality are often found in opposition to one another. As with the pragmatic and principle pair, one of these arguments reflects a preference for practical considerations, while the other reflects a moral commitment. Let's begin by looking more closely at the argument from quantity.

Arguments from Quantity

An advocate for sexual assault awareness writes:

> Every minute and a half someone is sexually assaulted in the United States. Each day more than 570 Americans experience sexual violence. This is an epidemic of sexual violence, and it must stop.

The **argument from quantity** is *an argument that affirms numerical considerations as an index of significance.* Such arguments judge events, organizations, problems and individuals on the basis of factors such as abundance and longevity, and reflect a disregard for things that do not exhibit such numerical indications of importance. Most of us are familiar with arguments using large numbers. For example:

Japan is unusual in the toy market in that a major portion of the toys sold are aimed at people who are twenty years old and older. Last year 27 percent of the enormous Japanese toy market was adults. That portion of the market is only going to grow as the median age in Japan continues to rise. Investors are thus pouring money into the three leading toy manufacturers in Japan.

The quantity argument can also be used to affirm the insignificance of small numbers. For example, a Harvard University astronomy professor, asked to justify the $600 million spent on the Hubble space telescope, responded:

Americans spend more than that amount each year on potato chips.

What's his point? The relatively small amount of money spent on the Hubble telescope—the "smallness" of the amount proved by the comparison to potato chip purchases—is insignificant, hardly worth mentioning. (Incidentally, analogy, discussed in Chapter 14, plays a role in this argument. Potato chip purchases are the evidence case; the telescope price is the conclusion case.)

Many advertisements use the quantity argument, suggesting that when a large number of people purchase a product or benefit from a service, this fact is evidence of the product's worth or of an organization's effectiveness. For example:

For the fifth year in a row, the Toyota Camry is the biggest selling car in America.

and

We performed our first heart transplant 25 years ago and have performed 11,151 since. (A leading hospital's advertisement.)

Arguing Relative Significance from Quantity

The "big numbers equal significance" and "small numbers equal insignificance" aspects of the argument from quantity are often combined to argue for the relative significance of two ideas or events. For example, an advocate for tighter seaport security argues by quantitative comparison:

There are 361 seaports in the United States, and 90 to 95 percent of all goods coming into and going out of this country pass through these ports. In the years since 9/11, the United States government has spent $8 billion to provide security for all 361 ports combined. Now, I know this sounds like a large amount of money, but consider that we spend that much every month in Afghanistan!

Notice that, as in an earlier instance, an analogy is used along with the argument from quantity in this example: spending on the Afghanistan conflict is the evidence case and spending for port security is the conclusion case. On the basis of this comparison of expenditures, it could be concluded that the United States needs to devote more resources to domestic port security.

Underlining a Problem

The argument from quantity is frequently used to underline or emphasize the magnitude of a problem. This argument is often followed by a call to action. For example:

Restaurants and stores throw away more than six billion pounds of edible produce each year in the United States. Such food waste is now at a level that demands action, including creating policies that would allow stores to sell or give away outdated and imperfect produce.

Quantity considerations are used in a wide range of contexts. Here is an example used to indicate the severity of a social problem:

The Children's Defense Fund reported recently that 6 million children in the United States live in single-parent families where the parent must work to avoid dependence on welfare. In addition, last year 12 million preschoolers, including 6 million infants and toddlers, spent all or part of their day being cared for by someone other than their parents, and 7 million children are left home alone on a regular basis. The Association for Child Care currently registers 37,000 people waiting for child care in Texas and Florida, and 25,000 in North Carolina. There can be no doubt that the United States is facing a child care crisis.

This example also illustrates how quantity considerations can be used to move an argument from considerations of fact to value claims (such as the one expressed in the last sentence of this argument), thus preparing the way for a policy claim.

Quantity and Hypothesis

Quantity arguments that emphasize the significance of a problem can also be used to introduce a hypothesis that explains the unusually large numbers.

Here is an example of the hypothesis and quantity reasoning being combined:

A new study confirms a twenty-year gap in life expectancy between rich and poor counties in the United States. "This enormous gap can no longer be ignored," said the study's lead researcher. The causes of the gap appear to be the prevalence of smoking and obesity in poor counties, health concerns that rich counties have successfully addressed.

Notice how this writer combined the argument from quantity with an argument for cause by analogy.

Small Changes, Major Consequences

Occasionally a version of the argument from quantity is used to argue that a relatively small change has significant impact when its effect is multiplied over a large number of cases or over a long period of time.

> A small change may have great impact when its effect is multiplied over many cases or over a long period of time.

Consider the savings that airlines realize each year from small cuts in their in-flight food service. A single bag of pretzels costs an airline pennies, but United Airlines cut pretzels from short domestic flights and saved $700,000 in one year. Recently British Air dropped its sandwich service on its flights to the European continent, resulting in a savings of more than $30 million in the first year. Here, then, is one way in which the quantity argument can be used to persuasive effect—by demonstrating what can happen when small effects are multiplied by large numbers.

The argument from quantity is often closely related to pragmatic concerns, as is evident from the following example.

A newly released Centers for Disease Control study indicates that 11 percent of all calories in the diet of an average adult in the United States now come from fast food, while the figure is 15 percent for adults aged twenty to thirty-nine. For young black adults the figure is even higher—21 percent. These are averages, and some of the eleven thousand respondents to the study said they never eat fast food. It's time we addressed the serious health implications of these alarming figures.

Let's consider some possible tests of the argument from quantity.

Testing the Argument from Quantity

The argument from quantity is an easy argument to understand. It simply affirms that things that exhibit quantity are desirable or significant and that things that do not, are not. There are two tests of the argument from quantity.

1. Is the quantity claim accurate? This question is directed to the numerical report in the quantity argument. For example, the statistics on the portion of adult calorie intake resulting from fast food consumption can be easily checked for accuracy on the Centers for Disease Control (CDC) website. This question also raises the issue of the accessibility of evidence, as described in the general tests of evidence in Chapter 6.

When we doubt the numbers in a quantity argument, we should seek some confirmation of the report. The most obvious approach in refuting a quantity argument is to show that the numbers are inaccurate. Another approach is to reinterpret the numbers to show that they are not as significant as they might at first appear. For instance, reports out of Australia argued that those who question the impact of popular culture on society should consider what happened in a recent Australian census, where more than seventy thousand people listed their religious preference as "Jedi," taking their cue from the massively popular *Star Wars* movies.

Other experts pointed out, however, that only about two thousand of these people take the fictional religion seriously. Most of the alleged Jedi faithful were responding to a prankster who organized the Jedi write-in campaign in the months leading up to the census. The much lower number of two thousand is not nearly as suggestive of an important Australian social phenomenon as would be the relatively large number of seventy thousand.

If we accept a numerical claim as accurate, we can still have means for testing or answering the argument. We must be confident that quantity is the central consideration in the case before us. A second test of the argument from quantity asks:

2. Are other considerations more important than quantity? We might object that a principle is at stake in the recommendation that follows a quantity claim, thereby answering the quantity argument with a principle argument. For instance, maybe a popular cosmetic product that boasts millions of users was developed through extensive testing on animals. In this event, purchasing the product would pose a question of principle for some people. Or perhaps we can show that some issue of quality is involved. The argument that a new housing and retail development in a desert area of Arizona will provide housing and shopping for several thousand people might be answered with the counter-argument that the desert is unique and would be destroyed.

The argument from quantity can itself be used as a rebuttal to certain other arguments, such as arguments from principle. For instance, Joel Barkin, press secretary for Congressman Bernard Sanders of Vermont, raised a question about the principle commitments of the US pharmaceutical industry when it resists permitting people to import lower-cost drugs from Canada. He pointed out that the real issue may not be the safety of Canadian drugs, but lobbying pressure. Barkin emphasized a strategic number, noting that there are 570 paid pharmaceutical lobbyists in Washington, DC, more than one for each member of Congress.[2]

FIGURE 16.1 Moral and Practical Arguments

Four familiar arguments based on moral and practical concerns:
- The Pragmatic Argument
- The Argument from Principle
- The Argument from Quantity
- The Argument from Quality

Arguments from Quality

An advertisement for a car features a photograph of the car above the caption, "The BXT is the fastest and most exotic car sold in the US." The caption connects some extraordinary qualities with an automobile. The goal, of course, is to create the sense that driving this particular car will make your life more interesting or "exotic." Similarly, a crystal manufacturer sells a line of expensive wine glasses using the phrase, "Once in a lifetime events don't just happen once in a lifetime." A company selling headphones that function both for listening to music and reducing external noise runs an ad reading, "Clearly these are no ordinary headphones."[3] Just behind these ads is the widespread belief that rare, beautiful, or unusual experiences or objects are, for that very reason, desirable.

The **argument from quality** is *an argument that affirms the inherent value in the unique, the beautiful, the rare, or the unusual.* Some advertising reflects the presence of the argument from quality:

> This railway excursion is among the most enchanting travel experiences available in the world today. You will enjoy the luxury of refurbished railway cars that reflect the elegance of a bygone era. You will experience the breathtaking beauty of the Siberian wilderness. You will be treated to sumptuous food and lavish accommodations in the grand tradition of the Tsars.

The persuasiveness of arguments from quality depends on a value for unusual or rare events, objects, and experiences.

Psychologist Robert Cialdini acknowledges the power of reasoning from quality when discussing a "weapon of influence" he labels "scarcity." Things that are rare or unusual, writes Cialdini, take on greater value. They are difficult to attain, and may be irreplaceable if lost. Consequently, to argue that an object, event, or resource is rare, unusual, beautiful, or irreplaceable can be highly persuasive.[4]

Testing the Argument from Quality

Like the argument from quantity, which it resembles and often opposes, the argument from quality can be tested by asking:

1. Is the indicated quality actually present? Often the argument from quality rests on assertions about the presence of an underlying attribute. Thus, these alleged qualities suggest a possible rebuttal. Let's return to the example of the "exotic" car. Whether a particular car actually is the fastest car sold in the US may be a testable claim, but how would we know the same car was the most exotic? A related approach is to challenge the undefined terms that accompany a quality claim. What, for example, is meant by the term "exotic?"

A second question to ask of the argument from quality is:

2. Is the quality more clearly represented elsewhere? Because the claims are about what is unique or rare, the argument from quality invites comparisons. We may agree that the BXT is fast and exotic, but still believe that it is not as fast or as exotic as the Vortex.

Finally, we might oppose the concern for quality because of greater concern for quantity, principle, or some other consideration. We can do this by asking:

3. Do other concerns outweigh this quality? Perhaps an exotic car is marketed using sexist appeals, offending a principle some people hold strongly. Maybe the very exclusivity of the product is distasteful to people for whom conspicuous consumption is offensive. In the beauty contest example, perhaps it would be appropriate to seek out other qualities, or maybe the contests violate a principle of not treating and judging women as objects. In response to the unusual qualities of beauty contestants, a critic might celebrate the characteristics of the much larger number of ordinary people— a quantity consideration.

CHAPTER REVIEW

Pragmatic arguments, frequently encountered in policy debates, urge us to do things that benefit us and avoid things that don't. So strong is self-interest that these arguments would almost always prevail were it not for the argument from principle, often advanced in response to pragmatic arguments. The argument from principle affirms adherence to a right, duty, value, or obligation. Because arguments from principle are vital to life in a free society, the argument from principle is potent and can be an effective response to the pragmatic argument.

Arguments from quantity reveal a preference for longevity, great amounts, or other numerical factors. Arguments from quality are often set forth to oppose arguments from quantity. The latter emphasize the unique or unusual qualities of some person, object, or idea. The four arguments described in this chapter are very common in advertising, but are also frequently encountered in all types of public discourse.

EXERCISES

A.   Identify the specific type of argument advanced in each of the following examples.

1. Five billion people on Earth have no access to the internet. That's why our plan to place balloons in the stratosphere to connect everyone on Earth to the internet is so urgent.

2. Available research does not provide clear guidance regarding marijuana, for several practical reasons. The only marijuana for government research comes from a single farm at the University of Mississippi. Commercially available marijuana has changed dramatically in recent years. These changes aren't reflected at the Mississippi growing facility. Regulations are also a problem. Federally funded marijuana researchers must get approval from the Drug Enforcement Agency and, in some states, a state board of medical examiners. In addition, testing the health effects of edible marijuana products that are marketed to consumers is illegal. Testing on lab animals is also illegal. All this leads to a severely limited body of reliable research. The system for administering marijuana research must be modernized. Barriers to doing good research must be removed.

3. Gwyneth Paltrow has told interviewers that she will not eat octopus. Her reason? The octopus is just too smart. The famed actress reasoned that these animals regularly demonstrate a high level of intelligence, which on principle makes her unwilling to treat them as food.

4. In a surprising and helpful development for the wind power industry, a majority of residents living in the vicinity of wind farms say they like the appearance of gigantic turbines. The enormous, slowly rotating blades and stately white towers are said to bring an air of majesty and tranquility to the landscape.

5. The World Wildlife Fund estimates that producing a single cup of latte requires two hundred liters of water. This figure takes into consideration the water used to grow the coffee, manufacture the cup and lid, produce the milk in the drink, and then brew the coffee. This number must be multiplied by the enormous number of lattes consumed each day. Practicing better conservation measures is the key to enjoying a cup of coffee without threatening our water supply.

6. Green roofs—roofs planted with grass, vegetables, and flowering plants—are the wave of the future, and for good reason. They decrease rain runoff, improve the energy efficiency of buildings, improve the urban landscape, and can even serve as a source of food.

7. Bryce Canyon must be preserved as a wilderness area because developing the canyon would threaten the last remaining bristlecone pines, the rarest and oldest trees on earth.

8. Wilderness areas in the United States should be preserved, not just because they are beautiful, but for a less well-recognized reason—they are intimately tied to the health of the people, who benefit physically from being outside.

9. Autism research is being hindered by a shortage of human brain matter for study. Thus, the regulations governing the use of human tissue samples in research should be revised to make more samples available for research purposes.

10. The cause of the massive die-off of California pine trees is the native bark beetle, whose population is exploding because of the five-year drought that weakened trees. There are now one hundred million highly flammable dead trees standing in the state's forests. We are one lightning strike away from a wildfire of unprecedented proportions. Whereas small forest fires come with some benefits, huge fires are not beneficial—they destroy soil and seeds, leading to erosion and landslides. Cutting the trees for lumber has just made the problem worse by extending the range of the beetle. Where can we turn for a solution? Some have suggested producing energy from the dead trees. One approach involves small, portable gasification power plants that turn trees into electricity. A by-product is a charcoal-like substance that can be used as fertilizer for young trees. The only drawback is cost—producing electricity this way costs slightly more than producing it by conventional means. Still, the state must weigh the benefits of reducing fire risk against the cost to consumers of more expensive electricity.

11. The Planetary Science Division of NASA says more than ten thousand large asteroids and four thousand small asteroids have been detected in the observable solar system. More than one thousand of these objects are each a kilometer in diameter, large enough to destroy human life on earth. While a few asteroids in our vicinity may not pose much of a threat, the laws of probability clearly suggest that thousands do. It's time we took seriously the threat posed to our safety by such enormous numbers of potentially deadly asteroids.

12. Wall Street executives were paid $18 billion in bonuses the same year the government bailed out many big banks and finance companies. This is simply unconscionable. It violates the average person's basic sense of right and wrong.

13. The National Parks receive more than four hundred million visitors a year, more than attend NFL, NASCAR, the NBA, and Major League Baseball events combined. Thus, the parks system deserves our financial support.

14. Dean Victor Gold, of Loyola Law School in Los Angeles, explained the school's decision to reduce the number of new admissions: "Reality has caught up to higher education . . . . We have a moral obligation not to just take tuition dollars and then turn a blind eye when our graduates can't find jobs."[5]

15. Tesla, under the direction of Elon Musk, has no technology that isn't available to anyone who wants it, and electric cars cost more to produce than consumers can afford. The one thing Tesla has going for it is that the Model S is one of the most beautiful cars ever made—that's it, design.

16. There are more than two billion smartphone users worldwide, 25 percent of whom live in one country: China. Marketers will be wise to target this emerging digital giant.

17. Once having acquired rights to the rare medication, the company increased the price of the drug by roughly 5,500 percent in one day. The cost to consumers rose to $750 per pill from the original $13.50. Two things struck pharmaceutical industry watchers as particularly immoral: that the drug has been unchanged for sixty-five years, and that many patients cannot live without it.

B. Which test of the pragmatic argument has been applied in the following example?

> Those who are lobbying for embryonic stem cell research are, in fact, hindering progress into stem cell research. That is, they are hurting their own cause. Let me explain. The protest against embryonic stem cells is founded on moral issues regarding the status of the embryo. Many biologists believe that it is not necessary to use embryos at all, because adult stem cells are available in bone marrow and other places in the body. The problem for researchers is that adult stem cells do not show the plasticity of embryo cells; that is, they are not capable of differentiating into different kinds of cells, but are programmed to become only one type of cell. Many experts agree that further research will allow scientists to induce plasticity in adult stem cells, thus completely eliminating the need for embryonic stem cells. Here's the irony: the controversy generated by current lobbying for the use of embryonic stem cells is drawing attention and support away from research into inducing plasticity in adult stem cells.

C. The following are arguments based on principles. For each example, state the moral principle being invoked. In addition, identify the action that is considered to be a violation of the principle.

1. Only about one in ten of those killed in US pilotless drone strikes is a targeted combatant. Our obligation to protect the lives of innocent civilians means that our current policies concerning pilotless drones in combat are unacceptable.

2. Pharmaceutical companies giving presents to medical students in order to convince them to prescribe company drugs after they graduate violates the ethical principle that corporate money should not play a role in shaping medical curricula.

3. Some robots and computers are intelligent enough to be self-aware, and thus qualify as machine persons. We have a duty to protect their rights as persons. Thus, arbitrarily turning off an intelligent machine is immoral.

4. Keeping a prisoner in solitary confinement is a violation of the constitutional guarantee of protection from cruel and unusual punishment.

5. It is wrong to deny the right to marry to gay people. Such a prohibition violates a fundamental human right to seek happiness.

6. The proposal that parents should be allowed to "design" their children by genetic engineering violates the moral limit on tampering with nature.

7. The United States has a moral obligation to promote human rights in other countries through its trade policies and diplomatic activities.

8. A recognizable model of a human face can now be constructed from DNA left on cigarette butts, chewing gum, or saliva on a coffee cup. This procedure—which has been successfully performed in at least one college art class—raises privacy concerns.

ENDNOTES

[1] Michael Sandel, "The Case against Perfection," *Atlantic Monthly,* April 2004, 51.

[2] Kate Long, "State Eyes Canadian Drugs," *Sunday Gazette* (Charleston, W.V.), October 20, 2003, http://www.wvgazette.com/section/Series/Everybody+at+Risk/2003101827.

[3] The advertisements are for Waterford Crystal and Bose Quiet Comfort 2 headphones.

[4] Robert Cialdini, *Influence: Science and Practice* (Boston, Mass.: Allyn & Bacon, 2000).

[5] Jason Song, "Faced with Job Complaints, Loyola Law School Accepting Fewer Students," *Los Angeles Times,* August 19, 2013, http://www.latimes.com/news/local/la-me-loyola-law -20130819,0,2313212.story.

RECOMMENDED WEBSITES

Informal Logic

Stanford Encyclopedia of Philosophy

plato.stanford.edu/entries/logic-informal

The arguments discussed in this chapter are among the most commonly encountered forms of reasoning in the marketplace of ideas. This entry in the *Stanford Encyclopedia of Philosophy* provides a detailed analysis of the informal logic of public discourse.

The Uses (and Abuses) of Influence

Harvard Business Review

http://hbr.org/2013/07/the-uses-and-abuses-of-influence/ar/1

Psychologist Robert Cialdini has explored six principles of influence, some of which are closely related to the four arguments discussed in this chapter. In this interview by Sarah Cliffe, Cialdini explains how basic principles of persuasion may be employed ethically in the workplace.

17 Essential Nature Arguments

Nature is often hidden, sometimes overcome, seldom extinguished.
Francis Bacon (1561–1626)
British philosopher

I am not at all the kind of person you and I took me to be.
Jane Carlyle (1801–1866)
British writer
in a letter to her husband, essayist Thomas Carlyle

KEY TERMS

argument from function

argument from intent

essential nature argument

genetic argument

person/act argument

visual argument

Carlos opposes placing large sea mammals in captivity for the purpose of entertainment. He tells a friend who sees no harm in the practice: "It is undeniable that whales and dolphins are highly intelligent creatures, expressing complex communication, emotional states, and a desire for freedom. It is a violation of their nature to place them in confinement. Such captivity deprives these creatures of the space and freedom they need to maintain their mental health. We should not be surprised when they occasionally act out their frustration by attacking a trainer or engaging in other aggressive behavior."

This chapter discusses **essential nature arguments,** *arguments that focus on the "essence" or unchanging nature of an organization, object, person, entity, or work of art.* As evidence of a defining essence, essential nature arguments consider such factors as origins, intentions, functions, and—in the case of people and groups—public actions. The essential nature of an object becomes crucial to assigning meaning, rendering moral judgments, and identifying appropriate uses. This chapter examines four essential nature arguments—the genetic argument, the argument from intent, the argument from function, and the person-act argument.

GENETIC ARGUMENTS

The genetic argument takes its name from an ancient word for beginnings or origins. **Genetic arguments** are *arguments that look to origins as evidence of essential nature.*

The genetic argument affirms the inference from origin to essential nature regardless of how much time has elapsed from the time of origin. For example:

> Modern science grew out of the efforts of medieval and Renaissance magicians to control nature by esoteric methods such as alchemy and astrology. The same impulse is at the heart of much modern science—a determination to control the natural world by discovering its secrets, to mold it to our purposes, to make nature do what we desire it to do.

Here the origin of a practice—modern science—is said to reveal its essence or nature, even though that origin is temporally and culturally distant. The evidence in this and similar arguments is a claim regarding origins, or history. The conclusion is that the essence of science renders it a questionable practice. Notice that the unstated connective in the argument is that essential nature is revealed in origins.

The genetic argument is often used in discussions of events and institutions. Here is an example from a debate about whether a university's commitment to a specialized type of research should be maintained:

> State University must maintain its commitment to range and soil science despite the lack of students in the department, because the school was founded as a land grant college with an agricultural mission.

In this argument, the origin of the university as a "land grant college" is invoked as bearing the essential nature of the institution. This essential nature, in turn, is considered to govern aspects of the university's day-to-day functioning.

Testing the Genetic Argument

The genetic argument relies on the assumption that origin reveals or perhaps determines essence. That assumption is open to question. We can ask:

1. Does origin reveal essence? Some experts question the basic assumption underlying the genetic argument, which is why it is sometimes referred to as the "genetic fallacy." The claim in our example is that the historical origins of Western science imparted to it an unchanging essence as a practice that aims to manipulate the natural world. Respondents to this claim, however, would argue that the origin of modern science in magical practices of the Middle Ages and Renaissance no longer affects how we think about scientific practices.

Whenever a historical claim is made, as inevitably is the case with the genetic argument, the claim may be inaccurate. Ensuring the accuracy of that historical claim is important, as far as this is possible. A second test of genetic arguments asks:

2. Is the origin account accurate? This test of the genetic argument often requires some historical research. Did modern science originate in the practices of alchemy, astrology, and related systems such as numerology several centuries ago? Many historians would affirm that these practices are indeed the origin of what we know as science. Moreover, the earliest of these scientific efforts often were efforts to control nature, thus making them a source of personal power. The origin account in this case, then, is largely accurate. However, in any case in which origins are being argued, it is important to check the claim against historical facts.

3. Are present meanings or uses more important than origin? Certainly meanings change over time. Can the same be said for the essence of a practice or an organization? The essence of science is found today in its role as a method of inquiry and investigation, which is far removed from esoteric practices now quite distant in time. It would be difficult at best to establish that science still reflects the essential interests of alchemists and astrologers. Science has taken on its own meanings, which are distinct from the practices from which it sprang.

ARGUMENTS FROM INTENT

Arguments from intent are *arguments that affirm that the meaning or essential nature of an object or document is revealed in the intended meaning of its authors or designers.* Such arguments may be advanced regarding objects, institutions, documents, or even nature itself. In the intent of an object's creator or designer is found its essential nature and, thus its meaning, uses, value, and interpretation. The following is an example of an argument from intent:

> It is ridiculous to prevent historians from using the Freedom of Information Act to access Pentagon documents on the Vietnam War. The people who drafted the act intended it to control access to recent documents that have a direct bearing on national security matters. These documents are now forty to fifty years old, and for that reason could not possibly affect national security.

The evidence in this argument is the assertion concerning the original intent of the authors of the Act, as well as the observation about the age of the documents in question. The conclusion is the statement about the inappropriateness of restricting historians from the documents on the basis of the Act. The unstated reason in this example is the assumption that the Act should be interpreted according to its authors' original intent.

> The argument from intent often occurs in debates about interpretations of the Constitution.

A common and important instance of the argument from intent occurs in debates over interpretations of the United States Constitution. The focus of such debates is usually on the framers of the Constitution: the nature or meaning of that document is considered to be revealed in their original intent. Most of us have encountered some version of the following argument:

> The Constitution guarantees the right of every citizen to "keep and bear arms." Thus, the framers' intent was to ensure that citizens would always have free access to arms with which to defend themselves and the country. Therefore, the right to own a gun must not be violated.

In response, some variation on the following argument often is advanced:

> The Constitution states that "a well-regulated militia being necessary to the security of a free state, the right of the people to keep and bear arms shall not be infringed." Thus, the framers' intent was to ensure the existence of a militia, like the National Guard. Therefore, no constitutional injunction against gun control is present.

The argument from intent almost always develops around a question of interpretation. The assumption that essential nature is discovered in the intentions of authors or designers links the evidence for a particular interpretation of a document or work of art to a conclusion. Such arguments are especially common in deliberations about legal matters or interpretations of the law, but they may appear in any argumentation about the correct interpretation of documents or artifacts. Arguments from intent are particularly crucial in controversy surrounding the interpretation of historical documents. They also show up in arguments about the design of nature, when God is posited as the "designer" of the physical world, as well as in discussions of works of art.

Testing the Argument from Intent

The argument from intent assumes that an author's or a designer's intent governs present meanings. This assumption is not always justified and can be called into question. The first test of the argument from intent asks:

1. Does the author's intent govern interpretation in this case? Though intent may be important to interpret an artifact or document accurately, it is not inviolable. We might reply to the argument about the Freedom of Information Act by saying that the authors' intent now is irrelevant, that all laws are adapted and interpreted in accordance with current need, and that the current need is for the act to regulate access to documents that are older than those to which the act originally controlled access.

A similar response could be made to either argument about the right of citizens to keep and bear arms under the Bill of Rights. Someone might argue that the intent of the framers is irrelevant to current interpretations of the Constitution, that circumstances in the United States have changed so drastically in the past two centuries that what Jefferson or Madison thought about citizens' right to bear arms is absolutely irrelevant to current applications of the Constitution. This rebuttal could be made by someone who believes strongly in constitutional government but who rejects the idea that interpretations of the Constitution ought to be governed only by reference to the framers' intentions.

Of course, the original intent of a designer or an author could have been wrongly understood. To know someone's intent in creating an artifact or document is difficult at best. Thus, a second test involves asking:

2. Has intent been represented accurately? The argument about whether the Bill of Rights ensures a right to own a gun is not an argument about whether the authors' intent ought to govern interpretation of the Constitution. On that point the disputants agree. What they disagree about is what the framers intended: each claims the other misrepresents that intent. That is to say, each of these people is employing the second test of arguments from intent. Resolving this dispute involves ascertaining, with as much accuracy as the situation allows, the framers' actual intent. Doing so may require a good deal of historical research, as terms such as "militia" and even "keep and bear arms" may change in meaning over time.

Finally, even when we are inclined to find some interpretive value in an author's intent, we can ask:

3. Do other considerations outweigh intent? Although the framers' intent is important, it might be argued, the need to control the number and distribution of firearms is even more important to our present social situation. This response advances social need as a consideration that outweighs original intent.

ARGUMENTS FROM FUNCTION

Arguments from function are *arguments that locate the essential nature of an object, event, or institution in its social or natural function.* Because the evidence for the function of an object or institution is often found in what it has been or done in the past, the argument from function may be advanced as support for a conservative point of view. However, as we shall see, this is not its only use. The argument from function is deployed in many cases to preserve the current order of things, to maintain an established meaning rather than searching for a new one.

Function arguments are encountered in debates about social institutions, such as the public schools, courts, police departments, and the military. The argument may reaffirm a function for an institution that is being contested, or use an already established function as the basis for drawing an additional conclusion. Consider the following example:

> The mayor is wrong to suggest that the police are not doing enough about the underlying causes of crime in our city. Police can do little or nothing about poverty, unemployment, access to guns, lack of proper role models for kids, abuse and neglect, and tolerance for drug use.

The argument lists problems that a police force—because of its established function—should not to be called on to address. It concludes that the mayor is wrong to criticize the police for not doing enough about the root causes of crime. The argument describes the police as having an essential nature that is revealed in the characteristic social function of law enforcement, but notice how the argument also limits any future development of additional police functions. The nature of the police is assumed to be fixed and unchanging.

In the following example, however, the argument from function exploits an established function—in this case, the function of campaigns—to *expand* the role of a social institution. Notice how the institution's essential nature is said to be preserved by allowing for a change:

> A political campaign, by its very nature, is supposed to allow a free exchange of a variety of views so that the public can make a fair and informed decision. To restrict the expression of views to two parties does violence to this important function of campaigns. Smaller parties must be included in debates and other public arenas where views are aired.

The argument from function can also be employed to identify a *natural* rather than a social function. For instance, consider how one scientist assesses the natural function or essential nature of leatherback turtles based on their design:

> Leatherbacks are built to travel. "On the beach, [leatherback turtles] look as out of place as a submarine in dry dock," but in the water "they are the most graceful creatures you have ever seen," says [biologist] Scott Eckert. "This is one of the most hydrodynamically designed creatures on the planet. They can probably swim as easily as rest."[1]

One of paleontologist Stephen J. Gould's most famous arguments developed from form to a natural function. In his collection of essays titled *The Panda's Thumb,* Gould argued that the form of a panda's thumb was an argument against its having been designed by God. He reasoned from the thumb's odd form to its function as a natural adaptation. The "thumb" is not a true thumb but a wrist bone adapted to stripping the bark from bamboo plants. This function placed the panda's thumb within the larger set of functions biologists refer to as evolutionary adaptations. According to Gould, that adaptation places the thumb outside the purposes of an intelligent creating divinity. He thus "removed" the unusual thumb as a potential argument from intent—that God created it that way—making it instead evidence in an argument from function.[2]

Testing the Argument from Function

Arguments about function can be tested by asking:

1. Has function been identified correctly? The basis for establishing function and attributions based on function can be called in question. Returning to our example regarding the function of the police, although dealing with social problems may not be their typical function, the police might still be expected to help address some of the problems mentioned. Though their job description might not include "providing a role model for children in the community," can they not legitimately be expected to help out in this regard? Another approach would be to ask whether some other aspect of police work has in the past extended their responsibilities beyond the usual law enforcement function.

This line of inquiry leads to a second test of the argument from function:

2. How is function derived? It is always possible to challenge attributions of function by examining how function has been assigned. In our example, the contention that certain activities are not functions of the police could be challenged by questioning the source of functions. If function has been derived from outdated or narrow views of police as only law enforcers, a different source of function—a broader, traditional view—might be affirmed. For instance, someone might reply:

> If we look at the police as peacekeepers rather than simply enforcers—a role we increasingly ask them to play—it seems that the police *do* have some responsibility to help control access to guns and the availability of drugs on the street. And why should we not expect the police to provide a role model for children in the community? To say that these things are outside the proper function of the police is to limit their proper function unreasonably, to an excessively narrow reading of their job description. Let's look at the broader tradition of police work.

Sources of Function

This last test raises the question of sources of function. Attributions of function may develop from a number of sources, four of which are particularly common:

1. Prescription: Function is sometimes prescribed; that is, spelled out in an official or authoritative manner. The function of a police officer, for instance, may be written down in a job description. This prescription of function may be referred to in developing an argument from function.

2. Common understanding: Many claims about function are based on a commonly understood function of a person, object, or institution. Thus, schools commonly are understood as functioning to provide education, police to enforce the law, hospitals to take care of sick people. Common understanding often is linked closely to tradition—the function of an object is known from what it has done in the past.

3. Form: Function may also be attributed on the basis of form. Thus, the police officer's "form"—a military-style uniform, weapon, and specially equipped car—indicates a function having something to do with enforcement, literally with the use of force to achieve compliance with the law. A school's form—seats arranged in rows, chalkboards, teachers addressing students—indicates a function of delivering something (education) to an orderly audience. As we have seen, the form of a natural object can also be used to argue for a particular function.

4. Current need: Claims about social function may be based on current need. Though police traditionally may be understood as enforcers of the law, current need may require them to function as mediators, role models, or educators. Many schools today invite police officers into classrooms to provide instruction in the law. Similarly, though the traditional function of schools may be seen as providing education, the current social situation may suggest that their function should be expanded to include personal counseling. As social needs change, institutional functions may change also.

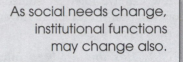

As social needs change, institutional functions may change also.

Knowing the source of a claim about function can assist in understanding or responding to an argument. For instance, if we know the claim is based on common understanding, we can point out either that common understanding may be too limited or that other ways of assigning function, such as current need, are perhaps more appropriate.

PERSON/ACT ARGUMENTS

Genetic, intent, and function arguments usually are advanced about objects, documents, and institutions. Occasionally they are also made about people. A fourth essential nature argument is used exclusively to evaluate the nature of a person or a group of people. The **person/act argument** is *an argument that looks to a person's or group's acts to find the true nature or character of that individual or group.*[3] The following is an example:

> Following his death in 2011, numerous efforts were made to identify the qualities of Steve Jobs's character that led to his great business success as the founder and leader of Apple. As testimonials to his vision, brilliance, and determination accumulated, however, so did alarming revelations about his personal relationships and managerial style. Petty and vindictive, a bully prone to outbursts of rage, Jobs was a boss willing to demean an employee's idea one day and take credit for the same idea the next. His arrogance, disregard for the feelings of others, and aloofness to the needs of those closest to him make it clear that Jobs was neither a commendable business leader nor a person worthy of emulation.

The person/act argument assumes that a reliable way to evaluate an individual's or a group's character is to look at what that individual or group has done. Probably we all accept the person/act argument in some instances, but we also know that all human acts require interpretation and that our actions can be deceptive or misleading. People frequently mask their true natures with behaviors that are not in keeping with them. We also know we are inconsistent in our own actions at times, kind to one person but perhaps cruel to another, so even a great act of generosity or a reputation for hard work might be called into question, especially if other acts attributed to the same individual seem to contradict it.

The person/act argument can be used to condemn as well as to commend. In an editorial piece, sports writer Jim Litke took aim at a Little League coach who bribed a player on his team to intentionally injure an eight-year-old autistic boy on the same team so he could not play in a game. One boy on the team said the coach "told me if I would hit [the autistic boy] in the face, he would pay me $25." Later, the coach told the same player, "go out there and hit him harder." The eight-year-old was hit twice with the baseball—once in the groin and once in the ear. When the injured player's mother approached the coach about the incidents he said casually, "The balls must be after

258 Part VI Types and Tests of Arguments

him. He should take the day off." Litke concludes that the coach, who was charged with criminal solicitation to commit aggravated assault, is one of a growing number of "sadistic Little League parent[s] and coach[es]."[4] Again, the person/act argument reasons from an individual's actions to conclusions about personal character.

Testing the Person/Act Argument

How can we interpret someone's actions? For example, is a refusal to answer a question an indication of anger or of shyness? The person/act argument should be tested by asking:

1. Has this act been interpreted accurately? Virtually any act is subject to more than one interpretation. One observer might view an individual famed for her support of a children's hospital as kindhearted, while another might interpret the apparent generosity as a means of avoiding taxes. Because almost any act can be part of an effort to create a false image or to divert attention from other events or activities, interpretation may require additional support, especially if the interpretation is questioned.

The second test of person/act argument recognizes that all people engage in a variety of activities, and that the nature of an individual is revealed more in a series of acts than in a single decision. Thus, we should ask:

2. Are the observed acts consistent with other acts by this person? For an act to indicate a person's nature, the act should be consistent with a pattern of behavior. If charitable giving is inconsistent with other things an individual has done, especially if these other acts are well known, the argument is severely weakened. The sports hero who is revealed as a spousal abuser will likely suffer a severe reduction in pubic esteem. Charging individuals or organizations with inconsistency is so common in public discourse—especially political discourse—that it deserves a closer look.

Charging Inconsistency

The goal of the charge of inconsistency is to suggest dishonesty or instability. We generally hold inconsistency to be a sign of a character flaw, such as indecisiveness, deceitfulness, or weakness of will. Some actions and statements are inconsistent in a way that should be pointed out to an audience. When someone alleges inconsistency, every effort should be made to establish that the inconsistency is actual and not contrived, apparent, or a result of intentional misinterpretation.

The charge of inconsistency may be aimed at showing a questionable duplicity in the opposition. Consider the following example:

> When Reagan called himself a citizen of the world, conservatives applauded. When Obama said the same thing, conservatives protested that he was not sufficiently American.

Again, the person/act argument may be directed at groups as well as at individuals.

Another goal of charging inconsistency is to force an opponent to take a stand on an issue to avoid appearing indecisive. This is a common tactic in political argumentation and other settings in which personal character is an issue.

Sometimes the goal of charging inconsistency is to force an opponent to admit to one of the inconsistent actions or statements. Inconsistency charges can be aimed at organizations as well as at individuals:

> The Freedom from Religion Foundation charges that teaching creation science violates the doctrine of separation of church and state, but in a recent

FIGURE 17.1 Visual Arguments of Essential Nature

Jonathan Bachman/Reuters

Supreme Court decision, its worldview of scientific humanism was ruled a religion. This religion is taught in all of our schools, and I don't hear the Foundation objecting.

VISUAL ARGUMENTS FROM ESSENTIAL NATURE

When Dr. Martin Luther King, Jr., presented his famous *I Have a Dream* speech in the summer of 1963, he stood on the steps of the Lincoln Memorial in Washington, DC. The setting was symbolic, as Dr. King mentioned in the introduction to his speech. Because of Lincoln's association with freedom and the end of slavery, his memorial provided a physical and visual representation of the essence of these and related ideas. Thus, for Dr. King to speak about the ongoing struggle for freedom and equality for all Americans from the steps of the Lincoln Memorial provided his listeners with visual reinforcement for his verbal argument.

So far the arguments considered in this text have all been constructed of words, but a moment's thought will suggest that an argument might be made musically, through dance, or even architecturally. What we will term **visual arguments**— *arguments conveyed through images or objects rather than words*—can be highly persuasive, often precisely because they are not immediately perceived as arguments at all. Visual arguments often achieve their effect through their capacity to present a concise summation of a situation, that is, to capture the essence of an event or set of circumstances.

Figure 17.1 is one example. Ieshia Evans, a nurse from Pennsylvania, traveled to Baton Rouge, Louisiana, to participate in a Black Lives Matter protest on July 9, 2016. The protest was a response to recent police shootings of two young black men, Alton Sterling and Philando Castile. This widely distributed photo constitutes a powerful

FIGURE 17.2 Visual Arguments of Essential Nature

Image courtesy of TEACH.org

visual argument for the courage and determination of the protesters. In contrast to the aggressive posture of several police officers, Evans calmly submits to arrest. The photo summarizes the essential nature of the protest and of the protesters.

In another example, in Figure 17.2, the essential nature of a dedicated young teacher is captured in this woman's expression and gesture. The photograph expresses confidence, determination, and idealism, summing up the nature of the situation more effectively than might a written argument about the excitement of entering teaching as a career.[5] The photo of a child refugee (Figure 17.3) captures the plight of fifty million displaced children throughout the world, and thus makes an effective argument from essential nature for humanitarian aid.

Visual arguments may convey their messages in a variety of ways, for example, by suggesting a similarity between two political candidates or by revealing that a moral principle has been violated. In this chapter, we will focus only on the important category of visual objects and images that achieve their effects by suggesting the essential nature of an institution, a nation, an event, or even of a person.

Another example, from the world of architecture, is intended to reveal the essential nature of a country. Three enormous new skyscrapers stand in close proximity to one another in the Chinese financial center of Shanghai. The first building is called the Jin Mao Tower. The second is called the Shanghai World Financial Center. The third is called simply the Shanghai Tower.

These buildings, taken together, constitute a powerful three-part visual statement to the world about the history, culture, and economic development of the

FIGURE 17.3 Visual Arguments of Essential Nature

Giorgos Moutafis/Reuters

People's Republic of China. As such, the three Shanghai skyscrapers may be thought of as a visual argument, a set of architectural premises in an argument about China's past, present, and future.

The Jin Mao Tower (1380 feet) is designed to reflect traditional Chinese architecture. Its pagoda-like lines suggest China's unusually long, rich history as a nation. As a visual argument, this tower makes the case that China is a lasting world power with a millennia-long history and well-established traditions.

The Shanghai World Financial Center stands near the Jin Mao Tower. Its great height (1614 feet), contemporary design, and striking 151-foot opening at its pinnacle assert visually that China is a modern nation with tremendous technological and financial resources.

At 2073 feet, the third structure, the Shanghai Tower, is the world's second-tallest building. Its futuristic twisting design—really nine separate buildings stacked one on top of another and covered in a glass skin—makes a powerful visual statement about China's importance as a world power in the coming technological and economic future.

Taken together, the three towers constitute a visual argument that moves us toward the conclusion that China is a nation with a long and illustrious history, a powerful contemporary financial presence in the world, and a promising future of international leadership. In order to arrive at such a conclusion we have considered elements of design, materials, and proximity. A much more elaborate interpretation could be drawn from specific architectural details of these buildings, but this overview can introduce us to the possibility that a persuasive argument need not be constructed of words.

In a more recent example, a visual argument invited a visual counter-argument. Sculptor Arturo Di Modica created the famous Charging Bull sculpture in 1987 as a symbol of US resilience, following the stock market crash that year. The sculpture, originally placed in front of the New York Stock Exchange, was intended to make a point: the United States is strong and will recover. However, a small addition transformed the bull statue into a premise in a rather different visual argument.

At the request of an investment firm, State Street Global Advisors, sculptor Kristen Visbal crafted a four-foot-tall bronze sculpture of a defiant little girl a few yards away, facing the popular bull. Visbal's public art made a provocative statement about the need for gender equality on Wall Street. "We were focusing on making a statement about the future of Wall Street," Visbal stated. "We wanted this wonderful contrast."[6]

The little girl's posture and facial expression are unmistakable symbols of determination, and as such reframe the bull as a metaphor of the largely male power of the market. A plaque at her feet reads, "Know the power of women in leadership. SHE makes a difference." ("SHE" is the common name of an index that measures the financial performance of companies in which women are well represented in leadership.)

The meaning of the bull was altered by Visbal's argumentative act. A piece of public art representing a financial fact—the resilience of the financial markets—was pressed into new service as a symbol of Wall Street's entrenched male power. Recognizing that the defiant girl reinterpreted his sculpture, Di Modica protested the placement of the new statue. As always, an argument invited a counter-argument, which in turn generated an additional argument.

Let's consider one more example of visual argument that suggests essential nature. Photojournalism is a means of making arguments—leading audiences to conclusions—by means of images. Photographs of a war, a famine, or a natural disaster can evoke the essence of the unfolding crisis in a way that verbal arguments might fail to do. Images of New Orleans following the Hurricane Katrina disaster, for example, confronted many people with the vast scope of the disaster. Similarly, photographic images of war or of famine can in some cases consolidate public opinion more quickly than a series of written or spoken arguments can. Most of us have seen the riveting images of civil rights advocates in the early 1960s being assaulted with fire hoses or attacked by police dogs. These pictures served to convey to the US public the essential nature of the struggle for racial equality for all citizens of the United States. Such images convey an emotional essence that can be difficult to achieve in more verbal argumentative approaches.

Evaluating Visual Arguments from Essential Nature

It is relatively easy to see how an image or an object might convey an argument to an audience, but it is not particularly evident how we would evaluate the strength of such an argument. A thorough evaluation would include questions about the aesthetics of the image or object in question, for example, its composition. It might also consider the artist's point of view, and what he or she has chosen to include in or exclude from the audience's visual field. However, let's look at how a visual argument might be evaluated *as* argument, beginning with the visual argument's inferential structure.

> In a visual argument, the image itself stands in the place of both evidence and conclusion.

In a visual argument, the image itself stands in the place of both evidence and conclusion in a verbal argument—we *see* rather than read or hear the evidence, then infer the conclusion. The artist communicating an argument by means of an image or object, thus, is taking something of a risk, for the audience may not immediately perceive the intent of the visual presentation. Here is one question to ask in evaluating such arguments:

1. Does the image or object clearly sum up the essence of the subject so as to convey the advocate's intended conclusion? For instance, the images of brutalized civil rights marchers mentioned earlier have stood for many years as a clear and powerful summary of the civil rights struggle at that time. The intended conclusion, for most audiences, is clear.

Whether we accept the visual argument's implied conclusion also depends on whether we share the values of the artist presenting the image, so we can also ask:

2. Is the intended audience likely to embrace the value or principle that leads from the image to its implied conclusion? Someone who was more concerned about the ordinary person and did not share a deep concern for the image being projected through the architecture of a rising world power might not be moved by an image of prominent buildings. It is possible with visual arguments, as with verbal ones, to frame a counter-argument or simply to fail to be persuaded by the argument.

Finally, because an image or object is necessarily a condensation of a more complex set of circumstances—thus, a reduction of something complex to something relatively simple—we will want to ask about the presence of other widely known and potentially contradictory facts or even images. Thus we might ask:

3. Is the visual argument weakened by widely known facts that contradict its central claim? For example, the government of North Korea distributes photographs and videos intended to create the impression of a well-ordered and prosperous nation inhabited by free and contented people. Reports to the contrary by members of the press and by North Koreans who have fled the country are common, however. As a result, the visual evidence supplied by the nation's leaders is widely dismissed by the outside world.

CHAPTER REVIEW

Some arguments seek the essential nature of a person, object, institution, or idea to justify judgments or interpretations. Five common means of establishing essential nature discussed in this chapter are the genetic argument, the argument from intent, the argument from function, the person/act argument, and the visual argument.

The genetic argument seeks essential nature in origins. Its underlying assumption is that origins indelibly stamp objects, events, and organizations with their essential nature.

The argument from intent respects the intent of designers, authors, legislators, and other creators of documents and objects. It assumes that essential nature is revealed in authorial intent.

The argument from function finds the essential nature of a person, object, or institution to be revealed in its evident function. Sources of function include prescription, common understanding, form, and current need.

This chapter has also noted that the nature of people and organizations is often held to be revealed in what they do, their acts. The person/act argument operates on the basis of this assumption. Although this argument is a common means of assessing a person's value, it is not always reliable. The charge of inconsistency is an effort to reveal a character flaw by demonstrating inconsistency in acts or statements.

Finally, this chapter has considered how an essential nature argument may be constructed from visual elements. We have seen how physical settings, images, and even the design of a building can convey a set of reasons that evoke the essence of a movement, a crisis, or a nation.

EXERCISES

A. Identify the specific essential nature argument advanced in each of the following examples.

1. It is clear from the design of an assault rifle that it has a military purpose, and thus should not be easily available to members of the general public. The very form of these weapons suggests that they are not for civilian uses such as hunting.

2. The founders of this nation believed that the citizen soldier was the best person to defend the country, so a volunteer army violates their vision for national defense.

3. The central goal of a public health system is to keep people well, not to make a profit. Thus, our current system of "health for sale to the highest bidders" should be overhauled radically to reflect its guiding purpose better.

4. The practice of downloading one song at a time has destroyed the aesthetic of the album, and thus something of the nature of rock and roll as an art form. At one time artists had to imagine the interaction of each song with the others on the album, and even the interaction of the music with the album cover. The album as a complex composition made an artistic statement. All that remains after the intervention of nonmusicians is a market-driven business model that reflects no sense of the nature of rock as an art form.

5. To interpret this poem correctly we must understand that the author intended it as a Marxist statement about the ongoing class struggle and the eventual triumph of the working class. Seeing it as a statement about personal struggle and overcoming obstacles may be meaningful to you, but that is not what the poem is about.

6. Christians should not give their children candy eggs and similar items as part of the Easter celebration. They should also refrain from throwing rice at weddings. Such symbols were originally signs of fertility in religious cults associated with fertility goddesses such as Ishtar, and therefore have no place in a Christian ceremony or celebration.

7. A fully autonomous robot or drone making decisions in a combat situation changes the essence of warfare. Instead of human beings making the ethically complex decision regarding whether to kill other human beings, a machine is making those decisions based on an algorithm. War involves human agents taking real risks and weighing their own lives against the lives of others. This is no longer the case when robots and drones take over the fighting.

8. The board of trustees has been critical of the boss, calling her insubordinate, self-centered, and aloof. As a twenty-year employee of the company, I know these charges about her character are not true. Her recent advocacy of raises for all staff members angered the board, but this action reveals a person who is caring and has her priorities straight. The fact that she will not stage company events to satisfy the board also shows that she has courage under pressure.

9. I favor allowing athletes to use performance-enhancing drugs. Everyone knows that sport is about pushing competition and performance to the highest level, which is precisely what these pharmaceuticals do. Why not allow athletes to compete at the peak of their abilities?

10. Keeping porpoises and dolphins in water parks violates their nature as intelligent and highly social animals.

11. The sports press has often covered up the misdeeds of celebrity sports figures. Its highly selective reporting cannot be excused as staying out of the players' private lives. Sports reporters reveal their own sexism when they ignore athletes' spousal abuse, and their disregard for law when they treat drug use as insignificant.

12. Human cloning deliberately severs a natural link between procreation and human sexual intercourse. This connection was established by the creator as part of the design of nature. It should not be broken through the artificial creation of human life.

13. The Declaration of Independence sets out citizens' rights to life, liberty, and the pursuit of happiness. It is the proper role of government to care for the vulnerable and marginalized—to protect their lives and chances for happiness—including the elderly. Thus, ensuring medical care and housing for an increasingly aged society is a proper role of government, and not the obligation of private organizations or even of families.

14. He is fundamentally authoritarian. This is not just a philosophy—it is who he is. He talks of overruling everyone who gets in his way. He ignores international law. He is even willing to send his opponents to jail on trumped-up charges. These are not just idle threats or casual bluster—they indicate a dictatorial personality.

ENDNOTES

[1] Tim Appenzeller, "Ancient Mariner," *National Geographic,* May 2009, 123–141, p. 134.

[2] Stephen J. Gould, *The Panda's Thumb: More Reflections in Natural History* (New York: W. W. Norton, 1992).

[3] For a detailed discussion of the relationship between persons and their acts, see Chaïm Perelman and L. Olbrechts-Tyteca, *The New Rhetoric* (Notre Dame, Ind.: University of Notre Dame Press, 1969), 293–305.

[4] Jim Litke, "Youth Sports Is Getting Uglier," MSNBC, August 1, 2005, http://www.msnbc.msn.com/id/8786437.

[5] If you would like to read more on the visual aspects of argument and public discourse, see: *Defining Visual Rhetoric,* ed. Charles Hill and Marguerite Helmers (New York: Routledge, 2004); Lawrence J. Prelli, *Rhetorics of Display* (Columbia, S.C.: University of South Carolina Press, 2006); *Visual Rhetoric: A Reader in Communication and American Culture,* ed. Lester Olson, Cara Finnegan, and Diane S. Hope (Thousand Oaks, Calif.: Sage Publications, 2008).

[6] Quoted in Danielle Wiener-Bronner, "Wall Street Crowds Bullish on 'Fearless Girl' Statue," *CNN Money,* March 9, 2017.

RECOMMENDED WEBSITES

Visual Rhetoric and Strategies of Persuasion

http://www.stanford.edu/~steener/f03/PWR1/research/visarg_samples.htm

This web site from Stanford University provides links to several examples of visual argument in both student essays and published papers.

Visual Rhetoric: Overview

Purdue Owl

owl.english.purdue.edu/owl/resource/691/01

This website, provided by Purdue University, overviews the concept of visual rhetoric.

18 Fallacies and Appeals

It would be a very good thing if every trick
could receive some short and obviously appropriate name,
so that when a man used this or that particular trick,
he would at once be reproved for it.
Arthur Schopenhauer (1788–1860)
German philosopher

The ruling passion conquers reason still.
Alexander Pope (1688–1744)
British poet

KEY TERMS

ad hominem fallacy

ad populum fallacy

appeal

appeal to authority

arguing from ignorance

arrangement fallacy

attacking a straw man

civil disobedience

continuum fallacy

emotional appeal

fallacy

linguistic conventions

majoring on minors

paralepsis

poisoning the well

question begging

reductio ad absurdum

rule of charity

selection fallacy

straw man fallacy

tu quoque fallacy

underdescription

Bill McKibben is a writer who has taken on the question of whether rapidly advancing technology is always good for us. Because of his views, he has been charged with being a Luddite, that is, an opponent of technology. "One danger of any critical writing about technology," McKibben notes, "is that it will be dismissed as Luddite." He adds, "That's a glib charge, as silly as accusing someone of being a prohibitionist because he'd rather leave a barroom with a warm glow than a spinning head."[1] In making his response, McKibben employs an appeal discussed in this chapter.

To this point we have considered arguments that are defined as reasons advanced to support conclusions. We have also discussed the criteria for assessing evidence and arguments, such as internal consistency, support, and linguistic consistency. In a few cases we have pointed out a weak form of an argument, or "fallacy." The topic of fallacies deserves greater attention, however, and is the subject of this chapter. We will consider several common fallacies along with some related issues in argument.

Some strategies that often appear in arguments are not clearly fallacious, but neither are they clearly an effort to persuade by offering reasons or arguments. An emotional appeal or an appeal to authority is sometimes a legitimate component in an argumentative case, but such appeals are also easily misused. We will begin the chapter with a consideration of some of the most common fallacies.

FALLACIES

A **fallacy** is *an argument that is invalid or otherwise so seriously flawed as to render it unreliable.* Fallacies would not pose problems in arguments if they were always easy to identify, but they can sound reasonable and often resemble reliable arguments. Recognizing fallacies is a key aspect of being a critical consumer of arguments and of avoiding fallacies when constructing our own arguments.

We will group fallacies under four headings based on similarities in the errors they introduce into argumentation. These are:

1. Fallacies of Faulty Assumption
2. Fallacies Directed to the Person
3. Fallacies of Case Presentation
4. Fallacies of Suggestion

Let's start with some of the most difficult fallacies to identify, the fallacies of faulty assumptions.

Fallacies of Faulty Assumption

A fallacy may result from inserting a faulty assumption in an argument. Three common fallacies of faulty assumption are arguing from ignorance, the continuum fallacy, and question begging.

Arguing from Ignorance

Among the most common fallacies of faulty assumption is **arguing from ignorance,** *falsely assuming that a conclusion can be reached on the basis of the absence of evidence.* One form of the argument from ignorance assumes that because an assertion has not been disproved, it has been proved. For example, if I were to reason that, because the existence of extraterrestrial life has never been disproved, it has therefore been proved, I would be committing the fallacy of arguing from ignorance. Similarly, some arguments from ignorance assume that the failure to prove an idea means that the idea has been disproved. Here is an example:

> Because there is no hard evidence that violence on television programs has an undesirable effect on children, we must conclude that it has no such effect.

Both examples argue from what we do not know, that is, from an absence of evidence or knowledge, but absence of evidence is not proof of a claim.

There are some interesting historical examples of this fallacy being used persuasively. Let's look at one:

> In 1751 a forgery of an ancient text was circulated in England. *The Book of Jasher* was advanced as a "lost" book of the Bible. Scholars immediately identified it as a fake, but it remained in circulation for a long time and had many defenders. One defender, Reverend Bond of Bristol, England, wrote in 1829 that the many efforts to disprove the authenticity of *The Book of Jasher* had

failed. This failure, he suggested, proved beyond doubt that the book was an authentic ancient manuscript that deserved to be included in the Bible. According to Bond, failure to disprove the book's claim to authenticity amounted to proof that *The Book of Jasher* was authentic.

The argument from ignorance assumes that an absence of evidence constitutes a kind of support, which is not the case. In order to establish a claim we need solid evidence in its support, as we discussed in our treatment of support as one of three criteria of a reasonable argument. Answering the argument from ignorance is usually as simple as pointing out this fact.

Continuum Fallacy

The **continuum fallacy** is *a false assumption that qualitative changes along a line of progression do not occur if we cannot agree about exactly where such changes occur.* For example:

> I'm not convinced that "poverty" is anything but an invented abstraction of the government. When is a family in poverty? When it makes less than $20,000 a year? Less than $15,000? Less than $7,000? We have no way of making a meaningful distinction between poverty and sufficiency of income.

This argument represents the basic structure of the continuum fallacy. It claims that, because no one can determine at which point in the progression from "adequate income" to "no income" a family crosses the "poverty line," "poverty" is an essentially meaningless term. Here is another example of the continuum fallacy:

> If hormone treatment need not be limited to those with hormone deficiencies, why should they be available only to very short children? Why shouldn't all shorter-than-average children be able to seek treatment? And what about a child of average height who wants to be taller so that he can make the basketball team?[2]

The fact that it might be difficult to determine who is deserving of growth hormone treatments on a continuum of height does not mean that meaningful distinctions could not be made by qualified people.

When controversies can only be resolved by compromising on an issue involving a continuum, it may be necessary to establish a point of agreement between differing parties at either end of the continuum. It is then possible to work gradually toward identifying the range of potential agreement. For instance, when do we consider a person to be disabled for the purpose of receiving special accommodation from an employer? If we imagined a continuum running from able-bodied to completely disabled, it might be difficult, if not impossible, to garner complete agreement even among experts about whether a particular person is "disabled." If this absence of agreement were taken to mean there is no difference between being able-bodied and being disabled, a serious practical problem might arise. Thus, the presence of a continuum should not be allowed to stop discussion, but should prompt efforts to achieve a compromise.

Question Begging

> A general defends the decision not to allow women to serve in certain branches of the Special Forces by arguing: "Women do not belong in the Special Forces because these forces have always been staffed by men."

Of course, the general has not addressed the question of whether women can serve effectively in these branches. He has *assumed* an answer to a question rather than addressing it. Similarly, the candidate who asks her audience, "Do we want four more years of liberal leadership in Washington?" is expecting a negative answer to her rhetorical question—but some of her listeners might prefer four more years of liberal leadership to the alternative.

Question begging is *a fallacy that assumes that a debatable question can be treated as already answered.* In this way the fallacy begs or avoids the question at issue. This fallacy's name can be misleading, as the term "beg" usually means to make an urgent request. A legislator argues that "in order to keep our health care system on a strict free-market basis, we must not allow the administration to pass its publicly funded system." The question of whether we should keep our health care system on a free-market basis is treated as having been answered affirmatively already. An opponent who objects to the notion of a free-market basis for health care would be correct to point this out as an instance of question begging.

Fallacies Directed to the Person

A second group of fallacies diverts attention from legitimate argumentative issues by focusing attention on an individual's personal character or circumstances. Because argumentative issues should be settled by reference to relevant issues and evidence, these approaches are typically treated as fallacious.

Ad Hominem Fallacy

African-American educator and author Dr. Walter Williams has criticized people he terms "poverty pimps and race hustlers" for drawing attention away from "the true connection between race and poverty."[3] Though Williams may have a point in arguing that race can be misused in analyzing the causes of poverty, his resort to harsh labels to condemn his opponents may itself distract attention from important issues.

We have all heard an advocate attack the opponent rather than the opponent's case. The **ad hominem fallacy** is *an intentional effort to attack a person rather than an argument, by damaging an opponent's character or reputation or by engaging in name-calling and labeling.*

If I call my opponent a "leftist socialist" or a "right wing fascist," a "heartless neoconservative" or a "tree-hugging environmentalist," I am engaging in *ad hominem* attacks. As we discussed in Chapter 17, an argument may legitimately discuss character qualities if they are actually relevant to a case. This is the nature of the person/act argument—to seek the essence of an individual through examining their choices and actions. The *ad hominem* fallacy does not address the merits of a case or of an individual, however. Rather, it attempts to discredit the person arguing the case. Because it diverts attention away from the opponent's case rather than answering it, the *ad hominem* fallacy deprives the audience of the opportunity to make a reasoned decision on the issue at hand. It can thus also be understood as a violation of the ethics of advocacy, which requires respect for the opponent as a reasoning individual.

Poisoning the Well

Closely related to *ad hominem* is what has been colloquially called **poisoning the well,** which means *dismissing an individual as unqualified to speak on a topic based on some accident of circumstance.* If a parishioner says to a priest, "You can't possibly know anything about rearing children; you don't have any yourself," the parishioner is poisoning the well. No matter how qualified the priest may be to speak about raising children, or how sound the priest's advice may be, the parishioner will not accept anything he says as true or accurate.

Tu Quoque Fallacy

Most of us strongly reject advice, directions, or recommendations that we consider hypocritical. The **tu quoque fallacy** is *falsely reasoning that someone who is guilty of an offense has no right to instruct others not to do something similar.* For example:

> How can you tell me to study harder and to apply myself at college? You weren't a standout student, and you spent more time golfing than studying.

Tu quoque means "and you also" in Latin. It usually is treated as a fallacy because it assumes that advice of a hypocritical nature cannot be good advice, but being guilty of a specific offense does not automatically render the guilty person's advice on the topic bad. The advice giver might be exactly right. Rejecting hypocritical advice may be satisfying for other reasons but generally does not represent a good inference.

Ad Populum Fallacy

The fallacy of *appealing to the audience and its sentiments rather than to the merits of the argument* has gone by various names, but is most commonly called the **ad populum fallacy**.

Wayne LaPierre, president of the National Rifle Association, crafted an *ad populum* appeal during a 2014 speech to his organization's membership in Indianapolis. LaPierre raised a number of concerns likely to resonate with his listeners' anxieties and frustrations. "Something has gone wrong. You feel it in your heart. . . . The core values we believe in, the things we care about most, are changing. Eroding. Our right to speak. Our right to gather. Our right to privacy. The freedom to work, and practice our religion, and raise and protect our families the way we see fit." Despite the fact that violent crime has been declining for the past twenty years, LaPierre raised the specter of "terrorists and home invaders and drug cartels and carjackers and knockout gamers" and other perceived threats to personal safety. LaPierre's appeal was addressed to audience fear and suspicion, rather than to specific issues such as the benefits or liabilities of carrying a gun, the risks associated with keeping a gun in one's home, or reasonable policies regarding purchasing a gun.[4]

Fallacies of Case Presentation

Most people recognize that presenting our own cases accurately is crucial to constructive public discourse. That means we should also seek to respond to a strong interpretation of an opponent's argument, rather than to a weak or misleading one. The following are some common fallacies of case presentation.

Straw Man Fallacy

Cal Thomas, a popular syndicated columnist, has characterized efforts to modernize educational practice as the work of "social experimenters . . . using kids as guinea pigs for their untested schemes." According to Thomas, schools are bogged down in the study of "sex education, or the environment, or any of today's trendy subjects that masquerade as a real education."[5] Thomas thus caricatures the efforts of many educators as misguided, politically motivated, and perhaps even damaging to students. In making his argument, however, he has not answered any actual argument in favor of educational reform, or responded to any justification for a particular educational practice such as sex education or education about the environment. Instead, he has offered his own easily dismissed representation of educational reform.

Thomas's response to his opponents brings to mind a principle of reasonable public discourse known as the **rule of charity,** or *the obligation to restate an opponent's argument so as to give it a strong interpretation.* One failure to observe this rule is called **attacking a straw man** or the **straw man fallacy,** *responding to a weakened version of an opponent's case.* Advocates often intentionally misrepresent their opponent's arguments in order to make them easier to refute.

Majoring on Minors

Majoring on minors is *a fallacy that focuses attention on minor or inconsequential points to draw attention away from important ones.* For example, an opponent of new health care legislation that requires all employers to provide minimum health care protection to their employees argues:

> This plan is clearly flawed. It doesn't spell out precise levels of coverage for some treatments. It also leaves unanswered questions of compensation to participating physicians for these treatments.

If the basic approach of the health care plan is accepted, details might have to be worked out. This argument, however, avoids major points: the need for more accessible health coverage, methods of paying for that coverage, and the individuals responsible for providing it. Instead, it presents relatively minor points—levels of coverage for specific treatments and questions of compensation to doctors for these treatments—as crucial to the proposal.

Similarly, weaknesses in a proposed plan may be hidden by drawing attention away from central issues to a side issue. When this happens, a respondent should bring the focus back to the important issues.

Underdescription

Underdescription is *the fallacy of creating a false sense of meaning by failing to fully describe a proposal or a crucial component in an opponent's case.* For example, a plan to close several factories might be described as "simply a cost-cutting measure," when it would actually disrupt the lives of thousands of people. An opponent of the plan would be correct to say that because the plan involves much more, "cost cutting" is an underdescription.

A racist organization that wants to place a float in a civic parade may defend the proposal by saying, "Look, this is just a matter of allowing people their right to freedom of speech." A question of freedom of speech may indeed be involved, but to say that it is "*just* a matter of allowing people their right to freedom of speech" does not account for other important questions that the proposal raises.

Another example of underdescription occurs when a student argues that affirmative action programs help students enter college on the basis of "some little nuance of their existence they have no control over, such as race." While it is true that we have no control over the race into which we are born, it is hardly accurate to refer to minority students' races as "some little nuance of their existence."

> Many tactics and fallacies risk violating argument ethics.

Many tactics and fallacies of case presentation risk violating argument ethics, as discussed in Chapter 4. As a critic or as an advocate, you are responsible for identifying and correcting any efforts at misrepresentation of your case, as well as for not advancing or responding to a weak construction of an opponent's case.

Fallacies of Suggestion

A conclusion, and even an entire argument, can be suggested without being stated directly. When an argument is only suggested, we might accept it uncritically because we have not recognized its full content. Moreover, we may accept bad reasoning or insufficient evidence on the basis of an advocate's unscrupulous and intentional use of suggestion. We will consider three common strategies of suggestion that can be used fallaciously to mislead an audience to accept conclusions they otherwise might not have been willing to accept.

All fallacies of suggestion are achieved by means of **linguistic conventions,** *recognized methods of expressing a meaning indirectly.* These conventions enable an advocate to say something implicitly without stating it directly. All suggestion depends on the linguistic conventions we learn at the same time we learn to speak a language. Particular conventions take on the nature of fallacies when we use them to mislead an audience or to misrepresent claims or arguments.

Paralepsis

Here is a famous example of the fallacy discussed in this section:

> Let me say, incidentally, my opponent, my opposite number for the vice presidency on the Democratic ticket, does have his wife on the payroll. And he has had her on the payroll for ten years—the past ten years. Now just let me say this. That's his business, and I'm not critical of him for doing that . . . but I have never done that . . . .

In this example from Richard Nixon's 1952 "Checkers Speech," the claim, "That's his business, and I'm not critical of him for doing that" is disingenuous. This paragraph contains an accusation masquerading as a simple observation. Nixon was actually saying:

> My opponent . . . does have his wife on the payroll. It is wrong for him to have his wife on his payroll, and I am critical of him for doing this.

As you can see, **paralepsis** is *the strategy of making a claim about an issue by stating that you will not bring up that issue or that the matter is insignificant.*

Selection Fallacy

Suggestion can also be achieved by the **selection fallacy,** *promoting a false interpretation by presenting only some of the relevant evidence in a case, while intentionally excluding other evidence that would contradict the suggested interpretation.* The selection fallacy actually involves intentional deception by excluding relevant facts. It is related to underdescription, which provides a picture of a situation that may be accurate, but is inadequate.

Suppose that Senator Wilson knows his opponent in the election, State Representative Clark, donated more than $30,000 of her personal income to medical charities and thus paid less in taxes than her income of $85,000 would otherwise require her to pay. In a campaign speech, Senator Wilson argues:

> Anyone who wonders whether Representative Clark can identify with the middle-income taxpayer should compare her income to her taxes. Last year she made over $85,000 but paid only $5,000 in taxes!

By selection—in this case, failing to provide the audience with a relevant piece of information of which he was fully aware—Senator Wilson suggested two related

FIGURE 18.1 Common Fallacies

Fallacies of Faulty Assumption
- Arguing from Ignorance
- Continuum Fallacy
- Question Begging

Fallacies Directed to the Person
- *Ad Hominem* Fallacy
- Poisoning the Well
- *Tu Quoque* Fallacy
- *Ad Populum* Fallacy

Fallacies of Case Presentation
- Straw Man Fallacy
- Majoring on Minors
- Underdescription

Fallacies of Suggestion
- Paralepsis
- Selection Fallacy
- Arrangement Fallacy (Association)

points: (a) that Representative Clark has not paid enough of her income in taxes, and (b) that she thus cannot identify with the middle income taxpayer. Though he is not lying in his presentation of evidence, he is being dishonest by creating the impression that Representative Clark has done something unscrupulous, perhaps even illegal. How does he accomplish this? By leading the audience to conclude that Representative Clark's deductions for charitable donations were similar to those of others with similar incomes when this was not the case.

Arrangement Fallacy

Suggestion is also achieved by the **arrangement fallacy**, *the fallacy that creates a false impression by ordering, associating, or grouping items in a misleading way.* This fallacy is also referred to as the association fallacy. We often assume that points placed next to one another in a statement have equal status, or that the ordering of items in a list reflects their relative merit. We may also assume that people who have been associated in some way, even if their names simply appear together on a list, share similar qualities. These are two of several assumptions that allow us to achieve suggestion by means of arrangement.

In the following example, the use of arrangement suggests a conclusion about the significance of the work done by a city's Committee on Human Relations:

> The Committee on Human Relations has, they tell us, important work to do. I doubt it. Listen to the three items on the agenda for the last meeting: (1) student relations at Jackson High School, (2) the language in the city's hiring policy, and (3) a new name for the mascot of Westland Junior High School.

Because the three items on the agenda are phrased similarly, one might assume that each has equal significance. Because the third item does not seem particularly significant, it has been used to make the other two sound less significant than they are. This item's inclusion trivializes the agenda. Moreover, placing the least significant item last is more effective in making it sound typical than would be placing it first or second. The last item heard or read tends to reflect on earlier items in a list.

In another example, suppose a candidate for president has been the governor of a small state and, in a debate, her opponent attempts to suggest the insignificance of the governor's qualifications by using the arrangement fallacy:

> If the governor's state had been a Fortune 500 company, it would have ranked 301st, just between Land O'Lakes Butter and Campbell Soup!

By noting the irrelevant fact that her state would rank between a butter company and a soup company, the governor's opponent sought to trivialize her political experience, but a politician's political experience cannot be adequately assessed by such contrived associations.

The arrangement or association fallacy may also be employed to falsely suggest admirable qualities. Suppose that a well-known athlete has been accused of spousal abuse. A defender claims that "he simply cannot be guilty of those charges. Last year he was named the league's Most Valuable Player, placing him among some of the country's most respected athletes." Such an association with virtuous individuals does not allow for the presumption of virtuous behavior by the accused.

APPEALS

We sometimes read advertisements that seem designed to engage our emotions. For instance, an advertisement for an environmental advocacy group might contain statements similar to the following:

> If we don't aggressively pursue solutions to the environment crisis, particularly to massive problems such as air pollution, water depletion, and global warming, we will pass along to our children a ruined planet. For the sake of subsequent generations, we must address these monumental environmental threats now!

Such powerful appeals are common not only to the world of advertising and sales, but to much political and religious discourse as well. We also encounter a range of appeals in many personal discussions.

An **appeal** is *a persuasive strategy directed to the audience's emotions, sense of humor, or deeply held loyalties and commitments.* As such, appeals often are not directed to the analytical thinking we call upon when assessing arguments.

Appeals are not fallacies, which are simply faulty or deceptive reasoning. Appeals can be part of a reasonable argumentative case. The potential for misuse, however, is present in all appeals. Three of the most common appeals are those to authority, to the emotions, and to the audience's sense of the absurd.

Appeals to Authority

An **appeal to authority** is *an appeal that urges compliance with the directive of a person, group, or document possessing power.* Authorities are many. They may include a judge, a religious leader, a teacher, the president, a parent, the Internal Revenue Service, or the law. For example, many DVDs carry the warning that reproducing the DVD is a violation of federal law, punishable by both fines and imprisonment. This is an appeal to the authority of laws and the people who enforce them. Telling an employee that if he blows the whistle on an unethical practice, the boss will fire him, is also an appeal to authority.

The following example illustrates the power of authority appeals:

> Fifty years ago, US social psychologist Stanley Milgram demonstrated how susceptible we are to authority. Subjects in his famous study delivered painful electric shocks to an unseen person who answered a question incorrectly. A new study shows that little has changed. Researchers at Poland's University of Social Sciences and Humanities found that seventy-two out of eighty subjects complied with a perceived authority's directions to administer electric shocks to a research subject in the next room. Subjects complied despite the fact that they could hear screams of terror coming from the supposed recipient of the shocks. Even though they were told they could end the experiment at any time, most complied with the authority figure's insistence that a stronger shock was needed.

An appeal to authority may also make reference to a document, as in this example:

> If you believe that no citizen should be able to purchase and possess assault rifles modified for civilian use, then you're denying the right to bear arms established in the Constitution.

A threat of sanction lurks in the background of many appeals to authority. The threat in turn is rooted in the authority's power to impose penalties if we refuse to comply or to give rewards for compliance. We may find it reasonable to heed authority under some circumstances, and yet find it unreasonable at other times and under different circumstances.

Some appeals to authority do not involve threats of reprisal. For example, a company's president may be known to support a local charity. The strong suggestion within the company is that employees should also support this charity. Though no sanction is connected with failing to contribute to this charity, some employees who have done so seem to have gained prestige or privilege within the company.

How can we know whether a particular appeal to authority should be heeded?

One question we can ask is:

1. Is there sufficient reason to heed this authority in this case? The great Renaissance artist and inventor, Leonardo Da Vinci, wrote that "Whoever in discussion adduces authority uses not intellect but rather memory."[6] What was Da Vinci's point?

> If authority is used as a support for a position, it should be done for a compelling reason.

Just this—that citing an authority to justify one's decisions is not a matter of thinking or even of arguing so much as it is simply repeating what someone else has said. If authority is used as support for a position on an issue, it should be done for a compelling reason.

We should be certain that we either ought to or want to heed authority in a specific case, that we find such a basis for making decisions to be reasonable in this situation. There are good reasons for heeding authorities. For example, we may wish to acknowledge and support the structures of an institution such as a church or government. We may have found the authority of an individual such as a physician to have been trustworthy in previous cases. We may simply wish to avoid sanctions the authority is in a position to mete out.

Still, there certainly are times when we should challenge or resist authority. Sometimes, deviating from the dictates of authority is the more reasonable course of action. You might choose not to comply with an authority for any number of practical or moral reasons. For example, perhaps what an authority is directing you to do violates the rights of other people. In recent well-publicized cases journalists have chosen not to reveal the identity of their sources, even when judges ordered them to do so, because they found a source's right to remain anonymous more compelling than a judge's authority.

Civil disobedience is *the intentional decision to disobey a law or directive of a government authority for moral reasons.* A compelling reason for rejecting authority is one that so outweighs the authority's ability to wield power that we are willing to endure the consequences. Not paying your income taxes because you wanted to use the money to buy a new car is not, for most people, a compelling reason to resist the authority of the IRS. However, refusing to pay taxes because some of your money will be used to buy military weapons is, for some people, a compelling moral reason for rejecting government authority.

In other cases it may simply be too costly in time or money to heed an authority's guidance. Suppose your boss has told you to invest some of your pay in company stock, something you feel you cannot afford to do. You may find yourself resisting authority for practical reasons.

A second important question to ask when facing an appeal to authority is:

2. Is this group or individual an authority for me in this case? The power of an authority to gain compliance is based on either voluntary or coerced acceptance of the authority. A parishioner following the directives of his priest is voluntarily heeding an authority. A Marine running an obstacle course when she would rather take the day off may feel coerced by military regulations to heed the authority of her commanding officer.

A religious authority may have a claim to authority over issues of doctrine or practices in the organization. When that same authority makes statements suggesting how we should vote, however, a line between legitimate and illegitimate exercise of authority may have been crossed.

One type of appeal to authority is sometimes employed in defense of a controversial action. Individuals may argue that they were simply "following orders"—from a supervisor, a superior officer, a religious leader, or even a spiritual entity—when the acts they committed have been questioned. In March 1968, for example, a company of United States soldiers under the command of Lieutenant William Calley killed more than two hundred residents of the village of My Lai in Vietnam. Calley argued that the orders to destroy the village had come from higher up in the army chain of command, so he was not directly responsible for what happened. His defense was a type of appeal to authority. (The defense was rejected, and Calley was found guilty of murdering at least twenty of the villagers.)[7]

Emotional Appeals

The nineteenth-century English novelist Charles Dickens recognized the power of human emotions. He once commented that "there are strings in the human heart that had better not be vibrated." Still, our emotions may sometimes guide our reasoning. When is it appropriate to engage an audience's emotions?

We are all familiar with **emotional appeals**, *engaging the audience's emotions for the purpose of persuading.* For example, an organization fighting for stronger legislation against texting while driving makes the following emotional appeal:

The American Automobile Association estimates that six thousand people die on our roads each year as a result of texting while driving, and nearly half a million are injured. But statistics like these don't tell the human story. Consider the case of the Missouri teenager who died during her first solo drive at the age of sixteen. She turned in front of a truck while texting friends about her new license. How many more tragedies like this one will it take before we enact serious legislation to stop texting while driving?

Fear, anger, and pity are three emotions that arguments appeal to. These appeals are often persuasive. How do they work? What tests are appropriate to evaluating them?

Fear appeals often derive from three concerns common to most people:[8]

1. Death or physical harm, either to self or to loved ones.

2. Loss of health, wealth, or security, as in loss of occupation.

3. Deprivation of rights or freedoms.

A person intent on persuading an audience may try to show that what we fear is likely to happen unless we take a certain action—or if we fail to take an action.

Anger appeals are often rooted in the suggestion that someone is doing or will do to us what we fear, or that injustices are being done to us or someone we care about. *Pity appeals* usually involve suggesting or stating that someone or something helpless is being harmed. These appeals are intensified if someone is perpetrating the harm carelessly or intentionally.

Emotional appeals are frequently dismissed as unreasonable, as having no place in rational argumentation. At times, however, we all use or are influenced by emotional appeals, finding them not only persuasive but reasonable. Often, such an appeal is the basis for a decision to take action on a matter.

Emotional appeals suggest that it is reasonable to experience emotion in certain circumstances. They may even imply that *not* to be guided by emotion would be unreasonable. If a person hears about a child being seriously and intentionally harmed by an adult and does not feel some anger, we might consider that person morally insensitive.

Many objections to emotional appeals are based on the power of these appeals to draw attention away from reasons and arguments. Emotional appeals might be used conveniently in the absence of other arguments or as a substitute for arguments. In most cases, it is reasonable to balance emotional appeals with other arguments that clearly display their evidence and conclusions.

Perhaps a good first test of emotional appeals is to ask:

1. Does the emotional appeal appear in the absence of other arguments and evidence? To make a decision strictly on the basis of an emotional appeal probably is not reasonable. Such appeals, however, tend to be embedded in and accompanied by other arguments and evidence. In the example about texting while driving, evidence is advanced concerning the number of fatalities and injuries attributed to texting drivers each year. We might wish for more evidence or other arguments before we accept the argument's conclusion, but some evidence is advanced.

Just as the emotional appeal probably should not be the sole support for a conclusion, it should not be presented so that the audience is distracted from exercising reason. Some speakers and writers are so skilled at arousing our emotions that they prevent critical thinking. Again, a balance between critical reasoning and the power of emotion is desirable. We can ask:

2. Is the appeal so powerful that the audience will have difficulty exercising reason? In most cases we would rightly object to an emotional appeal so powerful that it subverts reason. When issues are emotionally charged, we need to be careful about what we respond to and how we ourselves argue.

Perhaps the best defense of emotional appeals in argumentative cases is their ability to place an audience in the appropriate frame of mind for making a decision and acting on it. We should ask whether a given appeal is likely to accomplish this goal:

3. Does the appeal place the audience in the proper frame of mind for making a reasonable decision? Unless we reject all emotional appeals out of hand as fallacies, we may think these appeals can be properly employed at times, and even that they have a vital role to play in making reasonable decisions. Perhaps we should feel some anger and fear when making decisions about driving laws, some fear when deciding whether to smoke or not, some pity and anger when deciding how to deal with child abusers. This test asks us to consider whether a certain emotion is appropriate to consider in deciding an issue.

Reductio Ad Absurdum

Another type of appeal is directed to the audience's sense of the absurd or incongruous. The **reductio ad absurdum** (reduction to absurdity) is *an appeal that asks an audience to recognize an idea as either self-contradictory or as so unreasonable as to be absurd.* This chapter opens with an example of the appeal being employed by the author Bill McKibben.

There are two ways that the *reductio ad absurdum* is used to demonstrate that an idea or proposal results in a contradiction or an absurdity.

The first approach involves assuming that the idea is true and seeing where the assumption leads. For example, Callicles, a character in Plato's dialogue *Gorgias,* argued that the strongest person deserves to have the most and the biggest of everything. The philosopher Socrates employed a *reductio* against this claim by imagining where the argument, if accepted, would lead:

> So, then, the man who is best and most intelligent about shoes should have the advantage. The shoemaker should, no doubt, have the biggest shoes and walk about shod in the largest possible number.[9]

The second *reductio* approach involves setting up a parallel argument to the one advanced, in which the parallel is clearly unreasonable. For example:

> Some Google executives talk as if they're in the advertising business, but to say that Google's main business is selling advertising is like saying that Walmart's main business is providing their customers with checkout lines. Walmart's main business is providing consumers with inexpensive products that are of reasonably good quality. Google's main business is similar—providing consumers with helpful digital products at low or no cost. If Google loses sight of this central purpose, it will be vulnerable in the marketplace.

The *reductio ad absurdum* is best used when other approaches to rebuttal might fail to reveal a rational flaw in the original claim. When used carelessly to discredit ideas that deserve consideration, it can, like other appeals, be both misleading and powerful. You as critic and advocate must decide how the strategy is being used in any given case.

CHAPTER REVIEW

Fallacies are flawed arguments that persuade by appearing to be reasonable. Fallacies of faulty assumption include arguing from ignorance, the continuum fallacy, and question begging. Fallacies directed to people include *ad hominem,* poisoning the well, *tu quoque,* and *ad populum.* Fallacies of case representation include the straw man fallacy, majoring on minors, and underdescription. Fallacies of suggestion include paralepsis, selection, and arrangement.

Appeals—strategies of argument that are intended to engage our commitments or sentiments, but not aimed directly at our capacity to reason—also have persuasive powers. One powerful appeal is the appeal to authority. We should accept some people's directives on the basis of their positions, provided that we find no compelling practical or moral reasons for rejecting their direction.

Emotional appeals may also be appropriate and reasonable in some instances. These highly persuasive strategies—usually based on fear, anger, and pity—should be accepted with some caution, though. They should not appear in the absence of arguments and evidence, nor be so powerful as to prevent the exercise of reason. Emotional appeals can, however, put an audience in the right frame of mind for making a reasonable decision and acting upon it.

Finally, the *reductio ad absurdum* seeks to demonstrate a proposal's self-contradiction or absurdity by extension or comparison. It thus appeals to an audience's sense of what is irrational or self-refuting.

EXERCISES

A.   Identify any fallacies or potential fallacies in the following examples.

1. I don't believe in a personal God, but this does not mean that the vast plan that is unfolding on the earth is any less meaningful. We need to assist the growth of a world mind that developments such as the internet are bringing about.

2. There is no way I would condone his use of campaign funds to pay for vacations for himself and his family, but I also refuse to make that an issue in this campaign.

3. A movie reviewer writes: "This film lacks coherence in its plot and the acting is unconvincing. However, it is packed with action for those who are satisfied by colliding automobiles and mangled bodies." The movie's promoter uses the review as follows: "One reviewer writes that this movie is 'packed with action'!"

4. The First Baptist Church burned to the ground this morning. The causes of the fire are under investigation. Without speculating about the fire's origin, we should note that the church was recently insured for $2,000,000 and the congregation is known to have debts of about $1,500,000.

5. An advocate of sales techniques that included lying to customers about product availability and prices defended the practices by claiming, "This is simply a matter of making a persuasive sales presentation."

6. This new handgun registration proposal, which requires a waiting period of one week for purchasing a handgun, as well as a background check on all potential handgun owners, is badly conceived. It says nothing about whether holidays are to be counted as part of the week a person is required to wait.

7. Representative Baker's opinion on this matter should not be heeded. After all, he's a far left, tax-and-spend liberal!

8. Certainly I believe in UFOs. With all the efforts to disprove their existence, no one yet has succeeded in showing that these are not visitors from other planets.

9. Programs for the gifted are impractical, because determining a child's giftedness presents a critical problem. How are we to determine where to draw the line between the gifted child and others? If we draw the line at, say, a GPA of 3.85, do we deny gifted programs to children with a GPA of 3.83? Because these determinations are impossible to make, and because the gifted programs depend on making these determinations, gifted programs should be abandoned.

10. All Catholics should back this new legislation that pays for private schools through an additional city sales tax. Why? Because it will ensure that parochial schools maintain their tax-exempt status.

11. Your opinion on the new sexual harassment policy is irrelevant. After all, what can a man know about these things?

12. Concerns have been raised that artificially raising human intelligence by genetic engineering to levels that routinely exceed an IQ of 170 would usher in a new species—the post-human. However, there is no clear means of determining when such a new human has arrived, so I think these fears are unfounded.

13. Senator, will you continue to support the United States's essentially unjust anti-Israel policy in the Middle East?

B. Identify the appeal being employed in each of the following.

1. You say I should never take the advice of others. But that's ridiculous. If I accept what you are saying, I am taking your advice.

2. Illegal immigration must be stopped, and stopped now! It poses a threat to our health care system, our schools, our economy, and our workforce. It places citizens at risk. Unchecked immigration at our southern border could be the final, mortal blow to the United States as we know it!

3. Despite recent interest in our organization on the part of both the media and law enforcement agencies, all loyal members of the Omega Planetary Mission are required to refrain from any contact with the press. This pronouncement comes directly from President and Prophet Valentine M. Smith.

C. The straw man fallacy is common in public debate when an opponent is allowed to summarize an advocate's case. Provide an example from your own experience of the straw man fallacy.

ENDNOTES

[1] Bill McKibben, *Enough* (New York: Henry Holt, 2003), xii.

[2] Michael J. Sandel, "The Case against Perfection: What's Wrong with Designer Children, Bionic Athletes, and Genetic Engineering," *Atlantic Monthly*, April 2004, 53.

[3] Walter E. Williams, "Ammunition for Poverty Pimps," *Capitalism Magazine*, October 31, 2005, http://www.capmag.com/article.asp?ID=4460.

[4] Dan Friedman, "NRA's Wayne LaPierre Tells Supporters Guns and Contributions Can Protect Them from Murderers and Michael Bloomberg," *New York Daily News*, April 25, 2014, http://www.nydailynews.com/news/national/nra-wayne-lapierre-tells-group-guns-protect-murderers-bloomberg-article-1.1769560.

[5] Cal Thomas, "Schools Need to Go Back to Basics," *Jewish World Review*, June 9, 2005, http://www.jewishworldreview.com/cols/thomas060905.asp.

[6]Leonardo Da Vinci, *Leonardo Da Vinci's Notebooks* (London: Duckworth, 1906); *The Oxford Essential Quotation Dictionary* (New York: Berkeley Books, 1998), 226.

[7]George C. Herring, *America's Longest War: The United States and Vietnam* (New York: Wiley, 1979), 212, 236.

[8]See Aristotle, *Rhetoric,* Book II, especially chapters 2, 5, and 8.

[9]Plato, *Gorgias,* trans. W. C. Heimbold (Indianapolis, Ind.: Bobbs Merrill, 1952), 60.

RECOMMENDED WEBSITES

Common Fallacies in Reasoning

Robert Gass

http://commfaculty.fullerton.edu/rgass/fallacy3211.htm

Fallacies

The Writing Center

http://writingcenter.unc.edu/handouts/fallacies

These two websites, developed at California State University, Fullerton, and the University of North Carolina at Chapel Hill, provide extensive lists of fallacies common to everyday discussions.

Fallacy Theory

Stanford Encyclopedia of Philosophy

plato.stanford.edu/entries/logic-informal/#Fal

This website includes an interesting discussion of the history of evaluating fallacies.

Appendices

Developing and Adapting Your Case

A Policy Case Construction: The Structure of Debate

Many public controversies revolve around policies such as laws, rules, and regulations. At present, controversies ranging from regulating genetic engineering research to methods of reviving ailing public school systems demand the public's attention. Because argumentation about propositions of policy is so common and so important to democratic societies, we will take a close look in this appendix at how cases advocating policy change are constructed successfully. As we will see, these same principles inform classroom debates and competitive debate settings.

Recall that Chapter 2 introduces three types of claims or propositions: propositions of fact, value, and policy. Propositions of fact are those that report, describe, predict, or make causal claims. Propositions of value advance judgments about morality, beauty, merit, or wisdom. Policy statements urge that an action be taken or discontinued.

You may have noticed a logical progression to these three types of claims. In discussions of policy issues, propositions of fact are typically discussed or established first, followed by propositions of value that establish the importance of the facts or the severity of the problem. Propositions of policy are introduced only after the facts clearly establish that a problem exists and show the problem to be serious enough— an evaluation—to warrant action. Once issues of fact and value have been adequately addressed, an advocate may propose that a particular change in policy is the best way to solve the problem.

For example, a case for stronger gun control laws might follow this fact, value, and policy format:

Fact: More than thirty thousand people are killed each year by firearms in the United States.

Value: This high number of deaths represents a major public health crisis. And

Policy: More stringent gun control policies must therefore be enacted.

As you can see from this example, each type of statement has a role to play in establishing a policy case, that is, in making the case that a new policy is needed. Let's take a closer look at this process and at the place of fact, value, and policy claims in that process of arguing for policy change.

INFORMING AND PERSUADING

A good policy case, whether it is part of a public controversy or a formal debate, has an informative as well as a persuasive function. A sound policy case should inform the audience of the facts relevant to understanding the history and present state of the controversy. Even presenting facts can take on a persuasive quality, however. For example, we often find ourselves having to argue for a particular interpretation of the available facts. We may also argue that a certain set of facts is more important or more reliable than another.

A policy case also advances arguments to persuade an audience to a particular view of a problem. A convincing policy case should present the problem as serious and requiring immediate attention. It should also advocate a workable plan, which usually involves helping the audience to understand both the details and the benefits of the proposed plan.

In sum, a well-developed policy case should accomplish at least the following goals:

1. Establish the presence (fact) and severity (value) of a *problem*.

2. Advance a clear and workable *plan* (policy) for dealing with the problem.

3. Present the *benefits* of adopting the proposed policy.

When time allows, a persuasive policy case will also seek to

4. Answer counter-arguments. (In a formal debate, such counter-arguments often come up during a period of cross-examination.)

5. Suggest actions that the members of the audience can take.

Whatever else is accomplished, the basic problem-solution-benefit format is typical of many cases supporting propositions of policy. The same obligations face public advocates in important policy debates.

PRESUMPTION AND BURDEN OF PROOF

Before urging any policy change in a debate, it is important to establish that (1) a problem exists, (2) it results directly from present policies, and (3) the problem is serious enough to necessitate immediate action to alleviate it.

At this point we can introduce several concepts that are important to formal debate, but that are also relevant to any situation in which a new policy is being proposed. **Status quo** is a Latin phrase referring to *the way things are done now, the policy presently in place*. The status quo is the starting point for any policy case debate. The status quo is said to have or to "enjoy" presumption over any new policy that would alter it in any substantial way.

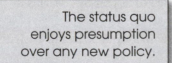
The status quo enjoys presumption over any new policy.

Presumption is *the tendency for an accepted idea or practice to be assumed to be true or adequate—and thus not requiring proof—until sufficiently challenged*. Our most familiar example of presumption is the presumption of innocence in criminal cases.

This presumption means the accused is assumed to be innocent, and does not need to prove his or her innocence.

When a policy, practice, or idea enjoys presumption, it is considered useful, accurate, or true until enough evidence has been advanced to raise a reasonable doubt about that usefulness, accuracy, or truth.

Presumption affords a definite privilege to currently accepted ideas and policies. We might even say that democratic societies adopt a conservative attitude toward policy change—we alter established ways of doing things slowly, and only in response to a strong case. Thus, a requirement called the **burden of proof**—*the obligation to provide sufficient evidence in support of an assertion*—is a responsibility of those seeking change, of advocates wishing to promote new policies or ideas. Those defending current systems have no such burden of proof, giving them a clear initial advantage in debate.

The burden of proof is considered to have been satisfied or "met" when a certain standard of proof is satisfied. The initial standard of proof required of a policy case is termed a **prima facie case,** or *a case that, prior to being challenged, appears to provide sound evidence for an assertion.* "Prima facie" literally means, "at its first appearance," so this case is not required to satisfy rigorous critical tests. Advancing a prima facie case does not mean you have developed a conclusive or irrefutable argument against the status quo, only one strong enough to raise a substantial question regarding the truth or efficacy of the status quo. That is, a prima facie case raises considerable questions about whether the status quo reflects a practical and reasonable policy.

In a debate, *a series of arguments—a case—challenging the status quo* is traditionally referred to as an **affirmative case.** Such a case "affirms" the need for a change. A **negative case,** on the other hand, is *a series of arguments supporting the status quo* in response to the assertions of the affirmative case. Again, the negative side in a policy debate enjoys a presumption in favor of its ideas and policies. According to traditional rules governing debates about policy issues, the negative side is not required to advance a case of its own, or even to offer a rebuttal, until the affirmative side has satisfied the burden of proof, that is, raised significant questions regarding the way things currently are done.

A few technical points are associated with challenging the status quo, so we should take a closer look at what a successful affirmative case must accomplish to meet the burden of proof.

STOCK ISSUES

The *criteria governing the soundness of an affirmative case,* the standards that an affirmative case must satisfy, are called **stock issues.** Stock issues provide direction for organizing an affirmative case in a policy debate, and can serve as a means of checking the thoroughness of the case. The four stock issues are inherency, significance, solvency, and topicality.

The affirmative case in a debate has the obligation to demonstrate the existence of **harms,** *problems or liabilities resulting directly from the status quo, the policy currently in place.* This means the affirmative case must first address two of four stock issues: the inherency and significance of the problems associated with the status quo. The affirmative side must also eventually address the solvency and topicality of the plan it advances.

The stock issue of **inherency** asks *whether* serious *problems are inherent, resulting directly from the status quo, not from extraneous or accidental circumstances.* There are two kinds of inherency: attitudinal and structural. **Attitudinal inherency** refers to *current attitudes or beliefs that contribute to the harms created by the status quo.* **Structural inherency** refers to *current laws or regulatory structures—or their absence— that result in the harms caused by the status quo.* Advocates often try to establish both kinds of inherency in their efforts to build a strong case that the status quo causes serious problems.

Second, the affirmative case must address the stock issue of **significance,** that is, it must demonstrate that *the current policy results in serious danger, waste of resources, or potential loss.* Minor problems attend any policy, but serious or consequential problems must be addressed, and can indicate the need for new policies. As part of its effort to establish significance, the affirmative case should argue for the **imminence** of the harms. This is a time-related criterion that asks *whether the status quo is already producing serious, undesirable consequences, or is likely to do so in the near future.* Why the need to satisfy the criterion of imminence? When an audience believes that a serious problem will not materialize for a long time, it is more difficult to persuade them to take action or to accept a change in policy.

A third stock issue that the affirmative side must address is **solvency,** which asks *whether the plan advanced represents an effective and practical solution to the problems created by the status quo.* A policy case must forge a clear link between these problems and the improvement resulting from the proposed solution. Focusing on solvency creates this link by demonstrating that the new plan will address root causes of the present problems and their associated harms. A plan that does not address root causes, that deals only with symptoms or superficial consequences, is inadequate. Such a plan does not solve problems; it merely masks their presence.

For a plan to address the stock issue of solvency requires that it demonstrate **practicality,** which asks *whether the plan addresses the problem expediently and is capable of overcoming financial and other obstacles to its implementation.* To practicality, many affirmative cases will add arguments for the benefits the proposed plan will bring with it.

As already noted, stock issues are a way of organizing an affirmative case in a policy debate, and can also serve as a means of checking the thoroughness of the case. These issues are intended to enforce the concept of **topicality,** the fourth stock issue, or *keeping the debate focused on issues relevant to the topic being debated.* Participants in a formal debate typically have to respond to a carefully worded proposal called a resolution. The resolution serves as a common starting point for both sides. Debaters are required to address the resolution directly and not deviate from standard definitions of key terms important to the topic. Topicality reminds advocates that the policy case must focus on the issue reflected in the resolution, and not on extraneous considerations. Topicality is a guard against errors such as strategies of distraction, irrelevant arguments, unusual definitions, appealing to the audience's emotions, or *ad hominem* attacks.

Having a basic grasp of the stock issues of inherency, significance, solvency, and topicality can teach us critical thinking skills such as organizing an argument carefully, and asking about the relevance and quality of evidence.

SAMPLE ESSAY ANALYSIS

We can explore several aspects of policy case development by examining an essay on human trafficking by a student named Leah. We'll consider how she develops the presence of a problem, evaluates the problem's seriousness, and advances a solution. Leah begins with an introduction that captures her audience's attention, explores the scope of the problem she is addressing, and announces her thesis.

Twenty-First Century Slavery

Introduction New York is America's largest city, with an official population of nine million people. That's a big city! Four million people live within the city limits of Los Angeles, our second largest city. Coming in at number three is Chicago, with more than three million residents. If we combine the populations of these three largest American cities we come up with the impressive figure of sixteen million people! I mention the populations of these great cities for the sake of comparison. You have heard of human trafficking, but you may not have understood the enormity of the problem. There are almost twenty-one million victims of sex trafficking in the world, according to the nonprofit International Labor Organization.[1] Let that staggering number sink in. That's five million more people in slavery today than live in New York, Los Angeles, and Chicago!

We have made great advances over the past one hundred years when it comes to equal treatment of women. For the first time in our history a woman received the nomination for US president from a major party. While this is a step forward, politicians and other leaders ignore a catastrophic problem that plagues the modern world, and that affects mainly women and girls: human sex trafficking. It is morally necessary to end this practice in the twenty-first century.

Analysis of Introduction

Leah relies on an argument from quantity to secure her audience's attention and to make the point that trafficking is a major problem. She employs a statistic—almost twenty-one million trafficked people worldwide—but also interprets this statistic for clarity with a striking comparison to the populations of several major US cities. Leah makes a point of citing the source of her statistic. Her thesis treats trafficking as an immoral practice that must be stopped. The thesis is a statement of policy; it is simply and clearly phrased.

In the next section, which begins the body of her essay, Leah continues to develop her analysis of the problem:

Body One would think that in an era in which we hear so many calls for equality for women, the public would be outraged by continuing female slavery in the form of sex trafficking. Is it not morally outrageous that, according to the United Nations Office on Drugs and Crime, 71 percent of trafficked individuals are woman and girls—yes, children—bought and sold in the underground sex industry?[2] Why are we as a nation willing to sweep this issue under the rug while simultaneously claiming that we are advocates for women and children?

We may think that trafficking only takes place in third world countries, so the moral responsibility cannot fall on the United States. If you think this way, you're wrong—it's here. More than 1.5 million people are enslaved in our great nation alone. Moreover, according to the U.S. Department of State, between 14,500 and 17,500 sex-trafficking victims are brought into the United States each year.[3]

Another major cause of the problem, according to a trafficking survivor named Alma, is inequality. "When women are not given equal opportunities for employment or education, their options are limited and they grow desperate." Due to economic desperation, women "are constantly driven into the sex industry."[4]

Analysis of Problem Development

Leah relies on the argument from principle in developing the problem: human trafficking is morally outrageous. She develops additional statistical evidence to emphasize the magnitude of the problem, and adds evidence from lay testimony. Her argument is also causal in nature: Leah advances a hypothesis to explain the causes of a persistent moral and social problem. She shows that trafficking is both serious and imminent—it is occurring in the United States, and the number of victims is staggering. Leah mentions sources for her statistics and testimony, but relies on the audience's own sense of the immoral nature of the practice.

In the next section of her essay, Leah analyzes the causes of inaction. She addresses attitudinal and structural reasons that the practice of trafficking persists. These issues are matters of the inherency of the problem:

> **Cause of problem/inherency** So why is the United States not doing anything? Because the war on sex trafficking would be much like the war on drugs: a difficult fight against an enemy that is hard to identify and that operates in an underground market. In addition, the sex industry is extremely lucrative to those at the top, and money is spent to protect this degrading business. Nevertheless, we are without excuse.
>
> We are not outraged because we think trafficking does not affect our lives directly. How much easier, and more selfish, is it to fight to raise the minimum wage when you personally have those two dollars an hour to gain? We focus on policy change that is self-serving, and ignore a moral offense bigger than New York, Los Angeles, and Chicago combined. Remember: a single human life is more important than ten dollars more in your next pay check.
>
> Our media are more focused on political scandal than on human suffering in the United States. Media outlets must pay attention to this issue; otherwise the public will remain ignorant and uncaring. I found virtually no news coverage on this topic. Why is an issue this big left to a few nonprofit organizations to combat?

Analysis of Problem/Inherency

In this section, Leah develops several analogies: to the war on drugs, to issues that are more personally relevant to her audience, and to media attention to political scandal. In each analogy, she compares her evidence case to the conclusion case of human trafficking: it is as difficult as fighting drug abuse and more morally relevant than a slight increase in a paycheck, and deserves more media attention than does political scandal. This section drives home the point that attitudinal and structural barriers keep the practice of trafficking alive.

In the last section of her essay, Leah proposes a solution or plan with several components:

> **Plan** There is hope, however, if we turn our inaction and carelessness into focused action. There are organizations fighting human sex trafficking, and we can learn from reading their research and supporting them financially.
>
> The Polaris Project is just one of the many that work to help trafficked victims and raise money to oppose the practice. Its goal is to "help survivors restore their freedom, prevent more victims, and leverage data and

technology to track traffickers."[5] Volunteer to work with such organizations, and donate money to their work. Remember, it's on us!

There are also ways to report information about suspected trafficking, but they must be improved. We need to update existing hotlines by linking them directly to law enforcement organizations and to a national data base.

Finally, each one of us needs to be vigilant in looking for and reporting signs of trafficking. Educate yourself: read the publications of activist organizations. Volunteer to staff a hotline. Let your representatives know that you care about human trafficking!

Analysis of Plan

Leah's plan is specific and practical. It includes proposals for audience involvement and for policy change. She has taken attitudinal and structural barriers into consideration, and provided the audience with a clear plan for addressing the problem she sets out earlier in her essay. She has sound connections to the earlier sections.

Leah is now prepared to conclude her argument:

Conclusion Human trafficking is a major tragedy, one that affects us directly, and one that is too seldom talked about. Trafficking competes for our attention with a host of serious moral issues, including civil rights and social equality, but it deserves more of our attention and action than it currently receives. There are actions each of us can take—educating ourselves, urging policy changes, and donating time and money.

It is my hope that more people would be willing to fight for helpless and marginalized victims of trafficking. My fear is that these exploited woman and children, who cannot even claim freedom of their own bodies, would continue to suffer. Let's not allow them to suffer simply because we did not pay attention to their plight, because we were distracted by other issues, because we simply weren't aware.

Notes

[1] Polaris, https://polarisproject.org/human-trafficking, (Accessed March 22, 2018).

[2] United Nations Office on Drugs and Crime, Global Report on Trafficking in Persons 2016, https://refugeesmigrants.un.org/majority-trafficking-victims-are-women -and-girls-one-third-children---new-un-report.

[3] U.S. Department of State, Office to Monitor and Combat Trafficking in Persons, Trafficking in Persons Report, Introduction (revised), June 14, 2014, https://www.state.gov/j/tip/rls/tiprpt/2004/34021.htm (Accessed April 24, 2018).

[4] Alma, Equality Now, https://www.equalitynow.org/campaigns/trafficking-survivor -stories/alma (Accessed March 22, 2018).

[5] As described by Connecticut Coalition to End Homelessness, http://cceh.org /human-trafficking-prevention (Accessed March 22, 2018).

Analysis of Conclusion

In her conclusion, Leah returns to the argument from principle—trafficking is a major moral issue that confronts us all and that challenges our inaction. Analogies to other social and moral issues are again featured. Finally, Leah brings the focus back to the victims, and repeats her call for audience action. She closes with an urgent plea for their attention, awareness, and action.

REVIEW

Cases advocating changes in policy are often encountered in public controversies. The policy already in place, the status quo, is said to enjoy presumption—it is assumed to be true, useful, or accurate until adequately challenged. Such a challenge is called a prima facie case. Developing such a case is the task of the affirmative side in a debate, the side challenging the status quo. The negative side defends the status quo. When a solid prima facie case has been advanced, the burden of proof is said to have been met.

A persuasive and reasonable policy case addresses stock issues: It establishes the inherency and significance of the problem associated with the status quo. It should also argue that the plan shows solvency—that it has the potential for actually addressing the root causes of current problems. Finally, the case must exhibit topicality, or a concern for keeping the debate focused on issues relevant to the topic being debated. You can also enhance a policy case by showing the benefits of following the proposed plan and addressing counter-arguments that may occur to the audience.

B Adapting Arguments to an Audience

KEY TERMS   audience analysis   dispositional analysis

demographic analysis   values analysis

Though our reasoning may be largely private, our arguments are usually presented in public. This means that they must be constructed with an individual or group—an audience—in mind. Audience adaptation is important whether we are presenting an argument to a friend, the local board of education, or a national television audience. We all adapt our arguments to audiences, but we may not always be quite certain how to go about this process effectively.

Creating a successful case, a case that is persuasive to an audience, requires having a command of the relevant information on your topic and integrating that information into arguments that satisfy the three criteria we have discussed—support, validity, and linguistic consistency. Your arguments should also be arranged into a carefully constructed presentation that addresses the relevant issues for establishing a proposition of fact, value, or policy.

Successful case presentation requires effective **audience analysis,** *seeking an accurate sense of the nature of the audience so you can adapt your arguments to that audience.* This basic point is often overlooked and so is worth restating. Arguments are typically addressed to an audience, so the most compelling arguments are those that have been skillfully adapted to their particular audiences. The goals of clarity, propriety, and persuasiveness dictate that we adapt our arguments, as well as the language in which they are cast, to an audience. Even a well-constructed argument may fail to convince if it is not adapted to your actual audience.

Adapting arguments to an audience means that we must know something about the audience we are addressing. The process of audience adaptation begins with an effort to construct an accurate profile of the audience members that considers such factors as their age, race, and economic status; their values and beliefs; and their attitudes toward you and your topic. Thorough audience analysis, then, involves demographic analysis, values analysis, and dispositional analysis.

DEMOGRAPHIC ANALYSIS

Demographic analysis is *an effort to create a picture of the audience that focuses on descriptive information such as age, race, gender, and economic status.* It can be simple or complex, but it always seeks to locate audience members socially. Demographic analysis involves asking questions about your audience such as:

Age: How old are the audience members?

Economic status: What is their income level?

Geographical location: Where do audience members live?

Gender: What percentage of the audience is female or male?

Race: What racial and ethnic groups are present in the audience?

Occupation: What professions are represented?

Demographic analysis is not intended simply to uncover interesting facts about an audience. Demographic information helps you as an advocate to develop a fundamental sense of an audience's likely interests, resources, aspirations, and experiences. For example, younger audiences are likely to be interested in the availability of jobs, while middle-aged and older audiences may be more strongly interested in interest rates. Elderly people are likely to be concerned with the stability of the Social Security system and controlling medical costs, while high-school and college students are more likely to have an inherent interest in the environment or the risk of reinstating a military draft. Parents will typically be concerned about the quality of schools and other matters affecting their families. Audiences in California and Arizona may be more concerned about water issues and immigration laws than are audiences in Wyoming. People who are well-to-do will likely pay closer attention to arguments about estate tax laws than will people working for fixed hourly wages, while the latter group may listen more intently to a speech on minimum wage regulations. Virtually everyone is concerned about the health of the economy.

> Demographic information helps you develop a sense of an audience's interests, resources, aspirations, and experiences.

In some cases demographic analysis may suggest that you need to do additional audience research. Some questions about an audience simply cannot be answered through demographic analysis. For instance, do young people or older people care more about surveillance and the security of personal information? Does geography affect whether an audience is concerned about policies restricting freedom of expression? Does gender play a role in audience beliefs about seat-belt laws? Does race influence attitudes toward the rights of gay people? Sometimes the challenge of effective argument comes in skillfully adapting a topic to an audience that is not already interested in that topic, or in crafting a convincing argument for conclusions that are contrary to an audience's beliefs. An audience's values and beliefs—crucial information when developing arguments—may not be revealed by demographic analysis. This last point brings us to the second major category of audience analysis, values analysis.

VALUES ANALYSIS

One theme in this text has been the important role that values and other commitments play in argumentation. We interpret evidence and draw conclusions from that evidence largely on the basis of our values. **Values analysis** is *the effort to ascertain an audience's beliefs, values, and other moral commitments.* Knowing something about what an audience values can assist you greatly in adapting arguments to the specific audience you are addressing.

Values analysis is less straightforward than demographic analysis, but may reveal more about an audience's actual commitments. In doing values analysis, you may wish to ask about an audience's personal values, religious affiliations, beliefs, political principles, and political affiliations.

Personal values: What personal values do audience members hold that bear on your topic and your position on the topic? Personal values are deep moral convictions that people acquire from family, cultural background, religious training, and personal experience. An example of a personal value derived from culture would be a high priority on the extended family. A personal value derived from personal experience might be that volunteer work for a charitable organization is more important than financial success.

Religious affiliations: To which religious organizations do your audience members belong? Religion remains an important source of values for the majority of people, as revealed in polls and in the extraordinary efforts that political parties devote to connecting their agendas with the public's religious commitments. An example of religious affiliation affecting moral commitments on a topic might be a devout Catholic objecting to human cloning research, on the basis of Church teachings about human beings as special creations of God.

Beliefs: What beliefs does your audience hold that are relevant to your topic? Beliefs are personal convictions about a range of practical issues that reflect an individual's life experiences. Examples would be a belief that military force should be used infrequently (or frequently), a belief that extensive surveillance of citizens is justified (or unjustified), a belief that the police exist to protect citizens (or to control them), and a belief that large corporations usually have (or do not have) the best interests of their employees in mind.

Political principles: What political principles do your audience members adhere to? Political principles are personal convictions rooted in legal or political ideas. An example would be a commitment to broad freedom of access to information, the individual's right to own firearms, equal rights for all people residing in the country, the freedom to express unpopular ideas openly, or the principle that the government should not place restraints on the operation of market forces.

Political affiliations: To which political parties and organizations do members of your audience belong? In addition to people who belong to the two major political parties, an increasing number of voters are independents or associated with smaller parties such as the Green Party. People might also belong to other political organizations, such as Amnesty International, the National Rifle Association, or Human Rights Watch. The parties or organizations to which an audience member belongs are good indicators of basic political beliefs and commitments. In most cases, political affiliations and political principles are closely related.

Demographic analysis may be relatively straightforward, but assessing beliefs and attitudes often requires more astute insight on the writer's or speaker's part. Because argumentation is rooted in political, religious, and cultural values, an effective advocate makes an effort to ascertain the beliefs and commitments that shape an audience's thinking. Effective advocates also try to stay informed about contemporary controversies and the various positions articulated on those controversies. A key to values analysis is to be actively involved in reading, listening, and thinking about a range of current issues.

DISPOSITIONAL ANALYSIS

In addition to demographic and values analyses, dispositional analysis can help you adapt arguments to your audience. **Dispositional analysis** is *audience analysis aimed at discovering audience attitudes toward your topic and perhaps toward you as an advocate.*

Here are some questions to ask, along with some suggestions as to how to adapt to specific situations:

Attitudes toward the topic: Is the audience likely to be hostile or friendly toward your position on this topic? A topic such as gun control, health care reform, or immigration will elicit strong feelings in audience members. An advocate needs to be aware of this possibility. Highly technical topics such as how the Federal Reserve sets interest rates, however, are less likely to encounter strong attitudes in an audience. In most cases you will have some idea about your audience's attitudes toward your topic on the basis of indicators such as news coverage, public reaction to the topic, and your demographic and values analysis.

Level of interest: Is this audience likely to be interested in this topic? If you are speaking to university students about the penalties for defaulting on student loans, you will probably have their interest without much extra effort on your part. If you are speaking to the same people about how membership in the European Union will affect the Baltic States, however, you will probably need to explain why they should be interested.

Some topics are of interest to virtually any audience. Health, personal well-being, monetary gain, and happiness are universal concerns. Can your topic be connected directly to any of these matters? Perhaps you can forge a link between the audience's beliefs or values and your topic. Your audience may have little interest in a new casino in the county, but be deeply concerned about local schools. Does introducing casinos to an area have a negative impact on schools?

Need for information: Does the audience need to know more about the topic? For instance, people being asked to approve a new property tax measure will want information about what the new taxes will be used for. If so, you may need to devote extra research to discovering basic information on your topic. Elderly people listening to a speech about Medicare guidelines for prescription drugs need information, so they will likely be attentive to a talk on this topic. It might be necessary, however, to convince the same people that they need information on investment scams that take advantage of the elderly.

Need for decision: Must the audience members make a choice on the topic? Parents of small children must decide whether to send their children to public or private schools, or perhaps whether to homeschool them. A speech on education systems might be adapted to their need to make a decision. If students must decide whether to provide volunteer and financial support to an environmental protection effort, you would want to adapt your argument on this topic to assist them in their decisions.

When people are faced with a decision, you may devote less time to developing their interest in the topic and more time to urging them to a particular action. For example, elections require people to make a choice, so candidates and their supporters devote most of their energy to giving voters reasons to select a particular candidate or measure.

In some cases audience members may not realize that they face a decision; they may have to be shown. For instance, many people do not have a written will. Many lawyers and others who are familiar with the settlement of estates know that is a risky situation, but most other people must be persuaded that a choice is truly important.

Attitudes toward the advocate: What are the audience members' dispositions toward you as a speaker or writer? Questions to consider include: Do they already know you? Do they view you as "one of their own," a friend, a guest, an outsider, or

FIGURE B.1 Audience Analysis

Thorough audience analysis involves:
- Demographic analysis
- Values analysis
- Dispositional analysis

an opponent? Does the audience consider you to be a credible source on the topic? Your age, reputation, qualifications, and position on a topic can all influence how an audience is predisposed to respond to your message. It is a great advantage to approach audiences with whom you enjoy credibility, but few speakers and writers have that advantage initially. You may be able to win over an audience that is neutral toward you as an advocate, however, if you can affirm similarities between yourself and the audience.

Addressing a hostile audience poses special problems, whether that hostility is tied to your topic or your relationship to the audience. Imagine that you are assigned to present the case for reducing a company's health insurance coverage to an employee group, or that you want to persuade Greek organizations to back the administration's effort to address hazing on your campus. What should you do? A well-supported and carefully written case is important, but even a strong case may not change the audience's disposition.

Here are a few suggestions for adapting your message to an unfriendly audience. First, candor is often an effective approach when facing a hostile audience. That is, you may want to begin by admitting that you recognize a difference of opinion exists between you and your audience. Second, it can help to tell your audience that you take its concerns seriously. The tone of your remarks as well as your willingness to answer questions can indicate your openness to audience concerns. Third, audience members' hostility may be reduced if you can connect your topic to their values or interests. For example, when speaking to the employee group, it may help to talk about the value of working together to preserve the company's financial integrity through hard times. With the Greek organization, it might be useful to connect your remarks to particular statements in their constitution about promoting the welfare of their members.

With these considerations in mind—demographic analysis, values analysis, and dispositional analysis—you should be able to make some intelligent guesses about your audience's interests, beliefs, and attitudes toward you and your topic. Let us consider a brief scenario in which audience adaptation might have saved a speech.

A CASE STUDY IN AUDIENCE ADAPTATION

Brad prepared an argumentative speech about art censorship for two different audiences. An art major at the university, Brad has been bothered by conservative Congress members' suggestions that the National Endowment for the Arts (NEA) should be restricted from providing funding for artists whose work is offensive to some members of the public. Here is a brief profile of Brad's two audiences:

First audience: The audience is Brad's classmates in a course called "Art in Society," which enrolls thirty-five students. About half the audience members are art majors. The other half represent a cross-section of the college, a large, public institution located in a major eastern city with a liberal political tradition. About twenty-five of the students are between ages eighteen and twenty-three. The others are older, ranging in age from twenty-four to fifty. The class is evenly divided by sex. About half the class members are of racial and ethnic minorities. Brad is an active member of the class who is well liked by the other students.

Second audience: This audience is a local service club in Brad's hometown. The club is known to be politically conservative. It often invites members of the community to speak on a variety of topics. A typical meeting attracts about fifty people, of whom the majority—forty or more—are male. All but a few members are white. Most are over the age of thirty-five; many are over sixty. Nearly all the club members are active in local religious organizations. Most own or work for businesses in the town. The town has a population of fifty thousand and is located in a central midwestern state. Brad is not a member of the club, and as a student just returned home from his junior year at a major urban university, he may be viewed with a little suspicion.

Brad addressed both groups, presenting arguments in opposition to restricting NEA funding on the basis of the content of artists' works. He probably would not have made exactly the same arguments before each group. His linguistic tone would likely have been different for each, too. For which group would the following portion of his argumentative case have been more appropriate?

> Most people behind the drive to censor artists by limiting their federal funding are narrow-minded conservatives with strict religious views. Their political and cultural bigotry should not be allowed to prevail in these matters. They are put off by important works of art that seek to expand their limited personal perspectives—such as Andres Serrano's photograph of a crucifix in a jar of human urine. Because these works offend them, they want to prevent artists from exercising their right to artistic expression. This is wrong, and the religious right needs to be put in its place! Therefore, I propose that artists represent a majority of the review board for all NEA funding of art projects. This is the only way to assure that bigotry will not prevail, and that great art and freedom of expression will!

Brad actually presented this argument to the second audience, which was not receptive. Having written the speech originally with his university class in mind, he made no changes in the presentation when speaking to the service club.

You could look at this situation in two ways. You might say, "Good—they needed to hear that!" If you do you are accepting that little or no persuasion took place and the argument was rejected. Or you might conclude that, with some efforts at audience adaptation, the speech could have been much more persuasive without sacrificing its point or its integrity as an argument. What could Brad have done differently while remaining true to his belief that the NEA should not restrict funds on the basis of artistic content?

Keeping the balance between conviction and content in mind, Brad might have adapted his argument more carefully to his second audience. He could have taken audience members' demographic factors and values into consideration: they are middle-aged, religiously oriented, white males living in a large town in the Midwest. They also belong to a group known for its political conservatism. Their values are likely to be influenced by all of these factors.

Moreover, they may hold to the belief that artists should not get federal support for art that offends some members of the general public. Had Brad considered dispositional analysis, he might have realized that his audience was more concerned with federal spending—which they likely understand as taxation—than artistic freedom. He should also have known that he was coming as something of an outsider, and one advocating an unpopular position. Nevertheless, the fact that he was born and reared in the town might have worked to his advantage if approached correctly.

Knowing these things about his audience, what could Brad have done differently while still remaining true to his convictions? Almost certainly, Brad should not have used labels such as "narrow-minded" to describe those favoring restrictions on the NEA, and labels such as "bigotry" to describe their attitudes. Members of his second audience might feel that they themselves are being attacked by such labels.

In addition, Brad could have sought to identify with his audience—to connect with them and their values—in several ways. First, he might have linked his value for artistic freedom more clearly to values the audience accepted, such as freedom of speech or the value of differing points of view in a democratic society. Had he given more thought to his audience's values and anchored his arguments in those values, his case probably would have been received better.

Brad might also have identified himself as a member of the community and as a person who understands some of the reservations the members have about provocative works of art.

He should have chosen his examples more carefully, especially because the examples he did choose are no more representative of the art causing the concern than are other examples that might have been less offensive to his audience, or he might have introduced some less startling examples to balance the effect.

Brad should also have introduced testimony from sources that the club members were likely to find credible, sources affirming either the value of freedom of expression or the need not to tie federal funding to local preferences.

Finally, Brad could have developed an analogy to a case on which the people in his audience are likely to have strong views already. For instance, he might have developed an analogy to the federal government telling business people what kinds of products they can sell and to what groups, dictating how they can advertise, and imposing other limitations on what they might see as their ability to compete.

These are just a few ways that Brad might have adapted his argument to a new and different audience. You can probably think of other ideas that would have helped make his arguments more effective before this audience. Though Brad's failure to consider his audience led to a rather obvious error, such incidents are not uncommon. By taking some time to think about your audience as you prepare your arguments, you can avoid many of the more obvious mistakes.

> By taking some time to think about your audience, you can avoid many obvious mistakes.

REVIEW

In the process of adapting arguments to a particular audience, you can get a picture of the audience through demographic, values, and dispositional analyses. Adapting arguments to an audience involves connecting you and your topic with the members of the audience by various means. These means can include emphasizing the values you and they have in common, linking your topic to values they already hold, and using candor with a hostile audience.

Glossary

A

Acceptance: One possible response to an argument; the agreement to accept the argument as presented; that is, to find it persuasive, or at least lacking in any major flaw.

Accessibility: As a test of evidence, the availability of evidence for examination.

Adequacy: As a test of evidence, whether the evidence presented, when taken together, is sufficient to support its claim.

Ad hominem **fallacy:** An intentional effort to attack a person rather than an argument, by damaging an opponent's character or reputation or by engaging in name-calling and labeling.

Ad populum **fallacy:** Appealing to the audience and its interests rather than to the merits of the argument.

Advocacy: The activity of promoting or opposing an idea in public settings.

Affirmative case: In a policy debate, a series of arguments challenging the status quo.

A fortiori **argument:** A literal analogy that asserts that what is true of its evidence case is even more likely or even less likely to be true of its conclusion case.

Ambiguity: More than one meaning of a word or phrase in a single context.

Analogy: For the sake of supporting a claim, a comparison of something with which we are familiar to something with which we are less familiar, or about which we have some question.

Antecedent: The "if" clause in a conditional statement; "that which comes before."

Appeal: A persuasive strategy directed to the audience's emotions, sense of humor, or deeply held loyalties and commitments.

Appeal to authority: An appeal that urges compliance with the directive of a person, group, or document possessing power.

Arguing comparative advantages: A response to a pragmatic argument or policy proposal; arguing that an alternative course of action carries greater practical advantages than the proposed plan does.

Arguing from correlation alone: A fallacy; attributing cause simply on the basis of events occurring or varying simultaneously.

Arguing from ignorance: A fallacy; falsely assuming that a conclusion can be reached on the basis of the absence of evidence. One form of this argument assumes that because something has not been disproved, it has therefore been proved.

Arguing from succession alone: A fallacy; attributing cause simply on the basis of one event preceding another. Also called "arguing *post hoc,*" an abbreviation of the Latin phrase, *post hoc ergo propter hoc,* which means "after this, therefore because of this."

Argument: A claim advanced with a reason or reasons in its support.

Argumentation: The cooperative activity of developing and advancing arguments and of responding to the arguments of others.

Argumentative contexts: The spaces, venues, and relationships in which arguments are made and heard.

Argumentative definition: A definition employed strategically to categorize an object or event so as to support a particular conclusion to an argument.

Argument from direction: An argument that strings together two or more conditional statements to predict a remote result from a first step.

Argument from example: An argument that draws a conclusion about an entire class of objects or events based on a particular instance or a limited number of cases, rather than about a single member of a group.

Argument from function: An argument that locates the essential nature of an object, event, or institution in its social or natural function.

Argument from intent: An argument that affirms that the meaning or essential nature of an object or document is revealed in the intended meaning of its authors or designers.

Argument from principle: An argument that affirms that we should abide by values, principles, and duties, and avoid actions that violate the same.

Argument from quality: An argument that affirms the inherent value in the unique, the beautiful, the rare, or the unusual.

Argument from quantity: An argument that affirms numerical considerations as an index of significance.

Argument from sign: An argument that reasons from an effect back to a cause.

Argument virtues: Those moral qualities and skills that help people think and act morally in an argumentative situation, and thus pursue argumentation in a manner that promotes and improves its practices.

Arrangement fallacy: The fallacy that creates a false impression by ordering, associating, or grouping items of evidence in a misleading way.

Attacking a straw man: *See* straw man fallacy.

Attitudinal inherency: In policy debate, the inherency that shows that current attitudes or beliefs contribute to the harms caused by the status quo.

Audience: The people for whom we develop our arguments.

Audience analysis: Seeking an accurate sense of the nature of the audience so you can adapt your arguments to that audience.

B

Backing: a foundational assumption or presupposition that supports a warrant (Toulmin model).

Biased testimony: Testimony from individuals who stand to gain if what they say is accepted.

Burden of proof: In policy debate, the obligation to provide sufficient evidence in support of an assertion.

C

Case: A series of arguments, all advanced to support the same general contention or set of conclusions.

Categorical argument: An argument composed of three categorical statements—two statements that are its reasons, or premises, and one that is its conclusion. Also called a categorical syllogism.

Categorical statement: A statement that establishes a relationship between two categories, or classes, of objects.

Categorical syllogism: *See* categorical argument.

Causal agent: In a hypothesis, a testable element in the alleged cause that is capable of producing an observed effect.

Causal generalization: An argument that affirms a causal relationship between two categories, or classes, of events.

Circular definition: A definition of a term by reference only to factors inherent in or strongly implied by the definition itself.

Civil disobedience: The intentional decision to disobey a law or directive of a government authority for moral reasons.

Claim: The assertion being advanced (Toulmin model). A statement the advocate believes or is in the process of evaluating.

Coherence: A test of narrative arguments that asks whether the components in a story create a meaningful and consistent whole.

Common usage: As a source of definition, the meaning of a term in everyday language.

Complementary reasons: A pair of reasons that must work together to lend support to their conclusion.

Conclusion: A claim that has been reached by a process of reasoning.

Conclusion case: In an analogy, an instance in the argument about which a claim is being advanced.

Conclusion relationship: In a figurative analogy, the relationship being urged in connection with the conclusion.

Concurrent testimony: Testimony that is consistent with other available sources of testimony on the topic.

Conditional argument: An argument built around an "if-then" statement or an equivalent. Also called a hypothetical syllogism.

Conditional statement: The "if-then" statement in a conditional argument.

Connectives: Reasons that consist of beliefs, values, assumptions, or generalizations that link evidence to a conclusion.

Consequent: The "then" clause in a conditional or "if-then" statement; an event that follows from or is a result of another event.

Consideration: One possible response to an argument; an agreement to think about the argument further, to withhold any final judgment about its quality for the time being.

Continuum fallacy: A fallacy; a false assumption that qualitative changes along a line of progression do not occur if we cannot agree about exactly where such changes occur.

Control group: As one means of assessing a causal generalization; a group, paralleling the experiment group, in which the suspected causal agent is withheld or eliminated.

Conversion: In a universal negative or particular affirmative statement, the process of switching the statement's subject and predicate terms in order to create an equivalent statement.

Convertible statement: A statement in which the subject and predicate terms are distributed similarly. Universal negative and particular affirmative statements are convertible.

Cooperation: As a virtue of ethical advocacy, a willingness to engage the argumentative process so that a rational resolution of the issues can be achieved.

Correlated: Occurring together with regularity.

Courage in argument: As a virtue of ethical advocacy, a willingness to accept the risks associated with open advocacy of one's position, even when that position is unpopular or dangerous.

Credibility: As a test of evidence, a source's reputation for accuracy and reliability.

Criteria of evaluation: The standards on which a value judgment is based.

Cues: Words or phrases that signal something, other than a reason or a conclusion, about the content of an argument.

D

Dangerous precedent: A basis for a series of undesirable exceptions for similar cases.

Data: The evidence presented in support of a claim (Toulmin model).

Deductive arguments: Arguments that lead to necessary conclusions when their reasons are true. The typical structure of a deductive argument involves moving from a general principle (sometimes called a "major premise") and a more specific observation (sometimes called a "minor premise") to a conclusion that applies the general principle to a particular case.

Define: To advance a meaning for a word or to classify an object, person, or act.

Definition report: A noncontroversial definition that all parties to a debate agree upon, or that states a generally accepted or agreed upon meaning.

Demographic analysis: A type of audience analysis; an effort to create a picture of the audience that focuses on descriptive information such as age, race, gender, and economic status.

Diagramming: A tool of argument analysis that involves mapping an argument, using only the letters assigned during scanning, and drawing lines from reasons to the conclusion they support.

Dialogic perspectives: Ethical perspectives that elevate efforts to preserve the two-sidedness of public discourse.

Digital literacy: The capacity to skillfully navigate and employ online resources.

Dilemma: A strategy of argument that forces a choice between limited and undesirable options.

Disjunctive argument: An argument that presents limited options: two enumerated alternatives, or disjuncts, often marked by an "either-or" statement.

Dispositional analysis: Audience analysis aimed at discovering audience attitudes toward your topic and perhaps toward you as an advocate.

Distinction without a difference: A definition that suggests that a category exists, without adequately explaining how objects in this category differ from objects in similar categories.

Distributed term: In a categorical argument, a term that, in a statement, refers to every member of the category of objects it represents.

E

Editorial process: A careful review of submitted research reports that provides an important check on the quality of research published in a periodical.

Emotional appeal: Engaging the audience's emotions for the purpose of persuasion.

End terms: In a categorical argument, the two terms that appear once in a reason and once in the conclusion.

Enthymeme: Aristotle's term for a truncated or abbreviated categorical argument, missing one or more of the basic components, such as a reason or a conclusion.

Enumeration argument: An argument that sets out alternative explanations or options and then follows a process of elimination.

Equivocation: A problem of definition; changing meaning of a key term in the course of an argument.

Essential nature argument: An argument that focuses on the "essence" or unchanging nature of an organization, object, person, entity, or work of art.

Etymology: As a source of definition, the origin of a word.

Euphemism: A strategy of definition; a less objectionable and often less accurate term exchanged for a harsh, condemning, or emotionally charged term.

Evidence: A reason rooted in observation.

Evidence case: In a literal analogy, a familiar or widely established instance that is used as the basis for the argument.

Evidence relationship: In a figurative analogy, the familiar relationship pair that is used as support for the conclusion.

Exclusive disjuncts: In a disjunctive argument, two alternatives that cannot both be true at the same time.

Expert testimony: The judgment or opinion of a qualified specialist in a discipline about matters relevant to that discipline.

Extent of the generalization: In a generalization from a sample, the portion of the population that is said to exhibit the particular property.

External consistency: As a test of evidence, the requirement that evidence must not be sharply at odds with either the majority of evidence from other sources or with the best evidence from other sources.

F

Fact: A claim that can potentially be verified as either true or false.

Fact, proposition of: A statement that reports, describes, predicts, or makes a causal claim.

Fallacy: An argument that is invalid or otherwise so seriously flawed as to render it unreliable.

Fallacy of hasty generalization: A generalization based on a sample that is too small to support it.

Fallible sign: An effect with more than one possible cause, though one cause is typical.

False dilemma: A fallacy; a dilemma argument that uses artificially limited options to mislead an audience.

Falsifiable: A criterion of evaluation for a hypothesis; capable of being shown false.

Fidelity: A test of narrative argument that takes us outside the story and into our own experiences to ask whether the story reflects what we know to be true about life experiences and human nature.

Figurative analogy: A comparison between things that are not of the same type, that come from different realms of experience; a metaphor.

Finding: In the process of sampling from a population, what was observed about members of the sample.

G

Generalizations from a sample: Claims that take as their evidence a sample drawn from a population, and advance a conclusion about members of the entire population.

Genetic argument: An argument that looks to origins as evidence of essential nature.

H

Harms: In policy debate, problems or liabilities resulting directly from the status quo, the policy currently in place.

Honesty: As a virtue of ethical advocacy, a commitment not to willingly mislead, and generally a regard for what is or what we take to be true.

Human nature perspectives: Ethical perspectives that develop around one or more essential qualities of human nature.

Hypothesis: An explanatory statement affirming that one or more events cause another event to occur.

Hypothetical syllogism: *See* conditional argument.

I

Imminence: A test of a policy case; whether the status quo is already producing serious, undesirable consequences, or is likely to do so in the near future.

Inclusive disjuncts: In a disjunctive argument, two alternatives that might both be true at the same time.

Indicators: Words and phrases such as "because" and "therefore" that provide important clues to identifying reasons and conclusions in an argument.

Inductive argument: An argument whose reasons lead to probable conclusions. Inductive arguments typically move from specific observations to general claims.

Inductive leap: A process in which the conclusion of an argument moves beyond its stated evidence.

Infallible sign: An effect that virtually always and only accompanies a particular cause.

Inference: The rational movement from a particular reason or reasons to a particular conclusion.

Inherency: A test of a policy case; whether serious problems or "harms" are inherent, resulting directly from the status quo, not from extraneous or accidental circumstances.

Intermediate conclusion: A conclusion in an argument that is then used as a reason for some additional conclusion.

Internal consistency: As a test of evidence, the requirement that evidence and sources must not contradict themselves.

J

Judicial analogy: A literal analogy that insists on similar treatment for people, ideas, or institutions in similar circumstances.

L

Labeling: A strategy of definition; characterizing a person, group, idea, or institution by introducing a suggestive name or term.

Lay testimony: A report of personal observation, experience, or opinion on a topic not requiring special expertise.

Linguistic consistency: One of the three tests of an argument, along with support and validity; the clarity of the argument's language and its use of terms in the same way throughout the argument.

Linguistic conventions: Recognized methods of expressing a meaning indirectly.

Linguistic link: A repeated phrase or term that links statements to one another.

Literal analogy: A direct comparison between two allegedly similar items or cases.

Logical sense: One's sense of how arguments develop.

M

Majoring on minors: The fallacy that focuses attention on minor or inconsequential points to draw attention away from important ones.

Mean: The arithmetical average; the sum of a set of figures divided by the number of figures in the set.

Median: The figure that exactly divides the top half from the bottom half in a range of figures.

Metaphor: A comparison between things that are not of the same type, that come from different realms of experience; a figurative analogy.

Metonymy: The use of one object to represent another associated object, or of a single attribute to represent a complex object.

Middle term: In a categorical argument, the term that appears in both reasons and not in the conclusion.

Mixed metaphor: A linguistic combination of images that do not belong together.

Modal qualifier: a term that indicates the intended strength of a conclusion (Toulmin model).

Mode: The most frequently occurring observation or response in a sample.

Modus ponens: Affirming the antecedent in a conditional statement to create a valid conditional argument; "mode that affirms."

Modus tollens: Denying the consequent in a conditional statement to create a valid conditional argument; "mode that denies."

N

Necessary conclusion: A particular conclusion to which the reasons or premises in a deductive argument— when accepted as true—unavoidably lead.

Necessary condition: A condition without which another event cannot occur.

Negative case: In a policy debate, a series of arguments supporting the status quo.

News and commentary publications: Periodicals that specialize in reporting news and presenting informed editorial opinions.

O

Observational study: Study based on the examination of existing data sets in an effort to discover correlations.

Original intent: As a source of definition, the meaning of a word or phrase in its original context, or what the initial definer of a term meant by it.

P

Paradigm case: As a source of definition, a representative example of the term or category in question; a typical member that defines the entire category.

Paralepsis: The strategy of making a claim about an issue by stating that you will not bring up that issue or that the matter is insignificant.

Particular affirmative statement: In a categorical argument, a claim that attributes a specified quality to only some members of a category.

Particular negative statement: In a categorical argument, a claim that denies that some members of a category possess a specified quality.

Person/act argument: An essential nature argument that looks to a person's or group's acts to find the true nature or character of that individual or group.

Pluralism: The variety of moral and ethical perspectives present in contemporary societies.

Pluralistic culture: A society composed of groups who see the world from different perspectives, value different activities, hold disparate religious beliefs, and aspire to different goals.

Poisoning the well: A fallacy; dismissing an individual as unqualified to speak on a topic based on some accident of circumstance.

Policy, proposition of: A statement that urges that an action be taken or discontinued.

Political perspectives: Ethical perspectives that rely on the essential values of a political system for their criteria of ethical assessment.

Popular magazines: Periodicals intended to provide pleasure reading and advice on a range of personal and professional issues.

Population: In a generalization from a sample, the group or class to which the generalization is intended to apply.

Post hoc fallacy: *See* arguing from succession alone.

Power: The capacity to wield influence, to shape important decisions that affect the lives of others.

Practicality: A test of a policy case; whether the plan addresses the problem expediently and is capable of overcoming financial and other obstacles to its implementation.

Pragmatic argument: An argument that recommends or discourages a course of action on the basis of its practical consequences.

Predicate term: The second term in a categorical statement, the term that attributes or denies a quality to the members of the category represented in the subject term.

Predictive: Making claims about the future.

Premise: A reason in a deductive argument. Also a reason in a conditional argument, an enumerative argument, or a categorical argument.

Presumption: In policy debate, the tendency for an idea or practice to be assumed to be true or adequate—and thus not requiring proof—until sufficiently challenged.

Prima facie case: A case that, prior to being challenged, appears to provide sound evidence for an assertion.

Probable conclusion: A conclusion that can be shown to be more or less likely, but not necessary; a name for the conclusion of an inductive argument.

Procedures: The rules or guidelines according to which argumentation will take place.

Property: In a generalization, a quality projected from the sample to the population.

Public discourse: Open discussion of those issues that potentially affect everyone.

Q

Qualify the source: State a source's credentials or give reasons for its credibility.

Question begging: A fallacy that assumes that a debatable question can be treated as already answered.

R

Random sample: A sample in which every member of a given population had an equal chance of being selected for the sample.

Randomized study: Research study intentionally designed from the outset to answer a single causal question.

Reason: A statement advanced for the purpose of establishing a claim.

Rebuttal: A possible answer or exception to the inference being drawn (Toulmin model). A counter-argument, a reasoned answer that addresses specific points made or evidence advanced in the original argument.

Recency: As a test of evidence, the requirement that evidence be up to date and not superseded by more timely evidence.

Reclassification: Strategic placement of an object, person, or idea under a new heading.

Reductio ad absurdum: An appeal that asks an audience to recognize an idea as either self-contradictory or as so unreasonable as to be absurd; "reduction to absurdity."

Redundancy: Unnecessary repetition of an idea or term.

Refereed: As a description of a publication; reviewed by two or more qualified readers before publication. Scholarly books and journals are typically refereed.

Refutation: A thoroughly successful response to an argument, one that clearly demonstrates a damaging flaw to the satisfaction of a relatively objective listener or reader.

Regard for contexts: As a virtue of ethical advocacy, a willingness to create and preserve settings for argumentation to occur, cultivate the relationships in which it occurs, and allow the argumentative process to continue as long as necessary to ensure reasonable resolution of issues.

Relevance: As a test of evidence, whether the evidence advanced has any bearing on the argument's conclusion.

Reluctant testimony: Testimony from sources who will lose something as a result of their testimony.

Representative: Of a statistical sample; accurately reflects the presence of a particular quality in the entire population.

Repudiation: One possible response to an argument; dismissal of an argument without serious consideration.

Reservation: A statement in an argument that acknowledges the existence of an argument, evidence, or an attitude opposing the conclusion being advanced.

Respect for persons: As a virtue of ethical advocacy, a regard for others as reasoning persons.

Rule of charity: The obligation to restate an opponent's argument so as to give it a strong interpretation.

Rule of justice: The connective in a judicial analogy; the idea that similar cases should be treated similarly.

Rule of parsimony: A rule that directs us to look for the simplest or least complex causal explanation that still accounts for the observed facts.

Rule of reason: The agreement to engage in the cooperative process of argumentation rather than to resolve disagreement by other means.

S

Sample: In a generalization, the members of a group actually observed or consulted during the sampling process.

Sample size: In a generalization from a sample, the number of members in the sample.

Sampling: Statistically selecting and observing members of a group or population who are taken to be representative of the rest of the group.

Scanning: A tool of argument analysis that involves identifying and marking the statements in an argument, as well as underlining indicators and cues.

Scholarly journals: Periodicals that feature essays and studies by experts, scholars, and researchers who are qualified to conduct research in their own fields.

Selection fallacy: Promoting a false interpretation by presenting only some of the relevant evidence in a case, while intentionally excluding other evidence that would contradict the suggested interpretation.

Semantic ambiguity: The ambiguity that occurs when a word or phrase carries more than one meaning in a particular context.

Sign: An effect of a well-known cause, one that allows us to reason back to the cause with some confidence.

Significance: A test of a policy case; whether the current situation results in serious danger, waste of resources, or potential loss.

Significant: Of a correlation; cannot be explained on the basis of chance or simple coincidence.

Situational perspectives: Ethical perspectives that identify ethical considerations or principles inherent to each unique communication setting.

Slippery slope argument: An argument from direction urging that the first step in a progression not be taken.

Solvency: A test of a policy case; whether the plan advanced represents an effective and practical solution to the problems created by the status quo.

Special-interest periodicals: Periodicals that focus on specific topics but are written for wider audiences than scholarly journals are.

Special pleading: The claim that an exception should be made to the rule or principle that would otherwise apply.

Standardizing: A tool of argument analysis that involves making each statement or implied statement in the argument a complete sentence, changing indefinite references such as pronouns to the definite nouns they represent, and placing reasons above the conclusions they support.

Statement: Any phrase or sentence that supplies a portion of the argument's content or meaning.

Statistics: Numerical evidence from records, studies, reports, surveys, polls, and the like.

Status quo: In policy debate; the way things are done now, the policy presently in place.

Stock issues: The criteria governing the soundness of an affirmative case.

Stratified sample: A sample that adequately reflects the various groups that introduce variation within the population.

Straw man argument: A weak interpretation of someone else's argument in order to make it easier to refute. *See also* straw man fallacy.

Straw man fallacy: A fallacy; responding to a weakened version of an opponent's argument.

Structural inherency: The type of inherency in a policy case that shows that current laws or regulatory structures—or their absence—result in the harms caused by the status quo.

Structure of inferences: The relationships among the reasons and the conclusions in an argument.

Subject term: The first term in a categorical argument, the subject or principal focus of the argument.

Succession: As a test of causal reasoning; assurance that the suspected cause consistently occurs before the alleged effect.

Sufficient condition: A condition that will bring about another event.

Support: One of three tests of a reasonable argument, along with validity and linguistic consistency; the strength and accuracy of the argument's evidence.

Syntactic ambiguity: The ambiguity that occurs when the structure or grammar of a sentence renders the meaning of a term or phrase uncertain.

T

Term: A noun or noun phrase that represents a category of objects in a categorical statement.

Testimony: As evidence; personal report of direct experience, expression of personal opinion, or judgment based on expert knowledge.

Topicality: The stock issue in policy debate that requires keeping the debate focused on issues relevant to the topic being debated.

Tu quoque fallacy: Falsely reasoning that someone who is guilty of an offense has no right to instruct others not to do something similar.

U

Unbiased testimony: Testimony from individuals who will neither gain nor lose if their testimony is accepted as true.

Underdescription: The fallacy of creating a false sense of meaning by failing to fully describe a proposal or a crucial component in an opponent's case.

Universal affirmative statement: In a categorical argument, a statement that makes a positive claim about every member of a particular category.

Universal negative statement: In a categorical argument, a claim that denies a specified quality to every member of a category.

V

Valid argument: An argument whose structure connects its reasons to its conclusion in a reliable manner.

Validity: One of the three tests of a reasonable argument, along with linguistic consistency and support; a solid internal structure that allows for reliable connections between evidence and conclusions in an argument.

Value, proposition of: A statement that advances a judgment about morality, beauty, merit, or wisdom.

Values: Deeply held moral commitments acquired from family, cultural background, religious training, and personal experience.

Values analysis: A type of audience analysis; the effort to ascertain an audience's beliefs, values, and other moral commitments.

Variation: Relevant differences among members in a population—the degree to which members of a population vary in ways that may be relevant to the quality being tested in a generalization.

Virtues: Personal qualities that assist us in making ethically good choices.

Visual argument: An argument conveyed through images or objects rather than words.

W

Warrant: The broader assumption linking the claim and the data (Toulmin model).

Worldview: An entire system of interconnected assumptions and beliefs.

Index

About the Author

James A. Herrick is the Guy Vander Jagt Professor of Communication at Hope College. He received his B.A. from California State University, Fresno; his M.A. from the University of California, Davis; and his Ph.D. from the University of Wisconsin–Madison.

Professor Herrick regularly teaches courses in argumentation, rhetorical criticism, and the history of rhetoric. He has received the John and Ruth Reed Faculty Achievement Award for excellence in teaching and research.

Herrick is the author or editor of eight books, on topics ranging from the history of rhetoric to modern mythologies. His co-edited collection of essays, *After the Genome: A Language for our Biotechnological Future,* received the edited volume of the year award from the Ethics Division of the National Communication Association. His latest book is *Visions of Technological Transcendence: Human Enhancement and the Rhetoric of the Future* (2017).